Baldrige Award Winning Quality

Fourth Edition

How to Interpret the Malcolm Baldrige Award Criteria

Mark Graham Brown

QUALITY RESOURCES ®
A Division of The Kraus Organization Limited
White Plains, New York

ASQC
Quality Press
® Milwaukee, Wisconsin

This text is independently produced by Quality Resources and is not an official document created by or endorsed by the Secretary of Commerce nor the National Institute of Standards and Technology or any other organization, governmental or private, having official recognition and/or association with the Malcolm Baldrige National Quality Award.

Printed in the United States of America

98 97 96 95 94   10 9 8 7 6 5 4 3 2 1

Quality Resources
A Division of The Kraus Organization Limited
One Water Street, White Plains, New York 10601

ASQC Quality Press
611 East Wisconsin Avenue
Milwaukee, Wisconsin 53202

Library of Congress Cataloging-in-Publication Data

Brown, Mark Graham.
    Baldrige award winning quality : how to interpret the Malcolm
Baldrige Award criteria / Mark Graham Brown.—4th ed.
      p.   cm.
    Includes bibliographical references.
    ISBN 0-527-76250-4
    1. Malcolm Baldrige National Quality Award. 2. Total quality
management—United States—Awards. I. Title.
HD62. 15.B76   1994
658.5'62'07973—dc20   94-19996
                                 CIP

ISBN 0-527-76250-4

CONTENTS

INTRODUCTION   vii

CHAPTER 1

Understanding the Malcolm Baldrige National Quality Award   1

- Has Interest in Quality Peaked in the U.S.?   2
- Who Can Win the Award?   5
- Application and Evaluation Process   6
- What the Examiners Are Really Looking For   10
- The Baldrige Has Given Rise to Internal Awards   12
- Responsibilities and Benefits of Winning the Baldrige Award   13

CHAPTER 2

Preparing an Application for the Baldrige Award   15

- General Outline of the Major Components of the Application Package   16
- How to Write the Application   17
- Managing the Application Development Project   19
- How to Write the Application Report   26
- Ten Common Mistakes to Avoid When Writing Your Application   26
- Ten Rules to Use When Preparing Graphics For Your Application   33
- Length of Application Report Sections   43
- Producing the Final Copy of the Baldrige Application   44

CHAPTER 3

Key Themes and Relationships Among the Criteria   45

- The Baldrige Criteria as a System   46
- Core Values in the Baldrige Criteria   47
- Key Relationships Among the Seven Categories   51
- Summary of Key Relationships Among the Criteria   60

CHAPTER 4

Understanding the Baldrige Award Scoring Scale   63

- The Truth   64
- Misinformation   64
- How Do Baldrige Applicants and Winners Score?   65

- What it Takes to Win   65
- Understanding the Scoring Scale   65
- Approach, Deployment, and Results   67
- Scores of 0%   68
- Scores of 10-30%   69
- Scores of 40-60%   73
- Scores of 70-90%   76
- Scores of 100%   80
- Additional Scoring Guidance   81

CHAPTER 5

Interpreting the Criteria for Leadership (1.0)   85

- Senior Executive Leadership (1.1)   87
- Management for Quality (1.2)   95
- Public Responsibility and Corporate Citizenship (1.3)   102

CHAPTER 6

Interpreting the Criteria for Information and Analysis (2.0)   113

- Scope and Management of Quality and Performance Data and Information (2.1) 115
- Competitive Comparisons and Benchmarking (2.2)   124
- Analysis and Uses of Company-Level Data (2.3)   133

CHAPTER 7

Interpreting the Criteria for Strategic Quality Planning (3.0)   145

- Strategic Quality and Company Performance Planning Process (3.1)   147
- Quality and Performance Plans (3.2)   156

CHAPTER 8

Interpreting the Criteria for Human Resource Development and Management (4.0)   163

- Human Resource Planning and Management (4.1)   165
- Employee Involvement (4.2)   173
- Employee Education and Training (4.3)   181
- Employee Performance and Recognition (4.4)   191
- Employee Well-Being and Satisfaction (4.5)   200

CHAPTER 9
    Interpreting the Criteria for Management of Process Quality (5.0)   209

    • Design and Introduction of Quality Products and Services (5.1)   211
    • Process Management: Product and Service Production and
      Delivery Processes (5.2)   218
    • Process Management: Business and Support Service Processes (5.3)   228
    • Supplier Quality (5.4)   237
    • Quality Assessment (5.5)   245

CHAPTER 10
    Interpreting the Criteria for Quality and Operational Results (6.0)   249

    • Product and Service Quality Results (6.1)   252
    • Company Operational Results (6.2)   260
    • Business and Support Service Results Process (6.3)   265
    • Supplier Quality Results (6.4)   270

CHAPTER 11
    Interpreting the Criteria for Customer Focus and Satisfaction (7.0)   273

    • Customer Expectations: Current and Future (7.1)   275
    • Customer Relationship Management (7.2)   285
    • Commitment to Customers (7.3)   304
    • Customer Satisfaction Determination (7.4)   308
    • Customer Satisfaction Results (7.5)   314
    • Customer Satisfaction Comparison (7.6)   318

CHAPTER 12
    How to Audit Your Organization Against the Baldrige Award Criteria   323

    • The Audit Cycle   324
    • Phase I: Planning the Quality Audit   325
    • Phase II: Conducting the Audit   336
    • Phase III: Reporting Audit Findings   345
    • Phase IV: Correcting Audit Findings   350
    • Conclusions   357

CHAPTER 13
   Using a Baldrige Assessment as a Strategic Planning Tool   359

   • Assessment Alternatives   360
   • Using the Baldrige Assessment to Drive Improvement   364

FURTHER READING   369

APPENDICES
A. 1994 Award Criteria: Malcolm Baldrige National Quality Award
B. 1994 Application Forms and Instructions

INTRODUCTION

The Malcolm Baldrige Award is seven years old in 1994. By now, just about every company in the United States has heard something about the award and is at least somewhat familiar with this new approach to running a company, called Total Quality Management, or TQM. Since 1988, there have been literally hundreds of articles published on the Baldrige Award, and how companies are using the award criteria to improve their operations. When the present book was first published in 1991, it was the only one of its kind on the market. Now there are at least four others, and chapters in many quality management books, that address the award.

Growth of the Quality Movement

The Malcolm Baldrige National Quality Award was initiated in 1987 to promote TQM as an increasingly important approach for making products and services in the U.S. among the best in the world again. The award recognizes small and large service and manufacturing companies that demonstrate exemplary performance in both the way they run their companies and in the quality of their products and/or services. The award has greatly exceeded the expectations of its initiators at the Department of Commerce and the National Institute of Standards and Technology. Since 1988, almost a million copies of the award criteria have been distributed, and about 500 companies have applied for the award. More importantly, it appears that TQM is having an impact on improving the quality of American products and services. In the 10/15/92 edition of *USA Today*, writer John Hillkirk reports that:

- *Among U.S. . . . automakers, average defects per vehicle have declined from 7.3 in 1981 models to 1.5 in 1992 models. That's almost as good as Japanese cars, on average.*

- *Just 1% of U.S. steel products contain defects, vs. 8% in 1981.*

- *U.S.-made semiconductors are better. In 1980, almost 3,000 chips failed for every 1 billion hours of active computer time. Today, fewer than 100 fail under the same usage. (p. 1-B)*

Baldrige Winner Files for Chapter 11

In recent years, stories have arisen about problems that Baldrige winners have faced subsequent to winning the award. The first and most serious story concerns the Wallace Company, a 1990 Baldrige winner. Wallace is a Houston-based distributor of pipes valves and related equipment and parts for oil and chemical plants. The newspaper and business magazine stories presented dire headlines sounding like:

Baldrige winner goes in toilet while executives make speeches about quality.

The newspaper stories explain that the company got into financial trouble because no one was minding the store while the executives traveled all over making speeches, and the folks back home were too busy conducting tours for and talking to the thousands of companies who wanted to know how they too could win the Baldrige Award. In January, 1992, the Wallace Company's troubles became so bad that they filed for Chapter 11.

When, however, you talk to the people at the Wallace Company you get a very different story than the one in the newspapers. Their side of the story is that in mid-1991, a large bank bought the bank that Wallace had done business with for many years. Consequently, Wallace got assigned a new loan officer. Wallace is a highly leveraged business, so they had had a close relationship with their previous banker. During 1991, a couple of Wallace's biggest competitors filed for bankruptcy because the recession had caused business to drop off so severely that sufficient cash was not coming in to allow them to stay in business. Good news for Wallace, right? Unfortunately, Wallace's new banker looked at what happened to these other companies and decided that Wallace might be next. Wallace was losing business because their customers were buying up inventory from the two bankrupt competitors at greatly reduced prices. Wallace's customers said, "We like you people and will continue to buy from you in the future, but the company down the street's going out of business, and has the same parts for half what you want for them."

Observing this, Wallace's new banker decided to call their loan. By the end of 1991, Wallace had temporarily lost much of its business due to the misfortune of its competitors, and then had to pay off a huge loan all at once. Since they didn't have the cash to pay off the loan or the resources to keep afloat until the customers bought all of the competitors' inventory and came back to Wallace, there was only one solution. In January, 1992, Wallace filed for bankruptcy. Since then, Wallace has been purchased by a larger company who is willing to infuse the necessary cash to get the business going again.

According to Wallace officials, to suggest that their winning the Malcolm Baldrige Award, or their total quality effort more generally, had anything to do with their financial troubles is ridiculous. As quoted in the January, 1992, issue of *The Quality Observer*, former CEO Michael Spiess puts it this way:

> *To be real blunt, winning the Malcolm Baldrige National Quality Award had absolutely nothing to do with the position that Wallace finds itself in today. In fact, had it not been for the fact that we embraced total quality management, we wouldn't be around . . . to enjoy the '91 recession. (p. 12)*

Problems of Other Baldrige Winners

Other Baldrige winners have also experienced troubles. IBM, whose Rochester, Minnesota plant won the award in 1991, had a very bad year in 1992. Yet, under new CEO Gerster, IBM is still using the Baldrige criteria to assess and improve the organization. General Motors, whose Cadillac Division won in 1990, closed many of its plants in 1992 and 1993 due to sluggish sales and excessive labor and overhead costs. Both of these companies had one division or plant of their organizations win the Baldrige Award. When the entire parent company is having trouble, though, people forget that it wasn't IBM or General Motors as such that won the Baldrige Award. The IBM plant that won continues to be successful despite its troubles, as is the Cadillac division of General Motors. Cadillac's 1992 Seville STS won most of the major annual automotive awards, and levels of Cadillac's customer satisfaction and sales continue to improve.

Other Controversies Surrounding the Baldrige

In an October 14, 1992 *Wall Street Journal* headline, the process used to select winners is questioned by a unit of Westinghouse that feels it should have won the award, but did not for political reasons:

> *In an action never previously reported, the Commerce Department blocked a recommendation by the contest's expert judges to award a Baldrige to Westinghouse Idaho Nuclear Co., a unit of Westinghouse Electric Corp. that processes nuclear material for the federal government. The veto appears to mark the first time since the competition began in 1988 that the department, which administers the award, has rejected the advice of the nine-member judging panel. (p. B1)*

The Commerce Department has always had the final say on the selection of winners, but since this is the first time the Department has ever overruled the judges' recommendations it raises questions about the credibility of the entire process. Prior to selecting winners, a thorough investigation of the finalists is conducted, looking at records from the police, the FBI, the IRS, and other regulatory agencies. The purpose of this review is to make sure that the company does not have any skeletons in its closet that might come out after the company won the award. As I understand it, the Westinghouse facility had received several safety violations from the Nuclear Regulatory Commission, and the Commerce Department did not feel that a company that received such violations would be a good role model for other businesses in the country.

Another controversy arose in late 1992 when the winners were announced. One 1992 winner was AT&T Universal Card Services, a company that won in the service category. Cries of protest arose because this company has only been in business since 1990. Baldrige Examiners are generally taught to look for at least three to five years' worth of data in the sections that call for results. Three to five data points are important for several reasons. First, one cannot determine whether a trend exists by looking at two data points only. Statisticians generally believe that seven data points are the minimum necessary to establish any kind of trend in data. The second reason is that the criteria call for evidence of *sustained positive results*. Critics argue that AT&T Universal Card Services had only two years' worth of data at the most, which is hardly enough to establish any kind of trend, and certainly not a sufficient time period to suggest that results can be sustained. In fact, since winning the award, it's been reported that AT&T Universal Card Services is losing significant market share to General Motors' new credit card. (However, this is almost certainly due to advertising and better terms/benefits. The GM card has not been out long enough for customers to experience service levels.)

In responding to these concerns about how a two-year-old company could possibly win the award, Baldrige officials explain that while trends and ability to sustain results are important, so are the levels of performance as depicted on graphs. AT&T's results were so powerful and at such high levels, officials explain, that this offset the fact that the company could provide only two years' worth of data. While this response sounds reasonable, and is consistent with the scoring scale, it doesn't satisfy many of the critics.

Beyond the Headlines—The Real Payoff of Using the Baldrige Criteria

The bad news about Baldrige winners and finalists seems to make it to the front page, whereas the good news ends up in small print in the back of the paper. The real test of whether or not the Baldrige criteria are a road map for running a better company is whether companies that win the award are better off financially than those who do not apply for the award.

Consultant B. Ray Helton reports in the September/October issue of QPMA's newsletter *Discovery* that investing in Baldrige winners pays off better than you might expect. Helton created the hypothetical Malcolm Baldrige Mutual Fund, which consisted of all publically-traded Baldrige Award winners from 1988 to 1992. The Baldrige Mutual Fund outperformed the general stock market by more than double. According to Helton: $1,000 invested in each of the Baldrige winners after they won the award would have yielded an 82% increase in principal. The same money invested in the S&P 500 stocks on the same dates would have yielded a 34% increase. The Baldrige stocks did almost three times better than the S&P 500. This is in spite of losses that were seen in the stock values of IBM and Westinghouse. Some Baldrige winners have shown phenomenal growth in their stock value. Motorola's stock has gone up over 400% since winning the award in 1988, and Solectron, a 1991 winner has shown a 226% increase in the value of its stock.

The lesson to be learned is that investing in quality really does pay off. If you ignore the headlines and look at the real data, you will find that there is a great deal of evidence that following the Baldrige criteria not only makes a company more successful in the long run, but also helps to ensure a healthy bottom line in the short-term.

In short, it's working. Most companies are now working to improve their products and services and are grateful for a road map that leads them on their journey. U.S. products and services continue to improve, but the question is: are they improving fast enough? Only time will tell. Some companies will obviously drop out, being unable to compete; but many will survive. To quote the CEO of 1991 Baldrige winner, Zytec Corporation:

> *If you're not on the quality journey now, you better get on it. Only those companies that are on this journey will be around in the future.**

The Baldrige Award Has Served its Purpose Well

In spite of all the criticism about fairness in judging, and whether or not meeting the criteria predict financial success, the Baldrige has done more to improve the quality of U.S. products and services than anything that has come before it. Quality is now something that almost every company in America is working on. The biggest benefit of the Baldrige criteria is that we now have a common framework for making sense out of all of the theories, tools, and approaches that are part of the quality movement. We have a common language and a common way of understanding where to apply all of these theories and techniques. Another benefit of the Baldrige has been that companies are now sharing and talking to one another to help one another get better. This sharing and helping almost never occurred five years ago—companies kept to themselves, and shared only those practices that they were certain would not help a competitor. The Baldrige Award has been successful beyond the greatest expectations of its founders. It has given rise to 18 similar awards in other countries, 5 of which are modeled exactly on the Baldrige criteria. Thirty-two states in the U.S. have either established their own quality awards or have an effort underway. Through these "baby Baldriges," quality is being deployed even more pervasively than through the Baldrige by itself. In fact, the existence of state-level quality awards is one of the primary reasons why Baldrige applicants dropped from around 100 in previous years to 76 applicants in 1993.

---

* Schmidt, Ronald. *American Interests*. "The 1991 Malcolm Baldrige National Quality Award Winners Share their Secrets." Washington, DC: aired 2/22/92.

Interpreting the Baldrige Criteria

One problem for users of the Baldrige Award criteria is that they can be difficult to interpret. The criteria are written to be very general, because they must apply equally to both service and manufacturing organizations, and they must apply to organizations ranging in size from a few hundred employees to many thousands. Because the criteria are so general, they are difficult to interpret. The other thing that makes the criteria hard to use for assessment is that they are non-prescriptive. In other words, they don't tell you how you should be implementing TQM. In my work as a management consultant and as a Baldrige Examiner, I've encountered many instances where people had difficulty interpreting the Baldrige criteria. Other examiners and quality improvement consultants I've spoken to report similar observations.

The purpose of this text, then, is to provide readers with a better understanding of the 89 Areas to Address that make up the Baldrige Award criteria. The book is designed to aid organizations that are actually preparing an application for the Baldrige Award, as well as the many organizations that will be using the award criteria as a way of improving their quality improvement efforts.

How to Use This Book

Generally, there are two types of uses for this book:

1.   As a guide for individuals who are responsible for coordinating or actually writing a Baldrige Award application.

2.   As a tool for individuals who wish to audit or assess their organization using the Baldrige Award criteria, or who wish to apply for an internal award based upon the criteria. Individuals who are responsible for developing TQM implementation plans based upon the Baldrige criteria will also find the book useful.

The specifics of the book are directed primarily toward the individuals of the first category, with information provided on how to write various sections of the Baldrige Award application. Chapters 1 and 2 provide general information on understanding the Award and on preparing the application. Chapter 3 explains how the seven categories of criteria work together as a system, and covers the overall themes carried throughout the criteria. Chapter 4 includes information on the scoring scale. The next seven chapters cover the seven main categories in the Baldrige criteria. Each of these chapters includes an overall explanation of the main category and definitions of the Examination Items and the Areas to Address. Also provided are sections entitled "What They're Looking For Here," which describe the criteria as seen by the Examiners. This section is followed by a listing of "Key Indicators" or evaluation factors provided to further assist you with the interpretation of the criteria. Naturally, I assume that those companies seriously considering challenging for the Award have had a quality system in place for several years and that their use of this text is to help them best represent their quality systems and demonstrate compliance with the Baldrige criteria.

This information is also helpful to individuals using the criteria for the second purpose. For this second type of user, the various "indicators" that are listed for each of the 91 Areas to Address are helpful in devising TQM audit instruments and in developing plans rooted in each of the seven categories in the Baldrige criteria. Chapter 12, explains how to plan and conduct an organization audit using the Baldrige criteria as a baseline. The final chapter outlines alternative assessment approaches and how to use such assessments as an input to your strategic planning process.

Complete copies of the 1994 Award Criteria and Application Forms and Instructions are included in Appendices A and B respectively. If you are not already familiar with the criteria, I suggest that you quickly review them as a means of preparing for reading and working with this text. If you are interested in actually applying for the award, you might want to obtain the *original* 1994 Award Criteria and the Application (two separate documents) so that you can work with the original entry forms. For the purpose of actually applying for the award, you should familiarize yourself with *all* the information in both forms. These two documents are available free of charge through the National Institute of Standards and Technology, Route 270 and Quince Orchard Road, Administration Bldg., Room A537, Gaithersburg, MD 20899-0001.

How the Information For This Book Was Compiled

The information in this book was compiled on the basis of my experience as a Baldrige Award Examiner from 1990 through 1992. My experience as an examiner enabled me to review actual applications, discuss the examination process and award criteria with numerous other examiners, and participate in the Examiner Training Workshop in which examiners are trained to interpret the criteria. The text is not an official publication of the National Institute of Standards and Technology, and the suggestions and opinions in it are my own.

The information in this book also draws upon my consulting experience, in which I help companies develop their own quality improvement processes based upon the Baldrige criteria.

The third edition of this book was based upon the 1993 award criteria, and has been revised here to reflect the changes made for 1994. Although the number of Areas to Address has been changed from 92 to 91, the criteria remain mostly unchanged from 1993. Almost all of the changes involve word changes to clarify the Areas to Address, along with the addition of many notes. (Further details on changes from the 1993 Examination appear on page 12 in the 1994 Award Criteria booklet.) In the few instances where the criteria were actually changed, I have provided my interpretation of the new criteria.

Additional Notes to The Reader

Because the Baldrige Examiners are not allowed to disclose any information contained in award applications, all of the examples used in this text are fictitious. Some are based upon actual applications but are thoroughly disguised so as to protect the anonymity of the applicants. Some companies have volunteered or have made public specific information about their experiences in challenging for the Award. These companies have been mentioned by name.

Future Volumes

Revised and updated editions of this work are planned for each year, assuming that the Baldrige Award criteria continue to be revised and improved each year. Suggestions on how we might improve the 1995 version of this book are welcome, and should be directed to:

Mark Graham Brown
c/o Quality Resources
A Division of The Kraus Organization Limited
One Water Street
White Plains, NY 10601

Chapter 1

Understanding the
Malcolm Baldrige
National Quality Award

HAS INTEREST IN QUALITY PEAKED IN THE U.S.?

According to some executives I have talked to, interest in quality peaked in 1992. Some companies have tried TQM for a while and have abandoned it in favor of a back-to-basics approach that concentrates on results rather than process. However, the problems that created the need for a new way of running organizations are still present. Our factories still aren't as productive as some other countries'; our cars still aren't as good as Japanese cars, and service is still poor in many of the service companies in this country. Healthcare and education costs are skyrocketing, yet quality is getting worse. There is still a great need to improve quality in most U.S. companies.

If interest in quality has peaked, which I think is doubtful, it is due to the realization that this approach called TQM or Total Quality requires a great deal of hard work, time, and major changes in the way companies operate. The prize to win for all this effort is not the Baldrige Award. The prize is staying in business and being a successful company. The evidence that I see shows that interest in TQM is still on the upswing. The American Society for Quality Control, the largest and oldest professional organization for those in the quality field, has more than doubled its membership since 1987. There are now well over 100 books and at least 8 regular periodicals that specifically address Total Quality Management. From what I've seen there's not much evidence to suggest that interest has peaked. Since the Baldrige criteria were first published, over a million copies have been distributed. Sales of the present book have been greater in 1993 than in 1992, even though there were several other books on the Baldrige Award available in 1993. Yet, the number of companies that applied for the Baldrige in 1993 is down by about 25% from 1992 levels.

To help encourage U.S. companies and reward them for providing high quality products and services, the Malcolm Baldrige Award was created in 1987 through an act of Congress. According to the 1994 Award Criteria, the award is designed to promote:

- *awareness of quality as an increasingly important element in competitiveness*

- *understanding of the requirements for quality excellence*

- *sharing of information on successful quality strategies and the benefits derived from implementation of those strategies (p. 1)*

According to Harvard professor, David A. Garvin:

"In just four years, the Malcolm Baldrige National Quality Award has become the most important catalyst for transforming American business. More than any other initiative, public or private, it has reshaped managers' thinking and behavior." (1991, p. 80)

The existence of the Baldrige Award is based upon Public Law 100-107, which creates a public-private partnership designed to encourage quality from American companies. The Findings and Purposes sections of Public Law 100-107 state that:

1. The leadership of the United States in product and process quality has been challenged strongly (and sometimes successfully) by foreign competition, and our Nation's productivity growth has improved less than our competitors' over the last two decades.

2. American business and industry are beginning to understand that poor quality costs companies as much as 20 percent of sales revenues nationally and that improved quality of goods and services goes hand in hand with improved productivity, lower costs, and increased profitability.

3. Strategic planning for quality and quality improvement programs, through a commitment to excellence in manufacturing and services, are becoming more and more essential to the well-being of our Nation's economy and our ability to compete effectively in the global marketplace.

4. Improved management understanding of the factory floor, worker involvement in quality, and greater emphasis on statistical process control can lead to dramatic improvements in the cost and quality of manufactured products.

5. The concept of quality improvement is directly applicable to small companies as well as large, to service industries as well as manufacturing, and to the public sector as well as private enterprise.

6. In order to be successful, quality improvement programs must be management-led and customer-oriented, and this may require fundamental changes in the way companies and agencies do business.

7. Several major industrial nations have successfully coupled rigorous private-sector quality audits with national awards giving special recognition to those enterprises the audits identify as the very best; and

8. A national quality award program of this kind in the United States would help improve quality and productivity by:

   A. Helping to stimulate American companies to improve quality and productivity for the pride of recognition while obtaining a competitive edge through increased profits;

   B. Recognizing the achievements of those companies that improve the quality of their goods and services and providing an example to others;

C. Establishing guidelines and criteria that can be used by business, industrial, governmental, and other organizations in evaluating their own quality improvement efforts; and

D. Providing specific guidance for other American organizations that wish to learn how to manage for high quality by making available detailed information on how winning organizations were able to change their cultures and achieve eminence.

The Award is managed by the National Institute for Standards and Technology (NIST), which is part of the Department of Commerce.

The actual award is quite impressive. It is a three-part Steuben Glass crystal stele, standing 14 inches tall, with an 22 karat gold-plated medal embedded in the middle of the central crystal. This prestigious award is presented to winners by the president of the United States at a special ceremony in Washington, D.C.

So what happens to the thousands of sets of criteria that get sent to companies who don't end up applying for the Baldrige Award? Some get thrown in the trash, but from my experience and conversations with clients and colleagues most become dog-eared and are photocopied many times over. They are being used by all types and sizes of companies as the standards by which their own quality improvement efforts and activities are assessed.

Robert Galvin, former chairman of Motorola (1988 Baldrige Award winner), is quoted in the April 23, 1990, issue of *Fortune* as saying:

> *If all eligible companies in the U.S. went for the Baldrige, the natural growth rate of the GNP would rise by an extra half a percentage point. (p. 101)*

So, the value isn't necessarily in winning the award as much as in providing a common set of standards for implementing total quality management.

WHO CAN WIN THE AWARD?

The award program is set up so there can be a maximum of six winners each year—two large manufacturing companies, two large service companies, and two small businesses, which may be either manufacturing or service. In the five years that the award has been given out, the maximum number of winners has been five, in 1992. In 1989, only two companies won the award, both being large manufacturing companies. The winners from the last five years are listed in the box below.

AWARD WINNERS: 1988 to 1993

1993 Award Winners

Manufacturing
Eastman Chemical Company
Kingsport, TN

Small Business
Ames Rubber Corp.
Hamburg, NJ

1992 Award Winners

Manufacturing
AT&T Network Systems Group
Transmission Systems Business Unit
Morristown, NJ

Texas Instruments, Inc.
Defense Systems & Electronics Group
Dallas, TX

Service
AT&T Universal Card Services
Jacksonville, FL

The Ritz-Carlton Hotel Company
Atlanta, GA

Small Business
Granite Rock Company
Watsonville, CA

1991 Award Winners

Manufacturing
Solectron Corp.
San Jose, CA

Zytec Corp.
Eden Prairie, MN

Small Business
Marlow Industries
Dallas, TX

1990 Award Winners

Manufacturing
Cadillac Motor Car Company
Detroit, MI

IBM Rochester
Rochester, MN

Service
Federal Express Corp.
Memphis, TN

Small Business
Wallace Co., Inc.
Houston, TX

1989 Award Winners

Manufacturing
Milliken & Company
Spartanburg, SC

Xerox Business Products and Systems
Stamford, CT

1988 Award Winners

Manufacturing
Motorola, Inc.
Schaumburg, IL

Westinghouse Commercial
Nuclear Fuel Division
Pittsburgh, PA

Small Business
Globe Metallurgical, Inc.
Cleveland, OH

One thing that has happened over the last few years is that an increasing number of service companies and small companies have applied for the Baldrige Award. One of the indicators that TQM is being further deployed across the U.S. is the number of small companies that apply for the award. In 1993, many of the 76 applicants were small companies that apply for the award. In 1993, many of the 76 applicants were small companies. The winners in 1991 were all fairly small companies. This fact encouraged a number of small businesses across the country, who realized that you don't have to be a Xerox or IBM to win the award. In fact, it is probably easier for a small company to implement an approach like TQM. Many companies were scared off when Xerox reported that it took them 800,000 labor hours to prepare their winning Baldrige application in 1989. Ronald Schmidt, CEO of 1991 award winner Zytec Corporation, reports that they spent a total of $8900.00 on their application. They did not hire any consultants to help them, and the executives completed the application themselves.

APPLICATION AND EVALUATION PROCESS

Applicants for the Baldrige Award must write up to a 85 page application (up to 70 pages for a small business) that explains how they have implemented total quality in their organization and the results they have achieved. The report is divided into seven sections, corresponding to the seven categories of criteria for the award:

1. Leadership	(9.5%)
2. Information and Analysis	(7.5%)
3. Strategic Quality Planing	(6%)
4. Human Resource Development and Management	(15%)
5. Management of Process Quality	(14%)
6. Quality and Operational Results	(18%)
7. Customer Focus and Satisfaction	(30%)

Each category is weighted according to its importance in the overall evaluation. As you can see, Customer Satisfaction is worth a full 30% of the evaluation, whereas category 3, Strategic Quality Planning, is worth only 6%.

Each of these seven categories is further broken down into 28 Examination Items, which are themselves broken down into 91 Areas to Address.

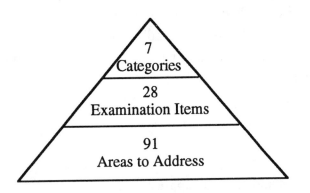

Figure 1.1: Hierarchy of Award Criteria

The application report needs to address each of the 91 Areas to Address separately. All Areas to Address should be covered by all organizations. However, an applicant does not lose credit if one or more Areas to Address does not pertain to his/her business. If an item is not relevant, the applicant must explain why, however. Chapters 5 through 11 of this book explain each of the criteria in detail, so that you can better understand what the examiners are looking for.

What's New For 1994

Essentially, not much. There has been very little change to the criteria from 1993 to 1994. What has changed is the wording of the Areas to Address. Many unnecessary words were deleted, and two 1993 Areas to Address from Item 5.2 were combined into one. This makes the total number of areas 91 rather than the 92 that were there in 1993. The basic Baldrige system has not changed. The points are still allocated with about two thirds of the points for your approaches and the deployment of the approaches, and one third for the results an organization achieves. The specific breakdown of points for each of the 28 Items has not changed either.

The biggest change has been the addition of a great many notes to explain the 91 Areas to Address. While many of these notes help to clarify what is being asked for in the criteria, they also make the criteria longer and more difficult to read. Over the last six years the Baldrige criteria have grown from being a basic set of items to test for the presence of Total Quality to a comprehensive set of criteria concerning what it takes to run a successful organization. I hold that the 1994 Baldrige criteria are the most comprehensive set of standards available for evaluating the health of an organization. Unfortunately, however, the criteria have also become more like a typical government document. They are too long, too detailed, too hard to read, and contain too many points, sub-points, and sub, sub-points. It is with this in mind that I and my publisher offer this new book for 1994 as a quick reference guide to understanding the Baldrige criteria. The book was written because the Baldrige criteria still need to be interpreted to make sense to most people in most organizations.

Evaluation

Figure 1.2 depicts the prescreening process and the four-stage review process that occurs once an organization has submitted an application.

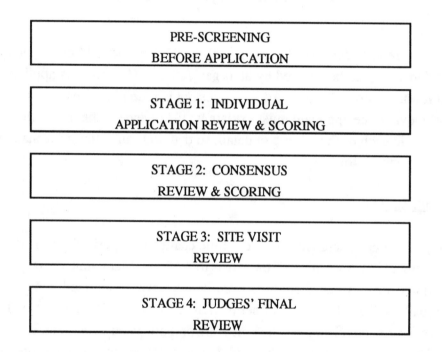

Figure 1.2: Four-stage Review Process

All applications are reviewed by six to eight members of the Board of Examiners. The board is composed of approximately 250 examiners selected from business, professional and trade associations, universities, and government. All members are recognized experts in the quality field. When assigning board members to review applications, the experience and industry background of the examiner are matched to the applicant, provided that there is no conflict of interest. Examiners with manufacturing backgrounds receive applications from manufacturing companies and examiners with service industry experience receive service company applications. Board members must follow strict rules regarding the confidentiality of applications, and must agree to abide by a code of ethics, which includes non-disclosure of information from applicants. Examiners are not even allowed to reveal the names of companies that have applied for the award.

In Stage two, the scored applications are then submitted to a Senior Examiner who reviews the variability in scoring, identifies major discrepancies, and schedules a consensus meeting. Much like a jury, the examiners must reach consensus on your score. A consensus meeting is held via conference call or in person, and is led by a senior examiner. Senior examiners are responsible for supervising the team of examiners assigned to review each company. A recommendation is made as to whether or not a site visit is warranted. A panel of judges decides whether or not to accept the recommendation, or to have the application reviewed by other examiners.

Of the 1,000 points possible to earn on an application, the majority of applications receive scores of less than 500 points. As a general rule, if an application receives a score of 601 or above, the organization is considered to have made it to the semi-finals, and might qualify for a site visit. The 600 or above points is not a hard rule about who receives a site visit, only a general guideline based on what's happened in the past. During a site visit, a team of five or more examiners spends approximately three to five days in your facilities touring, conducting interviews, and reviewing data and records. Applicants are asked to make introductory and concluding presentations. The site visit is similar to having an audit done. The purpose of the site visit is to verify and clarify the information included in your written application and to resolve any issues or uncertainties that came up in reviewing your written application. The examiners may have accepted what you said in your written application at face value, but now they want to see proof of your claims.

The findings of the site visit are summarized in a site visit report that goes to the Baldrige Award judges for the stage four review. It is during this review that the judges decide which applicants they will recommend in each category to be award winners. The panel of judges makes its recommendations to the National Institute of Standards and Technology, which makes final recommendations to the U.S. Secretary of Commerce. Those serving as judges are known nationally for their expertise in the quality field and have typically served as examiners or senior examiners in the past.

At the end of the calendar year, feedback reports are sent out to all Baldrige Award applicants. Regardless of the score, each applicant receives a detailed feedback report that summarizes the strengths and weaknesses identified by the examiners in their review of the application. Feedback reports are probably the most valuable result of applying for the award because they provide very specific information on the areas in which you excel and the areas that you need to work on. In fact, the feedback report is probably the best bargain in consulting services that you could buy. It costs $4,000 for large companies to apply for the Baldrige Award and $1,200 for small businesses. For that fee, you get five to six highly trained quality experts to review your company and prepare a detailed analysis of its strengths and weaknesses. If you wanted to purchase this service from an outside consulting firm, it may cost between $10,000 and $25,000, depending upon the size of your organization and the number of consultants involved. So, for $4,000 you receive a wealth of valuable information. In fact, many organizations realize that they are far from being at the level required to win the Baldrige Award, but apply anyway. That way, they can find out exactly where they need to focus their improvement efforts in the next few years.

WHAT THE EXAMINERS ARE REALLY LOOKING FOR

The three factors (or "evaluation dimensions") that the Baldrige Examiners look for in each section of an application are your:

- Approach

- Deployment

- Results

Approach refers to the processes you use to achieve quality products or services. Clearly there are certain themes that the Baldrige people look for in your approach:

- The degree to which the approach is prevention-based

- Focus on continuous improvement

- The appropriateness and effectiveness of the methods, tools, and techniques to the requirements

- The degree to which the approach is systematic, integrated, and consistently applied

- The degree to which the approach embodies effective evaluation/improvement cycles

- The degree to which the approach is based upon quantitative information that is objective and reliable

- Degree to which approach is based upon cooperation and participation of all levels of employees

- The indicators of unique and innovative approaches, including significant and effective new adaptations of tools and techniques used in other applications or types of businesses

Deployment refers to how well your approach has been executed. It is possible that an organization has an exceptional approach, but it has only been implemented in a few areas. Some of the overall indicators for assessing deployment are:

- The appropriate and effective application of the stated approach to all product and service features

- The appropriate and effective application of the stated approach by all work units to all processes and activities

- The appropriate and effective application of the stated approach to all transactions and interactions with customers, suppliers of goods and services, and the public

Results are clearly *not* asked for in all of the 91 areas to address or 28 Examination Items. Many of the areas to address ask only for information on your approach and the deployment of that approach. Other areas to address ask only for results. Within the Leadership category, results are asked for in 1.3d, which asks for trend data demonstrating improvements in measures of public responsibility and corporate citizenship. No results are asked for in either categories 2.0 or 3.0. Results are asked for in the following areas to address in the Human Resource Development and Management section (4.0):

- 4.2d Trends in the effectiveness and extent of employee involvement

- 4.3d Trends in the effectiveness and extent of quality and related training and education

- 4.4c Trends in the extent and effectiveness of employee reward and recognition

- 4.5d Trends in key indicators of employee satisfaction and well-being.

Results are also asked for in the following Examination Items:

- 6.1 Product and Service Quality Results

- 6.2 Company Operational Results

- 6.3 Business Process and Support Service Results

- 6.4 Supplier Quality Results

- 7.5 Customer Satisfaction Results

- 7.6 Customer Satisfaction Comparison

Some specific factors that are examined when evaluating results are:

- Current and past overall quality and performance levels

- The demonstration of sustained improvement or sustained high-level performance

- Demonstration of cause/effect between quality improvement efforts and quality results

- The rate/speed of performance improvement

- The breadth and importance of performance improvements

- Significance of quality improvements to the company's business

- The quality and performance levels relative to appropriate comparisons and/or benchmarks

Each of the 91 Areas to Address that are described in Chapters 5–11 of this book are identified as to whether they pertain to approach, deployment, or results (see brackets [ ]).

THE BALDRIGE HAS GIVEN RISE TO INTERNAL AWARDS

Many organizations have been using the Baldrige criteria to evaluate and improve their own companies, without ever intending to apply for the award itself. Among some of the organizations that use the criteria for assessment are:

- Air Products & Chemicals
- Appleton Papers
- McDonnell Douglas
- Baxter Healthcare
- Bell Atlantic
- Pacific Bell
- AT&T
- Boise Cascade
- Northrop
- NYNEX
- Bell South
- IBM

- Roadway Express
- Northern Telecom
- U.S. Airforce

- Kodak
- Cargill Corporation
- Westinghouse

A few of these organizations have made some changes to the Baldrige criteria to customize them for their own organizations, but most use the criteria as is.

RESPONSIBILITIES AND BENEFITS OF WINNING THE BALDRIGE AWARD

Winning the Baldrige Award may be the dream of a number of companies' CEOs and executives. However, winning brings with it a great deal of responsibility. One price of winning is that you must share your approach to quality with others. As an award winner, you will be inundated with requests for information, tours, etc. Everyone will want to know how you did it, how much money you spent implementing total quality management, how much time it takes, and how they can take what you have done and apply it to their own companies. According to an article in the April 23, 1990 issue of *Fortune*, Richard Beutow, Motorola's vice president for quality, made 352 speeches to conventions and corporations, and answered requests for information from over 1,000 companies (p. 109). All of the award winners report similar interest and responses. So if you win, you must be prepared to share your secrets of success with the world, and be prepared to devote several full-time people to the task of responding to requests for information on how you won the Baldrige Award.

The benefits of winning, however, far outweigh the costs. Winners are allowed to publicize the award as much as they want to their customers. Xerox, for example, includes the Baldrige logo on all of its correspondence and product literature. This does wonders for promoting their image as a quality company. Motorola has taken similar advantage of the opportunity to advertise its quality achievements. Winners receive a great deal of peer recognition from other executives, competitors, and the entire business community. Winning is probably the best thing that can happen to a company to promote a positive quality image. Another benefit of winning is the impact the award has upon employee morale. Employees of Motorola, Xerox, Ritz Carlton, Federal Express, AT&T, and the other award winners have long known that they worked for a quality company. But did the world know? Winning the award tells their business relations, neighbors, relatives, friends, and competitors that they work for one of the best companies in the country.

Chapter 2

Preparing an Application for the Baldrige Award

Preparing the written application for the Baldrige Award is a great deal of work. In fact, Xerox, one of the 1989 winners, claims to have spent over 800,000 labor hours gathering data and developing their application. Don't be scared off by the time spent by Xerox. The president of Globe Metallurgical, the 1988 small business Baldrige Award winner, says that he did most of the work on their application over a long weekend (*Fortune*, April 23, 1990, p. 103). It is important to spend a fair amount of time completing the application report because it will be all the examiners have to evaluate your company. Most award applicants never receive a site visit, as you need to score in the high 600s or better before you are scheduled for a site visit. Therefore, your application needs to be written in a thorough and comprehensive enough manner to achieve a qualifying score for a site visit.

The quality level of Baldrige Award applications vary considerably. Some are expertly written, contain only pertinent information, and are printed in four colors, so they look like an annual report. Others are poorly written, are missing information, and are typed on an old typewriter. The quality of your company is being judged based upon the quality of this report, so it is crucial that the application report be complete, clear, and error-free. In this chapter, I outline some major issues on how the application should be written and provide guidelines concerning mistakes to avoid when preparing your application. Examples are provided to help illustrate what to do and what not to do.

As a special note to readers, I suggest that the information provided in this chapter be reviewed in conjunction with the information contained in the 1994 Criteria and Application Forms and Instructions for the Malcolm Baldrige National Quality Award. Reproductions of these documents appear in the back of this text. An original set is available free of charge from the National Institute of Standards and Technology (see Appendices A and B).

GENERAL OUTLINE OF THE MAJOR COMPONENTS OF THE APPLICATION PACKAGE

Your 1994 application package must contain all required forms including (1) the Eligibility Determination Form (which must already have been approved); (2) the Application Form; and (3) the Site Listing and Descriptors Form. These forms are available in the 1994 Application Forms and Instructions booklet, as are complete instructions on how to prepare them.

Your application package must also contain an application report. The application report consists of a four-page overview of your business and a 70-85 page document that is generally divided into seven major sections, corresponding to the seven categories of criteria. In this document you must respond to and address all of the Examination Items and Areas to Address as presented in the criteria. If you are in the small business category your written document is limited to 70 single-sided pages, or 85 pages if you are a large service or manufacturing business (the four-page overview is not counted as part of the page limit). This 70 or 85 page limit includes charts, graphs, tables, and any supporting materials you decide to attach to your application. The examiners are very strict on this guideline. If your application report contains 95 pages, the Baldrige administrators will probably tear off the last 10 pages before sending the application to the examiners to review.

You may also be required to submit Supplemental Sections as a part of your application report. According to the Award Criteria, these are required when the applicant is a unit within a company that is in many different businesses. The criteria provide more details on this.

The major components of your application package should be organized into logical and clearly defined sections, such as:

- Application and Other Forms
- Overview
- 1.0 Leadership
- 2.0 Information and Analysis
- 3.0 Strategic Quality Planning
- 4.0 Human Resource Development and Management
- 5.0 Management of Process Quality
- 6.0 Quality and Operational Results
- 7.0 Customer Focus and Satisfaction
- Supplementary Sections (if required)

HOW TO WRITE THE APPLICATION

The way most internal users and award applicants approach writing the application is to form seven teams to work on each of the seven sections in the application. A project manager oversees the effort and attempts to edit the final document to make it appear as if it were written by one person. Although by far the most common approach, it is also the reason why most internal users and award applicants receive such low scores. *Using seven teams and/or individuals to work on each of the seven sections in the application is a major mistake.*

The seven categories of Baldrige criteria work together as a *system*. They are not seven independent factors. One of the most common problems appearing in Baldrige applications is what I call "disconnects." Disconnects are inconsistencies between sections. For example, an applicant might report in section 2.1 that they collect data on three different measures of customer satisfaction, but include no goals for these measures in section 3.2 and no graphs of results in section 7.5. *All seven sections need to be consistent and work together as a system.*

So, how do you ensure that all sections work together effectively? One answer is to have one person write the entire application. While this is not feasible in many large and complex organizations, it has been done. Marty Smith, of New England Telephone was the primary author of that company's Baldrige application. Marty had a committee that assisted in gathering information in writing the application, but he did the majority of the project coordination and writing himself. Several small companies that have won Baldrige Awards submitted applications written primarily by the CEOs.

In most large complex organizations it simply is not practical to have a single person write the application, so some type of team must be formed. But if forming teams around each of the seven Baldrige categories is not the way to organize the effort, how should it be done? A recent client of mine put together an application for the award by forming teams as follows:

> TEAM A: Section 1.0 Leadership
> TEAM B: Section 4.2-4.5 Human Resource Development and Management
> TEAM C: Sections 2.0, 3.2, 5.5, and 7.4 Measures and Goals
> TEAM D: Sections 3.1, 4.1, 5.1, and 7.1 Planning
> TEAM E: Sections 5.2-5.4, 7.2, and 7.3 Process and Customer Relationship
>   Management
> TEAM F: Sections 6.0, 7.5, and 7.6 Results

Sections 1.0 and 4.0 in the Baldrige system are the easiest ones to work on independent of the other sections. The approach of dividing up into the six teams as listed above worked fairly well in this case, but Teams C, D, E, and F had to work closely with one another. Team F (results) did not write its sections until the measurement team (C) finished its section.

Another organization I worked with organized two small teams and one large team to prepare their Baldrige Award application:

TEAM A: 1.0 Leadership
TEAM B: 4.0 Human Resource Development and Management
TEAM C: 2.0, 3.0, 5.0, 6.0, 7.0

This approach also worked well and helped to ensure that the seven sections flowed together well. Granted, the third team that had five sections had a lot of work to do, but it was a larger team that the other two and was prepared for the bigger effort.

MANAGING THE APPLICATION DEVELOPMENT PROJECT

Regardless of how you choose to put together teams to write the application, you will undoubtedly need a steering committee to oversee and approve the application, as well as a project manager to coordinate the effort. The steering committee should consist of 4-7 executives, including the CEO and his/her direct reports. These individuals may not have any involvement in writing the application, but they should provide access to any data needed by those writing each section and review the completed report. The steering committee members allocate resources to write the application and make any decisions regarding policies and the divulgence of confidential information. Steering committee members should plan on attending a minimum of two 4-8 hour meetings and spending an additional 6-8 hours reviewing various sections of the application.

Once the steering committee has been formed, select a project manager. In some organizations, the vice president of quality is chosen. In others, a function manager or director fills the position. The job this individual currently has is not important. What is important is that this individual have a good overall knowledge of the entire organization, know quality concepts, have good rapport with other managers, and pay great attention to detail. The project manager is responsible for seeing that the individuals working on various sections of the application meet their deadlines and adhere to key quality standards. The project manager serves as the liaison between the steering committee and a group of representatives from the teams who will make up an award application committee.

The number of people who participate on the award application committee will depend upon the size and complexity of your organization and how you decide to divide into teams. Figure 2.1 depicts a typical structure of the teams/committees that work on preparing the Baldrige application.

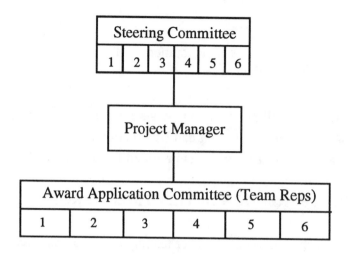

**Figure 2.1: Typical Organization Structure for
Baldrige Application Committee/Team**

Select people to work on the award application committee who are knowledgeable of the area/category they have been assigned and possess excellent writing skills. This will consume a great deal of time over the months that it takes to polish the application, so it is important that their bosses release them from some of their other responsibilities.

It is also a good idea to form a team of individuals responsible for editing and formatting the various sections of the application, creating graphics, doing word processing, and coordinating the reproduction and binding of the application. These tasks are time consuming, yet important. And it is important that the application look good and be error free. The leader of the application production team should be a member of the award application committee and attend all key meetings.

The first task on the project manager's and the award application committee's agenda is to hold a meeting to create a project plan for the development and production of the application. A project plan is a detailed list of tasks, resources estimates, and deadlines. It specifies the person(s) responsible and the amount of time allocated for performing each task. This serves as the basis from which a project can be built. The project plan can be created during a meeting facilitated by the project manager. An example of such a plan is shown in Figure 2.2. The numbers listed in the columns represent the time estimates (in days) for the various people who will work on the application. The plan presented is based upon using a seven-person award application committee. Time estimates apply to each person on the committees, and are based upon the assumption that quality assurance systems are already in place.

Project Plan
Baldrige Award Application

Tasks	Responsibilities & Time Requirements						Schedule
	PM	AAC	PROD	EDIT	SC	REV	
1. Project Planning Meeting							
a. Prepare for meeting	0.75	-	0.25	-	-	-	
b. Conduct/attend meeting	1.0	1.0	-	-	-	-	
c. Write Project Plan	1.0	-	1.0	0.25	-	-	
d. Review/Revise Project Plan	0.25	0.25	0.25	-	0.25	-	
2. Conduct Interviews and Gather Data	2.0	3.0	-	-	-	-	
3. Write First Drafts of Application Sections	2.0	2.5	5.0	4.0	-	-	
4. Review First Drafts	-	-	-	-	1.0	1.0	
5. Complete Mock Evaluations	0.5	-	-	-	-	2.0	
6. First Draft Feedback							
a. Assemble Reviewers' comments and evaluations	2.0	-	1.5	1.0	-	-	
b. Conduct/attend Feedback Meeting	2.0	2.0	-	-	-	-	
c. Document meeting outputs	1.0	-	2.0	-	-	-	
7. Write Second Drafts of Application Sections	1.5	1.5	-	3.0	-	-	
8. Production of Application Report							
a. Prepare and conduct/attend Production Planning Meeting	1.0	-	0.5	-	-	-	
b. Produce artwork, graphics, and printing specifications	1.5	-	4.0	0.5	-	-	
c. Printing of Final Award Applications	0.5	-	1.0	-	-	-	
9. Review Final Materials, Complete Forms, Prepare Overview, and Submit Application	1.5	0.5	1.5	0.5	0.5	-	4/3
TOTALS (days)	18.5	10.75	17.0	9.25	1.75	3.0	

KEY   PM   = Project Manager   EDIT = Editors
          AAC = Award Application Committee   SC   = Steering Committee
          PROD= Production/Graphics   REV = Reviewers

Figure 2.2: Project Workplan

As you can see in Figure 2.2, the plan includes a detailed list of tasks for each committee member or subcommittee. This plan is the project manager's tool for tracking the progress of the committee members. Many applicants don't bother to create such a plan and end up missing deadlines or having to race around at the last minute to complete the application in order to get it out by the April 1 deadline.

The best way to approach the application report is to look at each Examination Item and Area to Address separately. For each one, make a list of the data or resources needed for reference in order to prepare your response. For any Area to Address that asks for trends or data, you should also make a list of the graphs or charts you will need to prepare. This can be done in the committee meeting by listing the information on flipcharts, as demonstrated in Figure 2.3.

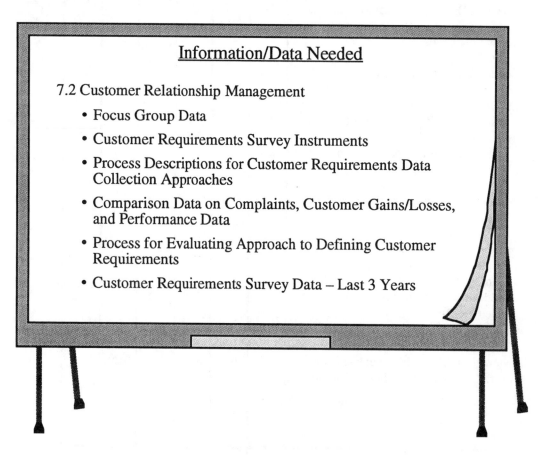

Figure 2.3: Example Flipchart from Planning Meeting

If you are working with several subcommittees, it may be necessary to assign information-gathering tasks to specific individuals. At the conclusion of the initial meeting, the project manager should formalize the project plan and distribute it to all award committee and steering committee members.

Gathering the information necessary to write the various sections of the Baldrige Award is the most difficult and time consuming task. Rarely will an organization have all the data needed readily at hand. Some data may not exist anywhere in the organization and may need to be collected. A number of departments and individuals within the organization may need to be contacted to collect all of the information needed to write each section of the application. The biggest problem experienced by committees working on the Baldrige application is lack of cooperation from other employees and managers who must dig up the information or data needed. This is one of the reasons that it is important to have high-level individuals on the steering committee. If the CEO or one of the vice presidents calls a manager to ask him or her where the data are that you requested in order to write your section of the award application, you can bet that the delinquent manager will get the information quickly.

All first drafts of sections of the application report should be turned in to the project manager, who will review them for accuracy, completeness, and clarity. He or she will return the edited copy of first drafts to the committee members who wrote them. The writers will then make the corrections suggested by the project manager and resubmit the application sections. If the project manager is satisfied that all of the necessary changes have been made, the material will be turned over to an editor who will edit the grammar, consistency, headings, readability, and other factors. After the sections have been edited, they will be turned over to production for word processing and preparation of graphics.

Once the report has been produced, internal copies should be prepared and distributed to the steering committee members and other key managers and technical professionals for their review. It is also a good idea to give the application to a few relatively new employees who have industry experience but little knowledge of the organization. These individuals can review the manuscript and the practices of your organization more objectively.

In addition to having many different people review the application and provide their feedback, it is also a good idea to train a group of people to actually evaluate the application against the Baldrige criteria. This might be a group of outside quality consultants or a group of your own employees. Whoever you select to perform this evaluation should be familiar with quality improvement concepts and tools, and be objective in their evaluation of the organization's application.

Feedback from reviewers and evaluations of the application should all be returned to the project manager by a specified date. After assembling and summarizing all of the comments, suggestions, and scores of the evaluators, the project manager should plan a two-day meeting with the award application committee to review the feedback and discuss changes and additions needed to each of their sections, as well as any overall comments that pertain to all sections. As each section is reviewed, the project manager should record the changes needed in each Area to Address to satisfy the reviewers' suggestions and to improve on the scores given during the mock evaluation.

Following the meeting, the committee members revise their assigned sections based upon the action items and suggestions outlined in the meeting. Final drafts are submitted to the project manager for review and to the editor for final editing. The entire application should then be given to production so that the layout, cover, tabs, and any other aspects of the final document can be designed. Some applicants custom-design a cover and special tabs for their applications, but this is definitely not necessary. In fact, an application that looks *too* slick may make the examiners suspect that the applicant is perhaps substituting flash for substance. Final artwork is then done, the materials are thoroughly proofread, and the application is printed and bound.

Then, the tough part comes—the waiting. Applications are due on April 1st and you won't receive feedback for many months. This can be very frustrating, but the review process takes a long time.

Figure 2.4 provides a graphic representation of the major steps involved in completing an application. The exact process you use will no doubt vary somewhat from this. A mock evaluation by people trained on the Baldrige criteria is an important step that you should not leave out. Many organizations don't do this because they lack time or expertise. Lack of time shouldn't be a problem if you prepare the application far enough in advance. Lack of expertise is no excuse either. Universities and professional associations such as the American Society for Quality Control and the Association for Quality and Participation offer workshops on how to interpret the Baldrige criteria.

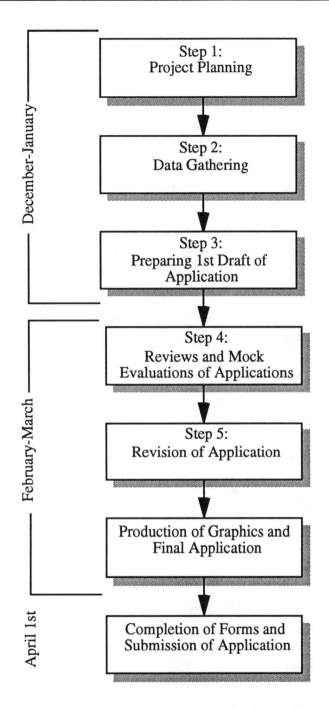

Figure 2.4: Application Development and Production Process

HOW TO WRITE THE APPLICATION REPORT

The main reason for writing this book is that many applicants and others using the Baldrige Award Criteria misinterpret what the Areas to Address are requesting. Reading chapters 5-11 of this book and using them as a reference when writing your responses to each of the 91 Areas to Address should help you to interpret the criteria accurately. In writing your report, it is important that you don't make the same mistakes made by many of the previous Baldrige Award applicants.

Pages 35–38 of the 1994 Baldrige Award Criteria provides some fairly specific instructions and advice about the best way to write your application. Make sure that you read these pages thoroughly and understand all of the guidelines. An important guideline that bears repeating is to make sure that you reference each section with the appropriate numbers and letters. It is helpful to the examiners if you include the Examination Items in your response, for reference. An example is shown below.

3.2 Quality and Performance Plans

3.2c. Anacon's long-term quality goal is to achieve 100% customer satisfaction. Some related long-term goals are to possess 40% of the domestic market for automated teller machines, and 60% of the domestic market for POS terminals. One of the requirements we must address is to improve the reliability of our products. We need to work on improving the mean time between failures as well as our overall product lifespans.

Several applicants have labeled each section with a number to correspond to the Examination Item (e.g., 4.2, 3.1, etc.). But when this is done without indicating *letters* for the Areas to Address, it is difficult for the examiners to find the information that pertains to each Area. You should denote responses to Areas by underscoring the Item/Area number and letter (e.g., 3.2c).

TEN COMMON MISTAKES TO AVOID WHEN WRITING YOUR APPLICATION

The general guidelines on how to write the application report (which appear in the Application Forms and Instructions package) are clear and well written. However, sometimes general guidelines are not enough to effectively guide performance. Judging by some of the applications received, many applicants either misunderstood the guidelines or chose not to read them. The purpose of this portion of the book is to list and explain some of the mistakes made by previous applicants. By reviewing this information, you should be able to avoid making some of the errors that others have made in the past. I have listed and discussed ten of the most common mistakes in the pages that follow. Some of these are minor errors, but most are mistakes that may cost you a large percentage of the points which otherwise might have been earned for a particular item.

Some of the information in this section is based upon the Baldrige Award Criteria. Other information is based upon my own and other examiners' experience in reviewing applications.

Mistake #1: Reiteration of Words From the Criteria

This is a technique that can enhance your score only if the examiner is not paying much attention to what he/she is reading. Examiners all have other jobs, so frequently they must review the applications in the evenings, after a long day of work. If your response includes some of the same words from the criteria, at first glance, it sounds like your response meets the criteria well. An examiner who is tired might just skim your response and give it a high score because it "sounds good." However, you must remember that up to six different examiners review each application. For every one or two who give you a higher score because your response includes words from the criteria, there will be others who will take points away for this. Repeating the criteria in your response is unnecessary.

Mistake #2: Use of Examples Rather Than Descriptions of Processes

This commonly occurs when the applicant does not have a systematic process to describe. A typical response starts out with a general statement such as: "We identify customer requirements in a variety of different ways". This is then followed by a detailed example of one situation where customer requirements have been identified. The problem with responding this way is that it doesn't tell the examiners how you identify customer requirements. If you do not describe a well-defined process in your response, chances are that you do not have a process, and customer requirements are identified in a casual and unsystematic manner. Whenever the criteria ask about processes, respond with a fairly detailed description of a step-by-step process or with a detailed flowchart.

Mistake #3: No Examples When They Will Help to Illustrate a Process

This is just the opposite of Mistake #2, using an example as your response. Including an example or two helps to clarify a flowchart or process description. Examples add interest and credibility to your process descriptions; just be certain that you have adequately described the process(es) before the example is used. When you use examples, make sure that you label them as such, and explain whether or not the situations you described are typical. Remember that the examiners have never seen your company and may not even be very familiar with your industry. Examples help to paint a picture for the examiner, making it easier for him/her to understand how your quality-related processes work.

Mistake #4: Lack of Specificity

Of all the mistakes made by applicants, this is the most common and the most severe. Answering all of the 91 Areas to Address thoroughly within 70 or 85 pages is tough. It is obvious that many applications have been ruthlessly edited to include only the most necessary information. Often, too much information is eliminated. A vague and general description of a process will earn few points from the examiners. An example of a non-specific response is shown in the following box.

7.3b How the company evaluates and improves its commitments, and the customers' understanding of them, to avoid gaps between customer expectations and company performance. Include: (1) how information/feedback from customers is used; (2) how product/service performance improvement data are used; and (3) how competitors' commitments are considered.

At our annual planning meeting we review our product guarantees and other commitments to customers and revise them as necessary. For example, in 1991, we re-wrote the warranty statement for our washers so that the document was 50% shorter than in the past and much clearer.

There is nothing particularly wrong with what is said in this example. The problem is that the response is vague and nonspecific. It also includes an example of an isolated incident, rather than describing a system or process. The response is about as long as the criteria, and not enough information is provided to adequately judge how well the applicant is doing on this Area to Address. When a response is vague or nonspecific, examiners are taught to assign a low score. You don't need to provide pages and pages of information in response to each area. However, a sentence or two is usually not enough.

Mistake #5: Presenting Data on Only a Few Quality Indices/Measures

This is also a very common occurrence, and one that will cause you to lose a significant number of points. If you collect data on over 40 different indices of quality and report on only five or six of them, the examiners might assume that you have chosen to report on only the measures for which your performance is good. Data not reported are often assumed to be negative. In one case study used to train the Baldrige Examiners, the applicant claims to have 160 indices that are used to measure quality. Yet, the application presents data on only three or four of these indices, and says nothing about performance levels for the other 150+ measures. While it may not be practical to present data for 160 indices, a great deal of information can be summarized in a table or chart. Examples of how to do this are presented in Chapter 10: Quality and Operational Results.

Mistake #6: Too Many Cross-References to Other Sections

According to the directions in the 1994 Award Criteria, you should:

Cross-reference when appropriate.

> *Although applicants should seek to make individual responses self-contained, there may be instances when responses to different Items are mutually reinforcing. In such cases it is appropriate to reference responses to other Items, rather than to repeat information presented elsewhere. In doing so, applicants should make the reference specific by using Item and Area designators, for example, see 4.2c.*

The criteria further explain that you should not repeat information included elsewhere. You can cross-reference information if it will help enhance your response to a particular Area to Address. Make sure that you cite the page number, the Examination Item (number) and the specific Area to Address (letter). For example:

> *"Additional information on our overall approach to human resource management is presented on page 28, in section 4.1a."*

You should minimize the amount of cross-referencing that you do, however. It is very frustrating to the examiners to have to constantly flip back and forth from section to section. Because each of the Areas to Address is designed to stand on its own, it should not be necessary to cross-reference very often.

Mistake #7:   Responding With Words When You Should Respond With Data

Many of the Areas to Address in categories 4, 6, and 7 ask for trends and results. Any time you see the words "trends," "results," or "data" in the criteria, this should be your clue to make sure your response includes graphs and data. It is surprising that this is misinterpreted, but applicants sometimes describe a *process* when the criteria specifically ask for *trends (data)*. Or, they give a narrative summary of their results with no graphs or statistics. An example of a poor response is shown below.

6.2a Trends and current levels for key measures and/or indicators of company operational performance.

We track many different indices that relate to operational performance factors used in our business. These measures have shown continuous improvements over the past five years, with significant improvements being demonstrated in the last year. We also track conformity of our support processes to quality standards. These measures, too, have shown improvement over the past few years.

Note that no graphs or statistics are included. Words and phrases such as "significant improvements" do not impress the examiners—they want to see the data. A narrative summary of the information included in graphs is good, but it is not a substitute for hard data.

Mistake #8:   Responding With Information That is not Relevant to the Area to Address

This is also one of those mistakes that occurs quite frequently in the applications. It seems that either the applicants misunderstand some Areas to Address, or that they understand them but have little to say in their response. Rather than admit something like: "We have not identified a process for tracking the degree to which customer requirements are met," applicants respond with some quality jargon that may sound good at first glance. But in reading it a second or third time one realizes that the response has nothing to do with what was asked for in the Area to Address.

An example of a response that is unrelated to the Area to Address is shown in box 7.3a (following).

> **7.4a How the company determines customer satisfaction. Include: (1) a brief description of processes, and measurement scales used; frequency of determination; and how objectivity and validity are assured. Indicate significant differences, if any, in processes and measurement scales for different customer groups or segments; and (2) how customer satisfaction measurements capture key information that reflects customers' likely future market behavior, such as repurchase intentions or positive referrals.**
>
> Customer satisfaction is our number one priority at Baker Industries. Every employee is expected to meet customer expectations for timely service and high quality products. We work in a collaborative fashion to systematically identify the ever-changing demands and expectations of our customers, and find ways of meeting those demands. Our quality and levels of customer satisfaction are unsurpassed in our industry, and continue to improve each year.

The Area to Address asks you to explain how the organization measures customer satisfaction. The example in the box does not discuss how customer satisfaction is measured. It only includes various "well written" phrases, which is typical of an application submitted by an organization that does not have the data to respond to an area. A response such as the one in the example would not earn any points, because there is no information that tells the reader how the company segments its customers and measures customer satisfaction.

Mistake #9: Use of Too Many Acronyms

I was once interviewing a man from AT&T on a consulting project, and I asked him to describe a particular process he was involved with, without using acronyms in his description. He just stuttered and couldn't explain the process without including a myriad of acronyms. Use of acronyms is very frustrating to the Baldrige Examiners. Everyone in your company may know what certain company-specific acronyms stand for, but the Baldrige Examiners won't. Spelling out what an acronym stands for the first time you use it will not solve the problem either. An examiner will forget and have to refer back to previous sections to recall what the CASE or AIP programs are. Avoid acronyms entirely if you can. This is tough for many large companies that have an acronym for every process, document, and program. An example of an acronym-laden response is shown in the following.

Our CEO, CIO, and CQO all strongly support the TQM effort at BMI through the initiation of a variety of programs such as the CCF (Customers Come First), AQP (Assessment of Quality Processes), and PTM (Participative Team Management). Our IIS and OEM Divisions have thoroughly implemented QFD using a variety of QITs (Quality Improvement Teams).

Mistake #10: Use of Too Much Industry, Quality, or Management Jargon

This irritates many of the Baldrige Examiners because it appears as though you are trying to impress them with your vocabulary. The application should be written at a fairly low reading level, about the same level used in an annual report to shareholders. It should not be written like a college textbook or a technical paper for a professional journal. Use of complicated words and jargon should be thoroughly discouraged. The Baldrige Examiners are probably as unfamiliar with your industry jargon as they are with your acronyms. To eliminate jargon, it is a good idea to have someone outside of your company, or new employees, review the application before it is finalized.

Even though the Baldrige Examiners may be familiar with quality jargon such as Quality Function Deployment or Taguchi Method, it is best not to overuse these terms either. Write the application as if it were to be read by shareholders or the general public. A tenth- to twelfth-grade reading level is appropriate. This is the same level as a magazine such as *U.S. News and World Report.*

Similarly, you may want to avoid using trendy management words and phrases such as

- Intrapreneuring
- Cross-functional management
- Participative team process
- De-layering

TEN RULES TO USE WHEN PREPARING GRAPHICS FOR YOUR APPLICATION

Up to this point we have been discussing the writing style of the application and common mistakes made when preparing the written response. Let's now turn our attention to graphics, which are also a big part of the application. So many of the applications contain poor and hard-to-read graphics that this subject warrants separate treatment and guidelines. I have outlined ten rules to keep in mind when preparing and discussing graphics in your application.

Rule #1: Explain Graphics in the Text

Some applicants have responded to an Area to Address that asks for data by simply including a graph, with no explanation of what the graph shows, or what kind of results are shown. A graph or chart should never be included without at least some explanation or reference in the text of your application. For example, you might say something like:

> *Figure 6.3 presents a summary of our major quality results compared to our foremost competitor: DMI. As you can see, we are superior to them in each of the six measures of quality results depicted in the bar graph.*

Always explain what the graph represents and summarize the conclusions that can be drawn from the data depicted on the graph. Even though it may seem obvious, the examiner may miss the significance of certain data unless you call his/her attention to it.

For example:

> *The data in Figure 7.8 show that our levels of customer satisfaction have improved by over 80% in the last two years. We have shown steady improvements over each of the last five years.*

Rule #2: Don't Duplicate Information from Graphics in the Text

This is just the flip side of the first rule. Graphics should be explained and referenced, but the information contained in them need not be duplicated in the text that accompanies them. This is simply a waste of valuable space and an insult to the examiner's intelligence. Figure 2.5 shows what *not* to do when explaining graphics.

As you can see in the graph below, the levels of customer satisfaction began at 78% satisfied in 1988, rose to 83% in 1989, dropped back to 79% in 1990, and rose again to 86% in 1991. In 1992, levels of customer satisfaction rose to 88% and to an all-time high of 92% in 1993.

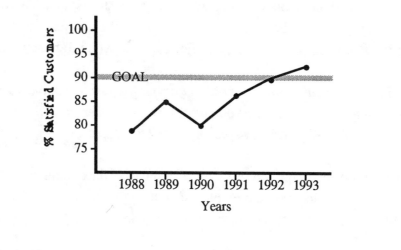

Figure 2.5 What *Not* to Do When Explaining Graphics

Rule #3: Don't Include More than Two Lines of Data on Any One Graph

In an attempt to conserve space, some applicants have tried putting four or more lines of data on a single graph. This is also done in an attempt to show interrelationships among different quality indices. You should never include more than two lines of data on a single graph. Figure 2.6 shows the right and wrong ways to present data graphically.

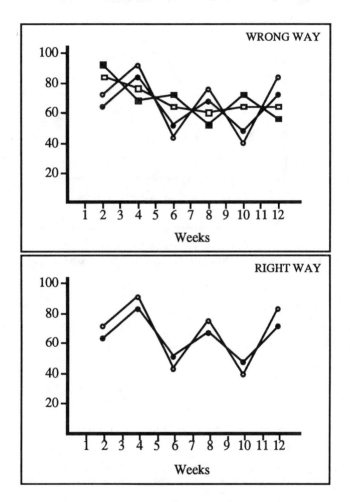

Figure 2.6: Put No More Than Two Lines of Data on a Graph

Rule #4: Graphs Should Depict Goals or Standards

A graph without a line to indicate a goal or standard is very difficult to interpret.
Standard or goal lines should be drawn on all graphs to indicate how close actual
performance is to desired performance. Figure 2.7 presents an example.

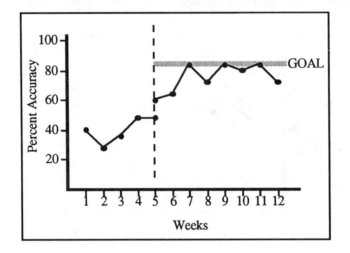

Figure 2.7: Goals Should Always Be Shown on Graphs

Rule #5:   Graphs of Performance Indices Should Show Improvement Using an Ascending Line

We are all taught that results are better when the line on a graph slopes up, representing an upward trend, and that a negative trend is indicated by a downward sloping line. Yet many applicants report positive quality results using negative indices such as number (or percent) of errors. Wherever possible, quality data should be presented in a positive fashion, so the line moves up as performance improves. Rather than graphing errors, graph the number or percentage of products *without* errors. Figure 2.8 shows the right way and wrong way to graph quality data.

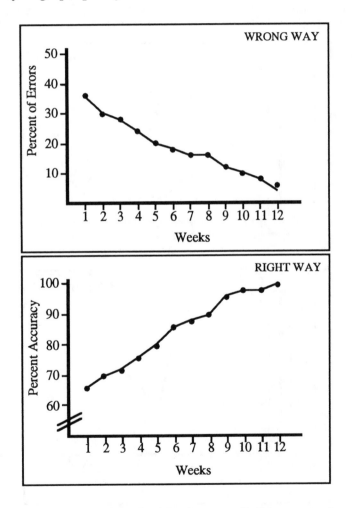

Figure 2.8: Graph Desired Performance So Improvements Appear as an Ascending Line

Rule #6:   Scales on Graphs Should Be Set Up to Show Maximum Variability in the Data

For your own benefit, it is important that you set up performance scales on graphs to show the maximum degree of change or variability in quality performance. For example, if customer satisfaction ratings are done on a percentage scale, you would not set up the scale from 0 to 100%, unless there were that much variability in the data. If scores over the last five years have ranged from 80% to 95%, you might set up the graph with a scale that goes from 70% to 100%. As you can see in the "Wrong Way" example in Figure 2.9, very little variability is seen in the data scale on the graph from 0 to 100%. The second graph with the smaller scale, however, shows a great deal of variability.

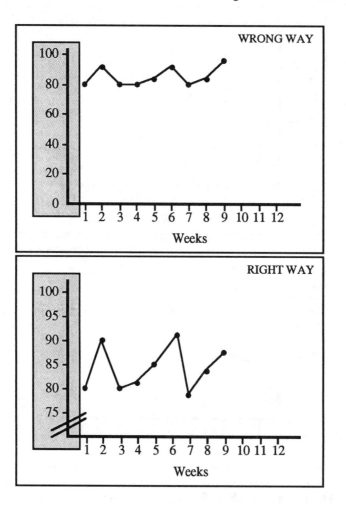

Figure 2.9: Setting Up the Scale for Performance on the Vertical Axis

Rule #7:   Separate Baseline Data From Post–Quality Improvement Data

Baseline data are data on levels of quality or other measures before a countermeasure or change has been introduced to improve performance. In many of the Areas to Address it is important that you demonstrate a cause-effect relationship between improvements in quality results and the introduction of quality improvement efforts or programs. In order to do this, you need to show quality levels both before and after you began your quality improvement effort. When depicting the data on a graph, separate the two phases using a dotted vertical line and do not connect the last baseline data point with the first post-improvement data point.

Figure 2.10 shows a sample graph that depicts the impact of goals and feedback on the percent accuracy.

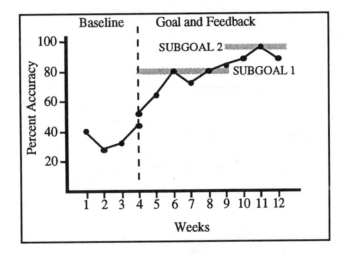

**Figure 2.10: Graph Showing Baseline Performance and
Percent Accuracy After Goals Were Set and Feedback Began**

Rule #8: Use Standard Graphing Formats

Use of strange or exotic graphing formats should be discouraged. Several applicants included graphics that this examiner, for one, had trouble interpreting. Almost any type of quality data can be presented using either a bar graph or a line graph. Bar graphs are most effective when comparing summary data. Line graphs are most effective for showing trends and for showing data over time. Figure 2.11 shows a line graph that has been appropriately labeled.

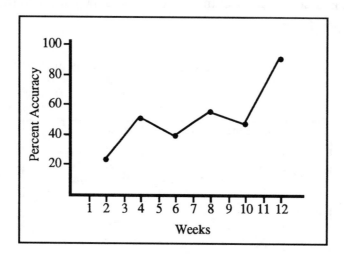

Figure 2.11: Line Graph Appropriately Labeled

Other acceptable formats include pie charts, cumulative line graphs, and scatter diagrams. Examples of these formats are shown in Figure 2.12.

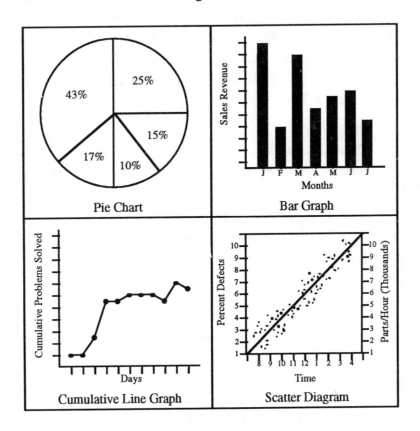

Figure 2.12: Various Ways of Graphing Performance

Rule #9: Graphs Should be Clearly and Specifically Labeled

Every aspect of the graphs included in your application should be appropriately and completely labeled. The two axes should indicate the quality dimension that is being depicted and the measure of time. Goals and subgoals should be labeled, along with the phases in your quality improvement efforts. An example of an appropriately labeled and easily read graph is shown in Figure 2.13.

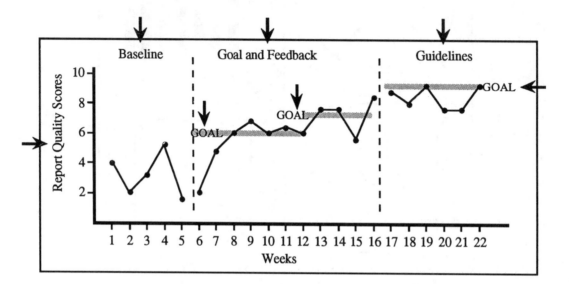

Figure 2.13: Graphs Should Be Clearly and Specifically Labeled

Rule #10: Graphs Should Be Simple and Free of Clutter

Some people tend to make a graph as informative as possible. Pointing out significant increases or improvements, indicating where key events have occurred that have impacted the data, and including other relevant information is thought to help the reader interpret the data better. This seems good in theory, but it often results in cluttered graphics that are difficult to read. A sample graph that includes a great deal of information is shown in Figure 2.14; it is cluttered and very hard to read.

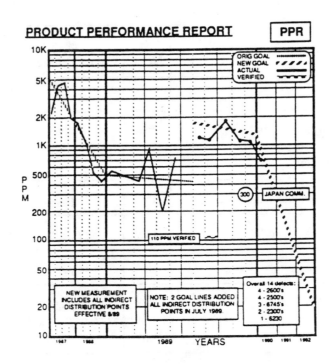

Figure 2.14: Graph is Cluttered and Very Hard to Read

This graph includes four different lines, too many notes, and scales that are very difficult to read. The spacing between years is unequal, as is the PPM scale on the vertical axis. Furthermore, we don't know what PPM means, nor whether the scale is number of defects, ratio of defects, or something else. In general, this graph represents a perfect example of what *not* to do when preparing your own. It violates at least four of the ten rules we have discussed.

LENGTH OF APPLICATION REPORT SECTIONS

If you are a large manufacturing or service organization, you are allowed a maximum of 85 single-sided pages. If your company is a small business, you are allowed 70 pages. These limits do not include the four page overview, the table of contents, tab dividers, and covers. Appendices and attachments are included in the 85 or 70 page limit, however. In deciding how much space to allocate for each of the seven sections of the report, you should keep in mind the weight given to each of the categories. The Customer Focus and Satisfaction category (7.0) is worth 30% of the evaluation, so it should be allocated the most pages. The Strategic Quality Planning category is worth only 6%, so relatively few pages are needed for this section. A suggested breakdown of the number of pages to allocate for each of the seven sections of the application report is as follows.

CATEGORY/SECTION	% Value	Length Large Organization	Length Small Organization
1.0 Leadership	9.5%	9 pages	7 pages
2.0 Information and Analysis	7.5%	8 pages	6 pages
3.0 Strategic Quality Planning	6%	7 pages	5 pages
4.0 Human Resource Development and Management	15%	13 pages	11 pages
5.0 Management of Process Quality	14%	12 pages	10 pages
6.0 Quality and Operational Results	18%	16 pages	13 pages
7.0 Customer Focus and Satisfaction	30%	20 pages	18 pages
TOTAL	100%	85 pages	70 pages

PRODUCING THE FINAL COPY OF THE BALDRIGE APPLICATION

The appearance of the application is not formally one of the criteria by which it is evaluated, but appearance does give the examiners an overall impression of your organization. If the application is sloppy, poorly laid out, and includes typographical and other errors, this doesn't portray a positive image about the company's level of quality. The appearance of the applications ranges from corner-stapled applications that have been typed on old typewriters, to application reports that have been typeset, printed on expensive paper, and include four-color photos and graphics throughout.

It is certainly not necessary that the application include color photos or that it be typeset. Most laser printers and desktop publishing packages can produce written materials that look as good as those that have been typeset—for a fraction of the cost. The 1993 Application Forms and Instructions provide specifics on the type style and size that must be used in the application. Be sure to review this information before writing your application.

The Baldridge officials also discourage using 3-ring binders for your application. I suggest using a Cerlox plastic spiral binding. With this type of binding, the application can be opened flat on a desk and does not take up much space or hinder movement.

Be certain to include a table of contents, and to separate each of the seven main sections of the written report with tab dividers. I also suggest that pages be numbered sequentially within each tab, and that graphics and exhibits be integrated into the text and not placed at the end of each section or in appendices. Finally, material should be printed on both sides of each page to lessen the bulk and weight of the application.

Chapter 3

Key Themes and Relationships Among the Criteria

THE BALDRIGE CRITERIA AS A SYSTEM

The Baldrige criteria are made up of seven Categories, which are further divided into 28 Examination Items and 91 Areas to Address. While each of the seven Categories is evaluated separately, there are relationships (or "linkages") between the seven and they function together as a system.

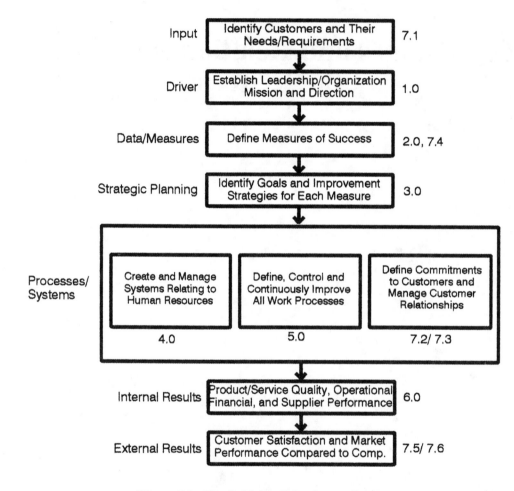

Figure 3.1: The Baldrige Criteria as a System

As you can see from Figure 3.1, the "driver" or beginning of the Baldrige assessment is not Leadership, but customers and their requirements. Baldrige suggests that an organization needs first to define its customers and markets, and then identify what is important to each of those groups of customers. Customers and their requirements are asked for in Item 7.1 of the Baldrige criteria. Once markets and needs have been identified, the company can develop its mission and direction, which is what is asked for in the Leadership (1.0) section. Once the mission and direction of the organization have been defined, you need to identify measures of success. Measures are asked for in Section 2.0, Information & Analysis, and Item 7.4, Customer Satisfaction Determination. Short- and long-term goals and plans then need to be developed, relating to each of the performance measures. Planning is asked about in Section 3.0 of Baldrige. Based upon the goals and improvement strategies outlined in the organization's plans, you need to develop systems/processes: Section 4.0 asks about human resource systems; Section 5.0 asks about work processes in the direct and indirect areas of the organization; and items 7.2 and 7.3 ask about the processes used to manage relationships with customers. All of these systems/processes should work together to produce internal (6.0, Quality and Operational Results) and external results for customers (7.5 and 7.6).

CORE VALUES IN THE BALDRIGE CRITERIA

Even though there are 91 different Areas to Address in the criteria, there are a few key themes or "core values" that underlie many of the items and categories. These recurring themes or values are:

Customer-Driven Quality

This is one of those concepts that every company today talks about but few actually follow in practice. Most companies assume that they can know what the customer wants and that they can define quality for the customer. Satisfying the real needs of customers is what this theme is about, as well as occasionally "delighting" customers with something they didn't ask for or expect. This theme runs throughout the criteria, involving the way executives set up the company's values and goals, as well as the method executives use to decide what data to collect, how to design new products/services, and how to improve relationships with customers. This area involves an assessment of how well you really know what customers want and expect, and how you manage your organization so as to meet or exceed those expectations on an ongoing basis.

Leadership

Every single company that has won the Baldrige Award has a CEO, president, and often an entire team of senior executives that are completely committed to TQM in both their heads and their hearts. For them, customer satisfaction and quality are regarded with as much, if not more, importance than other key measures of the company's operational and financial health. For example, AT&T Universal Card Systems, a winner in 1992, not only has top executives that are committed to customer satisfaction but has built its whole management approach and systems around the Baldrige criteria. In contrast, executives in most companies review financial and operational data at least once a month, if not every week. Quality and customer satisfaction data are often never reviewed by the senior executives unless there is a major problem that gets called to their attention.

Continuous Improvement

Back in 1991 the Baldrige criteria used to have a separate Examination Item that asked about continuous improvement. In 1992 this item was eliminated to reflect the fact that continuous improvement is not a separate activity. Instead, it is a theme that should run through every function and every process in an organization, and it should be integrated into all of the award criteria that ask for information on systems and processes. This is exactly what has been done with the Baldrige criteria from 1992 to 1994. Evidence of continuous improvement is asked for throughout all of the categories. Continuous improvement is also expected in those categories and items that ask for results. Standards are continually being raised in most industries. I recently read that the 1993 Cadillacs are designed to go 100,000 miles before their first tune-up! No one would have believed this was possible even five years ago; it's the result of continuous improvement.

Employee Participation and Development

For a company to be truly customer-focused, every employee needs to be service-oriented. Karl Albrecht explains in his book, *Service Within:*

> *If you're not serving the customer, your job is to serve somebody who is. (p. 3)*

Companies that have been successful with their quality efforts have found that in order to get high levels of customer satisfaction, it is important to also have high levels of employee satisfaction. The 1994 Baldrige Award Criteria Booklet explains:

> *A company's success in improving performance depends increasingly on the skills and motivation of its workforce. (p. 3)*

Employee participation is often interpreted to mean that the Baldrige criteria require the use of teams. Teams are only one way of getting employees involved in improving quality and performance, and they often have been used inappropriately. I know of one organization that worked for five years to get to the point where 100% of its employees were on quality improvement teams. During this same five years overhead costs went up and quality went down. Teams should be used when they are appropriate, but they should not be viewed as a cure-all or the only way of getting employees involved. Employee development is also an important theme in the criteria. Employees are about the only asset an organization has that can't be copied by competitors.

Fast Response

When the quality movement first began to take hold in the U.S. in the early 1980's, quality meant an absence of defects. Companies began collecting statistics on the number of defects they found and then instituted new processes to improve the level of quality in their products and services. The problem that many found was that quality takes time. If quality was the priority rather than production or some other measure, deadlines were often missed. In 1992, the Baldrige criteria began to concentrate on cycle time or fast response as well as on quality and customer satisfaction. To customers in many businesses, timeliness is as important or more important than quality. Cycle time is also critical when introducing new products or services. Being the first one to introduce a new product can often make the difference in its success.

Design Quality and Prevention

Early efforts to implement quality improvement techniques usually focused on plant floor employees in manufacturing companies and customer contact employees in service businesses. The problem with this method is that most quality problems are caused during the design phase, not while in the factory or while interacting with customers. Designing quality in is the approach that is being encouraged with this theme, as opposed to fixing problems once they are uncovered down the road. This is a more preventive approach to quality.

Long-Range Outlook

Companies that are the most successful today are those that anticipate trends in the economy, as well as customer preferences and demographics, and design their products and services to meet those future needs and demands. Many companies simply react to trends. The Baldrige criteria expect to see that a company predicts the trends accurately, using a more proactive approach. The term long range, in the sense that it is being used here, refers to 10 years or more in the future, not a year or two. A long-range outlook is also reflected in how the company manages its business. Investments in research, employee development, and cultivation of relationships with suppliers are all indicators of a long-range focus. Evidence that the company manages strictly according to quarterly financial results is the approach that the Baldrige Examiners do not want to see.

Management By Fact

The Baldrige criteria call for evidence of a scientific approach to management. What this means is that they want to see evidence that a company manages using data and analysis, rather than by following instincts. I once worked on a project for the newly opened Toyota plant in Georgetown, Kentucky. The project involved teaching U.S. workers and managers to solve problems and manage Japanese-style. When I talked to the Japanese people and asked them how they managed differently than we do, they explained that we both collect a lot of data. The difference is that Japanese managers make decisions based on analysis of the data. American managers make decision with their "guts," or based on their feelings and instincts. This latter approach is the one that the Baldrige criteria discourage. Throughout many of the categories and examination items you will find that the criteria ask for evidence of a systematic, planned approach that has been based on the analysis of key data.

Partnership Development

Another theme that is characteristic of recent Baldrige Award winners is that they develop partnerships with various inside and outside groups and individuals. One way of doing this internally is the development of service pacts or agreements between a support function and its internal customers. The two groups get together and draw up an agreement regarding the levels of performance that the support department will adhere to, and the measures that the internal customer will use to evaluate the support function. The agreements also usually specify what the responsibilities of the customer are. The criteria also look for evidence of partnership development with outside groups such as suppliers, unions, and educational institutions. Many large corporations have adversarial relationships with employees, unions, suppliers, and essentially anyone from whom they buy goods or services. Suppliers are threatened so that the company will pay the lowest possible price, and employees are laid off whenever the company has a bad year. These companies have the attitude that suppliers and employees are a replaceable commodity. This is just the opposite of the attitude that the Baldrige Examiners are looking for in this theme.

<u>Corporate Responsibility and Citizenship</u>

The last theme that one sees in the criteria is evidence that the company is a good corporate citizen. Since Baldrige winners are held up to the world as role models of how to run a successful organization, it is important that they demonstrate exemplary performance in the areas of:

- Ethics
- Public health and safety
- Environment

Evidence is asked for that illustrates how the company develops improvement plans for these areas, as well as how it performs compared to other companies. Just contributing money to charities is not the essence of this theme. Rather, it is whether or not the company demonstrates concern for the community and the environment in everything it does. There are many large corporations, for example, that have terrible records in the areas of environmental protection and concern for public welfare that nevertheless donate millions to charities and educational institutions. A preventive approach is what is expected regarding this theme. Your responsiveness to problems when they occur is considered important, but so is what you did to prevent the problems from occurring in the first place.

KEY RELATIONSHIPS AMONG THE SEVEN CATEGORIES

Although each of the 28 Examination Items is given a separate score and evaluated independently, performance on one item clearly affects performance on other items. Something that the Baldrige Examiners routinely do is to look for what I call "disconnects" or missed linkages among items in different categories. The more of these missed linkages that are found, the more likely it is that an applicant will receive a low score. A lack of consistency across the categories and items shows a system that is flawed, or at least an application that was not well planned and written. In the next few pages I will discuss the linkages that should be addressed for each of the seven categories, and the common "disconnects" that I have found in the Baldrige Award applications I've reviewed in the last three years.

<u>1.0 Leadership—Key Relationships With Other Criteria</u>

Compared to some of the other six categories, the Leadership category is fairly independent. However, there are a few things to check for in terms of overall consistency. Item 1.1, which asks about Senior Executive Leadership, should be consistent with information in Item 1.2, which asks about how the company's values and customer focus are integrated with its overall approach to managing the company. In other words, what the Examiners are looking for is consistency between the management approach used by senior executives (1.1) and the approach to management defined in Item 1.2. Another thing to look for is the linkage of 1.1b, which asks about how the company's values and customer focus serve as a basis for communication, and 7.2, which asks about customer relationship management. The values defined in 1.2 should reflect the company's approach and priorities for managing relationships with customers.

Item 1.2c asks about how plans and performance are reviewed. This item should be checked for consistency with 3.1c, which asks about how plans are deployed. The processes described in these two sections of the application should be consistent with one another.

2.0 Information and Analysis—Key Relationships With Other Criteria

This is really the foundation of the entire application. Although this category is only worth 75 points, a low score here can affect your scores in categories 3.0, 5.0, 6.0, and 7.0. Item 2.1 asks for information on what you measure—what indices you have in your data base for tracking performance in the areas of:

- Customer satisfaction and retention
- Product/service performance
- Operational performance
- Supplier performance
- Cost and financial performance

A linkage that is commonly missed is that between 2.1 and 3.2. Whatever indices you list in 2.1 should be the variables on which you set long- and short-term goals, which is what is asked for in 3.2. I often see measures listed in 2.1 for which there are no goals in 3.2. Or, a more serious error, goals are listed in Item 3.2 for measurement indices that are not listed as part of the company's data base that is described in 2.1. Another common problem is a lack of consistency between the measurement indices listed in 2.1 and the data presented in Items 6.1, 6.2, 6.3, 6.4, 7.5, and 7.6. In other words, Item 2.1 lists key measures for which there are no data presented in the items that ask for results. This is a warning sign for the Baldrige Examiner. It says that the company collects data on some important measures that it has neglected to present in sections 6.0 and 7.0. The implication is that performance must be poor or the data would have been included. Make sure that the performance indices that are listed in Item 2.1 all have goals in Item 3.2, and that you present results for all or at least most of these measures in sections 6.0 and 7.0. This is probably the most common type of error I see, and it can have a devastating effect on your score.

Another linkage to check for is that between Items 2.2 and 5.2 and 5.3. Item 2.2 asks about your competitive comparisons and benchmarking activities. What the Examiners want to see is that the processes that you have chosen to benchmark and report on in Item 2.2 are the same as the key processes that you have identified in Items 5.2 and 5.3. Often I see benchmarking done on processes that are not identified in category 5.0 as being the key processes that the organization needs to manage.

Item 2.3 is characterized as the "central intelligence item" within the Baldrige criteria. The importance of this item is demonstrated by the fact that an entire page in the 1994 Award Criteria booklet is devoted to explaining it. Item 2.3 asks for information on how you aggregate and analyze key data. You need to make sure that the aggregation of your data that you define here is consistent with the graphs and statistics you present in categories 6.0 and 7.0. For example, let's say that you describe in Item 2.3 how you aggregate eight different indices of customer satisfaction into a single customer satisfaction index. Yet, for Item 7.4 you don't present any aggregated customer satisfaction data. Similar relationships would be expected in your description of how financial, operational, and quality data are aggregated, and how the data are presented in category 6.0.

3.0 Strategic Quality Planning—Key Relationships With Other Criteria

Category 3.0 asks for information on how you develop and deploy plans in your company. I've already mentioned that there should be a relationship between 1.2c, which asks about how plans and performance are reviewed, and 3.1c, which asks about how plans are deployed. Consistency should also be present between annual, or short-term, goals asked about in 3.2b and the longer-term goals asked about in 3.2c. I often see completely different sets of goals for the short and the long term. Both sets of goals should be measured on the same indices, and these measurement indices should be the same ones that are mentioned in Item 2.1. In other words, if you list market share as a key measure, you should have both an annual and a long-term goal for market share.

Another relationship to check is that between 3.2d, which asks about projections of 2–5 year improvements in quality and operational performance, and 7.1b, which asks for information on how the company determines future requirements and expectations of customers. Both of these items ask for projections regarding the long-term future of the company and its customers. Information should be consistent for both sections.

Another commonly missed linkage I am always surprised to see is that between the goals listed in Item 3.2 and the goals presented on the graphs that appear in categories 6.0 and 7.0. For example, Item 3.2 might list the goal for product defects as .003, but the graphs in section 6.1 show the goal to be .005. This is a warning flag for the Baldrige Examiners.

4.0 Human Resource Development and Management—Key Relationships With Other Criteria

Category 4.0 is more independent than any of the other six sections. However, there are a few key relationships to check for. Item 4.1 asks for information on your human resource plans, which should be derived from the goals and plans outlined in section 3.0. The Examiners will look for how your human resource goals are derived from your overall business goals. Often there is not a clear relationship between HR goals and business goals. HR goals often specify things such as: "All employees will receive a minimum of 20 hours of quality-related training in 1994." Your response for Item 4.1 should explain how this goal will help you achieve one or more overall business goals as listed in Item 3.2. There should also be consistency between the HR goals listed in Item 4.1 and the HR activities described in Items 4.2, 4.3, 4.4, and 4.5.

Item 4.2 asks about the strategies you employ to get employees involved in improving organizational performance. The information in this section should be consistent with the information presented in Item 3.1b, which asks about efforts to reengineer work processes and improve productivity. Information in Item 4.2 also should be consistent with information presented in 1.2, which asks about how quality and customer focus is integrated in the management of the organization. For example, if you describe self-directed work teams in section 4.2, this should also be mentioned in 1.2, where describing roles and responsibilities of different levels within the company (1.2a).

Items 4.2d, 4.3d, and 4.4c all ask for data on the effectiveness of your employee involvement, training, and recognition/reward systems. Measures of the effectiveness of these strategies should be consistent with and possibly the same measures as those listed in Item 2.1. For example, one measure of the effectiveness of quality improvement teams is their impact on the quality of the company's products or services. Hence, in Item 4.2 you might present a graph that shows quality data before and after the team effort. If, in Item 4.4, you discuss your approach to linking customer satisfaction to employee compensation, you might include a graph that shows how levels of customer satisfaction have improved as a result of linking it to compensation.

You might also draw attention to your strategies to link recognition and compensation to customer satisfaction and quality, on the one hand, and what you discuss in Item 1.1 when explaining approaches you have used to make sure that executives are committed to quality.

Item 4.5, which addresses employee satisfaction and morale, should be compared to Item 1.3, which asks for information on how you address public health and safety. The approach you take toward public safety should be compatible with your approach to employee safety, which is discussed in Item 4.5. It is important, however, that you omit presenting employee safety data in 1.3, and public safety data in section 4.5.

5.0 Management of Process Quality—Key Relationships With Other Criteria

Item 5.1 asks about how you design new products and services. Your response to this section should build upon and be consistent with your response to Item 7.1, which asks about how you determine customer requirements. Item 7.1 does not ask what you do with the requirements once you gather them, and Item 5.1 does not ask how you gather data on customer requirements. In Item 5.1 you should explain how you take the customer requirements data and translate them into product and service designs. Your response to 5.2 and 5.3 should identify your key processes and how you measure them. The processes identified in Items 5.2 and 5.3 should be consistent with the processes identified for benchmarking discussed in 2.2. The measures of the key processes described in Items 5.2 and 5.3 should also be consistent with the key measures identified in Item 2.1. Your answer to Item 2.1 need not list all of these process measures, but they should be consistent. For example, you might explain in Item 2.1 that one of your overall process measures is cycle time. More detail might be presented in Item 5.2 when discussing how cycle time is measured for specific processes.

There should also be a very close relationship between your responses for 5.2 and 5.3. These two Examination Items ask for essentially the same information. Item 5.2 asks about how you manage the process in the line organization, and Item 5.3 asks about managing processes in support functions. Both management approaches should be basically the same.

Categories 5.0 and 6.0 are fairly closely linked. Category 5.0 is strictly an approach and deployment category, and 6.0 asks for results only, relating to the approaches discussed in section 5.0. Item 5.2 asks about how you manage the key processes in producing your products or delivering your services, while Item 6.1 asks for results on the quality of your products or services, and Item 6.2 asks for operational and financial performance data. Item 5.3 asks about managing support processes, and Item 6.3 asks for data on the results you have obtained in support functions. Similarly, Item 5.4 asks about how you manage suppliers' performance, and Item 6.4 asks for data on supplier performance. A summary of these linkages is shown in the box below.

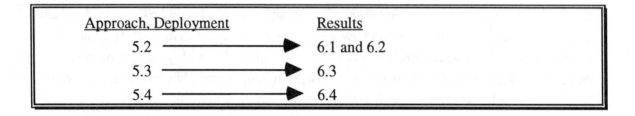

6.0 Quality and Operational Results—Key Relationships With Other Criteria

We've already discussed most of the relationships between category 6.0 and others, but some bear repeating here because of their importance. The most important link is between 2.1 and 6.0. The key measurement indices for the company that are presented in 2.1 should be the indices for which data are presented in sections 6.1–6.4. We also mentioned how goals described in Item 3.2 should be consistent with the goals presented on the graphs in category 6.0. Something else to check for is consistency between what you state in the overview regarding when your quality journey began and what you present as starting points in the data for category 6.0. If you explain that the quality initiative began in 1989, and all of your graphs start with data from 1989, there is no way to evaluate the impact of the quality initiative. In other words, there is no baseline data against which to compare your current performance.

7.0 Customer Focus and Satisfaction—Key Relationships With Other Criteria

I've already explained the relationship between Items 7.1 and 5.1, which ask about determining customer requirements and about how those requirements are used to design products and services. There also should be a relationship between Area 7.1b, which asks about determining future customer requirements, and your response to 3.2d, which asks about two-to-five year projections on the future of the company. There may also be a relationship between Area 7.1c, which asks how you evaluate and improve your approach to determining customer requirements, and 7.4c, which addresses how you evaluate and improve your approaches to measuring customer satisfaction. Many companies use some of the same data to determine customer requirements as used to measure customer satisfaction.

Examination Item 7.2, which deals with how you manage relationships with customers, crosses over into a number of other areas to address. Area 7.2a asks you to identify the key processes that bring employees into contact with customers. It also asks for measurement indices relating to these processes. The processes and measures discussed here should be consistent with those discussed in Item 5.2. These two sections certainly do not ask for the same information, but the processes described should be compatible.

Service standards, which are inquired about in 7.2b, should be consistent with goals that are outlined in Item 3.2. Sometimes a few macroservice standards are the same things as goals. For example, you might discuss in Item 3.2 that your 1994 goal is to receive an average rating of 4.75 on your 5-point customer satisfaction rating scale. Information in Area 7.2b should be consistent with this. I sometimes see customer-related goals in category 3.0 that are at different levels from the standards described in section 7.2.

Area to Address 7.2f asks about how you select, develop/train, empower, and reward customer contact personnel. All of the information requested here is very similar to what is asked for in Items 4.1, 4.2, 4.3, 4.4, and 4.5. These items in category 4.0 ask about the same sorts of human resource activities, except they ask about all employees. Area 7.2f asks only about customer contact employees. It is quite likely that you will have some common HR strategies that are used for all employees. Do not repeat this information in 7.2f. Simply refer back to category 4.0 and talk about what you do that is unique to customer contact employees. Again, be careful to look for any inconsistencies between these two sections. The HR practices discussed in category 4.0 should be compatible with those discussed in Area 7.2f.

Examination Item 7.4 asks about how the company measures customer satisfaction. The most important items to check this one against are 2.1 and 2.3. In Item 7.4 you need to identify the specific measurement instruments and methods used to collect data on customer satisfaction. Ideally, you will have a mix of soft measures such as surveys, and hard measures such as repeat business or gains/losses of customers. The measures that are described here should be the same as the measures of customer satisfaction that are defined in Item 2.1. You would be surprised at how many times different customer satisfaction indices are reported in these two sections. This is usually due to different individuals or teams writing the two sections and not bothering to talk to each other. The customer satisfaction measurement indices discussed in Item 7.4 should also be consistent with your description of how customer satisfaction data are aggregated in Item

2.3. If you discussed in detail how customer satisfaction data are aggregated in Item 2.3, you need only to refer back to that section, rather than repeating the information in Item 7.4.

The last two Examination Items (7.5 and 7.6) ask for customer satisfaction results. First of all, make sure that you present data for the measurement indices that you list in sections 2.1 and 7.4. I often see a complete list of customer satisfaction measurement indices in section 7.4, but data on only a few of those measures presented in Item 7.5. This is such an obvious omission that you would think that it couldn't happen, but it does. Often the applicant is trying to get a good score in Item 7.4 by listing all of the different measures of customer satisfaction for which they collect data. Yet the data do not all show improvement, so the applicant either doesn't discuss the measures in Item 7.4 or fails to include the data covering those measures in Item 7.5 or 7.6. Sometimes linkages are missed on purpose. In general, it is better to present data for all the major indices that are discussed in section 7.4. The Examiners will be more lenient in scoring if a few of your graphs show downward or flat trends than they will if key data are completely missing.

It is also important to present points of comparison on the graphs that are included in sections 7.5 and 7.6. The best graphs have three or four points of comparison. They show how your level of performance compares to:

- Your annual and long-term goals
- Key competitors
- Industry averages
- Benchmarks

Something to watch for in presenting these points of comparison is that they be consistent with information in other sections. Specifically, the goals in Item 3.2 should be the same goals that are depicted on your graphs. What sometimes happens is that performance doesn't look very outstanding compared to your own goals, so goals are simply adjusted. However, the writers of the applications sometimes forget to go back to change the goals that are outlined in Item 3.2. This is why it is so important to have many sources of comparison to use in evaluating your performance. Your own goals are completely arbitrary, and some companies set goals at levels they're sure they will be able to reach without much trouble.

The number of years for which data are presented is also important. If you began your quality initiative in 1987 and all graphs present data from 1990 on, the Examiners will wonder what happened to the missing years' data. They also won't be able to evaluate the impact of the quality movement, because there are no baseline data—no data from before 1987. The data you present in Items 7.4 and 7.5 should, moreover, be checked against the data presented in category 6.0. What I see happening in some service applications is that the data presented in Item 6.1 (Product and Service Quality Results) are the same as the data presented in Area 7.5b, which asks for data on key dissatisfaction indicators. For example, one company I worked with that ships cargo across the Pacific was confused as to where to put data on claims for damaged freight. This is a standard indicator for which they collect data, and it is clearly related to levels of customer satisfaction. Yet it is also a very strong indicator of customer dissatisfaction. So, does it go in 6.1 or 7.5b? The answer is that it goes in Item 6.1, because it is a measure on which the company itself collects data. If it had data on customer opinions of how the shipping company does in preventing freight damage, that data would go in Area 7.5b.

Similarly, market share and gains/losses of customers are sometimes thought to be operational or financial data that should be reported on in Item 6.2, not 7.6. The data need not go in both places, even though these are important measures. These data belong in section 7.6b and 7.6c.

SUMMARY OF KEY RELATIONSHIPS AMONG THE CRITERIA

When Reviewing These Criteria	Check For Correspondence With These Criteria
1.0 Senior Executive Leadership	
1.1	1.2, 7.1
1.1b	7.2
1.2c	3.1c
2.0 Information and Analysis	
2.1	3.2
2.1	5.2, 5.3
2.1	6.1, 6.2, 6.3, 6.4
2.1	7.5, 7.6
2.2	5.2, 5.3
2.3	2.1
2.3	6.1, 6.2, 6.3, 6.4
3.0 Strategic Quality Planning	
3.1c	1.2c
3.2b	3.2c
3.2b, 3.2c	6.1, 6.2, 6.3, 6.4
3.2b, 3.2c	7.5, 7.6
4.0 Human Resource Development and Management	
4.1	3.1
4.1	3.2
4.1	4.2, 4.3, 4.4, 4.5
4.2	3.1b
4.2	1.2a
4.2d, 4.3d, 4.4c	2.1
4.4	1.1
4.5	1.3

(continued)

SUMMARY OF KEY RELATIONSHIPS (continued)

When Reviewing These Criteria	Check For Correspondence With These Criteria
5.0 Management of Process Quality	
5.1	7.1
5.2, 5.3	2.1
5.2, 5.3	2.2
5.2	5.3
5.2	6.1, 6.2
5.3	6.3
5.4	6.4
6.0 Quality and Operational Results	
6.1, 6.2, 6.3, 6.4	2.1, 2.3
6.1, 6.2, 6.3, 6.4	3.2
6.1, 6.2, 6.3, 6.4	Overview
7.0 Customer Focus and Satisfaction	
7.1	5.1, 1.1, 3.2
7.1b	3.2d
7.1c	7.4c
7.2a	5.2
7.2b	3.2
7.2f	4.1, 4.2, 4.3, 4.4, 4.5
7.4	2.1, 2.3
7.5, 7.6	2.1, 7.4
7.5, 7.6	3.2
7.5b	6.1
7.5, 7.6	Overview
7.6b, 7.6c	6.2

Chapter 4

Understanding the
Baldrige Award Scoring Scale

According to a major quality consultant's data base from a survey they conduct on the Baldrige criteria, "corporate America" rates 560 points out of the 1000 on the Baldrige scale. An organization I consulted with scored themselves at 700/1000 on a Baldrige self-assessment survey, and was shocked when they got knocked out of the first round upon actually applying for the Baldrige Award. The truth is that most companies think they rate much higher on the Baldrige scale than they really merit. If corporate America were really at an average level of 560 on the Baldrige scale, U.S. products and sevices would be beating everyone else's in quality.

THE TRUTH

The truth is that corporate America is nowhere near 560 points on the Baldrige scale. If we define corporate America as including small and large service and manufacturing companies, corporate America is really around 150 points or less. As a Baldrige Examiner, I evaluated a company last year that received a score of 26 points out of 1000. Another Examiner gave an applicant 60 points out of 1000. These are companies that thought they had a chance at winning a Baldrige!

MISINFORMATION

One of the major reasons for this gap between where companies think they are and where they really stand on the Baldrige scale is the popularity of surveys as a means of self-assessment. I've written one myself that has been published for the last four years in the June issue of the *Journal for Quality and Participation*. If you review the advertisements in any of the quality journals, you can find ads for at least half a dozen companies with surveys that claim to tell you "where you really stand" on the Baldrige scale. The problem with all of these surveys, not excluding my own, is that they are all based upon internal company opinions and self-report data. Consequently, they are all questionable measures of your status on the Baldrige scale. Some of them look very scientific. They are computer scored and you receive a detailed report showing you a variety of different breakdowns of the data. But no matter how many computers are used or how many data comparisons are done, much of it is doubtful because it is based upon people's opinions of themselves and their work. People tend to think that they are further along applying Total Quality than they really are.

Using one of these surveys to assess your Baldrige status is like filling ut a questionnaire to determine your level of health and physical fitness, rather than actually getting a physical. A survey is an inexpensive method of determining where you stand, but chances are you will not get an accurate assessment. Companies such as Northrop, Westinghouse,

TRW, Coldwell Banker, and Nevada Bell use a more thorough approach to evaluation against the Baldrige criteria by simulating the Baldrige Award process. Applications are prepared and scored just like they are in Baldrige, using internal and external Examiners that have been through several days of training. Some of these organizations even conduct site visits of the best scorers to validate the information contained in the written application. An approach like this is likely to give you a score that is within 10% of the score you would receive if you actually applied for the Baldrige Award.

HOW DO BALDRIGE APPLICANTS AND WINNERS SCORE?

When you look at the breakdown of scores over the last few years, you find that most of the Baldrige Award applicants score less than 600 points out of a possible 1000. In fact, about 80% of applicants score between 0 and 600 points. The rule used to be that you needed a score of 600 points or greater to receive a site visit, but this is not a hard rule. In the last few years, there were several organizations that received site visits that scored less than 600. Receiving a site visit with less than 600 points is still not common, but it is possible—especially if you are a small business. The Baldrige Examiners are taught to be less stringent in their scoring of small companies. Examiners learn not to expect as much evidence of a systematic approach to everything. Informal approaches sometimes work very well in small companies.

WHAT IT TAKES TO WIN

People I talk to at workshops I teach on the Baldrige criteria generally believe that it takes a score of 900 or better to win a Baldrige. Last year's distribution of scores indicates that this is far from the truth. The companies that won in 1991 received scores that were less than 750. None of the applicants received scores in the eight or nine hundreds, as might be expected. When deciding on a winner, the nine Baldrige Judges look less at the scores than they do the comments on strengths and areas for improvement, and how these factors relate to the business the applicant is in.

UNDERSTANDING THE SCORING SCALE

Scoring for the Baldrige is done using a scoring scale of 0-100%. Scores are generally done in multiples of 10, using guidelines provided by the Baldrige Award Office. The chart below provides a summary of the scoring scale that appears on page 34 of the 1994 Award Criteria Booklet.

SCORING GUIDELINES

SCORE	RESULTS
0%	■ no results or poor results in areas reported
10% to 30%	■ early stages of developing trends; some improvements and/or early good performance levels in a few areas ■ results not reported for many to most areas of importance to the applicant's key business requirements
40% to 60%	■ improvement trends and/or good performance levels reported for many to most areas of importance to the applicant's key business requirements ■ no pattern of adverse trends and/or poor performance levels in areas of importance to the applicant's key business requirements ■ some trends and/or current performance levels — evaluated against relevant comparisons and/or benchmarks — show areas of strength and/or good to very good relative performance levels
70% to 90%	■ current performance is good to excellent in most areas of importance to the applicant's key business requirements ■ most improvement trends and/or performance levels are sustained ■ many to most trends and/or current performance levels — evaluated against relevant comparisons and/or benchmarks — show areas of leadership and very good relative performance levels
100%	■ current performance is excellent in most areas of importance to the applicant's key business requirements ■ excellent improvement trends and/or sustained excellent performance levels in most areas ■ strong evidence of industry and benchmark leadership demonstrated in many areas

SCORE	APPROACH/DEPLOYMENT
0%	■ no systematic approach evident; anecdotal information
10% to 30%	■ beginning of a systematic approach to the primary purposes of the Item ■ early stages of a transition from reacting to problems to a general improvement orientation ■ major gaps exist in deployment that would inhibit progress in achieving the primary purposes of the Item
40% to 60%	■ a sound, systematic approach, responsive to the primary purposes of the Item ■ a fact-based improvement process in place in key areas; more emphasis is placed on improvement than on reaction to problems ■ no major gaps in deployment, though some areas or work units may be in very early stages of deployment
70% to 90%	■ a sound, systematic approach, responsive to the overall purposes of the Item ■ a fact-based improvement process is a key management tool; clear evidence of refinement and improved integration as a result of improvement cycles and analysis ■ approach is well-deployed, with no major gaps; deployment may vary in some areas or work units
100%	■ a sound, systematic approach, fully responsive to all the requirements of the Item ■ a very strong, fact-based improvement process is a key management tool; strong refinement and integration — backed by excellent analysis ■ approach is fully deployed without any significant weaknesses or gaps in any areas or work units

APPROACH, DEPLOYMENT, AND RESULTS

You will notice that three factors are assessed as part of the scoring scale. <u>Approach</u> refers to the systems you have in place to improve quality and customer satisfaction. Some of the factors Baldrige examiners look at when assessing your approach are the degree to which your approaches are:

- Systematic, planned, logical, and tailored to your key business factors
- Prevention-based versus inspection and correction-based
- Based upon thorough analyses of needs and constraints
- Systematically evaluated and improved over time
- Innovative and unique

<u>Deployment</u> essentially means the extent to which your approach has been implemented across the organization. Many companies have unsystematic approaches that are fully deployed. Obviously, this won't earn you a high score. What the Baldrige Examiners would like to see is a sound approach that has been implemented in all parts of the organization. Simply having a sound approach by itself does not earn a high score. When assessing deployment, the Baldrige scale looks at implementation of your approaches across:

- All transactions with customers, suppliers, and the public
- All operations, facilities, and businesses
- All products and services
- All levels and functions of employees

<u>Results</u> are the third aspect of the Baldrige scoring scale. Results refer to data. Results are asked for and assessed in the following items and areas to address within the 1994 Baldrige criteria: 1.3d, 4.2d, 4.3d, 4.4c, 4.5d, 6.1, 6.2, 6.3, 6.4, 7.5, and 7.6. These Areas/Items ask only for results—no information on approach or deployment is requested. When evaluating your results, the Baldrige Examiners look at:

- Your overall level of performance
- How your performance levels compare to competitors and to benchmarks
- Rate of improvement, or the slope of trends in your data
- The breadth of the data, whether improvements are shown on all key measures of performance
- The degree to which results have been sustained and show continuous improvement over time.

If you refer back to the scoring scale above, you will notice that scores are grouped into five bands, with descriptors for each of these bands, across the three factors: approach, deployment, and results. I will explain, below, what a Baldrige Examiner is likely to see in an organization when a score is assigned for each of the ten levels from 0% to 100%.

Scores of 0 on Approach /Deployment

Scores of 0 are actually given out quite frequently by Baldrige Examiners when they evaluate each of the 28 Examination Items. Companies that assess themselves, however, rarely give zeros in any area. Part of this discrepancy stems from a lack of understanding of what constitutes a zero. The scoring scale uses the word "anecdotal" for the approach, deployment, and results factors when describing what a zero looks like. This means that the only evidence provided consists of stories, or anecdotes, illustrating how the company does in meeting the criteria. No matter how impressive, examples or stories are not worth anything on this scale.

Most of the items that ask about your approach are looking for a *system*. A score of zero would indicate that you probably have no system. You may also receive a score of zero if you have plans for a sound system, but you have not yet implemented it. This would indicate no deployment. Plans and intentions will not earn you points on the Baldrige scale until you have deployed the system. Most companies that do self-assessments tend to score themselves between 10 and 30% for good intentions in the future. A score of zero may indicate that the organization has some "pockets of excellence," but these pockets are tied to key individuals rather than the existence of a systematic approach. In general, the company's approach to quality tends to be the traditional inspection/correction approach.

Scores of 0 on Results

A score of zero in an Area to Address or Examination Item that asks for results would indicate that one or more of the following conditions are present:

- There are no results other than anecdotes—no graphs or data
- Data presented are irrelevant to the criteria/requirements of the item
- Data show that performance on key measures has gotten worse, or has not improved at all since the company began its quality effort

Scores in the 10-30% Range

This is the range in which many Baldrige applicants fall, and the range in which most U.S. companies probably fall on the Baldrige scale. This is also the range in which there is the most misunderstanding on how to score. The biggest reason for this lack of consistency in scoring and misunderstanding is that the descriptors in the scoring scale are the same for all scores in this range. In other words, there is no distinction to indicate how a 10% score differs from a 20% or 30% score.

When I recently worked on a project where I teamed up with a group of internal examiners at Northrop, we found that most of our scoring disagreements centered around what was a 10, 20, 30, or 40 percent. The scoring guidelines provided little help, so we decided to construct our own. Once this matrix was constructed, the consensus discussions took less than than half the time because we all were in agreement about what a 10% looked like versus a 30%. The scale of the 10-30% range is presented below for your reference. It is not the official Baldrige-approved version, but I think that you will find it useful as a guideline.

SCORE	APPROACH	DEPLOYMENT	RESULTS
10%	Beginnings of a systematic approach but lacking in several major areas	Implementation in one or two major areas or functions	Very slight improvement, or only one data point showing improvement; data on many major indices are missing
20%	Sound, well thought-out approach (more than a beginning) that shows some evidence of being prevention-based	Deployment of system(s) to 10-30% of the major functions or facilities in the organization	A couple of data points showing some undramatic improvement in at least 50% of key measures. Other graphs show no improvement and some key data are still missing from the application.
30%	Early stages of a prevention-based approach based upon thorough analysis. No real integration yet; immature systems	Deployment to at least half of the major functions or facilities in the organization	A few data points that show the beginnings of positive trends in more than half of key indices. Slow steady progress in many areas.

Scores of 10% on Approach/Deployment

An organization at this level is likely to have only the very beginnings of an approach to Total Quality Management. They have probably been working on this effort for a year or two. The systems that they do have in place often contain major "holes" and lack maturity and completeness. It could be said that a company at this level is off to a good start in the design and implementation of systems to promote Total Quality Management. Deployment at the 10% level would involve implementation in at least a couple of the company's major business units or facilities. For example, if the company consisted of six different business units with a total of 35 facilities, we might expect to see the system deployed to a couple of the business units or at least 10% of the facilities. An organization at the 10% level would probably not have any deployment to support functions.

Scores of 10% on Results

Results at the 10% level will be minimal. The graphs of major performance indices are likely to show very slight improvements, or perhaps one or two data points that show only the beginnings of a positive trend. At the 10% level we might also see that the data show some measures to be improving, some to be getting worse, and some to be remaining about the same.

Scores of 20% on Approach/Deployment

This level of performance would indicate more than just the beginnings of a systematic approach. Companies at the 20% level tend to have well-designed systems that are at least partially prevention-based. The scope of the approaches at the 20% level tends to be broader, but may still lack several necessary components. Companies at this level have generally been working on implementing Total Quality for more than a year to two. The exception to this may be a small company that can implement changes much faster than a large company. A small business might get to this level in a year if they are very serious about the effort. Wallace Company, a small company that won a Baldrige Award in 1990, went from the 20% level to winning the award in about two and a half years.

Deployment of systems and approaches tends to be somewhat greater at the 20% level when compared to companies that score 10%. A company at this level has done more than just pilot tested the system in one or two major areas. Implementation is well under way at the 20% level. We might expect to see that the sytematic approaches have been implemeted in between 10% and 30% of the company's major functions or facilities. As with the 10% level, we would not expect deployment of Total Quality to any of the support functions at the 20% level.

Scores of 20% on Results

Results at the 20% level will show more than a data point or two showing slight improvement. To give a score of 20% for results, the Baldrige Examiners would expect to see at least a couple of data points showing improvement in at least half of the key measures in the organization. At this level, it is clear that positive results are starting to materialize. Trends have not really been established yet, and results are not consistent across all measures, but it is clear that improvements are happening. The level of improvements tends to be undramatic at the 20% level. We might see a couple of data points showing slow steady improvement rather than major jumps in the data.

Scores of 30% on Approach/Deployment

This is the level at which a great number of companies fall. This should be considered to be a good score, indicating more than a good start with implementing Total Quality Management. In order to receive a 30% score, your approaches need to be based upon thorough analyses of needs, indicate a fairly strong prevention-basis, and be quite complete. At this level, your Total Quality effort is still seen by many employees as a program or add-on structure, rather than a way of life. What this means is that integration has not yet occurred. The test of integration is to ask employees how much time they spend on TQM activities and how much time they spend doing their jobs. If you get an answer like: "I spend 4-8 hours a week on TQM activities" you know that integration has yet to occur. TQM is invisible in organizations that have fully integrated it. Systems tend to lack maturity at the 30% level, but they are well designed and clearly indicate transition toward a prevention-based approach.

Deployment at the 30% level will be to at least half of the major functions or facilities in the company. Again, we would probably not see implementation in the staff functions or support departments. A 30% score would indicate that roughly half of the employees are working to implement the TQM approach in the company.

Scores of 30% on Results

The difference between results at 20% and 30% is that a 30% company would show the beginnnings of positive trends in *more* than half of the company's major indices of performance. Typically, most graphs will contain at least three data points, showing the beginnings of a trend, and the trends will be mostly positive. The level of results are not that impressive yet, and the company may not be doing better than all competitors, but they are getting better each year. You might still expect to see that some of the graphs show no improvement. You may also see inconsistencies in the data at this level. Even though more than half of the graphs show the start of an improving trend, other graphs show no trends, flat performance, even that performance on a few indices has gotten worse. The bottom line is that more than half of the key indices show the start of positive trends for this level of scoring. At the 30% level there may be key data that are still missing from the application.

SCORE	APPROACH	DEPLOYMENT	RESULTS
40%	Beyond the early stages of a preventive approach, but no refinement or integration of approach yet. Evidence of innovation in design of systems/approaches	Implementation at beginning stages in some functions and more advanced in others. Many major functions show fairly complete deployment	Beginnings of positive trends can be seen in areas deployed, and there are no significant adverse trends
50%	Some evidence of a more refined, prevention-based approach. A fact-based improvement process in place for key areas addressed in the item. Integration beginning to occur	Deployment to all major functions in the company —no gaps in deployment to major areas. Beginnings of deployment to several support functions	Clear positive trends seen on many graphs of key measures addressed in the item. Some trends can be evaluated against relevant comparisons and benchmarks
60%	Systematic prevention-based approach that has been evaluated and improved at least once. Some systems may show two or more iterations based on evaluation. Integration shown across several major areas	More than deployment to a few support functions. Most major support departments show at least the start of deployment. Deployment is more advanced in major functions than at 50% level	Majority of graphs show slow, steady improvements over several years or sustained high levels of performance. Many graphs show competitor and/or benchmark data and applicant's performance better than at least half of these comparisons

Scores of 40% on Approach/Deployment

This is the top end of the band that indicates that you are off to a good start with your TQM effort. Systems at this level of scoring tend to be more comprehensive and more innovative. Approaches are based upon thorough analysis and sound logic, and are tied into the key business and cultural factors in the organization. Companies at the 20-30% level tend to have systems that do not show creativity and tailoring to their individual organization's needs. They may have copied their systems from others. Organizations with scores at the 40% level tend to have developed their own "home grown" approaches and systems that are characterized by being innovative, truly prevention-based, and tailored to their company. Systems may still lack maturity at the 40% level, with no evidence of evaluation and improvement cycles. We would also expect to see that TQM has not yet been integrated, even though systems are fairly advanced.

Deployment of approaches will be to many major functions and/or facilities, which means more than half of the plants or service delivery areas of the business. The support department employees have yet to adopt a TQM approach, even though they may be familiar with the concepts through education and training. The organization has probably been working hard on implementing TQM for several years to achieve a score at this level.

A large company may have been working at TQM for 3–5 years and still receive a score at the 40% level.

Scores of 40% on Results

The differences between results at this level and at the 30% level are:

- Lack of significant adverse trends
- Consistency of results across all key indices where TQM has been deployed
- Number of data points indicating trends
- Overall level of results
- Slope of trend lines or rate of improvement

We would not expect to see sustained world-class results to give a 40% score for results. Graphs in most or all of the areas where TQM has been deployed will show positive trends that are not yet conclusive. Statisticians generally believe that seven data points are needed to establish any kind of trend. We would not expect this yet. Three or four data points that show the start of a good trend is more of what we would see at this level.

Scores of 50% on Approach/Deployment

In the Baldrige scale, a score of 50% is not considered average. A 50% is considered to be quite a high score and is fairly difficult to achieve. If you recall the distribution of the scores we discussed earlier, the majority of Baldrige applicants received a score of less than 50%. It must be remembered that this is still a 100% scale. Even though a score of 50% or higher is very hard to achieve, it is possible. In a set of scoring guidelines prepared for Baldrige Examiners, award director Dr. Curt Reinmann describes the 50% score as follows:

> *The 50% point represents a sound approach for accomplishing the principal purposes addressed in the Item. The basic approach should be the way the company actually operates and should affect most of the people and operations addressed in the Item. The approach should project reasonable confidence that over time, there are very likely to be further learning and more complete deployment.*

In order to receive a 50% score for your approach, two characteristics separate it from a score in the 10%-40% range. First of all, your approach will include at least one evaluation and improvement cycle. In other words, there will be evidence that you have assessed how well your approach or systems are working, and made changes or enhancements to the systems, based upon this assessment. If your approach has not been improved or changed over the years, you will not receive a 50% score. The second characteristic of a 50% score for approach is some evidence of integration. Many companies approach implementation of TQM as an add-on approach by creating teams, committees, and reports/plans. This is contrasted with the organization that approaches TQM as a different way of running the organization rather than an add-on structure. Integration is not complete yet at the 50% level, but is beginning to occur. As Dr. Reimann says, "The basic approach should be the way the company actually operates."

Deployment at the 50% level is characterized by implementation of TQM in most major areas of the business, and at least some of the support functions. Scores below 50% tend to show no deployment to departments such as finance, facilities, maintenance, HRD, material, procurement, and other support departments. What we are likely to see at this level is that several major support functions are in the early stages of implementing a customer-focused approach

Score of 50% on Results

In addition to having no significant adverse trends, results at the 50% level should clearly show improvement trends in most of the major indices asked about in the Examination Item. Not all graphs will show clear trends, but many will. Another factor that differentiates results at this level is that the company's levels of performance on some graphs compare favorably to key competitors and possibly benchmarks. There is usually a lack of comparative data in results below 50%. Or, the company's performance is below that of key competitors and benchmarks. At 50% there is not only comparative data, but the applicant's results are better than levels exhibited in the comparative data. We're certainly not expecting that the company show world-class results on all measures at the 50% level, only that some of the graphs of key measures have comparative data, and that the applicant's performance is at least slightly better than points of comparison. Again, not all graphs will show strong positive trends. Some graphs may still be flat or show slow steady improvements.

Scores of 60% on Approach/Deployment

Companies that receive an overall score of 60% or 600 points on the Baldrige scale are among the best companies in the country on the Baldrige scale. These companies tend to have been working at implementing TQM for a number of years, and show a degree of maturity in their approaches. Companies at this level tend to be finalists in the Baldrige competition, and receive site visits. The major difference between a 50% and 60% score in approach is the degree of:

- Integration
- Evaluation and improvement

Evaluation may be informal and lack rigor, but there is evidence that the company performs some evaluation of approaches, and uses the feedback from these assessments to improve its approaches. At the 60% level, we might expect to see at least one iteration of minor enhancements or changes to a number of major systems in the company. Integration of TQM as a way of life is occurring in a number of major areas in the company as well. This tends to occur in the areas or facilities that have been working at TQM the longest, and integration is not yet deployed across the company.

Scores at the 60% Level on Results

Results at the 60% level tend to be quite impressive. The majority of graphs depicting results will show either slow steady improvements over several years, or sustained high levels of performance over a number of years. Graphs at the 60% level also tend to show a lack of variability in the data, indicating that the company has these key measures in control as much as possible. Results at this level also tend to be superior to a number of different points of comparison. Most graphs will include two or three comparison points (e.g., industry average, largest compeititor, and benchmark). Performance of the applicant will be better than industry averages, key competitors, and other comparison points on many graphs. Results may even approach or exceed benchmark levels on a few graphs.

Scores in the 70% to 90% Range

The problem with using the matrix in the Baldrige Award Guidelines for scoring is the same as the problems with the 10%–30% for 40%–60% ranges—there is no guidance given for the individual scores at 10% intervals. This isn't much of a problem because very few companies fall into the 70% to 90% range. One of the problems that has occurred with the Baldrige scale over the last five years is that Examiners have gotten increasingly stingy in their grading. Examiners function as if the scale were a 0–70% scale rather than a 0-100% scale. In other words, Examiners almost never give out scores of higher than 70%. Scores for outstanding companies tend to be in the 60%-75% range rather than in the 80-95% range as one might expect with a 100% scale. A great deal of emphasis was placed on this in the 1992 training of Baldrige Examiners, and some overcompensated—especially when evaluating small companies. One consensus call that I participated in had many items where there was a 0-100% range across the six Examiners. Those who gave out the zeros saw no evidence of a systematic approach, and those that gave out 100% felt that we should give them the benefit of the doubt because they were a small company. A score in the 70% to 90% range should never be given out without serious scrutiny and evidence of a sound systematic approach. However, the company does not need to have a perfect world-class system with 100% deployment to receive a score in this range. (See chart on following page.)

SCORE	APPROACH	DEPLOYMENT	RESULTS
70%	Systematic approach with thorough evaluation and evidence of several iterations of improvement. Good integration of approach into the day-to-day operation of the company	Deployment is complete in at least 75% or more of major functions and facilities, as well as more than half of all support functions. Few support areas have yet to implement approach, even though integration levels may vary	Majority of graphs show dramatic improvements or sustained high levels of performance over several years. Few or no graphs show flat or declining performance. Many to most graphs show that performance is better than competitors' and industry averages. Benchmark level results on some key indices
80%	Excellent integration of an approach that has been systematically evaluated and improved several times. Indication of a mature system that shows innovation	Deployment to more than 75% of major functions and between 60 and 75% of all support functions. All departments show some deployment of Total Quality approach, and integration is complete in most areas/elements	Good to excellent trends in almost all graphs with demonstrated ability to achieve world-class results in industry over a sustained period of time. Many graphs show that company is at benchmark levels for key indices
90%	A sound systematic approach that has gone through a number of iterations showing evaluation and improvement. Integration is near complete. World-class approach that demonstrates many innovations	Deployment is complete to all major functions/facilities and to at least 75% of the support functions/departments. All areas of the company have implemented prevention-based approaches	Excellent trends showing either dramatic improvements or ability to sustain benchmark level results over a number of years. Results clearly superior to all competitors on most indices

Scores of 70% on Approach/Deployment

At this level, we are approaching a world-class organization in its approach, deployment, and results. A company at this level may be a year or two away from winning a Baldrige Award. Approaches and systems tend to be very mature and demonstrate at least two iterations or evaluation and improvement cycles. A 70% company usually has been working on TQM for more than three or four years, and is getting to the point where TQM is invisible. In other words, TQM is not an add-on structure or viewed as a program or initiative. It is viewed by employees as a way of life and just good common sense. Quality efforts and measures are blended with financial and operational efforts and measures. The approach to quality has filtered down and resulted in changes to the company's major systems such as:

- Leadership

- Business Planning

- Information

- Human Resource Development

- Compensation

- Quality Assurance

- Customer Relationship Management

An organization will never achieve this level if it looks at TQM as consisting of training, quality improvement teams, and measurement of customer satisfaction using some surveys.

Deployment in companies at the 70% scoring level is complete in at least 75% or more of the major product manufacturing or service delivery functions and to more than half of all the support functions in the organization. There are still a few areas where TQM has yet to be implemented. For example, we may find TQM absent in the law department or the finance department, where there is a tendency of resistance to the ideas of process control and measurement of internal customer satisfaction.

Scores of 70% on Results

Results in companies at this level tend to show dramatic improvements in performance or sustain very high levels of performance over many years. Most graphs show performance levels to be superior to industry competitors and may even be approaching benchmark levels in some areas. Few or none of the graphs show flat or declining performance and cause/effect relationships are clearly demonstrated. Results in support departments also show very positive trends or sustained high levels of performance.

Scores of 80% on Approach/Deployment

These are companies that achieve scores high enough to win a Baldrige Award. This does not mean that there is nothing that they could do to get better. Their approach has been evaluated and improved three or more times and shows a great deal of refinement and maturity. Major changes have already been made and they are at the point where minor enhancements are all that are needed each year to continue to improve the approaches. Approaches are probably very innovative and clearly tailored to the organization's culture and business factors. All systems show evidence of a prevention-based or proactive approach to quality and customer satisfaction. Integration is complete in at least 75% of the company.

Approaches have been completely implemented or deployed in more than three-fourths of all functions in the company, and all departments/functions are working to improve quality and customer satisfaction.

Scores of 80% on Results

Results show good to excellent trends in almost all major measures, with demonstrated ability to achieve world-class or benchmark level performance on a number of important measures. Results at this level of score need to go beyond just being the best in the industry. Trends tend to show at least 5-7 data points that are almost exclusively positive. Results at this level demonstrate that the company can keep improving over the long run. It is relatively easy to show two or three years' worth of data that show improvement. It is very difficult to demonstrate continuous improvement over a five or more year period. This does not mean that all graphs need to show five to seven years' worth of data. However, you do need to provide enough data to show *sustained* improvement over time.

Scores of 90% on Approach/Deployment

While it may be next to impossible to earn an overall score of 900 or more on the overall Baldrige scale, it is possible to receive a 90% or even 100% on an individual Examination Item. Your approach will demonstrate many evaluation and improvement cycles, and integration is nearly complete. Total Quality Management is almost completely invisible in an organizatin at this level. Employees don't need a flip chart for meeting to trigger their use of quality improvement tools. Employees at all levels have internalized these tools and approaches to the point that they now think differently. Concern with internal and external customers has become second nature and no longer requires committees, meetings, and forms to make it happen.

Deployment is complete in all major functions and facilities of the company and in almost all of the support functions. The systems in support functions may still require some additional evaluation and improvement, but they are well along in their efforts to concentrate on quality and customer satisfaction. The TQM approach has been fully integrated in most of the major systems in the company.

<u>Scores of 90% on Results</u>

Results at the 90% level would show world-class levels of performance in many major areas. Performance is clearly better than all competitors on most indices and is as good or better than world-class benchmark levels.

Scores of 100% on Approach/Deployment

It's a little tough to say what an organization at this level would look like, because I've never seen one. Some of the early Baldrige winners such as Motorola and Federal Express may be approaching the 100% level in a number of areas. An overall score of 1000 points should be considered impossible to achieve. However, it is possible to receive a score of 100% for an individual Examination Item. Your approach would need to be truly innovative, and show many cycles of evaluation and improvement. Systems at this level should require only minor adjustments over time. The Award Guidelines explain that the approach should show:

> *Excellent improvement trends and/or sustained excellent performance levels in most areas. (p. 34)*

The guidelines also explain that your approach should address all of the requirements of the Examination Item at the 100% level. Deployment is complete at the 100% level. All employees, facilities, and functions in the organization have implemented a customer-focused preventive approach to quality. Integration is so complete that employeess can barely remember what it was like before the company adopted this new approach to management. Total Quality is truly second nature and intuitive at this level of scoring.

Scores of 100% on Results

It's impossible for any company to have all of its measures show perfect results and trends, but that's close to what's expected at the 100% level. The Award Criteria Booklet defines the following characteristics of results at the 100% level:

- *Current performance is excellent in most areas of importance to the applicant's key business requirements*

- *Excellent improvement trends and/or sustained excellent performance levels in most areas*

- *Strong evidence of industry and benchmark leadership demonstrated in many areas (p. 34)*

SCORING AREAS TO ADDRESS

When assigning scores, Baldrige Examiners are taught to score an organization on each of the 28 Examination Items and not the 91 Areas to Address. This often leads to inconsistencies in scoring because each Examiner puts a different value on each of the Areas to Address (or subpoints) within a single Item. For example, Item 1.1 includes Areas to Address a–d. Let's say that the applicant does a great job (70%–80% on a and b), but does a poor job (10%–20%) in responding to c and d. How will this be scored? Some Examiners assume that all Areas to Address are equal; since there are four in this Item, each is worth 25%. This, however, can be a faulty assumption. Generally, the a's and b's tend to be more important than the c's, d's, and other Areas to Address.

To increase the amount of precision in the scoring process, some organizations have internal examiners score on Areas to Address as well as the 28 Items. To aid them in doing this, I developed a straw model of values to assign to each of the 91 Areas to Address. These values are expressed in percentages, and are based on my professional experience regarding the importance of each Area to Address. This is not, therefore, an official part of the Baldrige scoring process—and some examiners might even frown upon the assignment of such percentages to the Areas to Address. If, however, you are evaluating internal improvement applications, you could stand to benefit from using this scoring approach. I recommend that you start with these weights and then assign your own based on the situation in your own organization. (Note that I have not assigned separate percentages for the a's and b's in section 6.0. This is because both ask for data that generally appear on the same graphs. The a Areas to Address asks for your trends, and the b's ask for comparative trend data. Since both your data and competitor/benchmark data are evaluated together, these two Areas to Address cannot be scored independent of each other.)

1994 WEIGHTS OF AREAS TO ADDRESS

1.1	A. 45%	B. 10%	C. 20%	D. 25%			
1.2	A. 30%	B. 30%	C. 25%	D. 15%			
1.3	A. 25%	B. 15%	C. 35%	D. 25%			
2.1	A. 65%	B. 15%	C. 20%				
2.2	A. 30%	B. 35%	C. 20%	D. 15%			
2.3	A. 35%	B. 25%	C. 20%	D. 20%			
3.1	A. 30%	B. 20%	C. 30%	D. 20%			
3.2	A. 20%	B. 40%	C. 25%	D. 15%			
4.1	A. 50%	B. 30%	C. 20%				
4.2	A. 35%	B. 30%	C. 10%	D. 25%			
4.3	A. 30%	B. 30%	C. 20%	D. 20%			
4.4	A. 50%	B. 30%	C. 20%				
4.5	A. 25%	B. 15%	C. 25%	D. 35%			
5.1	A. 50%	B. 30%	C. 20%				
5.2	A. 60%	B. 40%					
5.3	A. 40%	B. 20%	C. 40%				
5.4	A. 30%	B. 35%	C. 20%	D. 15%			
5.5	A. 60%	B. 40%					
6.1							
6.2	The a's & b's cannot be looked at separately,						
6.3	hence there are no individual weights.						
6.4							
7.1	A. 55%	B. 30%	C. 15%				
7.2	A. 25%	B. 10%	C. 5%	D. 10%	E. 15%	F. 20%	G. 15%
7.3	A. 60%	B. 40%					
7.4	A. 55%	B. 25%	C. 20%				
7.5	A. 65%	B. 35%					
7.6	A. 65%	B. 20%	C. 15%				

Additional Scoring Guidance

No amount of guidance in a publication can take the place of practice and feedback in learning the Baldrige scoring scale. I encourage you to obtain a copy of the 1993 case study that was used to train current Baldrige Examiners. Score the case yourself, and then compare your score to the text book answer to see how your scoring differs from a group of Senior Baldrige Examiners who scored the case. By going through this exercise, you will gain a good understanding of what a 30% looks like, a 60%, an 80%, etc. A copy of the 1993 & 1994 case studies and text book answer are available by calling the ASQC at 800-248-1946. The 1994 case studies will be available in May, 1994.

Chapter 5

Interpreting the Criteria
for Leadership

OVERVIEW OF THE LEADERSHIP CATEGORY

The 1994 Award Criteria define the Leadership category as follows:

> The **Leadership** category examines senior executives' personal leadership and
> involvement in creating and sustaining a customer focus and clear and visible
> quality values. Also examined is how the quality values are integrated into the
> company's management system, including how the company addresses its public
> responsibilities and corporate citizenship (p. 14).

The 1.0 Leadership category is broken down into the following three Examination Items:

1.1 Senior Executive Leadership (45 points)
1.2 Management for Quality (25 points)
1.3 Public Responsibility and Corporate Citizenship (25 points)

As stated in the excerpt above, this category relates to the activities of the organization's
senior executives as well as the management system as a whole. The term "senior
executives" refers to the highest ranking official of the organization and the executives
that report directly to the CEO or president. This would seem very clear, but applicants
have been known to report on only the activities of their most senior executive, the CEO,
with no information being provided on the activities of any of the other executives in the
organization.

The sections below describe each of the Areas to Address, organized under each of the
three Examination Items in the Leadership category. Each section begins with a double-
ruled box containing the Examination Item, the point value, and any applicable Notes.*
Areas to Address falling under that Item follow in a single-ruled box. In the upper right
corner of each Area to Address box is an indication [brackets] of whether the Area
pertains to approach, deployment, or results. All definitions and information appearing
within these boxes is taken directly from the Baldrige criteria. Following each Area to
Address is an explanation defining what the examiners are looking for in assessing your
application. Next, I have supplied a list of indicators or evaluation factors that will assist
you in interpreting the criteria and in preparing your application.

---

* Item Notes that apply to a specific Area to Address are appropriately listed in the box containing that
Area.

1.1 SENIOR EXECUTIVE LEADERSHIP

Describe the senior executives' leadership, personal involvement, and visibility in developing and maintaining an environment for quality excellence.
(45 points)

Note:

(1)   "Senior executives" means the applicants' highest-ranking official and those reporting directly to that official.

AREA TO ADDRESS   [APPROACH, DEPLOYMENT]

1.1a Senior executives' leadership, personal involvement, and visibility in quality-related activities of the company. Include: (1) creating and reinforcing a customer focus and quality values; (2) setting expectations and planning; (3) reviewing quality and operational performance; (4) recognizing employee contributions; and (5) communicating quality values outside the company.

Notes:

(2)   Activities of senior executives (1.1.a) might also include leading and/or receiving training, communicating with employees, benchmarking, customer and supplier interactions, and mentoring other executives, managers, and supervisors.

(3)   Communication by senior executives outside the company (1.1a(5)) might involve: national, state, and community groups; trade, business, and professional organizations; and education, health care, government, standards, and public service/charitable groups. It might also involve the company's stockholders and board of directors.

What They're Looking For Here

What the examiners are looking for in this area to address is the degree to which senior executives are involved in the company's quality efforts. Many executives simply direct these efforts but fail to get personally involved. If all executives do is make speeches and hand out occasional awards for quality improvements, you will end up with a low score for this area. Evidence should be presented that the executives "walk the talk" when it comes to quality, or put into practice the values and approaches they recommend in their quality speeches. Employees judge executives' commitment based upon what they do, not on what they say. What the examiners want to see in your response to this item is that *all* senior executives spend a large percentage of their time participating in a *wide* variety of quality-related activities. Be as specific as possible, listing things such as the number and types of training courses attended by executives, the number of times executives lead quality team meetings, and so on.

In general, Baldrige Award applicants tend to score fairly well on Item 1.1. It's hard to find a company today where the executives are not committed to customer satisfaction and quality. However, many fall because most of the commitment and the activity is coming from the CEO, rather than from all senior executives. This is a common reason why Baldrige applicants receive lower scores on this item. Executives often see the quality effort as something they can delegate to others. The CEO appoints a Vice President of Total Quality whose job it is to manage the implementation of TQM throughout the company. The problem with appointing a position like this is that the rest of the executives feel they are off the hook. They don't need to worry about this quality business because that's the quality VP's job. Appointing a quality Vice President is not necessarily a bad idea. It only is a problem if it allows other executives to avoid involvement in the quality effort.

The three most important dimensions of involvement that are assessed in this item are:

- Types of quality-related activities executives spend time on
- Amount of time executives spend on these activities
- Extent to which all senior executives participate in these activities

I've seen companies that limit their executive involvement to only a couple of activities. For example, executives attend quality steering committee meetings and hand out quarterly quality awards. Other companies I've worked with show evidence that executives engage in a wide variety of quality-related activities, but overall spend very little time participating in these actions. Finally, I've seen companies that do a good job on the first two items, but there are a few executives that do most of the quality-related work, and a few executives who don't do anything. This is how deployment is evaluated in this area to address—by looking at the extent to which the activities are deployed across all the senior executives.

Indicators For Area 1.1a

- Evidence that all senior executives are involved in the quality effort

- Total number of hours executives have devoted in past year to quality-related activities

- Percentage of time executives spend in activities directly related to quality

- Breadth of quality-related activities in which executives are involved

- Amount of training/education that executives have received relating to quality

- Quality improvement projects that have been completed by executives

- Quality improvement teams and committees/task forces in which executives participate

- Time spent meeting with suppliers or customers discussing quality issues

- Time executives spend interacting with employees in the plant, field, or areas of the business where services are delivered to customers

- What employees say about visibility of executives and degree to which they are in touch with the business

- How often the executives review quality and customer satisfaction data

- Degree to which employees believe that executives are serious about quality effort

- Number and types of rewards/recognition items handed out by senior executives for achievements in quality and/or customer satisfaction

- Financial and other resources devoted to quality improvement effort

- Number of quality-related presentations made by senior executives to outside groups

---

AREA TO ADDRESS   **[APPROACH, DEPLOYMENT]**

1.1b Brief summary of the company's customer focus and quality values that serve as a basis for consistent understanding and communication within and outside the company.

<u>What They're Looking For Here</u>

In this section of the application you should briefly present the company's mission statement, overall goals, and any quality values you have written. What the examiners are hoping to see in your response is that the focus on satisfying customer needs is reflected in your overall mission for the organization, and that it is included in several of your overall goals and values for the company. When embarking upon a quality improvement effort, one of the first things an organization typically does is write a mission statement and set of values and post them throughout the company.

But just writing a clear set of quality values and posting them around the organization's facilities is not enough to receive a high score on this Area to Address.

It's one thing to write a mission statement, quality values, and goals, but an entirely different thing to make sure that this information is effectively communicated to all employees. For each of these three factors, the examiners look at both your approach and the deployment of the approach. In assessing your approach, they would look at the thoroughness with which the information is communicated, the variety of media used, the frequency with which employees are reminded of the values, and the visibility of the information. If every employee has a framed copy on his or her wall, and the information is displayed in common areas such as lunch rooms and lobbies, this would be a good example of high visibility. If employees also find out about the mission and goals through orientation, company speeches/meetings, training programs, and through the company newsletter, you would get high marks for thorough communication of this information. In assessing your deployment examiners look beyond your communication process to see how well employees know the mission and goals (without having to read them). If employees have to look up the mission statement, quality policy statement or goals, then quality values haven't been adequately communicated to employees.

It is also important that you communicate your quality values outside of your organizations. Executive speeches should mention quality values and relate how the company actually lives by these values. If articles about the company in the business press describe the organization in a way that is consistent with its values, this would be a good indicator of the effectiveness of communication.

<u>Indicators For Area 1.1b</u>

- Number of times average employee is exposed to mission and quality values

- Quantity and quality of communication of quality values outside of the company

- Extent to which external articles about the company indicate that it lives by stated quality values

- Existence of a clear and concise mission statement that includes "providing quality products/services that meet customer requirements" as part of the overall mission

- Inclusion of quality values in all appropriate employee training programs

- Existence of a set of quality values that emphasizes concepts such as zero defects, continuous improvement, prevention, and employee participation

- Use of a variety of media to communicate quality values to employees

- Extent to which mission and values are brief and easy to understand and remember

- Extent to which long-term goals for the organization integrate and are consistent with quality values

---

AREA TO ADDRESS   **[APPROACH, DEPLOYMENT]**

1.1c How senior executives regularly communicate and reinforce the company's customer focus and quality values with managers and supervisors.

What They're Looking For Here

Essentially what the examiners are looking for is evidence that the senior executives demonstrate the quality values through their behavior. It is important that the leaders manage the company and its people according to the quality values that the leaders espouse. A good way of responding to this Area to Address is to list the senior executives along the left side of a chart and the various actions of these executives along the top, to create a matrix. A sample matrix follows.

MATRIX OF ACTIONS OF SR. EXECUTIVES TO DEMONSTRATE QUALITY VALUES							
Executives	Speeches	Employee Orientation	Conf. Presentations	Staff Mtgs.	Team Mtgs.	Leadership Survey Action Plan	Lead Training on Values
CEO	X	X	X	X		X	X
V.P. H.R.	X	X	X	X		X	X
V.P. Finance	X		X	X	X	X	
V.P. Mkt.	X		X	X	X	X	
V.P. Operations			X	X	X	X	X

Several themes the Baldrige Examiners will look for in the leadership approach are:

- Employee participation

- Focus on continuous improvement

- Preventive approach to quality

- Management by "walking around"

Executives who do a good job on this Area to Address tend to spend a large percentage of their time walking around various facilities in the company, getting to know managers, supervisors, and employees, and asking them about quality improvement activities. Executives also tend to spend a fair percentage of time personally communicating with customers. This helps to:

- Keep executives in touch with customers and their needs

- Promote the company's quality orientation among customers

- Convince employees that executives are concerned with customer satisfaction

Indicators For Area 1.1c

- Evidence that executives have communicated quality values to all levels of employees

- Executives engage in a variety of activities to demonstrate their customer orientation and quality values

- Evidence that quality values are integrated into the organization's approaches to:
  - Planning
  - Decision making
  - Monitoring performance
  - Collection and analysis of data
  - Organization and job design
  - Workflow design
  - Performance planning and appraisal
  - Employee education and training

- Employees' view, at various levels in the company, of the extent to which managers and executives have integrated the quality values of the organization into their leadership approach

- Strategies in place to train managers to adopt new approaches to leadership and ensure that this behavior is reinforced in the work environment

- Degree to which major business decisions made in past several years are consistent with the quality values of the company

- Use of "management by walking around" by all executives

- Amount of time executives spend interacting with customers

- What managers, supervisors, and employees say about degree of executive commitment to quality

---

AREA TO ADDRESS [APPROACH, DEPLOYMENT]
1.1d How senior executives evaluate and improve the effectiveness of their personal leadership and involvement.

What They're Looking For Here

This is the first of many such Areas to Address that you will see throughout the various categories. It asks for evidence that the organization systematically evaluates how well the executives do in demonstrating their commitment to quality and customer satisfaction. Begin your explanation with a list of the specific measurement indices that you use to evaluate executives' performance in this area. Your measurement indices should be broad, including data from a variety of sources. Some example measurement indices might be:

- Employee survey items that address executive commitment to quality

- Percentage of time executives spend interacting with customers

- Employee focus group data

- Leadership survey executives complete with regard to each other and which executives' subordinates also complete

I've seen several Baldrige applicants mention that they use customer satisfaction data as the measure of the effectiveness of their leadership approach. But customer satisfaction data are impacted by too many other variables to be a good index of the effectiveness of the leadership approach. After listing the various leadership measurement indices, explain how you collect the evaluation data, how you aggregate the data, and use it to make decisions about what the executives need to do in the future to better demonstrate their commitment to quality. Finally you should provide several examples of changes that have resulted from evaluation data, and improvements you have made in your approach to getting executives to demonstrate quality in their leadership approach. The examiners are not only looking for a systematic approach to integrating total quality into their leadership approach.

Indicators For Area 1.1d

- Identification of a variety of measurement indices that can be used to evaluate executives' leadership and involvement

- Appropriateness and objectivity of measurement indices as indicators of executive leadership

- Extent to which measures directly relate to the effectiveness of leadership practices

- Evidence of a systematic approach to evaluation of executive leadership and involvement

- Clear explanation of how evaluation data are aggregated and compared

- System in place for follow-up planning in response to evaluation data

- Evidence of continuous improvements in executives' personal leadership and involvement based upon evaluation data

- Scope and breadth of changes that have been made over the last few years to improve executives' personal involvement and leadership

---

1.2 MANAGEMENT FOR QUALITY

Describe how the company's customer focus and quality values are integrated into day-to-day leadership, management, and supervision of all company units. (25 points)

AREA TO ADDRESS   **[APPROACH, DEPLOYMENT]**

1.2a How the company's customer focus and quality values are translated into requirements for all managers and supervisors. Describe: (1) their principal roles and responsibilities within their units; and (2) their roles and responsibilities in fostering cooperation with other units.

What They're Looking For Here

What the Baldrige Examiners look for in this area are job definitions, organization structure, and allocation of quality responsibilities. The "ideal" organization would hold everyone accountable for quality, but would have a hierarchy of specific measures and responsibilities based upon level, function, and position. The measures for the individual contributors should form the basis of the measures for the supervisors, which should form the basis of the measures for the managers, which should form the basis of the measures for the directors, etc. The two major criteria examined in this area are the extent to which all levels of employees are involved in and are evaluated on quality practices, and the extent to which the distribution of responsibilities is clear and systematic, with little or no overlap.

A common response for this area is to indicate that all employees are responsible for and evaluated on quality. But this is only to say that when everyone's responsible, no one's responsible. Responsibilities must be defined as specific indices over which the individual can exert a fair degree of control. In order to receive a high rating for this area, an organization would need to have job definitions outlining specific quality indices that are objectively measurable, and have a clear hierarchy of these indices at various job levels that lead to the overall quality measures for the company. Delineation of responsibilities should be clear in regard to who plays the primary, secondary, and support roles in achieving quality goals.

This Area to Address also looks at the extent to which the organization employs cross-functional management. In other words, do various functions or departments in the organization operate in isolation and work on their independent objectives, or do departments work as a team to accomplish common goals? Most responses for this area explain that all departments work as a team in a cooperative manner to achieve common goals. What the examiners want to see in your response is:

- Systems and procedures that are in place to encourage cooperation and cross-functional management (APPROACH)

- Evidence that the systems and procedures have been fully implemented and have produced positive results (DEPLOYMENT)

An important factor to look at in this area is the degree to which staff support departments are measured on the satisfaction of their internal customers. Staff departments have two types of customers: corporate and the line organization. They should be measured on how well they satisfy the requirements of both groups. Organizations that receive high marks in this Area to Address will have implemented a number of systems to promote teamwork and sharing among different functions and levels of employees.

Indicators For Area 1.2a

- Existence of job definitions that identify specific quality indices over which individuals have control

- Degree to which quality indices for various levels and functions are defined in a hierarchical fashion

- Degree to which all quality indices lead to ultimate quality measures for the entire organization

- Extent to which responsibilities relating to quality have been clearly delineated

- Degree to which all quality indices for employees and managers are objectively measurable

- Measurement of staff/support functions based upon internal customer satisfaction

- Degree to which *all* employees are measured on factors that contribute to the overall quality goals of the company

- Number of different systems and procedures in place to encourage cooperation

- Systems and procedures that encourage cooperation and teamwork are implemented in all areas of the organization

- Appropriateness of systems and procedures to the nature and size of the organization's business

- Use of techniques such as self-managed work teams, cross-functional teams, task forces

- Degree to which departments/functions work toward common quality goals

- Extent to which management of the organization encourages cooperation rather than competition between individuals, departments, and business units

- Employee opinion on the degree of cooperation between different departments and functions

- Amount of evidence to support claims made about cooperation between departments

---

AREA TO ADDRESS   **[APPROACH, DEPLOYMENT]**

1.2b   How the company's customer focus and quality values (1.1b) are communicated and reinforced throughout the entire work force.

Note:

(1)   **"Senior executives" means the applicant's highest-ranking official and those reporting directly to that official.**

What They're Looking For Here

At first glance this area to address appears to be very similar to 1.1c, which asks about how the executives communicate and reinforce the company's customer focus and quality values. This area to address also asks about communication and reinforcement of the company's quality values and customer focus. The difference is that area 1.1c asks about what senior executives do to communicate the values. This area to address asks about what the *company* does to communicate and reinforce the company's customer focus and quality values.

There are really two parts to this area to address that should be discussed separately. Begin your response by explaining how you communicate the company's focus on the customer and your values. An important dimension of how the values are communicated is the methods used for communication. Some companies simply post the values on plaques that are posted on walls all over the company. It is important that you use a variety of methods and media to communicate the company's values and customer focus. Employees need reminders of the values to help keep their behavior aligned with those values. Because of this, the frequency of your communication is also important. Values need to be communicated in speeches, newsletters, training programs, meetings, reports, plans, and various other ways in which the company conveys information to its employees. It is also important to vary the media used. One company I worked with programmed every computer terminal so that the company values would appear on the screen when employees signed on in the morning. Since almost every employee worked with a computer terminal, they saw the values every day. Yet, not one of the approximately 50 employees I interviewed could recite those values for me off the top of their heads. The lesson to learn here is that it is important to vary the communication media. People get used to seeing a plaque on the wall or words on a screen every morning, and don't really see it any more after a while.

The second half of the area, which I think is the more important part, asks about how you reinforce the customer focus and quality values. We first need to make clear what the word *reinforcement* means. Many will interpret this to mean how the company reminds employees of the quality values. Reminding is just more communication; it is not reinforcement. Reinforcement is being used in the Skinnerian sense here, to mean:

> How do you reward employee behavior that is consistent with your customer focus and quality values?

The company I mentioned above that has the values on the sign-on screen on the computer terminals may not communicate their values well, but they do an excellent job of reinforcing employee behavior that is consistent with the values. One way they do this is by putting all customer contact and many support employees on incentive pay. The incentive is based upon customer satisfaction scores. The company also gives out monthly and quarterly awards to employees for behaviors that are consistent with a focus on the customer. Employees may not be able to recite the words in the company's value statements, but they certainly live by the values, which is what's important.

Your response should explain the methods that you use to reward or reinforce employees for behavior that is consistent with your quality values. Describe the various methods used, the criteria for receiving the rewards, and the employees that are eligible for the awards. An ideal system would include methods for rewarding all levels and types of employees for following the values, as opposed to just the customer contact employees. An ideal system would also make sure that the items or actions that are used for rewards, are, in fact, rewarding to the recipients. For example, lunch with the boss is often used as a reward for individuals or teams in companies. Most employees I talk to find this to be more of a punishment than a reward. So, provide evidence that you tailor your rewards and reinforcement strategies to the likes and dislikes of the employee group being rewarded.

Indicators For Area 1.2b

- Number of times new employees are exposed to the company's quality values and customer focus during their first year on the job

- Number of different methods and media that are used to communicate the quality values

- Extent to which employees at all levels and in all locations are equally exposed to the values

- Evidence that media used to communicate quality values are continually changed to promote increased and continued awareness

- Extent to which employees know what the values are—not whether they can recite them word-for-word, but whether they understand the essence of the values

- Number of different techniques used to reward employee behavior that is consistent with the values

- Extent to which strategies exist for rewarding all categories and functions of employees for behavior consistent with values

- Evidence that items or activities chosen for rewards actually are rewarding to employees

- Use of innovative approaches to reinforce behavior consistent with values

---

AREA TO ADDRESS   **[APPROACH, DEPLOYMENT]**
1.2c How overall company and work unit quality and operational performance are reviewed.   Describe: (1) types, frequency, content, and use of reviews and who conducts them; and (2) how the company assists units that are not performing according to plans.

<u>What They're Looking For Here</u>

What is desirable in this area is a series of regularly scheduled, frequent meetings during which quality data are reviewed against plans. Organizations that receive low marks in this area might have monthly meetings in the quality control department to review quality data. Meetings might involve line people only when there are problems, or when quality is below standards. Every department in the organization should at least have monthly meetings where quality data and plans from the area are discussed. These are not quality circle or quality team meetings that are set up to work on specific problems or opportunities. These are more like staff meetings.

Along with regularly occurring meetings to discuss quality results, the examiners want to hear about the approach you take when goals or standards are not being met. What they want to know is that you assist departments or individuals not achieving their quality goals, not that you use a punitive approach. One applicant explained that when an individual or group is not hitting their goals, they had to "report this to the manager and have some pretty good reasons why the goals were not being met." This approach is a prime example of a punitive style of management that will earn few points with the Baldrige Examiners.

<u>Indicators For Area 1.2c</u>

- Frequency with which quality review meetings are scheduled and actually held

- Agendas from quality review meetings

- Extent to which quality reviews are integrated into reviews of other types of data such as financial and operational

- Deployment of quality reviews to all functions and facilities within the organization

- Degree to which all departments and functions in the organization hold regular quality review meetings, or review customer satisfaction/quality performance in regular staff meetings

- Use of a positive approach to assisting departments and individuals who are not meeting quality goals

---

AREA TO ADDRESS [**APPROACH, DEPLOYMENT**]

1.2d How the company evaluates and improves managers' and supervisors' effectiveness in reinforcing the company's customer focus and quality values.

Note:

(2) **Activities of senior executives (1.1a) might also include leading and/or receiving training, communicating with employees, benchmarking, customer and supplier interactions, and mentoring other executives, managers, and supervisors.**

What They're Looking For Here

Again, the examiners are looking for the existence of a systematic, data-based approach to assessing the effectiveness of integrating quality values into the management of the business and its people. Most organizations do nothing to evaluate the effectiveness of their management approach. What it would take to receive high marks in this area is an evaluation process that collects several levels of data on a regular basis and evaluates those data against standards to determine how well the management approach is working. Further, the examiners would like to see evidence that the results of these evaluations are used to implement changes in the management approach to achieve better results.

Indicators For Area 1.2d

- Existence of a systematic process for evaluating the integration of quality values into the management approach and the effectiveness of the management approach

- Reliability and objectivity of the data collected

- Comparison of data on management approach to established standards or goals

- Existence of a process for reviewing evaluation data and making decisions based upon the data

- Evidence that the management approach is adapted and changed to continuously improve its effectiveness

1.3 PUBLIC RESPONSIBILITY AND CORPORATE CITIZENSHIP

Describe how the company includes its responsibilities to the public in its quality policies and improvement practices. Describe also how the company leads as a corporate citizen in its key communities. (25 points)

Notes:

(1)   The public responsibility issues addressed in 1.3a and 1.3b relate to the company's impacts and possible impacts on society associated with its products, services, and company operations. They include business ethics, environment, and safety as they relate to any aspect of risk or adverse effect, whether or not these are covered under law or regulation.

(2)   The term "targets" as used in Item 1.3 and elsewhere in the criteria refer to specific performance levels, based upon appropriate measures or indicators.

(3)   Major public responsibility or impact areas should be addressed in planning (Item 3.1) and in the appropriate process management Items of Category 5.0.

(4)   Health and safety of employees are not included in Item 1.3. They are covered in Item 4.5.

AREA TO ADDRESS   **[APPROACH, DEPLOYMENT]**

1.3a How the company integrates its public responsibilities into its quality values and practices. Include: (1) how the company considers risks, regulatory and other legal requirements in setting operational requirements and targets; (2) a summary of the company's principal public responsibilities key operational requirements and associated targets, and how these requirements and/or targets are communicated throughout the company; and (3) how and how often progress in meeting operational requirements and/or targets is reviewed.

What They're Looking For Here

Being a Baldrige Award winning company takes more than having the right financial and customer satisfaction results and having the right systems in place. You also have to be a good corporate citizen. Examination Item 1.3 asks about how you develop plans and implement activities relating to corporate citizenship and public responsibility. What does this mean? It means factors such as environmental protection, charity, support of the arts, support of education, and help of the community. The only thing that is not included in this area to address is self-serving actions. For example, the money that a defense contractor donates to key congressmen's campaigns might be considered self-serving.

Begin your response for this area to address by describing how your company sets standards or goals relating to public responsibility and corporate citizenship. Explain the process for setting these goals and/or standards and who is involved in the process. Your discussion should also mention the key legal and regulatory requirements that must be adhered to. Explain how the levels of performance in your own standards or goals relate to required levels. Obviously it will be more impressive if your approach is to do more than just satisfy the requirements—you have no choice in this. The examiners want to see evidence of going beyond meeting basic legal and regulatory requirements in how you set your goals and standards. Also, you should explain how you evaluate risks and possible consequences when setting these standards or requirements.

Question 1.3a (2) asks for information about the key public responsibility areas that are relevant to your company. For example, factors relating to safety and environmental protection would be more important for an oil company or nuclear power company than a bank or retail store. Issues of honesty and ethics might be more important to a bank or brokerage firm. For each of the factors that are important and relevant to your company, describe how requirements are defined and integrated into policies and operating procedures. Finally, explain how these requirements are communicated to all appropriate employees in the company. Question 1.3a (3) asks about how your progress in the area of public responsibility is reviewed. Describe when review meetings occur, what is discussed, and who attends.

Indicators For Area 1.3a

- Response includes delineation of key measures of corporate citizenship and public responsibility that are relevant and important to the company

- A systematic process is used to define standards and goals relating to matters of corporate citizenship and public responsibility

- Goals or standards specify levels of performance that will lead the company to a world-class level of performance on these factors

- Evidence that risks and possible consequences are thoroughly assessed in the process of coming up with goals and standards in the area of public responsibility

- Evidence provided to demonstrate how key goals and standards for public responsibility and corporate citizenship are translated into operational policies and procedures

- Thorough communication of operational policies and procedures relating this item to all appropriate employees and locations within the company

- Regularly scheduled review meetings are held to discuss progress in meeting goals and standards in the areas of public responsibility and corporate citizenship

- Plans are revised as necessary based upon changes in requirements, the business environment, or other factors

---

AREA TO ADDRESS   **[APPROACH, DEPLOYMENT]**

1.3b How the company looks ahead to anticipate public concerns and to assess possible impacts on society of its products, services, and operations. Describe briefly how this assessment is used in planning.

What They're Looking For Here

The best companies are those that anticipate the future public concerns about their products or services and deal with those issues in a preventive fashion. Your response for this area should explain how you look into the future to identify trends that may impact your business, and how you plan for those trends.

An important aspect of judging your response to this area is the thoroughness and objectivity of your sources of information on future trends. Some companies rely on one or two sources of data. Others rely on a great many sources and devote a good deal of effort to predicting future trends that will impact their business. These tend to be the companies that are around for the long haul. Once you explain how and where you obtain data used to predict future trends, explain the process for using these data as inputs to your planning. An example or two will help to add credibility to your response, illustrating that you actually have used this data to change your plans.

Indicators For Area 1.3b

- Number of different sources of data company uses to predict future trends that may impact their products, services, or operations

- Objectivity of sources of data on future trends

- Evidence that company acts to prevent possible problems with their products/ services in the future, rather than to cover them up

- Amount and thoroughness of testing done on products/services sold by the company, and relevance of this testing to current and future public concerns

- Evidence that information on future trends in public concerns are incorporated into the company's planning process

- Existence of a specific process for integrating trends in public concerns into the planning process

---

AREA TO ADDRESS   **[APPROACH , DEPLOYMENT]**

1.3c How the company leads as a corporate citizen in its key communities. Include: (1) a brief summary of the types and extent of leadership and involvement in key communities; (2) how the company promotes quality awareness and sharing of quality-related information; (3) how the company seeks opportunities to enhance its leadership; and (4) how the company promotes legal and ethical conduct in all that it does.

Note:

(5)   **The corporate citizenship issues appropriate for inclusion in 1.3c relate to actions by the company to strengthen community services, education, health care, environment and practices of trade or business associations. Such involvement would be expected to be limited by the company's available human and financial resources.**

What They're Looking For Here

This area to address looks at two factors. First, it asks for information on what you are doing as a company to be a leader in demonstrating your corporate citizenship and involvement in the communities in which you operate. Second, it asks how you help other organizations in their quality improvement efforts. Sometimes these efforts overlap. For example, Baxter Healthcare, the world's largest manufacturer of medical supplies, recently held a workshop for area high school principals to teach them about Total Quality and how it may be applied in educational institutions. Since these principals are from the community surrounding Baxter's corporate offices, it is a community outreach effort. However, since it also involved helping promote Total Quality, it qualifies for the second half of this area to address as well.

A good way of responding to this area to address is to summarize in chart form the activities you engage in that make you a good corporate citizen. A sample of a portion of such a chart is shown in the example below.

ORGANIZATION	DESCRIPTION	NOTEWORTHY ACCOMPLISHMENTS
OPAR	Organization that funds and promotes AIDS research	• CFO is chairman • Company donated $50,000 in '93 • Meetings held at company facilities • Employees donated over 20,000 hours and $30,000 in '93
Portage Works Project	Workshop run by retarded	• All major mailings done by PWP • PWP one of our certified suppliers • Work from our company pays salaries of nine individuals from PWP
Juvenile Diabetes Foundation	Charitable organization for children with diabetes	• CEO is on the board • Company sponsors fundraising banquet each year, devoting many hours and dollars • Prepare all print advertising free for JDF • Company donates over $50,000 each year to JDF

In presenting information on the activities you engage in that make you a good corporate citizen, it may be helpful to provide some comparative data to help illustrate the importance of your accomplishments. For example, if your company donated $80,000 per quarter in 1993 to the United Fund, through employee contributions, and you have 18,000 employees, that works out to less than $5.00 per employee. The Baldrige Examiners may not know whether this is exceptional, average, or below par. Therefore, you might mention that for companies your size, it is typical for employees to average $3.20 per quarter in donations to the United Fund. This makes your performance look much better than the average company.

Once you've finished describing the activities that make you a good corporate citizen, you need to provide a similar explanation of the activities you engage in to promote total quality in other organizations besides your own. Some examples of relevant activities that might be listed here are:

- Speeches made by employees at quality meetings/conferences

- Quality-related articles written by employees and published in trade journals

- Speeches on quality-related topics made at your own trade association conferences

- Tours held at your company facilities to demonstrate implementation of TQM

- Quality-related workshops conducted by your employees for other organizations

- Extent to which your company is cited in books and articles about implementation of TQM

The key here is to be specific. Many Baldrige applicants respond with general words and phrases such as: "We have conducted a number of tours for outside organizations and frequently include suppliers and individuals from other companies in our quality courses." The problem with statements such as this one is that you sound like everyone else. In order to impress the examiners you need to list specifics such as: "Our employees gave 269 quality-related speeches to local and national professional organizations in 1993, our employes wrote 11 articles on TQM that were published in national periodicals, and we have conducted 640 tours and presentations on TQM for outsiders at our various facilities around the United States." These are the types of facts and figures that will impress the examiners.

This area to address also asks about how you seek to enhance your leadership in both corporate citizenship, and the promotion of Total Quality outside of the organization. Again, the worst thing to do is to present a general statement such as: "Our company continues to review and improve our approaches to corporate citizenship and promotion of TQM, and hope to continually enhance our leadership position in these areas in the coming years." Most examiners would read a statement like this and write a comment such as: "It is not clear how the company plans to seek and exploit opportunities for improving its leadership in the areas of corporate citizenship and promotion of Total

Quality." You need to get specific and explain how you intend to do this, and what your specific goals are for leadership in these areas.

Finally, 1.3c (4) asks how your company promotes legal and ethical conduct in all it does. Again, forget the general statements. Give us specifics of how you do this. For example, Northrop has an anonymous hotline number that employees can call to report unethical behavior or practices they have observed. This setup is combined with very thorough training for employees on what constitutes unethical behavior. These would be the types of activities that should be discussed here. Education and awareness are usually the first steps in the process, but there also needs to be measurement and control strategies in place to ensure that legal and ethical practices are followed on a continual basis.

Indicators For Area 1.3c

- Breadth and scope of activites that indicate that the company is a good corporate citizen and concerned with the public welfare

- Significance of the company's accomplishments in these areas

- Evidence from news media and outside sources that the company is, in fact, a good corporate citizen

- Comparison of the corporate citizenship and public responsibility activities of the applicant company to other companies that are similar in size

- Evidence that the company has increased its efforts to be a good corporate citizen over the last few years

- Number of presentations, tours, and publications that company employees have made that promote implementation of TQM

- Percentage of presentations that were done locally and percentage that required out-of-town travel

- Organizations at which presentations are made are a mix of quality, trade, civic, and educational

- Use of unique or innovative approaches for promoting Total Quality outside of the company

- Significance of the company's commitment to promotion of TQM

- Number of times the company is cited in books and articles on companies that have done a good job in implementing Total Quality

- Evidence that the company has sought opportunities to seek leadership positions in the promotion of TQM, and in being a good corporate citizen

- Specific strategies exist for attaining higher levels of leadership in these areas in the future

- Existence of a systematic approach to educating employees regarding legal and ethical behavior/practices

- Extent to which employees at all levels and in all locations are provided with this education/training on legal/ethical issues

- Existence of a system for monitoring extent to which employee behavior is consistent with legal/ethical guidelines

- Control strategies are in place to ensure that legal/ethical practices are followed

---

AREA TO ADDRESS   **[RESULTS]**

1.3d Trends in key measures and/or indicators of improvement in addressing public responsibilities and corporate citizenship. Include responses to any sanctions received under law, regulation, or contract.

Note:

(6)   If the company has received sanctions under law, regulation, or contact during the past three years, include the current status in responding to 1.3.d. If no sanctions have been received, so indicate. If settlements have been negotiated in lieu of potential sanctions, give explanations.

What They're Looking For Here

In case you missed it, this Area to Address asks for results or data. No information is requested on *how* you do anything. This item asks for evidence that all of the activities you talk about in the previous sections of this item really work. About a year ago the Wall Street Journal came out with a story about one of Westinghouse's nuclear power plants which was claiming that it deserved to win a Baldrige Award in 1992, and the judges recommended that it win. Westinghouse claimed that the Secretary of Commerce overruled the judges' recommendation in deciding that its facility should not be a winner. Westinghouse claims that the decision was political. The Baldrige people and Department of Commerce maintain that the Secretary of Commerce has always had the final say on the award winners and that it was not a political decision. The story as I understand it is that the nuclear plant had received several major safety citations by the NRC in the last few years, and that the Secretary of Commerce felt that, because of this, they would not be a good role model for other U.S. companies.

This may be part of the reason why this item now appears in the Baldrige criteria (it was first added in 1993). Whatever the reason, it is a worthy addition. What the criterion asks for are data to demonstrate your performance in the area of public responsibility and corporate citizenship. This does not mean singular pieces of data such as "We won the award from the American Heart Association in 1993 for highest contribution per employee in the state of Illinois." Accomplishments such as this should be listed in 1.3c (1), not here.

Time series data should be presented here so that trends can be determined. The specific indicators that you present are up to you. For example, every year, magazines like *Fortune* list the most and least admired corporations in America. Corporate citizenship is one of the determinants of these ratings. Being listed in the top 25 most admired corporations for five years in a row would be some important data to include here. Perhaps you track the number of complaints lodged against your company by the Better Business Bureau. These data might also be good to include here. Citations from the Environmental Protection Agency might be something else that is relevant.

Whatever indices you choose to present data on should be tailored to your industry and community. Your results will be assessed by first asking: Are these the important public responsibility indices for a company such as yours? Assuming that the indices are the correct ones, your performance will be assessed to determine the trends in the data, and how your current levels of performance compare with other data. The more sources of comparison the better.

The ideal situation would be a graph that shows that your company's performance is superior to:

- Your past performance
- Your goals
- Your competitors
- Other companies your size
- Benchmark organizations

Another aspect of your results that will be assessed is the number of data points on your graphs. Two or three years' worth of data represented by two or three data points is hardly enough to say what your trends are.

The part of your response for this area to address that requires words rather than data asks about your response to sanctions you may have received in the last few years. If you have not received any, simply state this. If you have, explain what they were for, and what you have done to correct the root causes of these sanctions so they don't recur. It would be wise to go into some detail on this if the sanctions were serious. The examiners are looking for evidence that you have mended your ways and have structured the work environment so that the problems the sanctions were for don't continue.

Indicators For Area 1.3d

- Number of different indices for which data are presented

- Extent to which indices are appropriate measures of public responsibility performance for a company of this type

- Trends in performance show continuous improvement over the last few years

- Company's performance on key indices is superior to other companies of similar size

- Company's performance on key indicators is superior to competitor's performance on public responsibility indicators

- Graphs include enough data to determine trends

- Comparison of company's performance on public responsibility indices to benchmark organizations

Chapter 6

Interpreting the Criteria for Information and Analysis

OVERVIEW OF THE INFORMATION AND ANALYSIS CATEGORY

The 1994 Baldrige Award Criteria define the Information and Analysis category as follows:

> The **Information and Analysis** category examines the scope, management, and use of data and information to maintain a customer focus, to drive quality excellence and to improve operational and competitive performance. (p. 16)

The 2.0 Information and Analysis category is worth a total of 75 points and is broken down into the following three Examination Items:

- 2.1 Scope and Management of Quality and Performance Data and Information (15 points)
- 2.2 Competitive Comparisons and Benchmarking (20 points)
- 2.3 Analysis and Uses of Company-Level Data (40 points)

The purpose of this category is to assess the types of data you collect relating to quality and company performance and to examine the process by which you analyze those data in order to make decisions. This chapter describes each of the three Examination Items and the eleven Areas to Address that fall under this category. Again, each section begins with a double-ruled box containing the Examination Item, the point value, and any applicable Notes.* Areas to Address falling under that Item follow in a single-ruled box. In the upper right corner of each Area to Address box is an indication [brackets] of whether the Area pertains to approach, deployment, or results. All definitions and information appearing within these boxes is taken directly from the Baldrige criteria. Following each Area to Address is an explanation defining what the examiners are looking for in assessing your application. Next, I have supplied a list of indicators or evaluation factors that will assist you in interpreting the criteria and in preparing your application.

This category forms the foundation of a sound quality system. If you have a poor information and analysis system, this will lead to a low score in the sections that deal with planning (3.0), human resource development and management (4.0), management of process (5.0), results (6.0), and customer satisfaction results (7.0). If you select the wrong indices to measure, this will lead to low scores in a number of different areas that ask for results. Even if your graphs look great, you won't end up with a good score for results if the performance indices on the graphs are inappropriate.

---

* Item Notes that apply to a specific Area to Address are appropriately listed in the box containing that Area.

The 1994 Baldrige application guidelines explain:

In simplest terms, Category 2.0 is the "brain center" for the alignment of a company's information system with its strategic directions. (p. 7).

Even though this category is only worth a possible 75 points out of 1000, it is critical to high scores in other sections. In fact, if you do a poor job on this section of your application it will have an impact on all of the sections that ask for *results*. Thus, section 2.0 actually impacts 75 points on its own, plus 335 points relating to results.

It used to be that this item asked for information on the *quality* data that a company collected. The focus now is on *all* important data that a company gathers and analyzes. Certainly quality and customer satisfaction data are still asked for. However, this category also asks for financial, operational, productivity, and any other type of performance data a company might gather and use in running the business.

2.1 SCOPE AND MANAGEMENT OF QUALITY AND PERFORMANCE DATA AND INFORMATION

Describe the company's selection and management of data and information used for planning, day-to-day management, and evaluation of quality and operational performance. (15 points)

Notes:

  (1)   Item 2.1 permits the applicant to demonstrate the *breadth and depth* of its data. Applicants should give brief descriptions of the data under major headings such as "internal operations and performance" and subheadings such as "support services." Note that information on the scope and management of competitive and benchmark data is requested in Item 2.2.

  (2)   Actual data should not be reported in Item 2.1. These data are requested in other Items. Accordingly, all data reported in other Items should be part of the base of data and information to be described in Item 2.1.

> **AREA TO ADDRESS**   **[APPROACH, DEPLOYMENT]**
>
> **2.1a   Criteria for selecting data and information for use in quality and operational performance improvement. List key types of data and information used and briefly outline the principal roles of each type in improving quality and operational performance. Include: (1) customer-related; (2) product and service performance; (3) internal operations and performance, including business and support services, and employee-related; (4) supplier performance; and (5) cost and financial.**

What They're Looking For Here

What the examiners are interested in seeing in this area is a systematic process for pinpointing the indices you use to measure and manage quality, from product/service inception through final delivery of products/services to customers. Many companies collect a great deal of data that end up in reports which no one reads. No one reads the reports because the data are not normally needed in making day-to-day decisions. An organization should, however, have a specific set of criteria it uses in selecting variables to measure and include this in its quality data base. At least one of these criteria should indicate that the dimension or index being used is there because of its importance to customers. A steel company, for example, might be in the habit of measuring the amount of dirt and oil present on finished and rolled steel. But customers may not care about this if they still need to wash the steel after delivery because it gets dirty en route. The Baldrige Examiners want to see evidence that you measure what is important, and not just what is easy to measure or what has traditionally been measured.

Another criterion that should be used in selecting measurement indices is the degree to which a variable impacts upon other variables that are considered important. For example, the customer may not care about the processing temperature, but processing temperature is one of the primary determinants of rigidity, which is something that customers care a great deal about.

The Baldrige Examiners also want to know about how measurement indices for internal support departments are selected. Specific quality measures should be selected based upon the degree to which they bear upon internal customer satisfaction.

Whatever criteria you have for selecting indices to measure and include in your company's data base, it is important that the criteria be narrow enough to serve as a good screen. In other words, the criteria should allow you to throw out all but the most critical variables. One Baldrige applicant listed their criteria as follows:

To be included in our data base, a measurement index should be:

- *Important to customers*

- *Measurable*

- *Related to other important measures in the company*

The problem with these criteria is that they are so vague and general, that you could make a case for measuring anything. These criteria would not allow the company to eliminate any extraneous data from their data base. Also, keep in mind that all indices may not be important to customers. For example, profits may not be something customers care about, but your executives, stockholders and board of directors certainly do. Keep in mind that this area to address refers to all data that the company collects, not just quality-related data.

In addition to learning about *how you decide* what to measure, the examiners want to know *what* you measure. Some of the criteria used to evaluate this portion of the application are:

- Scope of data collected
- Breadth of data collected
- Objectivity and validity of data collected
- Number of sources of data
- Who collects the data
- How data are summarized

Several Baldrige Award applicants have responded to this section by explaining their quality audit process. Having an auditing process is good, but if that is the only way you collect data on quality, you may get very low marks for this section. Further, an audit is a detection- and correction-based approach to quality, whereas an examiner prefers to see a preventive approach. In order to facilitate the prevention of defects, process data must be collected on a regular basis. The examiners look at the scope of the quality data you collect in order to determine whether it includes process and output data, and data on internal service functions. Many companies have very sophisticated quality measurement systems in place on the plant floor, but have no measurement systems in place for staff departments such as engineering, maintenance, and procurement. If you want to receive a good score for this area, you need to collect quality data on all functions/departments in the organization.

Another important factor assessed is the objectivity of the data collection methods you employ. For example, an important process in many service businesses is the interaction between customers and front-line service personnel. Many service companies measure this process by surveying customers or by using customer comment cards. Both of these techniques have poor reliability and have been shown to be based upon many subjective factors such as the sexes of the people involved, the appearance of the customer-contact personnel, the mood of the customer, etc. People are poor observers of their own and others' behavior.

In a manufacturing business, objectivity might refer to the degree to which you use scientific instruments to measure quality, versus the common "eyeball" approach to quality inspection. The more that human judgement is removed from the quality assessment process, the more objective the process will be. Measurement instruments need to be calibrated often, but they don't get bored or tired as humans do.

The objectivity of the quality data collected may be influenced by who collects the data. If the accounting department is measuring their own quality levels, this is not as objective as if the accounting department's quality were measured by the consumers of its services and products. Having a number of different sources of such data is important as well. The more varied your sources of quality data, the more thorough your measurement system.

Indicators For Area 2.1a

- Existence of specific criteria for selecting measurement indices for products and services produced for external customers

- Existence of specific criteria for selecting measurement indices for products and services produced for internal customers

- Degree to which measurement indices are selected based upon their impact on customer satisfaction

- Elimination from quality reports of any indices (and corresponding data) that don't meet selection criteria

- Degree to which internal and external customers are involved in identifying criteria for selection of measurement indices

- Degree to which data are collected on all important quality dimensions of the products and services produced/offered by the organization

- Degree to which data are collected on all important process dimensions relating to the manufacture of products or the performance of services

- Scope of data collected on quality indices in staff/support departments

- Objectivity and accuracy of devices/instruments used to measure process and output quality dimensions

- Degree to which quality data are collected from internal and external customers in order to evaluate products and services

- Collection of data from a variety of internal and external sources to ensure thoroughness and objectivity

- Extent to which data on the quality of goods and services from suppliers is collected

- Scope and objectivity of data on employee performance as it relates to quality

- Scope and objectivity of customer-related data

- Frequency, thoroughness, and objectivity of quality audits

- Extent to which the organization measures the cost of quality or the cost of nonconformance

- Data on cost and financial performance

- Collection of data on health, safety, and environmental issues

- Use of valid sampling and data collection techniques

AREA TO ADDRESS   **[APPROACH, DEPLOYMENT]**

2.1b How reliability, consistency, and rapid access to data are assured throughout the company. If applicable, describe how software accuracy and reliability are assured.

What They're Looking For Here

In the previous area we looked at how you select indices for measuring quality and the specific types of data you include in your reports. In this area (2.1b), the examiners analyze the processes used to ensure the validity of the data and the means by which valid data are disseminated to the appropriate employees. What the Baldrige Examiners want to see in this section is evidence that you use a variety of methods to evaluate and improve the accuracy of your measurement instruments and procedures. This pertains to automated measurement equipment as well as to instruments such as surveys, questionnaires, and checklists. All of these instruments need to be checked for reliability and calibrated on a regular basis.

In your response, if you explain simply that you check the accuracy of your measurement instruments periodically and adjust them as necessary, you won't receive a very high score. You must provide specifics. Give examples of how you assess different measurement devices. You might use both a hardware and non-hardware example.

A related aspect of this Area to Address pertains to the approach you use to disseminate the data to employees. What examiners are looking for here is that employees who need the data receive them in a timely fashion. If you don't receive a report on today's quality statistics until next week or next month, you can't do much about problems or deviations. Obviously, an on-line data system is the best way of getting data to employees when they need it. The availability of terminals used to access on-line data is also important. If there is only one terminal that fifteen employees must share, access to the data is limited.

The examiners also look at the standardization of data collection and reporting techniques. One manufacturing organization I worked with produced 24 different quality reports every week. The reports were produced independently by various departments (e.g., engineering, quality control, production, industrial engineering, etc.), and were all in different formats. What the examiners want to see is that quality reporting is standardized and that there is no overlap or redundancy in the data. Quality reports should be as brief and easy to interpret as possible. The use of graphs and charts to summarize data rather than printouts of statistics is preferable. The examiners also look at the recipients of each of the quality reports. Reports should only be sent to individuals who need the data to make decisions. Use of specific reports for specific levels and functions is a positive indicator, as compared with using a single report that attempts to meet the information needs of all levels of employees in all different functions.

Another factor that is examined in this area is the degree to which quality reports and on-line data are kept up-to-date and accurate. Many organizations have excellent reporting systems, but they don't maintain the database frequently enough, so the data are not current.

If appropriate, you should also explain how quality is assured for any software that is used to process data and generate reports.

Indicators For Area 2.1b

- Use of regular and systematic approach for testing and calibrating all automated and manual measurement equipment/devices

- Systematic evaluation, testing and calibration of non-hardware measurement instruments (e.g., surveys, checklists, etc.)

- Validity of methods used to evaluate accuracy of measurement instruments

- Use of evaluation and calibration techniques for measurement instruments used to collect quality data on staff/support functions

- Degree to which quality data available to employees is current and accurate

- Timeliness with which quality data are disseminated to employees

- Ease of employee access to quality data needed to do their jobs

- Standardization of quality data and report format across all functions/departments in the organization

- Readability and ease of use of quality reports

- Quality reports tailored to specific levels and functions so that employees only receive the data they need

- Use of graphs and charts to summarize quality data in reports

- Responses of employees regarding the usability and accuracy of the quality reports distributed

- Responses of managers and supervisors regarding the usability and accuracy of the quality reports

- Systematic process for ensuring that software used for various purposes is useful, accurate, and up-to-date

AREA TO ADDRESS   **[APPROACH, DEPLOYMENT]**
**2.1c How the company evaluates and improves the scope and management of
data and information. Include: (1) review and update;
(2) shortening the cycle from data gathering to access; (3) broadening access to
all those requiring data for day-to-day management and improvement; and
(4) alignment of data and information with process improvement plans and
needs.**

Note:

   **(3)   Improving the management of data and information (2.1.c) might also
            include company mechanisms and/or incentives for units to contribute
            and to share data and information.**

What They're Looking For Here

Your response for this Area to Address should explain how you systematically evaluate
your data collection systems and instruments. Describe how the evaluation is done, the
procedures used, instruments, etc. Don't respond with a statement such as: "We
regularly evaluate and improve the scope and accuracy of our quality data collection."
Be specific. Explain exactly how you evaluate the data collection system. Your
approach will be assessed based upon its thoroughness, objectivity, validity, and use of
accepted evaluation methodologies. You should begin by listing the specific indices you
use to measure the effectiveness of your data base. The measurement indices should
include internal customer satisfaction, process, and output measures. Follow this list with
a flowchart or list of steps involved in the evaluation process.

In this section you might also talk about any actions you have taken to get business units
and/or facilities to work together to develop common measures. If you have employed
any objectives or incentives to encourage sharing of data it would also be appropriate to
mention this here.

The Baldrige Examiners are also looking for evidence that you have taken actions to
streamline the information processing cycle and to implement countermeasures to
improve quality. Many organizations that have only just begun to work on total quality
management in the last few years find that quality improvement teams take a great deal of
time collecting and processing data before any corrective countermeasures are
introduced. While adequate data and thorough analysis are certainly important, too much

time can be spent on these activities. The examiners want to see that you are thorough, as well as efficient and improvement-oriented.

A typical response for this area is to describe that you have taken a number of steps to shorten the data gathering and processing cycle. As in the other areas, you need to be specific. Start out by explaining the situation in the past. Be sure to include some statistics if you have them. Your response to this area should also include an explanation of your efforts to broaden employees' access to data and information. The Baldrige people are looking for evidence that many employees are provided with access to the company's data base.

Question 2.1c (4) asks about how you have integrated your data base with process improvement needs and plans. What's being asked for here is evidence that your data base includes key process measures that you have decided are critical to control, in order to produce consistently high quality products/services. Your response for this portion of 2.1c should directly relate to and be compatible with your response to Item 5.2, which asks about your key processes, how you measure them, and how you control them. Your data base should not be limited to output measures such as defects, customer satisfaction, and financial accomplishments. Key process measures should also be included. What the examiners would like to see here is that the process indices you have chosen to measure are tied in to your key processes and key process variables that are discussed in Item 5.2.

Indicators For Area 2.1c

- Existence of a systematic approach for evaluating quality data collection systems

- Evaluation measurement indices include measures of internal customer satisfaction, process, and output quality

- Evidence that company has increased employees' access to data and information

- Validity and objectivity of evaluation instruments and methodologies

- Number of years during which evaluation has been done

- Evidence of improvements in data collection system based upon evaluation

- Evidence that data gathering, analysis, and reporting process has been streamlined over the last several years

- Amount of data indicating that cycle time of data collection and dissemination has been reduced

- Description of specific strategies and tactics that have been employed to reduce cycle time of collecting, summarizing, and disseminating data

- Degree to which projects completed by quality improvement teams require less time now than in the past

- Extent to which key process measures are included in the company's data base

- Process measures selected are consistent with process improvement needs and plans/goals

- Evidence of steps taken to closely align the company's performance measures with process improvement efforts

---

2.2 COMPETITIVE COMPARISONS AND BENCHMARKING

Describe the company's processes, current sources and scope, and uses of competitive comparisons and benchmarking information and data to support improvement of quality and overall company operational performance. (20 points)

Notes:

(1) Benchmarking information and data refer to processes and results that represent superior practices and performance and set "stretch" targets for comparison.

(2) Sources of competitive and benchmarking information might include: (1) information obtained from other organizations through sharing; (2) information obtained from open literature; (3) testing and evaluation by the company itself; and (4) testing and evaluation by independent organizations.

AREA TO ADDRESS   **[APPROACH, DEPLOYMENT]**

2.2a. How competitive comparisons and benchmarking information and data are used to help drive improvement of quality and operational performance. Describe: (1) how needs are determined; and (2) criteria for seeking appropriate competitive comparisons and benchmarking information—from within and outside the company's industry.

What They're Looking For Here

Benchmarking is a process of studying other organizations that are known to be the best in the country or the world at performing one or a series of functions. The data from benchmarking studies are used both to set goals and to determine what level of performance is possible, as well as to adapt some of the practices of the successful companies to one's own organization. The selected organizations against which one's company benchmarks will not necessarily be competitors, and may not even be in a related industry. Xerox Business Products benchmarked itself against many of the functions performed in a mail order clothing company—L. L. Bean, for example. This section of the application should begin with a description of your criteria for selecting competitive comparisons and benchmarks. Many applicants explain that they use specific criteria for selecting benchmarks, but don't list those criteria. Make sure that your response includes a list of your criteria, or at least the major criteria. Competitive comparisons are different from benchmarking. Competitive comparisons are simply comparisons of how your company does vis-à-vis your major competitors. Competitive comparisons should be selected based upon the similarities between the two organizations. The competitors you choose should be about the same size, have similar products/services, and operate in similar markets. Companies you select to benchmark yourself against need not be in the same business as your organization. Benchmarks should be selected based upon the level of quality they deliver in a particular area that is similar to an area in your own organization. For example, if your company is a computer manufacturer, you might compare your company to an auto manufacturer, because it may have the best inventory control system. The organizations you choose to benchmark or compare yourself against should be the best in the country or even in the world, in a particular area or function.

One factor on which your response for this item will be evaluated is the number of different functions or indices used to compare yourself to competitors and benchmark organizations. If you compare your company with one other competitor who is also one you benchmark yourself against, you won't receive a very high score for this Area to Address. Many organizations select one or two past Baldrige winners and compare every function in their organization to Xerox, IBM, Motorola, or one of the other winners. This approach will not necessarily be effective because being a Baldrige winner does not mean that every function in the company is world class. If, on the other hand, you have identified a dozen or more functions and compare yourself to world-class benchmarks on each function, you might end up with a perfect score in this Area to Address.

What the examiners want to hear about in your response for this Area to Address is how you select those organizations to which you compare your own performance and practices. It is important to do both competitive comparisons and benchmarks. You might select your direct competitors as the companies you use for benchmarking purposes, or you might select companies that are totally outside your industry. A good approach employed by many exemplary organizations is to collect comparison data on all major competitors and to benchmark yourself against a variety of different functions in a variety of different organizations. In this section (2.2), you need to explain the process by which you select comparative organizations or "benchmarking partners."

What is also considered important here is that the functions or processes you select as benchmarking and comparison targets must relate to your own goals and priorities for quality improvement, as outlined in the company's strategic and annual plans. Benchmarking is often done independently of the organization's quality improvement goals and plans. You should explain how the benchmarking and competitive comparison activities you engaged in during the past few years have supported your long-term and annual quality goals and priorities.

Within your response to this Area to Address, you should also explain how you determined which organizations were the best at performing a particular function. Some organizations do a much better job of self-promotion than others. It may be that the best organizations get overlooked in benchmarking studies because no one knows that they are the best. Explain what type and how thorough a job you did in identifying the world-class organizations used for benchmarking purposes. The more thorough your research the better.

Indicators For Area 2.2a

- Evidence of a systematic process for selecting competitive organizations for comparison purposes

- Scope and breadth of data collected on competitors

- Strong relationship between process/functions selected for competitive comparisons and benchmarking and quality goals and plans for the organization

- Thoroughness of research done to identify organizations that are the best at particular functions or processes

- Use of comparisons to both competitors and benchmarks for setting improvement goals

- Evidence that organizations selected as benchmarking partners are in fact world-class for the particular functions or processes studied

- Number and appropriateness of criteria used for selecting competitors with which to compare your organization

- Number and appropriateness of criteria used for selecting benchmark organizations with which to compare your organization

- Number of different functions or processes in the organization that are compared or benchmarked against others

- Objectivity and clarity of the criteria for selecting competitors and benchmarks for comparison purposes

---

AREA TO ADDRESS   [APPROACH, DEPLOYMENT]
2.2b Brief summary of current scope, sources, and principal uses of each type of competitive comparisons and benchmarking information and data. Include: (1) customer-related; (2) product and service quality; (3) internal operations and performance, including business and support services and employee-related; and (4) supplier performance.

What They're Looking For Here

Essentially what is listed in this Area to Address are the areas in which the examiners expect to see benchmark or competitor comparison data. The best way of responding to this item is to prepare a chart or table that lists the six types of data (as enumerated in area 2.2b) along the left side of the chart, an indication of the sources of the comparative data in the center of the chart, and a summary of the uses of the data along the right side of the chart. This is shown in the following example.

TYPES OF DATA	COMPARISON SOURCES	USES OF DATA
Product and Service Quality	J.D. Power Customer Satisfaction Surveys	Product Design Quality Planning
	Benchmarking study – Mercedes Benz	Product Design Quality Planning
Customer-Related	J. D. Power Customer Satisfaction Surveys	Improving Product Quality
	Dealership Customer Satisfaction Data	Improving Dealership Quality

What the examiners are looking for in this Area to Address is that you have many different sources of competitive and benchmark data. First of all, you should have data that are collected internally by your own employees. For example, an analysis of all the proposals you won and lost will provide a great deal of data on competitors. Look at the types of jobs/projects you win and lose, and the competitors to whom you've lost work. Another applicant used its own employees to gather data on competitors' prices and services by having people pose as customers. Marketing or market research employees can be a great deal of help in collecting data on competitors.

You should also have a number of different outside sources of data on competitors and benchmarks. Professional associations often publish reports outlining and categorizing the market their member companies serve. They also have data on market shares, sales, market penetration, and other pertinent information. Companies like Dunn & Bradstreet specialize in providing data on companies. Obtaining reports like those prepared by D&B is a good way of gathering data on competitors and benchmarking partners.

Companies that are well known for quality, such as past winners of the Baldrige or Deming awards, usually do an excellent job of communicating their successful strategies to others through tours, workshops, published articles, and seminars. This type of information is very valuable if you decide to benchmark yourself against a particular process or function in one of these award-winning organizations. The American Productivity and Quality Center in Houston is creating a data base for identifying companies to use for benchmarking purposes. If you wanted to know who has the best supplier invoice processing system, for example, you can access this data base to make your determination. Specific indicators that the examiners will look for when assessing your performance in this area are outlined below.

Indicators For Area 2.2b

- Number of different sources of data on competitors

- Objectivity and reliability of sources of data on competitors

- Number of different sources of data on benchmark organizations

- Objectivity and reliability of data sources on benchmark organizations

- Number of different functions and/or processes for which competitive or benchmark data are gathered

- Systems within the company to coordinate benchmarking activities to ensure consistency and avoid duplication of benchmarking efforts

- Clear explanations of how benchmark and/or competitive data are used

- Extent to which competitor and benchmark data are gathered on:
  - Product and service quality
  - Customer satisfaction
  - Supplier performance
  - Employee programs
  - Operations and support departments

AREA TO ADDRESS   **[APPROACH, DEPLOYMENT]**

2.2c How competitive comparisons and benchmarking information and data are used to improve understanding of processes, to encourage breakthrough approaches, and to set "stretch" targets.

What They're Looking For Here

What the Baldrige people want to see in this section is that you actually use the competitive and benchmark data as stimuli to encourage improvements. Many companies conduct benchmarking studies, review the findings, and go about business as usual. You need to have some sort of process in place for using the benchmarking studies and competitive comparisons as a way to improve processes in your company. Your response for this section should begin with an explanation of what happens to benchmarking studies and competitive analyses. Explain how studies are reviewed, who reviews them, and how action plans are developed to use the data to capitalize on improvement opportunities. As with many of the other Areas to Address that ask about processes, it may be a good idea to use a graphic of a process model that depicts your approach. What the examiners don't want to see is that you simply copy what other companies are doing. Rather, you should take what other companies are doing and adapt these practices to your own organization.

After explaining how studies are reviewed and action plans developed, you should provide a list of process improvements that have been made as a result of benchmarking studies or competitive comparisons. A matrix might be a good way of presenting this information.

COMPETITIVE/BENCHMARKING STUDY	COMPANY FUNCTION	ACTION PLAN
MBNA Benchmarking Study of Employee-Related Programs	Human Resources	Instituted "Parents Day" Concept in 1991
Boeing Supplier Certification Study (Competitive Comparison)	Procurement	Plan Developed for Implementation of Supplier Certification Process in 1992

Along with getting ideas of how to improve your own processes, another reason for gathering competitive and benchmark data is to determine how good performance can be on a particular dimension or process. This information is used to set goals or objectives for improvement. Goals and objectives should not be set in an arbitrary fashion. They should be based upon sound research that indicates that someone in the world has performed at the level of performance you have stated in your goal. For example, let's say that it takes your Human Resources function an average of 13 weeks to process a change of pay rate request for an employee. Two common ways of setting goals are to look at current performance and try to get 10-20% better for next year. (To reduce cycle time to 10 or 11 weeks, for example.) Another way of setting improvement goals is to set a "stretch" goal, by picking a number out of the air simply because it seems like a good one. For example: "Our 1995 goal will be to process all pay rate changes within 5 weeks." Why 5 weeks? Because it seems like a good number and it is much better than current performance? This is not the way to set stretch goals either. Stretch goals should be based upon research that indicates that someone has achieved this level of performance.

This is where benchmarking comes in. Benchmarking tells us what is possible. In benchmarking the company that seems to have the best compensation system, we may find that they process pay rate changes in two weeks. Our own stretch goal can then be based on reality—information that someone has achieved this level.

Stretch goals derived from benchmarking studies can then be used to encourage breakthrough approaches. To get the cycle time from 13 weeks down to 2 weeks will require major changes in the process used to review and approve these changes. Benchmarking should also help in figuring out how to do this. It may be that you can copy some of the ideas and approaches used by the companies in your benchmarking study.

Indicators For Area 2.2c

- Evidence that a systematic process is used to review and follow-up on competitive comparisons and benchmarking studies that are done

- Evidence that a consistent process is used to follow-up on benchmarking studies and competitive comparisons

- Training is done for key employees to teach them how to interpret and use competitive comparisons and benchmarking studies

- Breadth and scope of follow-up actions or changes implemented as a result of competitive comparisons and benchmarking studies

- Number of processes, systems, and programs currently in place that were initiated from competitive comparisons and benchmarking studies

- Degree to which the organization adapts, modifies, and customizes practices of competitors and benchmarkers versus simply copying what others do

- Evidence that competitive comparisons and benchmarking studies are used to set "stretch" objectives

- Breadth and scope of improvement goals/objectives that have been derived from competitive comparisons or benchmarking studies

- Evidence that benchmarking studies and competitive comparisons serve as a stimulus for "breakthrough" changes in processes

---

AREA TO ADDRESS   **[APPROACH, DEPLOYMENT]**
2.2d How the company evaluates and improves its overall processes for selecting and using competitive comparisons and benchmarking information and data to improve planning and operation performance.

What They're Looking For Here

In this section you should explain how you evaluate the scope and validity of your competitive analyses and benchmarking processes and data. You should describe a specific evaluation process and possibly provide an example or two to demonstrate how you have evaluated and improved your process for gathering and using benchmark data and data on competitors.

As in many of the previous Areas to Address, the examiners are looking for evidence that you plan to expand the scope of your data on competitive and benchmark organizations. A typical response for this section might be written as follows:

> *In the future we plan to expand the scope of the data we collect on competitors and benchmark organizations by gathering more information on a wider variety of companies that are known for their world-class quality products/services.*

While this response may sound promising, it lacks details and specifics. A response such as this would earn a score of no more than ten to twenty percent. Not enough information is provided to give credibility to the statements that the organization is expanding the scope of its data collection efforts. In order to earn a high score for this Area to Address, you might begin with an overall statement such as the one above, but follow it with a list of the specific actions or strategies you will employ over the next year or so to expand the scope of your competitive and benchmark data. This type of information will tell the examiners that you in fact have a plan for expanding the scope of your data collection and that you have identified specific strategies and actions.

Indicators For Area 2.2d

- Evidence that a systematic process is used to evaluate processes for gathering competitive and benchmark data

- Validity of evaluation methodologies and data collected to assess process for doing benchmarking studies and competitive comparisons

- Overall strategy for expanding the scope of data collection on competitors and on benchmarking organizations

- Documented plan for expanding the scope of data collection on competitors and benchmark organizations

- Specific actions that have been identified that will improve either the quantity or quality of information on competitors

- Specific actions identified that will improve either the quantity or quality of information on benchmark organizations

- Use of benchmarking data to help develop strategic quality and business goals

2.3 ANALYSIS AND USES OF COMPANY-LEVEL DATA

Describe how data related to quality, customers and operational performance, together with relevant financial data, are analyzed to support company-level review, action and planning. (40 points)

Note:

(1)   Item 2.3 focuses primarily on analysis for company-level purposes, such as reviews (1.2c) and strategic planning (Item 3.1). Data for such analysis come from all parts of the company. Other Items call for analyses of specific sets of data for special purposes. For example, the Items of Category 4.0 require analyses to demonstrate effectiveness of training and other human resource practices. Such special-purpose analyses are assumed to be part of the overall information base of Category 2.0, available for use in Item 2.3. These specific sets of data and special-purpose analyses are described in 2.3a and 2.3b as "other key data and analyses."

AREA TO ADDRESS　　　　　　　　　　　**[APPROACH, DEPLOYMENT]**

2.3a How customer-related data and results (from Category 7.0) are aggregated with other key data and analyses and translated via analysis into actionable information to support: (1) developing priorities for prompt solutions to customer-related problems; and (2) determining key customer-related trends and correlations to support reviews, decision making, and longer-term planning.

Notes:

(2)　　"Actionable" means that the analysis provides information that can be used for priorities and decisions leading to allocation of resources.

(3)　　Solutions to customer related problems [2.3a(1)] at the company level involve a process for: (1) aggregation of formal and informal complaints from different parts of the company; (2) analysis leading to priorities for action; and (3) use of the resulting information throughout the company. Note the connections to 7.2e, which focuses on day-to-day complaint management, including prompt resolution.

(4)　　The focus in 2.3a is on analysis to improve customer-related decision making and planning. This analysis is intended to provide additional information to *support* such decision making and planning that result from day-to-day customer information, feedback, and complaints. Examples of analysis appropriate for inclusion in 2.3a are:

- how the company's product and service quality improvement correlates with key customer indicators such as customer satisfaction, customer retention, and market share;

- cross-comparisons of data from complaints, post-transaction follow-up, and won/lost analyses to identify improvement priorities;

- relationship between employee satisfaction and customer satisfaction;

- cost/revenue implications of customer-related problems and problem resolution effectiveness;

- rates of improvements of customer indicators;

- customer loyalty (or positive referral) versus level of satisfaction; and

- customer loyalty versus level of satisfaction with the effectiveness of problem resolution.

What They're Looking For Here

A major portion of your data base should relate to customer satisfaction, customer retention, and market share. This Area to Address asks how you aggregate and use all of the customer-related data that you collect. What is expected in your response here is that you employ a systematic approach to analyzing and using these data to make decisions, decide on priorities, and establish goals and plans. Your response should begin with a list of the various customer-related indices for which you collect data. Following this list, explain how the data are reported, who receives these reports, and how you ensure that the data are acted upon for improvement. You should explain how you aggregate all of the data you collect that relate to customer satisfaction. Some organizations have developed a single measure called a Customer Satisfaction Index (CSI) that is derived from a number of different measures, including customer satisfaction, market share, and gains/losses of individual customers. An effective way of establishing an overall CSI is to assign a percentage weight to each of the separate indices you use. An example is shown below.

EXAMPLE CUSTOMER SATISFACTION INDEX

INDEX	% WEIGHT
Customer Satisfaction Survey	40%
Customer Focus Group Data	10%
Market Share	25%
Gains/Losses of Customers	25%
CUSTOMER SATISFACTION INDEX	100%

As you can see in the example, each of four different indices is assigned a percentage weight based upon its importance as an indicator of customer satisfaction. Establishment of a single CSI is certainly not a requirement; this is just an example of how an organization might aggregate and compare various customer-related measures.

After describing how you aggregate your customer-related data, explain how you analyze these data and use them to develop action plans. The criteria are fairly specific in indicating the specific types of actions you should report on in this section:

- Developing priorities for addressing customer-related problems
- Determining relationships between internal product/service quality data and customer-related data
- Using customer-related data to develop plans for improving performance.

I suggest that you use these three items as subheadings in your application, providing a brief explanation and an example or two for each one. Use a variety of different examples from various functions within your organization, which will help demonstrate how well you have deployed analysis of customer-related data.

Indicators For Area 2.3a

- Evidence that a systematic process is used to aggregate various customer-related indices

- Approach to aggregating and comparing various customer-related indices is logical and understandable by employees who must analyze and act upon these data

- Evidence that a planned and systematic approach is used to analyze customer-related data

- Deployment of analysis approach across the organization's various departments and functions

- Clear description and evidence to suggest that customer-related data are analyzed and used to establish priorities and develop action plans to improve customer-related problems

- Clear description and evidence to suggest that customer-related data are compared to internal product/service quality data

- Evidence that customer-related data is analyzed and used to develop goals and strategies for improving customer satisfaction, market share, and retention of customers

---

AREA TO ADDRESS   **[APPROACH, DEPLOYMENT]**

2.3b How quality and operational performance data and results (from Category 6.0) are aggregated with other key data and analyses and translated via analysis into actionable information to support: (1) developing priorities for products/services and company operations, including cycle time, productivity, and waste reduction; and, (2) determining key operations-related trends and correlations to support reviews, decision making, and longer-term planning.

Note:

(5)   **The focus in 2.3b is on analysis to improve operations-related decision making and planning. This analysis is intended to *support* such decision making and planning that result from day-to-day observations of process performance.**

         Examples of analysis appropriate for inclusion in 2.3b are:

- **how product/service improvement priorities are determined;**
- **evaluation of the productivity and cost impacts of improvement initiatives;**
- **rates of improvement in key operational indicators;**
- **evaluation of trends in key operational efficiency measures such as productivity;**
- **comparison with competitive and benchmark data to identify improvement opportunities and to set improvement priorities and targets.**

What They're Looking For Here

Most companies collect a great deal of data on the quality of the products and services they sell. What separates the exceptional from the average company in this Area to Address is how one aggregates and uses all of these data. As with the previous Area to Address, the Baldrige Examiners are looking for an explanation of how you interpret all of the data you collect. When Baldrige Examiners interview supervisors and managers during a site visit, they often find out that employees aren't really sure how to interpret and use all of the data in the reports they receive on quality. In this section of your application, you need to explain how the various measures of product/service quality are interpreted. If you compile several individual measures into something similar to a CSI, as I have described for area 2.3a, explain how this is done.

After explaining how quality results indices are aggregated, describe how these data are used to establish priorities for short-term quality and performance improvement. To add credence to your description, you might include a list of the various actions that were considered for short-term product/service quality improvement, showing how you prioritized these alternatives to decide which ones to take action on.

Make sure to provide specific examples of how analysis of results data was used to improve cycle time, productivity, and reduce scrap or waste. Your response for this Area to Address should also explain how you use quality results data to develop plans and strategies for future improvements. After describing the approach that you use, provide a couple of examples of key goals and strategies for achieving them that were initiated based upon analyses of quality results data.

Indicators For Area 2.3b

- Evidence that a systematic process is used to aggregate various quality results measurement indices in areas such as defects, cycle time, productivity, and waste/scrap

- Employees understand how to use and interpret quality results data on various indices

- Approach to aggregating and comparing various quality results indices is logical and consistently used throughout various functions in the organization

- Evidence that approach to analyzing quality results data is systematic and consistently used by employees in all parts of the organization

- Clear description and evidence to suggest that quality results data are analyzed and used to establish priorities for improving performance

- Clear relationship between plans to improve quality of products and services and analyses of quality results data

AREA TO ADDRESS [APPROACH, DEPLOYMENT]

2.3c How the company relates overall improvements in product/service quality and operational performance to changes in overall financial performance to support reviews, decision making and longer-term planning.

Note:

(6) The focus in 2.3c is on the linkages between improvements in product/service quality and operational performance and overall financial performance for company goal and priority setting. Analyses in 2.3c might incorporate the results of analyses described in 2.3a and 2.3b, and draw upon other key data and analyses.

Examples of analysis appropriate for inclusion in 2.3c are:
- relationships between product/service quality and operational performance indicators and overall company financial performance trends as reflected in indicators such as operating costs, revenues, asset utilization, and values added per employee;
- comparisons of company financial performance versus competitors based on quality and operational performance indicators;
- allocation of resources among alternative improvement projects based on cost/revenue implications and improvement potential;
- net earnings derived from quality/operational performance improvements;
- comparisons among business units showing how quality and operational performance improvement have improved financial performance; and
- contributions of improvement activities to cash flow and/or share holder value.

What They're Looking For Here

In previous years, the Baldrige criteria did not address financial data collection, analysis, or results. This has been one of the primary criticisms of the criteria as a measure of a successful organization. The critics have stated that if application of the criteria outlined by the Baldrige officials leads to a more successful company, then the Baldrige Examiners should look at financial, as well as other types of data. A study conducted by the U.S. General Accounting Office in 1991 suggests that adherence to the Baldrige criteria does lead to financial success.

This area to address asks about how you translate improvements in the quality of your products or services into financial measures. What the examiners want to see here is an explanation of how you measure the return on investment in your quality efforts. Let's say, for example, that you reduced the percentage of defects in your products from 2% down to .03%. The examiners will want to know how improvements in defect rates translate into financial benefits for the company. You also need to explain the relationship between key operational measures and key financial measures. A good way of presenting this data would be a matrix that lists your key financial measures along the top, and the key quality and operational measures along the left side. The matrix should indicate which quality and operational measures have a strong degree of impact upon the key financial measures. An example of such a matrix chart is shown below.

KEY MEASURES	PROFITS	MARKET SHARE	SALES	ROA
Customer Satisfaction Index	M	H	H	M
Product Defects	H	M	M	H
Design Cycle Time	L	M	M	L

A chart such as this should be supplemented with an explanation of how and why key measures of quality and operational indices lead to financial measures. You need to explain, for example, how your customer satisfaction index has a high degree of impact on both market share and sales.

Every organization collects financial data. The Baldrige Examiners are not simply asking if you collect and analyze financial data. What they are expecting to see in this section of your application is that you have a system for aggregating various individual financial measures and making sense out of a number of individual measures. One aspect of your financial data that you should explain is how you summarize and report these data. You might provide a description of what your financial reports contain, explaining whether they contain only financial data, or whether they also include other types of data. Financial reports should be designed with the readers in mind, being easy to interpret and easy to identify key changes in trends that require decisions or intervention of some sort. After describing how financial data are aggregated and reported, you should explain how these data are analyzed and how decisions are made based upon these data. If you review financial data in staff meetings or committee meetings, explain how often these meetings occur, who attends, and what process is used for analyzing the data. As with any other process that the examiners want to hear about, it will be helpful if you can summarize your approach to analysis of financial information in a process model or some type of graphic. Make sure that you also describe the process for decision making and planning that occurs, based upon a review and analysis of financial information. Be specific in describing how this does occur.

Following the explanation of the review and data-analysis processes, you need to provide some examples of how analysis of financial information has led to decisions or the initiation of changes that resulted in improved levels of operational results or improvements in customer satisfaction. The examples will add credibility to your process description. One of the major factors that the Baldrige Examiners look for once they have determined that you have a sound systematic approach, is deployment. A good way of giving them information on deployment is through a series of examples that include various functions and levels of employees in your organization. Space limitations will prevent you from listing as many examples as you might like, but matrices and charts are a good way of presenting a number of examples in a limited amount of space. You might create a four-column chart that looks like the following.

EXAMPLES - FINANCIAL ANALYSIS AND ACTION PLANS

FINANCIAL DATA	ANALYSIS	DECISION/ACTION	RESULTS
Loss of market share in Midwest region	11 new WalMart stores open in 1991	Increased newspaper & direct mail advertising More competitive pricing Increased staffing Additional service training	1st quarter results show improvements

---

Indicators For Area 2.3c

- Clear and systematic process for aggregating and interpreting financial data such as sales, profits, operating expenses, market share, return on assets, return on sales, etc.

- Systematic process for analyzing financial data

- Evidence of consistent use of financial analysis process throughout the organization

- Relationships have been clearly defined between quality and operational measures and financial results

- Degree to which analysis of financial data leads to decisions and action plans for improvements in performance

- Evidence of deployment of action plans based upon analysis of financial data

- Results that have been obtained from decisions and interventions designed to improve financial performance and performance on other key measures

---

AREA TO ADDRESS   **[APPROACH, DEPLOYMENT]**
2.3d How the company evaluates and improves its analysis for use as a key management tool. Include: (1) how analysis supports improved data selection and use; (2) how analysis strengthens the integration of overall data use for improved decision making and planning, and (3) how the analysis-access cycle is shortened.

What They're Looking For Here

Essentially what you are being asked to demonstrate in this Area to Address is that you evaluate and continuously improve your data-analysis processes. If you are using essentially the same analysis techniques as you've been using for the last five years, you are unlikely to receive a high score for your response to this area. The examiners are looking for continuous improvements in your approach to analyzing quality data. The best way of responding to this section is to begin by explaining how your analyses have led to changes and improvements in the types of data collected, the reliability of the data, and your analytical capabilities.

You should also explain how, through your analysis process, you have improved integration of all the various types of data you collect. It is important that you have processes in place to make sense out of all the various data you collect. Examples of these improvements may be improved reports or training on data interpretation and analysis. It may also involve development of ratios that compare various individual indices. For example, AT&T uses a metric called Economic Value Analysis that is a way of computing profit, including the cost of capital. This EVA index is one of the primary performance measures for AT&T.

The examiners are also looking for evidence that you have worked to shorten the cycle of data analysis and access to results. Some organizations spend a great deal of time analyzing data before any countermeasures are introduced. Again, while adequate data and thorough analysis are certainly important, too much time can be spent on these activities. This area balances areas 2.3a, b, and c, which assess the thoroughness of your analyses of various types of data. The examiners want to see that you are efficient and time-conscious in addition to being thorough. The quicker a countermeasure is introduced, the quicker the quality problem or deviation is corrected.

A typical response for this item is to describe how you have taken a number of steps to shorten the data-analysis and quality improvement cycle. As in the other items, you need to be specific. Start out by explaining the situation in the past. Provide some statistics if you have them. For example:

> *Our original quality improvement process model is depicted in the flowchart below. This approach required an average of 22 weeks to complete all seven steps in the process. We have since revised our model so that it includes the five steps depicted in the chart below. This new quality improvement process now requires an average of 16 weeks before quality improvements begin to materialize.*

Once you've explained how you go about improving your analytical methods, provide several examples. Make sure your examples vary. A manufacturing company should provide an example or two from the production department and a couple of examples from staff or support departments. Describe the benefits that have been realized as a result of improved analytical methods. Benefits may include things such as more precise measurement indices, more reliable data, improved analytical methods, shortened analysis time, etc.

Indicators For Area 2.3d

- Existence of procedures for evaluating analysis processes

- Trend of enhancements and improvements to analysis processes over the last several years

- Evidence that analysis data have resulted in changes and improvements in types of data collected and reliability of data

- Degree to which analytical capabilities have been improved over the last several years

- Trend of continuous improvement noted in approaches to analysis of quality-related data

- Evidence that quality data gathering, analysis, and countermeasure selection and implementation process has been streamlined over the last several years

- Amount of data indicating that data analysis and reporting cycle time has been reduced

- Description of specific strategies and tactics that have been employed to reduce quality improvement cycle time

- Example of quality improvement projects where time to complete each phase in the process has been documented

- Degree to which projects completed by quality improvement teams require less time now than in the past

- Specific improvements that have been made in approach for integrating customer satisfaction, operational, and financial data

- Track record of continuous improvements in processes for integrating customer satisfaction, operational, and financial data

Chapter 7

Interpreting the Criteria for Strategic Quality Planning

OVERVIEW OF THE STRATEGIC QUALITY PLANNING CATEGORY

Category 3.0 addresses the area of strategic quality planning, and is worth six percent of the total application, or a possible 60 points out of 1000. The Award Criteria define this category as follows:

> The **Strategic Quality Planning** *category examines the company's planning process and how all key quality and operational performance requirements are integrated into overall business planning. Also examined are the company's short- and longer-term plans and how plan requirements are deployed to all work units (p. 18).*

As expressed in this excerpt, the examiners are not so much concerned with planning being done in a particular way as they are with whether or not quality is integrated into your overall business planning process.

This category is divided into two Examination Items:

> 3.1 Strategic Quality and Company Performance Planning Process (35 points)
> 3.2 Quality and Performance Plans (25 points)

Following are the descriptions of each of the two Examination Items and the Areas to Address that fall under them. As before, each section here begins with a double-ruled box containing the Examination Item, the point value, and any applicable Notes.* Areas to Address falling under that Item follow in a single-ruled box. In the upper right corner of each Area to Address box is an indication [brackets] of whether the Area pertains to approach, deployment, or results. All definitions and information appearing within these boxes is taken directly from the Baldrige criteria. Following each Area to Address is an explanation defining what the examiners are looking for in assessing your application. Next, I have supplied a list of indicators or evaluation factors that will assist you in interpreting the criteria and in preparing your application.

---

* Item Notes that apply to a specific Area to Address are appropriately listed in the box containing that Area.

3.1 STRATEGIC QUALITY AND COMPANY PERFORMANCE PLANNING PROCESS

Describe the company's business planning process for the short term (1-3 years) and longer term (3 years or more) for customer satisfaction leadership and overall operational performance improvement. Include how this process integrates quality and operational performance requirements and how plans are deployed. (35 points)

Notes:

(1)   Item 3.1 addresses overall company strategies and business plans, not specific product and service designs. Strategies and business plans that might be addressed as part of Item 3.1 include operational aspects such as manufacturing and/or service delivery strategies, as well as new product/service lines, new markets, outsourcing, and strategic alliances.

(2)   Societal risks and impacts are addressed in Item 1.3.

AREA TO ADDRESS   **[APPROACH, DEPLOYMENT]**

3.1a How the company develops strategies and business plans to address quality and customer satisfaction leadership for the short term and longer term. Describe how plans consider: (1) customer requirements and the expected evolution of these requirements; (2) projections of the competitive environment; (3) risks: financial, market, technological and societal; (4) company capabilities, such as human resource and research and development to address key new requirements or market leadership opportunities; and (5) supplier capabilities.

<u>What They're Looking For Here</u>

The examiners are *not* looking for a separate quality plan that has been developed by the quality department. Yet, this is often what award applicants believe is meant by the criteria for this category. In fact, the title of this category should be "Strategic Planning." The word *quality* is misleading because this section refers to overall business planning. A strategic quality plan should not be a separate document prepared by one department in isolation of the others. Quality, customer satisfaction, and operational performance goals should be addressed with the same importance as financial goals in the overall business plan for the organization. It is expected that the specific process used to develop the quality and customer satisfaction goals for an organization will be tailored to the size of the company and the type of business it is in. The examiners are looking for evidence that a systematic process is used, that it is participative, that all major functions in the organization participate in the goal-setting process, that short- and long-term strategic quality planning are done, and that macro- and micro-level plans are well integrated.

One award applicant that received very high scores in this area presented a "systems diagram" that depicted inputs, processes, and outputs of their long- and short-term quality goal setting processes. This section of their application also described the various phases of the planning process depicted in the diagram and explained how quality factors were incorporated at each step.

Your response for this area should explain how customer requirements and current levels of performance gauged against your competitors' are used to set quality goals. Quality goals must not be set arbitrarily. Goals must be both reasonable and relevant to what customers expect, and to what is possible. Sometimes what customers want and expect is just not feasible, so you must look at performance levels that competitors in your same price range are able to achieve.

In preparing your response for this area, you should also explain how your overall business planning process is integrated into individual and departmental planning and goal setting. Often an organization has an overall business plan that isn't shared with most employees, while individual and departmental plans are developed without knowledge of what is in the macro-plan for the organization. This leads to conflicting goals and poor results. While it is not necessary that all employees receive the entire company plan, they do need to know the general direction of the organization and its major goals over the next few years.

All levels of plans in the organization, from those done by top executives to the performance plans for individual employees in the hourly work force, should be integrated into a common strategic plan. Quality goals should also be articulated for the short and long term at all levels, and with all functions of employees. Quality and customer satisfaction are not the responsibility of the quality control department and customer contact employees alone, but the responsibility of every employee. A flow diagram that shows how the outputs from one level of planning serve as part of the inputs for a lower level of planning is a good way to depict the integration of the various levels of planning.

An important aspect of your response for this Area to Address is to show that planning is not done in a vacuum, but that information from outside sources is used in the planning process. Probably the most important information to include is customer needs and requirements. Many organizations develop their strategic business plans without ever considering current or future customer requirements. Or they may think they know what customers want and require, but they never really ask the customers themselves. The Baldrige Examiners are looking for evidence that you gather data on customer requirements and use those data as an input to your planning process. In particular, quality improvement goals and strategies outlined in the plans should be based upon and tied to customer requirements.

Projections of changes in the competitive environment should also be addressed in your plan. For example, a new competitive company that is threatening your market share may have come on the scene. Various types of risks should likewise be addressed in your plans. Financial risks, market risks, and societal risks all need to be addressed. You might, for example, list what could go wrong with your strategies, and assess the probability of each of these events occurring and their relative seriousness. This type of explanation would help show the examiners that you systematically assess risks as part of your planning process.

Process capability data should also be considered in the planning process. I've seen many large organizations that will develop unrealistic goals and plans because they don't know or don't understand the limitations of their existing processes and technology. The examiners would like to see evidence that you have determined process and technology capabilities, and that the data are used in the planning process. It may be helpful to include an example of how these data are used.

The final type of outside data that should be used as an input to the planning process are data on supplier capabilities. This is especially important for organizations that depend heavily upon suppliers for goods and services. Just mentioning that you use supplier data in your planning process will not be very convincing. An example of how you gather and use supplier data to develop goals or plans will help add credibility to your response to this area.

One Baldrige applicant that received a very high score for this area presented a table that listed the various types of information used in the planning process, according to the five categories of data addressed in this area. A sample follows.

DATA USED IN PLANNING PROCESS				
Customer Requirements	Competitor Data	Risks	Company Capabilities	Supplier Data
• Focus group data	• Mascor Data	• Financial	• Telecommunication	• Northern Telecom
• Telephone survey	• Andress, Inc.	• Market	• Order processing	• NCR
• Mail survey	• J. Crew	• Societal	• Buying office	• Various

Indicators For Area 3.1a

- Degree to which quality and customer satisfaction goals, strategies, and issues are addressed in the long-term strategic business plan for the company/organization

- Degree to which quality and customer satisfaction goals, strategies, and issues are addressed in the annual business plan for the company/organization

- Degree to which short- and long-term quality and customer satisfaction goals are consistent with goals in other areas such as growth, profits, and markets/products

- Planning and goal-setting processes are systematic, well organized, and include all functions in the organization

- Evidence that customer requirements are thoroughly identified and that this information is used in developing goals and plans for the organization

- Quality and customer satisfaction goals are based upon current and future quality requirements of customers in key markets, as well as projections of changes in customer requirements

- Quality and customer satisfaction goals are set based upon performance of major competitors in target markets

- Planning is done in a hierarchical fashion and at all levels in the organization, starting from the top

- Availability of data on the capabilities of all important processes and technology in the organization

- Evidence that process and technology capabilities/limitations are taken into consideration when developing long- and short-term plans and goals

- Extent to which supplier data are used as an input to the planning process

- Degree to which the future competitive environment is addressed in the plan

- Evidence that financial, market, and societal risks are considered in the development of goals and strategies

- Evidence of systemic risk analysis being done as part of the planning process

---

AREA TO ADDRESS   **[APPROACH, DEPLOYMENT]**

3.1b How strategies and plans address operational performance improvement. Describe how the following are considered: (1) realigning work processes ("re-engineering") to improve customer focus and operational performance; and (2) productivity and cycle time improvement and reduction in waste.

Notes:

(3)   Productivity and cycle time improvement and waste reduction (3.1b) might address factors such as inventories, work in process, inspection, downtime, changeover time, set-up time, and other examples of utilization of resources such as materials, equipment, energy, capital, and labor.

(4)   How the company reviews quality and operational performance relative to plans is addressed in 1.2c.

<u>What They're Looking For Here</u>

This section should be similar to the previous section, in which you describe the process for developing plans to improve quality and customer satisfaction. This was a new area to address in 1993. In the 1992 criteria they simply asked about your planning process, rather than break it down into two types of processes. Most companies don't have separate processes for quality planning and for operational planning. Planning is planning. Most companies develop a strategic business plan that includes goals and strategies for customer satisfaction, quality, financial performance and key operational measures. If the process you use for operational planning is the same as the process used for quality planning, explain this in your response.

This area to address asks about "operational performance planning." In fact, you'll see the phrase "operational performance" used throughout the 1994 Baldrige criteria. Operational performance refers to aspects of performance that are not quality or customer satisfaction, and not financial. Operational measures may be either output measures or process measures. For example, percentage of on-time deliveries or pounds of scrap are output operational measures. Cycle time and productivity are process operational measures.

This area to address does ask for some additional information beyond how you do your operational planning. It asks about how you develop plans for improving work processes, or what is now being called "re-engineering". You should explain how the processes you are working on improving were selected, and what your long-term goals are for improvement. You should also explain how the levels of performance specified in your goals were determined.

This area to address also asks for information on any changes you have made in your organization structure. This information used to be requested in 1.2b in the 1992 Baldrige Award criteria, and it was moved here in 1993. Re-engineering often involves more than simply changing work processes. Re-engineering involves redesigning jobs and organization structure as well.

My personal experience is that most companies approach implementation of total quality as something they can add on to the existing structures in the organization. They form a number of different committees, but don't make any substantitive changes in the company's organization structure, job design, levels of authority, or procedures. Committees have a lot of meetings, but total quality has not changed the way the company does its work on a day-to-day basis.

 The criteria here also ask about how you develop plans for improving productivity and for reducing waste. Respond to this portion of the criteria with the same amount of detail as your explanation of how you develop plans and goals for process improvement.

Indicators For Area 3.1b

- Evidence of a systematic process being used to develop operational performance improvement goals and plans

- Extent to which operational improvement goals are congruent with goals for improving quality and customer satisfaction

- Inputs are obtained from all appropriate levels and functions in the organization prior to developing operational performance improvement goals and plans

- Customer requirements and supplier capabilities are considered in coming up with plans for improving operational aspects of the company's performance

- All appropriate variables are assessed in a risk analysis as part of the operational planning process

- Evidence that the company has integrated Total Quality principles with the way it structures its organization and designs jobs

- Evidence that the company has reduced bureaucracy by re-engineering the organization to facilitate a customer focus

- Extent to which the organization structure and work processes encourage empowerment and achievement of a customer-oriented culture

- Use of benchmarks and other comparisons to other companies as a way of initiating changes to organization structure, job design, and work processes

---

AREA TO ADDRESS   **[APPROACH, DEPLOYMENT]**
3.1c How plans are deployed. Describe: (1) how the company deploys plan requirements to work units and to suppliers, and how it ensures alignment of work unit plans and activities; and (2) how resources are committed to meet the plan requirements.

What They're Looking For Here

Many organizations do a commendable job creating strategic business plans, but few do a good job translating those plans into actions throughout the year. The plans get written, reviewed, and often end up in a file drawer until the end of the year or until a periodic review meeting occurs. This section of the application should describe the mechanisms and systems you have in place to ensure that plans do not remain in file drawers but are actually implemented. Explain how plans are reviewed by various levels of employees and translated into individual performance plans. All levels of goals and objectives should be based upon and contribute to the overall plans of the organization.

Your response should explain how plans drive regular and ongoing work activities. Explain how major projects as well as recurring work tasks relate to major business and quality goals. Be as specific as possible, citing an example or two to illustrate that plans really do drive day-to-day activities in your company.

There should be regular review meetings that occur among various levels of employees to review plans, discuss progress toward meeting the goals outlined in the plans, and change/update the plans as necessary. Describe when these meetings occur and who attends. Explain how plans have been revised based upon changing business conditions, changing customer requirements, or other factors. Also, explain what you do when performance is not reaching projected goal levels. Be specific. The examiners are looking for a positive approach rather than a punitive approach. One applicant who received a low score said, "Individuals who are not meeting their goals are talked to and reminded of the consequences to them of not meeting their goals." The mechanism for implementing strategies outlined in organizational plans may consist of projects, priority initiatives, task forces, teams, or other approaches. The specific approach you use is not important. What is important is that you have a clear and workable approach for translating your plans into actions and results. The leadership of the senior executives is critical to the success of implementing the plans.

This section of your application should also describe how requests for capital expenditures are evaluated and the extent to which improvement of quality is part of the criteria used to assess capital funds requests. Evidence should be provided to show that a large portion of the capital projects being undertaken in the organization will at least contribute to, if not directly improve, quality and customer satisfaction.

Indicators For Area 3.1c

- Existence of a well defined and workable process for deployment of long- and short-term plans in the organization to achieve quality and customer-satisfaction leadership

- Scope of deployment includes all functions and levels of employees in the development of individual improvement plans that support overall plans for the company

- Amount and objectivity of data to suggest that plan implementation/deployment process is successful in the organization

- Clear criteria for evaluating capital projects in relation to goals in long- and short-term plans

- Manner of assigning and deploying resources is consistent with long and short-term goals and quality priorities

- Evidence that plans are used to direct and control day-to-day work activity in the organization, with management involvement to ensure implementation and follow-up

- Plans are used to make decisions and control actions and priorities in the organization

- Process for deploying quality requirements to suppliers is systematic and timely

---

AREA TO ADDRESS [APPROACH, DEPLOYMENT]

3.1d How the company evaluates and improves. (1) its planning process; (2) deploying plan requirements to work units; and (3) receiving planning input from work units.

What They're Looking For Here

It's rare to find an organization that does any type of evaluation of its planning process, but that is exactly what the Baldrige Examiners are looking for in this Area to Address. If you do any kind of evaluation of your planning process, describe the sources of data you examine to determine how well the process is working. Evidence that you have adjusted your planning process based upon the evaluation data is also desirable. Like all other processes used in the organization, planning should show a cycle of continuous improvements. You need to evaluate not only the planning process itself, but how you deploy the plans to various work units in the organization. A major factor in the success or failure of planning is the extent to which plans quide day-to-day activity. Evaluation of this phenomenon should be part of your assessment.

Indicators For Area 3.1d

- Evidence that a systematic evaluation process is used to assess the organization's approach to planning

- Extent to which deployment of plans throughout the organization is part of evaluation

- Objectivity and thoroughness of process used to evaluate planning

- Changes made in the planning process as a result of the evaluation data

- Evidence of continuous improvement in the planning process over the last few years

- Changes made in the communication and deployment of plans throughout the organization

- Degree to which all levels of employees are involved in the evaluation of the planning process

---

3.2 QUALITY AND PERFORMANCE PLANS

Summarize the company's specific quality and operational performance plans for the short term (1-3 years) and the longer term (3 years or more). (25 points)

Note:

(1)   The focus in Item 3.2 is on the translation of the company's business plans, resulting from the planning process described in Item 3.1, to requirements for work units and suppliers. The main intent of Item 3.2 is alignment of short- and long-term operations with business directions. Although the deployment of these plans will affect products and services, design of products and services is not the focus of Item 3.2. Such design is addressed in Item 5.1.

AREA TO ADDRESS   **[APPROACH, DEPLOYMENT]**
3.2a For planned products, services, and customer markets, summarize: (1) key quality requirements to achieve or retain leadership; and (2) key company operational performance requirements.

What They're Looking For Here

This section of your application is designed to provide you with an opportunity to explain in narrative fashion what your vision is for the company and its products or services over the next few years. You might start out with an explanation of what is likely to happen to your industry over the next three to five years. For example:

> *The employee relocation business is expected to continue the shrinking trend we have observed during the past few years. Large corporations will be transferring fewer employees during the coming years because of escalating relocation costs and an increase in the number of individuals who refuse to accept frequent moves as simply a way of life in a large corporation. This means that there will be less business for all of us in the relocation business.*

You should explain not only what will happen to your industry in the future, but how customer needs are likely to change and how this will impact your products and services.

> *It appears that the reemergence of videodisc technology will have a major impact on the buying habits of consumers in the video market. Once thought to be a dead technology, discs and disc players will be the medium of choice for many consumers who are ready to replace old videotape units.*

Once you have explained what is likely to happen in your industry, and how customer requirements may change the market, you should explain what will be needed for a company in your industry to remain a leader in the future. It may be a matter of producing the best quality product, of being the first to introduce new products, or of having products that are sold at a more competitive price than the competition. If you are planning to introduce new products and/or services in the coming years, describe them, and explain how they will impact the market. Next, you should describe the requirements that your organization will need to meet in order to maintain its leadership position in the marketplace. Explain how you will need to change and what the key elements are likely to be to ensure your future success.

Indicators For Area 3.2a

- Clarity of explanation of changes that are likely to occur in the company's market during the next three to five years

- Evidence to support predictions about what will occur in the future for applicant's industry

- Explanation of how customer requirements and expectations are likely to change in the coming years

- Demonstration that company will be introducing new or enhanced products/services that will meet or exceed future customer requirements

- Evidence that company's approach is proactive versus reactive—company predicts trends and designs products and services to capitalize on trends

- Identification of key quality factors and requirements that will be necessary for success in the coming years in the applicant's industry

- Extent to which applicant has identified current strengths and weaknesses, and what changes are likely to be needed to continue to be successful during the coming years

---

AREA TO ADDRESS   **[APPROACH, DEPLOYMENT]**

3.2b Outline of the company's deployment of principal short-term quality and operational performance plans. Include: (1) a summary of key requirements and associated operational performance measures or indicators deployed to work units and suppliers; and (2) a brief description of resources committed for key needs such as capital equipment, facilities, education and training, and new hires.

<u>What They're Looking For Here</u>

Begin your response to this section with a list of your short-term quality and business goals. This Area to Address, and the next one (3.2c), should build upon the information contained in 3.2a. It should not, however, simply explain your financial goals. The goals described in this section should relate to quality, customer satisfaction, and related indicators such as market share. Summarize your annual improvement goals and explain how plans will be accomplished by the various work units in your organization. The phrase "summary of key requirements" simply means your quality goals or standards that must be achieved. "Performance indicators" are the measures or indices that are used to evaluate quality and assess progress.

As in many of the sections of your application, a good way of presenting this information is in a table or chart. An example is presented in the following to demonstrate how to present annual quality plans in a chart.

Quality Indicators	Goals/Standards 1992
• Customer Satisfaction Level	97%
• Defects Per Million	100
• Rejects of Plastic from Suppliers	< 0.05%
• Scrap Rate (Finished Product)	< 0.02%

After summarizing your annual quality and business goals, explain how these goals are deployed to both employees and suppliers. You also need to discuss the resources that will be committed to working on the goals outlined in this section. Resources for capital equipment, facilities, training, and other factors that will impact quality should be described. Resources are not only budget dollars, but people, equipment, and other resources. This may be difficult information to access, because you probably don't have a specific budget for quality improvement. If this is the case, simply estimate resources.

Indicators For Area 3.2b

- Inclusion of all major annual or short-term quality improvement goals in applicant's response

- Breadth of quality goals includes major products and/or services sold by the organization

- Quality improvement goals appear challenging, realistic, and achievable

- Addresses employee feelings on the reasonableness of short-term quality improvement plans

- Levels of resources dedicated to plans are realistic, given goals

- Evidence that resources for training, facilities, equipment, and personnel are based upon an analysis of requirements for meeting quality goals rather than simply past expenditures

- Evidence that plans are effectively deployed to all appropriate levels of employees and to suppliers, if appropriate

- Evidence that the capital expenditure budget is at least partially derived from quality and operational improvement goals and plans

---

> **AREA TO ADDRESS**   **[APPROACH, DEPLOYMENT]**
> **3.2c Outline of how principal longer-term (3 years or more) quality and operational performance requirements (from 3.2a) will be addressed.**

What They're Looking For Here

This area to address used to emphasize longer term *goals*. If you have specific goals for the next three to five years, this is still the place to list them. However, many smaller companies do not develop formal long-term goals or strategic plans. Baldrige does not suggest that all companies need to do formal long-term business planning. However, even if you are a company of 25 employees, you need to know where you want the company to go in the future, and how you intend to get there. The emphasis in this area to address is more on strategies than on goals. In section 3.2.a you should have described what will be important about your products or services in seeking to achieve or maintain your leadership position. You should have also explained your vision of where the company will be in the next five years or so in the markets that you serve.

In section 3.2.c of your application, you need to explain your major strategies for achieving your vision for the future. It is important that you be as specific as possible, given space constraints. For example, on Baldrige applicant explained that they were going to achieve their long term goals by spending $15 million on plant improvements and by providing employees with 40 hours of training a year. This is probably too vague. Think of yourself as a stockholder in your company, reading the annual report, trying to decide whether or not the company has a good future. Your response to this section should be similar to what you might tell stockholders to make them believe that your company will continue to hold its leadership position during the next three to five years.

Requirements for your success in the future might be to secure resources through a stock offering, or perhaps you plan to buy other companies to broaden your product offerings. Or maybe you are planning to build several new plants to make you more competitive. Sometimes information on the company's future strategies is highly guarded, even from its own employees. I worked with a company with a mature product in a mature market, and when I asked them how they would ensure their future survival, they said they couldn't reveal their plans (or they'd have to shoot me before I left). The Baldrige examiners understand the importance of keeping certain parts of your long-term strategy secret. However, you need to disclose enough to convince them that you have a strategy, and that it is likely to be successful. Simply saying "trust us, we know where we're going" will not get you much of a score.

Indicators For Area 3.2.c

- Response includes longer-term goals for key performance measures, if appropriate for size of the organization

- Strategies have been clearly articulated for all of the major product/service lines of the company, and the markets it serves

- Strategies are realistic and logical, given the future vision for the company that has been explained in section 3.2.a

- Likelihood that strategies will be successful in achieving the long-term vision for the organization

- Consistency between information in section 7.1.b, which concerns future changes in customers and requirements, and strategies outlined in this section.

AREA TO ADDRESS   **[APPROACH, DEPLOYMENT]**

3.2d Two- to five-year projection of key measures and/or indicators of the company's quality and operational performance. Describe how quality and operational performance might be expected to compare with key competitors and key benchmarks over this time period. Briefly explain the comparisons, including any estimates or assumptions made regarding the projected quality and operational performance of competitors or changes in benchmarks.

Note:

(2) Area 3.2d addresses projected progress in improving performance and in gaining advantage relative to competitors. This projection may draw upon analysis (Item 2.3) and data reported in results Items (Category 6.0 and Items 7.5 and 7.6). Such projections are intended to support reviews (1.2c), evaluation of plans (3.1d), and other Items.

What They're Looking For Here

In your response for this area, explain what you expect the benefits to be if you actually meet your quality improvement goals and achieve the goals outlined in your long- and short-term business plans. The examiners want to see statements such as:

- "By 1995, we will have at least 300 of the Fortune 500 companies as our clients, based upon our levels of service quality and customer satisfaction."

- "We will become the number one supplier of quality (products) in the world by the end of 1995."

- "We will produce the most defect-free (products) in the market."

- "By 1996, we will attain preferred vendor status from both Ford and General Motors."

Quality improvement should not be done for its own sake. It should produce quantifiable improvements in business success factors such as profits, sales, and market share. You should explain in this section what the specific benefits are that you believe will result from your quality improvement efforts. Don't do what one applicant did, who stated simply that, "We hope to improve the overall levels of quality of our products and to increase levels of customer satisfaction." This type of statement is far too general and vague. Be specific about the benefits you expect to see. The degree to which some of these benefits are already occurring will help add credibility to your statement of expectations. Mention any results achieved thus far that indicate that you are well on your way to reaching your overall goals. Also, be sure to explain how your projected level of performance will compare to that of your major competitors, and to organizations against which you have benchmarked your performance.

Indicators For Area 3.2d

- Scope/magnitude of changes in company's competitive position are based upon planned improvements in quality

- Description of expected benefits from quality improvement efforts is fully specific

- Evidence to suggest that the described changes in competitive position will occur if quality improvement goals are met

- Degree to which company will be more successful overall if quality plans are implemented and goals met

- Comparison of projections with major competitors' levels of quality

- Comparison of projections with performance levels attained by organizations against which company benchmarks itself

- Estimates or assumptions upon which comparisons are made are thoroughly explained

- Validity of sources of information used to make projections in company performance compared to competitors

Chapter 8

Interpreting the Criteria for Human Resource Development and Management

OVERVIEW OF THE HUMAN RESOURCE DEVELOPMENT AND MANAGEMENT CATEGORY

The fourth category of the Baldrige criteria is Human Resource Development and Management. It is worth fifteen percent of the evaluation, or 150 possible points. According to the Baldrige Award Criteria, human resource development and management is defined as follows:

> The **Human Resource Development and Management** category examines the key elements of how the work force is enabled to develop its full potential to pursue the company's quality and operational performance objectives. Also examined are the company's efforts to build and maintain an environment for quality excellence conducive to full participation and personal and organizational growth (p. 20).

As it is explained here, the Baldrige Examiners are not really concerned that you use a particular set of approaches or processes, but only that your human resource strategies are appropriate for your organization and that you have the data to demonstrate these strategies' effectiveness. Many applicants end with a low score in this category because their approach is not systematic and they lack data to validate its effectiveness. As with all of the categories, examiners are concerned here with your approach, its deployment, and the results you can demonstrate. A description follows of all five Examination Items and the Areas to Address that fall under them. Each section begins with a double-ruled box containing the Examination Item, the point value, and any applicable Notes.[*] Areas to Address falling under that Item follow in a single-ruled box. In the upper right corner of each Area to Address box is an indication [brackets] of whether the Area pertains to approach, deployment, or results. All definitions and information appearing within these boxes is taken directly from the Baldrige criteria. Following each Area to Address is an explanation defining what the examiners are looking for in assessing your application. Next, I have supplied a list of indicators or evaluation factors that will assist you in interpreting the criteria and in preparing your application.

---

[*] Item notes that apply to a specific Area to Address are appropriately listed in the box containing that Area.

4.1 HUMAN RESOURCE PLANNING AND MANAGEMENT

Describe how the company's overall human resource management plans and plans processes are integrated with its overall quality and operational performance and how human resource planning and management address fully the needs and development of the entire work force. (20 points)

AREA TO ADDRESS   [APPROACH, DEPLOYMENT]

4.1a Brief description of the most important human resource plans (derived from Category 3.0). Include: (1) development, including education, training and empowerment; (2) mobility, flexibility, and changes in work organization, work processes or work schedules; (3) reward, recognition, benefits, and compensation; and (4) recruitment, including possible changes in diversity of the work force. Distinguish between the short term (1–3 years) and the longer term (more than 3 years), as appropriate.

Note:

(1)   Human resource plans (4.1a) might include one or more of the following:
  • mechanisms for promoting cooperation such as internal customer/supplier techniques of other internal partnerships;
  • initiatives to promote labor-management cooperation, such as partnerships with unions;
  • creation and/or modification of recognition systems;
  • creation or modification of compensation systems based on building shareholder value;
  • mechanisms for increasing or broadening employee responsibilities;
  • creating opportunities for employees to learn and use skills that go beyond current job assignments through redesign of processes;
  • creation of high performance work teams;
  • education and training initiatives; and
  • forming partnerships with educational institutions to develop employees or to help ensure the future supply of well-prepared employees.

What They're Looking For Here

The 1994 Award Criteria booklet explains that item 4.1 is the "central intelligence" of the entire human resource category. The reason this area to address is so important is that it asks for information on all of your goals and plans that impact the employees in your organization. All aspects of the human resource function are included in this criterion.

The first point you need to make in your response for this area to address is how your human resource plans are derived from your business plans. The examiners want to see that your human resource goals are driven by the goals in your overall business plans. In some organizations the HR plan is developed by individuals who have no knowledge of the company's overall business goals. In order to receive a good score for this area, you need to demonstrate that there is a clear and logical relationship between your business plans and your HR plans. For example, if one of your business goals is to increase your market share in the telecommunications industry with more new products, this fact might lead to an HR goal that calls for increasing the levels of knowledge and skills among employees who design, manufacture, and market telecommunications-based products. You might also have a goal for recruiting more telecommunications experts into the company over the next few years. Examples will help the Baldrige Examiners see the relationship between human resources and overall business planning. Simply making a statement that, "Our human resource planning is based upon our goals for quality and operational performance outlined in our business plan," is obviously vague and will not elicit favorable comments from the examiners. In order to make your response more credible, you need to use illustrations and examples that are specific. Generalizing your response does not enable the examiner to get a true picture of how well you really meet the criterion.

Up to this point, we have been discussing ways to explain how your HR planning process is integrated with your overall business planning process. Now, you need to present information in your response on the specific types of HR goals and plans asked for in the criteria. This area to address asks about four different types of HR goals and plans:

- Employee development (including education, training, and empowerment)
- Mobility, flexibility, and work scheduling
- Rewards, recognition, compensation, and benefits
- Recruitment and selection

For each of these four areas of Human Resources, you should list both your long-term and short-term plans or goals. If you use a chart, all of this information can easily be summarized on a page or less. Along with a summary of the goals for these four HR areas, the chart might also include information on which business goals each HR goal is tied into. If you present all of this information, you will have a very strong response to 4.1a.

<u>Indicators For Area 4.1a</u>

- Demonstration that human resource plans and strategies are determined based upon long and short-term quality and operational performance goals of the organization

- Amount and credibility of evidence presented to suggest that business and HR planning are linked/integrated

- Human resource plans are developed as part of the overall strategic business planning process, rather than as a separate planning activity

- There are no arbitrary HR goals such as "Reduce head count by 10%," or "Every employee will receive 80 hours of training."

- Specific goals and plans exist for educating, training, and empowering employees

- Specific goals and plans exist for improving mobility, flexibility, and workforce organization

- Specific goals and plans exist for improving reward, recognition, compensation, and benefits

- Specific goals and plans exist for improving recruiting and selection

- Goals and objectives are measurable and specific

- Both long- and short-term plans are presented for all of the four major HR areas asked about in the criterion

- Clear relationship between long- and short-term plans for each of the four major HR areas asked about in the criterion

---

AREA TO ADDRESS   **[APPROACH, DEPLOYMENT]**

4.1b How the company improves key personnel processes. Describe key improvement methods for processes such as recruitment, hiring, personnel actions, and services to employees including support services to managers and supervisors. Include a description of key performance measures or indicators, including cycle time, and how they are used in improvement.

Note:

(2)   The personnel processes referred to in 4.1b are those commonly carried out by personnel departments or by personnel specialists. Improvement processes might include needs assessments and satisfaction surveys. Improvement results associated with the measures or indicators used in 4.1b should be reported in Item 6.3.

What They're Looking For Here

While Area to Address 4.1a asked about plans and goals, this Area to Address asks about your *strategies* for achieving improvements in human resources. The key words in the criteria are, "How the company improves . . ." Although the criteria do not call for this specifically, I would recommend formatting your response to 4.1b around the same four major HR functions that are listed in 4.1a. In fact, it may be a good idea to combine your response to 4.1a and 4.1b on one matrix chart. The chart would list your major HR goals by area, the indices used to measure your progress, and your major strategies that will be employed to reach the goals. A sample of a portion of such a chart is shown on the following page.

SUMMARY OF KEY HR GOALS & PLANS		
HR Goals and Performance Indicators	Improvement Strategies	Link to Business Plan Objectives
TRAINING, EDUCATION,& EMPOWERMENT 80% of hourly employees will have completed basic TQM course by end of '94 75% of employees will state on survey that they feel more empowered than in the past	Increase training budget Hire 3 new instructors Open 2 new classrooms in Midwest Trng. Ctr. Provide empowerment training Change policies & procedures that limit empowerment Define new decision making matrices for all functions Reduce unnecessary layers of management where needed	I a-c, III b,c, IV a, VI a-e I a-d, II b, III a-d, VII a, VIII a-c

As you can see in the sample chart, we have presented information on specific HR goals that fall under the first of the four categories of major HR activities outlined in 4.1a. (In this example, we have listed some of the goals of education, training, and employee empowerment that are asked about in 4.1a [1].) A good goal includes a performance indicator, so it would be redundant to list these separately. For example, if the goal is to reduce the time it takes to process changes in the HR information system data base from 12 days to 2 days, the index is obviously cycle time. If you feel it would be better to list the performance indicators separately, by all means do so. This action will help to ensure that the examiners don't miss this piece of information. Following the goals and performance indicators, the chart should present your strategies for achieving the goals. In most cases there will be a number of different strategies for each goal. Finally, the last column is used to show the linkage between the HR goals and the business goals defined in category 3.0 of your application. In this example, I simply listed the numbers and letters of the specific objectives rather than write them out. By writing them out you will make it simpler for the examiner, but you may not have the space to do so. A matrix such as this one can be used to present just about all the information that is requested in 4.1b. I would suggest, however, that you also include a few examples where you provide more details on the HR goals and improvement strategies for a few key areas. The advantage of the chart format is that you can present a wide breadth of information in a relatively small space. However, you also need to add some depth to your response by writing a few of these examples. This way you get both breadth and depth, which is something that the examiners will look for, as a general rule.

Indicators For Area 4.1b

- Information is provided on goals and improvement strategies for all key functions within HR (note that goals may have been presented in section 4.1a, so they don't need to be repeated here)

- Strategies are presented for achieving all HR goals

- Depth to which strategies are described

- Degree to which strategies appear to be likely to lead to achievement of goals

- Key performance indicators are defined for improvement of performance in all major HR areas/functions

---

AREA TO ADDRESS　　　　　　　　　　**[APPROACH, DEPLOYMENT]**

4.1c How the company evaluates and improves its human resource planning and management using all employee-related data. Include: (1) how selection, performance, recognition, job analysis, and training are integrated to support improved performance and development of all categories and types of employees; and (2) how human resource planning and management are aligned with company strategy and plans.

Notes:

(3)　**"Categories of employees" (4.1c) refers to the company's classification system used in its personnel practices and/or work assignments. It also includes factors such as union or bargaining unit membership. "Types of employees" takes into account other factors, such as work force diversity or demographic makeup. This includes gender, age, minorities, and the disabled.**

(4)　**"All employee-related data" (4.1c) refers to data contained in personnel records as well as data described in Items 4.2, 4.3, 4.4, and 4.5. This might include employee satisfaction data and data on turnover, absenteeism, safety, grievances, involvement, recognition, training, and information from exit interviews.**

(5)　**The evaluation in 4.1c might be supported by employee-related data such as satisfaction factors (Item 4.5), absenteeism, turnover, and accidents. It might also be supported by employee feedback.**

What They're Looking For Here

A typical response to this area is to explain, "Employee-related data are collected and evaluated to look for ways to continually improve human resource strategies and plans." What examiners want to see here, however, is specific information on how you *use* employee-related data. Examples will go a long way in convincing the Baldrige Examiners that you really do utilize your employee data to fine-tune your human resources strategies. You might explain, for example, how employee performance-appraisal scores are used to evaluate the quality of the company's selection systems and the quality of training and supervision. Show how selection systems have been improved and how that improvement has led to improvements in other dimensions such as reduced turnover and improved performance appraisal ratings.

As in many of the Baldrige criteria, the examiners are looking for an approach that is based upon the following sequence of activities:

1. Collection of objective data
2. Analysis of data
3. Feedback to employees who can improve performance on these indices
4. Change or improvement in practices to improve the indices being measured
5. Data-based evaluation and modification (if necessary) of improvement strategies

Your score in this area will depend upon the extent to which you have a systematic approach such as the one above, and can provide evidence that such an approach is really

followed.

This area to address also asks about how data on employee satisfaction or morale are used as indicators of the effectiveness of your efforts to improve performance on measures such as absenteeism, turnover, and so on. At first read, this seems like asking how one type of data (employee satisfaction) is used to influence another type of data (adverse indicators of employee satisfaction). With this interpretation the criteria make little sense. What they are really saying is: "How have your efforts to improve employee satisfaction had an impact on key measures of employee satisfaction?" This portion of the criterion seems to fit much better in item 4.5 than it does here, but it is here for 1994, so you need to respond to it.

The examiners are looking for information on the effectiveness of your efforts to improve employee satisfaction. For example, let's say that you redesigned your offices and put in new furniture and fixtures, using ergonomic experts to help you design a pleasing and productive environment for employees. You would describe that effort here, along with how the effort has impacted key measures of employee satisfaction. Does this mean that the examiners want to see data? No. This is an approach/deployment item only. What they want to know about is your approach to improving employee satisfaction, and how fully deployed this approach has been to all categories and levels of employees.

This area to address also asks about how you have improved your human resource planning process to better align it with business strategies and plans. Mention specific examples of how the HR planning process has been streamlined or otherwise improved over the last few years. Describe how the HR planning process is different or better in 1994 as compared to previous years.

Indicators For Area 4.1c

- Amount of employee-related data collected by the organization

- Extent to which indices currently being measured are good indicators of the success of the organization in the area of human resource management

- Length of time data have been collected for employee-related indices

- Objectivity of employee-related data

- Degree to which employee-related data are reported in a systematic and easy-to-understand fashion

- Evidence that employee-related data are periodically analyzed to identify causes of problems or deviations from standards

- Evidence that human resource plans and strategies are evaluated based upon employee-related data

- Regular reports of employee-related data are created and distributed to appropriate personnel

- Evidence that feedback on employee-related data is used to evaluate and improve human resource strategies, plans, and practices

- Extent to which evaluation includes data from all levels and types of employees

- Evidence that employee satisfaction factors are used to reduce adverse indicators of employee morale

- Changes that have been made to improve the HR planning process to make it simpler and better aligned with business strategies.

4.2 EMPLOYEE INVOLVEMENT

Describe how all employees are enabled to contribute effectively to meeting the company's quality and operational performance plans; summarize trends in effectiveness and extent of involvement. (40 points)

AREA TO ADDRESS   **[APPROACH, DEPLOYMENT]**

4.2a How the company promotes ongoing employee contributions, individually and in groups, to improvement in quality and operational performance. Include how and how quickly the company gives feedback to contributors.

Note:

(1)   **The company may use different involvement methods and measures or indicators for different categories of employees or for different parts of the company, depending on needs and responsibilities of each employee category or part of the company. Examples include problem-solving teams (within work units or cross-functional); fully-integrated, self-managed work groups; and process improvement teams.**

What They're Looking For Here

Applicants often assume that what is being asked for here is that a high percentage of employees be involved in process improvement teams. Teams are only one way of getting employees involved, however. If you happen to use problem-solving or process improvement teams in your organization, you should explain how employees get involved in the teams, and what they accomplish. One organization I've worked with has close to 100% of its employees involved in teams. The management believes that most of these teams waste time working on insignificant problems such as what color to paint the cafeteria. Management's current goal is to reduce the number of teams in the organization. Having a lot of teams is not by itself an answer.

Another effective way of encouraging employee involvement is a suggestion system. If you use such an approach in your organization, you should report on the effectiveness of the system. Statistics on number of suggestions per employee, acceptance percentage, and timeliness of feedback are important to include in your response. You should also explain how suggestions are evaluated and implemented. Many companies have suggestion systems that have no mechanism for implementing the acceptable ideas they receive.

It may appear that the criteria are actually prescriptive for this item, urging that you need to have a suggestion system and many process improvement teams. This, however, is not true. Teams and suggestion systems are only two of many other popular and effective mechanisms for encouraging employee involvement.

Although the Baldrige people claim not to be prescriptive in telling an organization how to achieve quality results, one approach that they do value and prescribe is teamwork. An organization demonstrating the highest order of teamwork might be organized into self-managed work teams without the traditional organizational hierarchy of supervisors and managers. This organization would also use a variety of teams such as task forces, quality improvement teams, customer teams, supplier teams, etc. The examiners are looking for the degree to which teamwork is a way of life in your organization. Almost all organizations have task forces, process improvement teams, or project management teams. Hence, they would not earn you many points by themselves. You will earn a high score in this area if teamwork is embedded in practically every function of your organization.

There is a big difference between an organization just getting started with teamwork or experimenting with some cross-functional teams to solve problems, and an organization that uses teamwork to achieve most key goals. The level of employee involvement on teams is an important criterion in assessing an organization's success in this area. Organizations just getting started in teamwork will have only a small number of the employees participating on any kind of team.

Indicators For Area 4.2a

- Degree to which the organization structure is based on teams rather than on a traditional hierarchy

- Existence of a suggestion system or similar way of obtaining improvement ideas from employees

- Effectiveness of suggestion system and extent to which it includes mechanisms for providing timely and accurate feedback to employees on their ideas

- Use of cross-functional teams to work on projects and products/services

- Employee opinion on the level of cooperation and teamwork that exists between departments

- Extent to which staff departments are evaluated and rated on the level of customer satisfaction they achieve from internal customers

- Involvement of internal and external customers on teams in the organization

- Involvement of suppliers on project and product/service teams in the organization

- Number and percentage of employees that participate in task forces, committees, quality improvement teams, and other similar groups

- Increased evidence of the use of teams over the last several years

---

AREA TO ADDRESS   **[APPROACH, DEPLOYMENT]**
4.2b How the company increases employee empowerment, responsibility, and innovation. Include a brief summary of principal plans for all categories of employees, based upon the most important requirements for each category.

What They're Looking For Here

What the Baldrige Examiners are looking for is evidence that you really do empower employees to make decisions and solve problems in order to satisfy internal and external customers. Empowerment is a practice that many organizations talk a great deal about, but don't always follow through on by giving employees much authority or autonomy.

The first thing the examiners want to see in this area is the existence of a plan for increasing the degree of empowerment in the organization. The plan should outline specific strategies to be employed to increase empowerment throughout line and staff functions in the organization. The empowerment effort should not be limited to the frontline personnel in the organization who interface regularly with customers; staff organizations should also be included in this effort.

The examiners will not only consider the plans and strategies you have employed to increase empowerment, but will be interested in what employees have to say about the degree to which they really are empowered to make decisions and solve problems. Employees will likely tell the true story about whether or not they have been given increased authority. Along with describing your approach to increasing empowerment, your response should include examples that illustrate how employees are empowered to satisfy customers.

The second half of this Area to Address relates to innovation, creativity, and risk-taking. This is another area where many organizations talk a good game, but fail to do much to encourage innovation and risk-taking. Most organizations reward employees for taking the safe approach rather than being creative and taking some risks—where the chance of failure is greater. Your response should describe the plan your company has in place to encourage innovation and risk-taking. Along with describing your approach, provide evidence that greater innovation and risk-taking is actually occurring. The more objective the data are that you present, the better. Data for indices such as the number of new products designed or patents obtained are preferable over survey data. Surveys to gather employee opinion on the extent to which the company encourages innovation and creativity, however, may be good to present.

Indicators For Area 4.2b

- Evidence of a clear plan for increasing employee empowerment

- What employees have to say about the degree of empowerment they have

- Degree to which employees in all functions have been given increased authority/empowerment over the last several years

- Breadth and scope of activities to increase empowerment include all types and levels of employees/management

- Credibility of examples provided to illustrate levels of empowerment

- Evidence of a clear plan for encouraging innovation/creativity

- Employee opinion on the degree to which management rewards innovation and risk-taking

- Whether risk-taking and innovation are part of the culture of the organization

- Quantity and objectivity of data that demonstrate increased innovation over the last several years

---

AREA TO ADDRESS   **[APPROACH, DEPLOYMENT]**

4.2c How the company evaluates and improves the effectiveness, extent and type of involvement of all categories and all types of employees. Include how effectiveness, extent and types of involvement are linked to key quality and operational performance improvement results.

What They're Looking For Here

The first thing the Baldrige Examiners are looking for in this area is whether or not you actually evaluate the extent and effectiveness of your efforts to increase employee involvement, empowerment, and innovation. Most organizations do little or nothing to evaluate their efforts in this area. The best response for this area would be to present a comprehensive evaluation system that includes a variety of different indices and that makes use of sound experimental designs to rule out alternative explanations for the improvements seen in involvement, empowerment, and innovation. At the very least, you should have a couple of different measures of the effectiveness of your efforts. The data should show that your efforts have been successful in changing employee behavior, levels of authority, and the culture of the organization.

A new sentence that was added to this area to address for 1993 asks about how the measures of employee involvement you use relate to key measures of quality and operational performance. This is a good addition because it seeks information on how you know that teams or whatever employee involvement method you are using leads to bottom-line results. In the January/February 1992 issue of the *Harvard Business Review,* consultants Schaffer and Thomson suggest that many employee involvement initiatives do nothing to improve meaningful measures of performance in companies.

> *This "rain dance" is the ardent pursuit of activities that sound good, look good, and allow managers to feel good—but in fact contribute little or nothing to bottom-line performance. (p. 80)*

What you need to explain here is the link between your measures of employee involvement and the quality and performance measures you listed in item 2.1 of your application. For example, one of your measures is the number of employee suggestions that are implemented. This measure might translate into dollars that have been saved by the organization due to employee suggestions. To consider another example, I know of a company that measures empowerment by the number of customer complaints that are received by supervisors and managers. The logic for doing this is that most complaints should be resolved by empowered customer contact employees. This measure is correlated to overall levels of customer satisfaction and repeat business for the company.

What the examiners want to see in your response is that you don't measure activities such as how many team meetings are held, unless you are sure that holding team meetings leads to improvements in key performance measures for the organization.

Indicators For Area 4.2c

- Measurement indices have been identified for evaluating effectiveness of employee involvement strategies

- Multiple measures are used, versus one measurement index, for assessing involvement

- Objectivity of data used to evaluate employee involvement

- Use of separate and specific indicators to evaluate each of the various methods used to encourage employee involvement

- Use of sound experimental design(s) to evaluate effectiveness of strategies/programs in these areas

- Scope of evaluation effort includes all categories of employees and all functions in the organization

- Evidence that employee involvement indices are linked to key quality and/or customer satisfaction indices

- Evidence that employee involvement indices are linked to key operational performance indices such as financial, productivity or cycle time

---

AREA TO ADDRESS   **[RESULTS]**
4.2d Trends in key measures and/or indicators of the *effectiveness* and *extent* of employee involvement.

Note:
(2)   Trend results (4.2d) should be segmented by category of employee, as appropriate. Major types of involvement should be noted.

What They're Looking For Here

In case you didn't notice, this area to address does not ask about *how* you do anything—it asks for *results*. Anytime you see the word "trends" in the criteria, you should know that they are looking for data or results. A narrative description of the wonderful things you have accomplished as a result of employee involvement and empowerment is not what is being asked for. What the examiners want to see is charts and graphs of data on two types of indices relating to employee involvement. One type of data is "extent" data. These data indicate the quantity of activities relating to employee involvement. Some typical "extents" for which previous Baldrige applicants have provided data are:

- Number of employee suggestions received
- Percentage of employees who submit improvement suggestions
- Number of quality improvement teams
- Percentage of employees who participate in quality improvement teams or committees relating to the improvement of quality and customer satisfaction
- Percentage of hourly employees involved on committees where policy decisions are made
- Number of self-directed work teams in place in the company
- Percentage of employees who work on self-directed work teams

These and other "extent" measures are measures of activity. Presumably, the more teams you have and the more suggestions that are submitted, the more employee involvement you have in your company. Activity measures are important, but by themselves they are not very meaningful. The criteria also ask for data on "effectiveness" measures. These are not activity measures, but data that indicate whether or not all this employee involvement produces any meaningful results. I've consulted with a number of companies who have a lot of teams, but whose quality has gone down since they implemented the quality improvement teams. What has gone up is their overhead costs, due to all the team meetings being held. I interviewed a team in one of these companies and asked them why they were having a team meeting, and they replied: "It's Friday at 2:00. We always have team meetings at this time—it sure beats working."

The graphs you present in this section should show several years' worth of data—the more the better. When the Baldrige Examiners look for trends what they want to see is more than two or three data points. Part of what will be assessed in looking at the results in this section is the validity of the measures for which you provide data. If the graphs look great, but the indices are poor, your results are not worth much. Conversely, you also need to have positive trends. If the measures are good but the data show flat or declining performance you will also receive a low score. It is also important that you present both data on the extent of employee involvement and the effectiveness of employee involvement efforts.

Indicators For Area 4.2d

- Number of different indices for which data are presented

- Data on employee involvement activities (extent) and the effectiveness of employee involvement activities are both presented

- Validity of measures of extent and effectiveness of employee involvement

- Stability of data shows that company has the measures in control

- Graphs show continuous improvement in measures of employee involvement extent and effectiveness

- Data are presented that indicate improving trends in empowerment, as well as in employee involvement

- Graphs present data from several years

- Slope of the trends—dramatically improving performance, as compared with slow, undramatic improvement

- Overall level of performance on graphs showing extent and effectiveness indicators

4.3 EMPLOYEE EDUCATION AND TRAINING

Describe how the company determines quality and related education and training needs for all employees. Show how this determination addresses company plans and supports employee growth. Outline how such education and training are evaluated, and summarize key trends in the effectiveness and extent of education and training. (40 points)

Note:

(1)   Quality and related education and training address the knowledge and skills employees need to meet their objectives as part of the company's quality and operational performance improvement. This might include quality awareness, leadership, project management, communications, teamwork, problem solving, interpreting and using data, meeting customer requirements, process analysis, process simplification, waste reduction, cycle time reduction, error-proofing, and other training that affects employee effectiveness, efficiency, and safety. In many cases, this might include job enrichment skills and job rotation that enhance employees' career opportunities. It might also include basic skills such as reading, writing, language, arithmetic, and basic mathematics that are needed for quality and operational performance improvement.

AREA TO ADDRESS   [APPROACH, DEPLOYMENT]

4.3a How the company determines needs for the types and amounts of quality and related education and training for all employees, taking into account their differing needs. Include: (1) linkage to short- and long-term plans, including company wide access to skills in problem solving, waste reduction, and process simplification; (2) growth and career opportunities for employees; and (3) how employees' input is sought and used in the needs determination.

<u>What They're Looking For Here</u>

Many organizations approach training and education by buying a series of packaged programs from vendors who tell them what their employees need. What the Baldrige Examiners are looking for in this area is that you conduct a systematic needs assessment to determine the specific knowledge, skills, and competencies needed by different categories of employees in your organization. A systematic needs analysis does not mean conducting a survey to ask employees which courses they would like to take. A training/education needs analysis is a process that involves an initial analysis of the functions and jobs, and then a determination of the knowledge and skills needed to do the jobs and functions correctly. Group or individual interviews are conducted to identify the specific tasks employees must perform in their jobs, as well as how quality tools and concepts can be integrated into those job tasks. The key to this process is that the knowledge and skills are derived from analyzing job tasks. From this, relationships are identified between particular job tasks and specific skills and knowledge.

It is also important that training needs are derived from an analysis of the company's business goals. Identification of key competencies that are needed to meet business goals is the first step. Current employee skills and competencies then need to be assessed. The gap between existing and needed competencies form the foundation for a needs analysis.

Some organizations adopt the one-size-fits-all approach to quality training/education. While it is true that all employees at all levels need education on the basic concepts of quality, such as prevention versus detection, not all employees need to learn about specific tools and techniques such as facilitating team meetings or the Taguchi method of conducting experiments. Giving all of the same quality courses to all employees only produces the result that:

- Training is not tailored to individual needs
- Time and money are wasted on training that is irrelevant
- There will be no discussion of job/function-specific applications of the quality tools and techniques
- Skills and knowledge learned in the classroom will not translate into changed behavior on the job

Needs analysis for education and training should also be based upon individual performance appraisals and developmental plans created for each type of employee. Succession plans also can provide key data to be used for training needs analysis. Area to Address 4.3a (3) asks about how employees' input is sought for the needs analysis process. This does not mean, as I mentioned earlier, that you should do a survey to find out which courses employees want to take. Instead, employees are involved in needs analysis through the techniques called job and task analysis that were discussed earlier. It is impossible to conduct a thorough training needs analysis without involving employees.

Indicators For Area 4.3a

- Evidence that a systematic needs analysis has been done to identify specific training needs of various functions and levels of employees

- Scope of needs analysis includes all functions and levels of employees, including executives

- Degree to which needs analysis is based upon the study of job tasks to identify the key knowledge and skills needed by various groups of employees

- Use of appropriate data gathering techniques, such as group or individual interviews, rather than surveys

- Use of appropriate needs analysis processes, such as job or task analysis

- Needs analysis identifies where and how quality and performance improvement tools and techniques will be utilized in specific job tasks

- Needs analysis is updated and changed as jobs, functions and training needs change

- Degree to which training need analyses are integrated with performance appraisal and individual employee development plans

- Training needs analysis linked to career development and succession planning as appropriate

- Extent to which employees are involved in the needs analysis process

---

AREA TO ADDRESS   **[APPROACH, DEPLOYMENT]**
4.3b How quality and related education and training are delivered and reinforced. Include: (1) description of education and training delivery for all categories of employees; (2) on-the-job application of knowledge and skills; and (3) quality-related orientation for new employees.

Note:

(2)   **Education and training delivery may occur inside or outside the company and involve on-the-job or classroom delivery.**

What They're Looking For Here

When describing the methods used for the delivery of quality and related education and training, it is important to explain why certain methods and media are used for particular audiences and topics. The examiners expect that the methods and media used are matched to both the audience and the content of the education. For example, use of reading assignments for a population with poor reading skills would not be advised.

When discussing on-the-job reinforcement of training, a typical response is to explain that "employees at all levels are encouraged to use the skills they learn in quality training throughout various aspects of their jobs." What the examiners are looking for here is that you have planned and implemented a systematic process for ensuring that skills learned in training are reinforced in the work environment. Most organizations have no such plan, and end up with a low score. I consult with many large organizations who spend millions of dollars on quality and related training and nothing on following up the training with coaching and reinforcement to make sure that the trainees apply the skills on the job. Consequently, the training fails to change job behavior or produce any improvements in quality. What usually follows is that the training itself is blamed, and the organization buys a different program, hires a different consultant, or develops a new program of their own. They usually find that the second or third training program works no better than the first one. All that a good training or education program can do is provide people with knowledge and skills. It cannot ensure that those knowledge and skills are applied and used on the job.

A lack of systematic and planned follow-up is the number one reason why training of any sort fails in organizations. As much—or more—time and money needs to be spent on what happens after the classes as is spent preparing and conducting the classes. In the beginning, it is good to teach all supervisors and managers how to reinforce their employees for applying the quality improvement tools and techniques on their jobs.

Another effective approach is to teach employees job-specific applications for the tools and techniques they learn. This will help in bridging the gap between the classroom and the job environment. A more formalized reinforcement program would result in an even higher score in this area. One award applicant describes a program whereby supervisors and managers hand out coupons and "thank you" notes to employees when they see them going beyond quality standards or making use of the quality improvement techniques learned in training courses. Coupons are posted on sheets, and completed sheets are used to earn symbolic recognition or a small monetary/privilege award. The existence of a program such as this, along with data on its effectiveness, would help to earn a high score in this area.

Indicators For Area 4.3b

- Use of a variety of methods for (if appropriate) for delivery of quality education/ training. For example, self-study, group instruction, video, case studies, etc.

- Education/training methods and media match characteristics of various target audiences within the organization

- Education/training methods and media match knowledge and skills to be taught

- Supervisors and managers have been trained to provide on-the-job reinforcement of employees' use of quality improvement tools and concepts

- Employee opinion about the degree to which supervisors/managers reinforce/encourage their use of quality tools and techniques

- Executives and upper management reinforce managers' use of quality tools and techniques

- Existence of a systematic plan to ensure that training/education courses on quality are followed-up with appropriate coaching and reinforcement

- Training is scheduled in a "just-in-time" fashion so that skills and knowledge have immediate application on the job

- Degree to which employees receive follow-up coaching on the use of quality and performance improvement tools and techniques

- Employees are given adequate time to practice and master quality improvement tools/techniques on the job after formal training is completed

- Existence and success of formal program to reinforce employees' use of quality tools/techniques

- Use of tangible and symbolic rewards to reinforce use of quality improvement tools and techniques by all employees

---

AREA TO ADDRESS   **[APPROACH, DEPLOYMENT]**

4.3c How the company evaluates and improves its quality and related education and training. Include how the evaluation supports improved needs determination, taking into account: (1) relating on-the-job performance improvement to key quality and operational performance improvement targets and results; and (2) growth and progression of all categories and types of employees.

Note:

(3)   **The overall evaluation (4.3c) might compare the relative effectiveness of structured on-the-job training with classroom methods. It might also address how to best balance on-the-job training and classroom methods.**

<u>What They're Looking For Here</u>

This Area to Address pertains to data you have on the quality and effectiveness of the education and training your organization does. This education and training should be evaluated on four dimensions:

- Reaction
- Learning
- Behavior Change
- Results

Reaction data are the most common, and are collected via questionnaires or surveys filled out by participants at the end of a class. The typical questionnaire asks the participants to rate the course, the instructor, the content, and the relevancy of the material on a five point scale. The Baldrige Examiners want to see that you have reaction data on all the quality and related courses/programs taught, and that the data show that participants rate the course quality high. They are also looking for a trend that shows improvement in these ratings over the last several years. Your response for this area may best be presented using several graphs of key reaction dimensions such as "overall course quality" or "relevancy." This type of information is what is typically used to evaluate the delivery of the education/ training.

The second education/training evaluation dimension is *learning*. This is another index that provides data on the effectiveness of the training delivery. This set of data should not simply report what the trainees/participants thought of the courses, but rather should indicate whether or not employees have mastered the material covered. Testing is the only appropriate means of measuring learning in an education/training program. Many large organizations do no testing in any of their quality courses, and hence have no data to demonstrate that participants learned any of the material. Testing does not have to consist of a paper-and-pencil, multiple-choice test. In any course in which skills are taught, performance tests are much better than written tests. A performance test might be a case study, a simulation, a role play, a demonstration, or any other situation where the trainee must demonstrate that he/she has mastered the skills taught in the course. Tests should be developed based upon the objectives of the courses, and should simulate how the trainees will use the skills in the job environment. For example, if fishbone diagramming is most often practiced in groups, it would be appropriate to test the trainees' abilities to construct a fishbone diagram in a group exercise with other trainees. Data on learning should also be presented in graphs or tables showing all percentage scores. Establishing a pass/fail criterion such as a score of 70%, and reporting only the number of trainees who passed the courses, is not the preferred way to present data on learning. It is better to show average or median scores of all trainees in all quality courses.

The third dimension of training/education evaluation is *behavior change*. This dimension considers whether trainees' behavior on the job has changed as a result of the training/ education they received. Many large and small organizations do not have data on behavior change. This type of data, however, is even more important than data on what was learned. If skills learned in training are not used on the job, quality will not improve, and the money and time spent on the training will have been wasted. The degree to which employees apply and use the knowledge and skills they have learned in training is usually a direct result of the strategies employed in doing follow-up coaching and reinforcement, which are discussed in the previous section (Area 4.3b). Data on behavior change are often collected via follow-up surveys of the trainees, their bosses, and their peers. An even more objective way of gathering such data is a measurement or audit of the actual products of people's behaviors and/or behavior changes. For example, an auditor might count the number of correctly prepared control charts posted in offices and work areas, or the number of quality improvement project reports that have been completed according to the criteria outlined in the training. A combination of process (behavior) and output (accomplishments/products) measures will earn high marks from the Baldrige Examiners in this area. Again, data should be presented in charts or graphs, and should include data from previous years as well as the current year.

The final type of evaluation data that should be collected on training/education programs and courses is data on quality *results*. Employees might like the course, master the tests, and apply the skills on the job, but quality may not improve. The major reason an organization invests in training and education is to produce better results from its employees' performance. If courses on quality improvement tools and techniques don't result in improved quality, something is wrong. The examiners want to see that you identify and measure key dimensions of quality that will be impacted by each course in your quality curriculum. You should compare quality results data both before and after the training to see whether the training has made any difference. Of course, various other activities occurring in the organization will also impact quality, so it is important that you use a sound, applied research/experimental design in your evaluation effort to rule out alternative explanations for the improvements seen in quality results. Present your response for this area using key graphs of major quality indices that have been impacted by the training.

In summary, the examiners are looking for four types or dimensions of evaluation data here. They are also looking to see that you can demonstrate clear cause-effect relationships between the quality education/training and improvements in both employee behavior and quality results.

Indicators For Area 4.3c

- Extent to which data indicating employees' reactions to quality-related education/training is positive

- Test scores demonstrate that the majority of employees who complete quality-related education/training courses have mastered the knowledge and skills covered in those courses

- Tests are developed to evaluate how trainees will apply and use quality skills/tools on the job

- Amount and objectivity of data collected that indicate the degree to which employees apply the knowledge and skills learned in quality-related courses on their jobs

- Data on behavior change is a combination of process (behavior) and output (accomplishment) measures

- Amount and objectivity of data that indicate that quality-related education/training produces measurable improvements in key quality results

- Sound experimental designs have been employed to demonstrate a cause-effect relationship between the education/training and improvements in quality results

- Satisfactory explanations provided for adverse trends or situations where training has had no impact upon quality results

- Evaluation data are fed back into the needs analysis process for education and training

- Evaluation data are collected to assess growth and development of all categories and types of employees

---

AREA TO ADDRESS   **[RESULTS]**

4.3d Trends in key measures and/or indicators of the *effectiveness* and *extent* of quality and related education and training.

Note:

   (4)   **Trend results (4.3.d) should be segmented by category of employee (including new employees), as appropriate. Major types of training and education should be noted.**

What They're Looking For Here

By now you should have learned that when the criteria say "summary and trends," examiners are looking for *data*, and not a narrative description of the number of classes you teach. In order to receive a high score for this area, you should provide statistics that demonstrate your organization's commitment to quality and related education and training. This Area to Address asks about "quality and related" education and training. This would clearly include all total quality or statistical process control types of courses. It may also include job skills training such as how to operate a piece of equipment, how to solve problems, or how to use a new software package. It may also include courses on leadership and managerial skills.

While it may be true that all education and training may partially contribute to quality in the organization, the examiners want to know about the training and education you do that is specific to quality concepts, tools, and techniques. It would *not* be appropriate to include the following training in this category:

- Sales training
- Product or service knowledge training
- General educational courses such as accounting, reading, math, engineering, etc.

Once you take out training on all of the areas listed above, you have probably removed more than 50% of the training and education that goes on in most organizations.

You will notice that the criteria ask for two types of data again: "extent" and "effectiveness." Data on the extent of training would include indices such as:

- Number of hours of training received by each employee

- Number and percentage of employees who have attended key quality-related courses

- Amount of money company spends per employee on quality-related education and training

More important is the data you present on the effectiveness of the training. The examiners want to see, for example, how you measure your ROI for quality-related education and training. They are interested in seeing how training has impacted key quality, customer satisfaction, and operational performance measures. As with any area to address that asks for data, the validity of the measures will be assessed, along with the trends depicted on the graphs.

Indicators For Area 4.3d

- Number of different indicators of extent of training for which data are presented

- Number of different indicators of the effectiveness of training for which data are provided

- Validity of measures of the extent and effectiveness of training

- Trends show that company has increased the amount of quality-related education and training it does over the last few years

- Overall level of quality-related training given to employees that approaches benchmark level for this size and type of company

- Data show increasing expenditures in quality-related education and training over the last few years

- Data show that there is a clear cause-and-effect relationship between quality-related training and improvements in key measures of quality and/or customer satisfaction

- Data show that there is a clear cause-and-effect relationship between quality-related training and improvements in operational performance measures

- Data provide evidence that the company has achieved a positive ROI for the dollars they have invested in quality-related education and training.

- Satisfactory explanations are provided for any adverse trends in the data

---

4.4 EMPLOYEE PERFORMANCE AND RECOGNITION

Describe how the company's employee performance, recognition, promotion, compensation, reward, and feedback approaches support the improvement of quality and operational performance. (25 points)

AREA TO ADDRESS   **[APPROACH, DEPLOYMENT]**

4.4a How the company's performance, recognition, promotion, compensation, reward, and feedback approaches for individuals and groups, including managers, support improvement of quality and operational performance. Include: (1) how the approaches ensure that quality is reinforced relative to short-term financial considerations; and (2) how employees contribute to the company's employee performance and recognition approaches.

Note:

(1)   **The company might use a variety of reward and recognition approaches—monetary and non-monetary, formal and informal, and individual and group.**

What They're Looking For Here

This Area to Address looks at four main factors:

- Performance Assessment and Feedback
- Compensation Systems
- Promotion Systems
- Recognition and Reward Programs

Performance feedback refers to the measures and data collected on individual and group performance. The examiners look for a performance feedback system that is built in a hierarchical fashion, starting with the top executives and working down to the individual contributors. Measures should be based on a combination of quality, quantity, cost, and timeliness dimensions. No employee should be evaluated on more than a few primary measures, and employees should be able to control or influence the measures for which they are responsible. Along with an identification of measures, data need to be collected for all indices and fed back to the appropriate employees in a timely fashion. Giving feedback once a year in a performance appraisal session does not constitute a performance assessment and feedback system that will earn you many points in this area.

The second factor examined in this Area to Address is *compensation systems*. Many organizations claim to be committed to quality, but they compensate employees based upon seniority, level, or job function. Few of the companies that have performance-based pay plans base the pay that employees receive upon quality. Performance-based pay is most often based upon sales, profits, and other financial measures. Some past Baldrige applicants have explained that they've implemented a gainsharing plan as a way of promoting improved quality. However, gainsharing in many cases is nothing more than profit sharing.

Based upon my own experience consulting with large companies, the ideal situation is that a large percentage of all employees' compensation is based upon their individual and group performance against quality goals and standards. Many organizations have bonus programs for executives and upper management, but not for other levels of employees. Three criteria are important in assessing the compensation systems in a company. First, a portion of employees' compensation should be based upon the degree to which individual and group quality goals have been met. The second criterion is that all levels and categories of employees should participate in quality-based compensation programs. Third and last, a large enough percentage of income should be based upon quality results to make a difference in motivating employees. Allowing employees who earn an average of $30,000 to earn an annual bonus of up to $500 for exceeding their quality goals is not going to do much to motivate them.

Promotion, career development, and succession planning is another factor examined in the Area to Address. You should explain how your decision-making and planning process relating to the promotion of employees helps to promote the implementation of total quality. Some organizations have defined specific criteria for evaluating candidates for managerial positions that assess the degree to which the candidates support total quality. Your response should explain how you ensure that employees who are promoted to leadership positions are truly committed to total quality in both their words and actions.

The fourth factor covered in this Area to Address is *recognition programs.* Recognition programs are similar to compensation programs in that both are systems for rewarding employees for desired performance. Recognition programs do not, however, make use of monetary rewards, whereas compensation systems do. Recognition programs make use of symbolic recognition—i.e., social or tangible awards such as gift items. They are designed to recognize individuals who go beyond standards in their performance. The first important consideration relating to recognition programs is the degree to which they are based upon quality measures. Some Baldrige Award applicants have responded to this section by describing the recognition programs they have in place such as sales contests, banquets to honor long-time employees for their seniority, etc. Your response for this section, however, should address *only* the recognition programs based upon *quality* and *operational* objectives. "Employee of the Month" or similar programs will not earn you many points in this area, unless the criteria for earning the award are quality or operational in nature.

Along with having a variety of recognition and reward programs based upon quality, it is important to present evidence of the effectiveness of the programs. Many recognition programs are thought to be successful by management, but viewed as a failure or an insult to the intelligence of many employees. Care must be taken in selecting the appropriate items to use for reward purposes. One of the Big Three auto companies had a quality recognition program for service technicians in its dealerships in which the technicians could earn a necktie if they exceeded quality goals. The program bombed. Not only did most of the male technicians not care about earning a tie—especially one with the company logo on it—but the award was an insult to women service technicians. The next year management used gold-plated tools as the award, and the program was a resounding success.

A final criterion relating to recognition programs is the percent of employees who receive recognition awards. If an average of one out of five hundred employees receives a recognition award, the program is not going to be very effective in motivating the other 499 employees.

Along with performance assessment, recognition, and reward systems, this Area to Address also looks at (1) how approaches to employee performance and recognition reinforce quality relative to short-term business considerations; and (2) the level of employee involvement in actively selecting approaches, measures, and rewards. What the Baldrige Examiners are looking for in this area is, first of all, a complementary relationship between the measures of quality and other overall measures of the organization's success. To respond to this area, explain your overall business goals for the short term, and describe how achievement of your goals in the area of quality will help (rather than hinder) results in other important areas such as growth, market share, sales, profits, employee satisfaction, safety, etc. It may not be obvious to the examiners how these goals are interdependent, so you should explain this. Don't assume that the examiners reviewing your application will be experts in your particular industry.

The second criterion included in this Area to Address is the degree to which all levels of employees are involved in the development of performance/recognition approaches. Obviously, the examiners are looking for a participative approach where employees from various levels and functions are all involved in deciding upon the specific performance approaches and measurement indices for evaluation and feedback. As we said earlier in section 4.4a., the performance measurement system should be created in a hierarchical fashion, starting with measures for the top executives. This does not mean that all the measures should be dictated by top management. It means that the measures for individual contributors should lead up to the measures for supervisors, which lead to the measures for managers, etc.

Indicators For Area 4.4a

- Existence of a performance measurement and feedback system for all levels of employees that has been built in a hierarchical fashion from top executives to individual contributors

- Employees are involved in developing performance measures for their own jobs

- No individual employee is measured on more than a few primary performance measures

- All employees receive regular and timely feedback on performance measures

- Employees have control or strong influence over the indices on which they are measured

- Extent to which compensation is based upon the achievement of quality goals

- Percentage of employees whose compensation is based upon achievement of individual and group/team quality goals

- Approach to deciding on promotions to leadership positions promotes customer focus and implementation of total quality

- Evidence that promotion decisions are based in part upon individual's demonstrated commitment to quality and customer satisfaction

- Percentage of total compensation based upon quality is large enough to motivate performance of various levels of employees

- Percentage of total compensation for all levels of employees that is at risk and based upon performance

- Degree to which recognition programs are based upon a combination of group and individual performance measures

- Extent to which recognition programs are based upon quality objectives, rather than other dimensions such as sales or profits

- Percentage of employees who receive recognition awards based upon their performance in the area of quality

- What employees at various levels have to say about the effectiveness and fairness of recognition programs designed to promote quality

- Quality recognition programs and the measures on which they are based are not contradictory to other measures and recognition programs designed to encourage success in areas such as sales, profits, and market share

- Extent to which employees at various levels and in various functions are involved in the development of quality performance measures for their own areas and jobs

- Extent to which employees at various levels and in various functions are involved in the development of quality recognition programs

---

AREA TO ADDRESS   [APPROACH, DEPLOYMENT]

4.4b How the company evaluates and improves its employee performance and recognition approaches. Include how the evaluation takes into account: (1) effective participation by all categories and types of employees; (2) employee satisfaction information (Item 4.5); and (3) key measures or indicators of improved quality and operational performance results.

Note:

(2)   Employee satisfaction (4.4.b) might take into account employee dissatisfaction indicators such as turnover and absenteeism.

What They're Looking For Here

By now you should have noticed a pattern in these Areas to Address. The final area under many Examination Items asks about the processes you use to evaluate strategies and programs you've implemented to improve quality. Systematic data-based evaluation, and focus on continuous improvement, are two extremely important concepts that underlie many of the Baldrige Award criteria. On this particular Area to Address, the examiners want to see evidence that you evaluate and improve the quality of performance measurement, compensation, and recognition programs. Some of the factors that will be examined are the number of different indices you use to evaluate these efforts, the objectivity of the data collected, and the level of specificity with which you describe the evaluation system. Most applicants respond to this area with one or two paragraphs describing the fact that they collect a variety of data to get feedback on how well their performance assessment and recognition programs are working. This type of response is too general. A flowchart or a graphic depiction of the process would be a better way of demonstrating your evaluation process.

A second part of this Area to Address relates to the degree to which you utilize the evaluation data to make changes and improvements in the performance measurement, compensation, and recognition programs/approaches. Many organizations prepare and submit evaluation reports that end up in a file cabinet without ever being read, let alone acted upon. In order for the evaluation data to do any good, a process must be defined for how you interpret the evaluation data, how you identify the causes of any problems, and how you specify and implement corrective actions. One such process might consist of periodic system-review meetings in which action plans are prepared and reviewed. Another process may delegate program/system updates to a particular group or individual in the human resources or another department in the company. How the follow-up is done is not important. What is important is that you *have* a follow-up system for constantly improving your performance assessment, compensation, and recognition programs over time. Providing some examples of how the systems/approaches have evolved over the years will help illustrate the fact that you really do constantly improve these systems based upon feedback and evaluation data.

Indicators For Area 4.4b

- Evidence that a systematic, data-based approach is used to evaluate the effectiveness of the performance measurement, recognition, and any quality-based compensation systems

- Existence of data that indicate levels of employee satisfaction with feedback, recognition, and performance-based compensation plans

- Objectivity and scope of data collected for evaluation purposes

- Degree to which employee feedback is solicited on a regular basis regarding performance, compensation, and recognition programs

- Evidence that a follow-up system exists for reviewing evaluation data and planning improvements in performance, compensation, and recognition programs

- Evidence that continuous improvements, changes, and enhancements have been made in all of these systems over time, as a result of feedback and evaluation data

---

AREA TO ADDRESS   **[RESULTS]**

4.4c Trends in key measures and/or indicators of the *effectiveness* and *extent* of employee reward and recognition.

Note:

(3)   **Trend results (4.4c) should be segmented by employee category, as appropriate. Major types of recognition, compensation, etc., should be noted.**

What They're Looking For Here

This area to address should look very familiar, as it is about the same as the others in category 4.0 that ask for results. Two types of data are being asked for:

- Extent data on reward and recognition deployment
- Effectiveness data that show the impact of reward and recognition actions on key measures of quality and operational performance

In asking to see extent data, the Baldrige Examiners are looking for statistics on the number, percentage, and different categories of employees who have received recognition awards for quality-related accomplishments over the last few years. They want to see increases in the number of employees by level and function/department who have received recognition awards. Many organizations limit awards to individual contributors or to employees who work in the line organization. Supervisors, managers, and employees at all levels in staff or support departments also need to receive rewards and recognition based upon their quality efforts. Make sure that your data show the range of employee levels and functions that have received rewards based on quality.

Extent data may also include rewards and recognition that are given to teams. However, in most organizations, not all work can be done by teams, so it is important to have a mix of recognition and reward data that is based on individual accomplishments and team results. In presenting extent data, make sure that you explain what is being presented on the graphs. I recall one application that had a graph showing the number of "special recognitions" given out each of the last three years. Nowhere in the application did it explain what "special recognitions" were.

More important than extent data is effectiveness data. Many companies hand out a lot of recognition items to employees for quality-related accomplishments. In fact, the Quality and Productivity Management Association had a display at a recent conference in southern California, where about a dozen major corporations presented what they did to reward quality in their organizations. Here's how they reward quality:

- T-shirts
- Plaques/certificates
- Lapel pins
- Hats
- Coffee cups
- Pens
- Paperweights
- Gift certificates

Your extent data might show that you give out huge numbers of rewards such as the items listed above. However, many employees I've talked to in these companies view these rewards as a slap in the face. The sentiment that I hear from many employees follows:

> *"Executives say that quality and customer satisfaction are important, but if I work my butt off for a year and improve levels of customer satisfaction, I get a $10 T-shirt and a 25¢ certificate without a frame. What's really important here is financial results. If an executive meets financial targets, he or she may receive a bonus of $50,000 to $150,000."*

Situations like this are one of the reasons the 1993 Baldrige criteria ask for data on the effectiveness of your attempts to tie in quality and customer satisfaction with compensation and reward systems. There is a lot of rewarding of quality going on in American companies, but most of it is ineffective. In this section you need to present data that shows that your reward and recognition efforts actually cause changes in key measures of quality and operational performance. The examiners will first assess the validity of the measures of effectiveness depicted on your graphs. Assuming that you have selected valid and objective indices, they will then assess the levels and trends in your data. As with any graph, they want to see enough data points to establish a trend, and want to see clear cause-and-effect relationships demonstrated between activities and results.

Indicators For Area 4.4c

- Number of different indicators of the extent of employee reward and recognition for which data are presented

- Number of different indicators of the effectiveness of employee reward and recognition for which data are presented

- Validity and objectivity of indices as measures of extent and effectiveness

- Extent to which data on employee reward and recognition represent all categories and functions of employees in all company locations

- Trends in data show steady increases in the amount of reward and recognition tied to achievement of quality and operational performance goals

- Overall levels of performance in extent of recognition and reward based on quality and operational performance approach benchmark levels for size and type of company

- Extent to which all levels and categories of employees have received increased reward and recognition for quality and operational performance achievements

- Trends showing compensation being based upon quality/customer satisfaction, operational results, and financial results, rather than almost exclusively on financial results and seniority

- Trends showing proportional mix of rewards and recognition given out to both teams and individual employees

- Trend showing increased percentage of employees whose compensation is tied to quality and operational performance results

- Trend showing increases in percentage of total compensation that is at risk for all levels and categories of employees

- Graphs display positive trends over the last few years in demonstrating the impact of reward and recognition on measures of quality and customer satisfaction

- Graphs display positive trends over the last few years when illustrating the impact of reward and recognition on measures of operational performance

- Degree to which a cause-and-effect relationship is demonstrated between introduction of rewards and recognition, and changes in measures of quality and operational performance

- Degree to which measures of the effectiveness of reward and recognition show sustained high levels of performance, or continuous improvement over several years

- Overall levels of performance on effectiveness graphs are approaching benchmark status, given the size and type of company

---

4.5 EMPLOYEE WELL-BEING AND SATISFACTION

Describe how the company maintains a work environment conducive to the well-being and growth of all employees; summarize trends in key indicators of well-being and satisfaction. (25 points)

AREA TO ADDRESS   **[APPROACH, DEPLOYMENT]**

4.5a How employee well-being factors such as health, safety, and ergonomics are included in quality improvement activities. Include principal improvement methods, measures or indicators, and targets for each factor relevant and important to the company's employee work environment. For accidents and work-related health problems, describe how root causes are determined and how adverse conditions are prevented.

What They're Looking For Here

It's not enough that a company follows the correct processes and achieves exemplary levels of product/service quality and customer satisfaction. The Baldrige officials feel that the company should also be seen as a good place to work by its employees. The case of a west coast department store chain known for service quality demonstrates that it is possible to achieve impressive levels of service quality while still (allegedly) exploiting employees. The store's approach to quality backfired over the long run, and they are faced with numerous lawsuits and a great deal of negative publicity about how they treat their employees. How a company treats its employees and the resulting level of morale greatly impact upon how employees treat internal and external customers.

The examiners are looking to see that your organization works on projects designed to improve safety, health, ergonomics, and employee morale and job satisfaction with the same degree of effort that you put into other quality improvement projects. Almost all companies, and literally all manufacturing companies, have some type of safety program. Having a good safety program may not earn you any points in this area, but you will certainly lose some if you don't have one. Programs intended to promote employee satisfaction and the use of ergonomics are much more rare and will be of interest to the Baldrige Examiners if the programs are well designed, creative, and properly implemented. The more specific you can get in your explanation of your organization's activities to promote employee satisfaction, health, and safety, the better.

What many organizations will do when they have an accident is to write a presumed cause, such as "employee carelessness," on the accident report and let it go at that. What the Baldrige Examiners are looking for in this Area to Address is that you employ a systematic process to arrive at the root causes of one or a series of any such accidents. This process should be similar to the approach used to diagnose the causes of quality problems. Having a space on your accident report form to list the cause does not qualify as an analysis. The examiners want to know how you investigate the causes of individual accidents and whether accident data are analyzed to identify trends that indicate serious safety hazards needing correction. A flowchart or diagram describing your process for analyzing the causes of accidents would serve as a good response to this section.

Having a proactive approach to the identification and correction of safety problems would also earn you points from the examiners. A good system of analyzing the causes of accidents once they occur is necessary, but a preventive approach is even better. Organizations that conduct detailed safety audits and correct any problems identified often have the beginnings of a preventive system. The scope, frequency, and objectivity of the safety audits have a lot to do with how well this approach works. The success of this approach also depends upon the degree to which the audit findings are acted upon. In addition to describing your process for analyzing the causes of actual and potential safety problems, it is a good idea to provide an example or two to illustrate how you have identified the cause(s) of a real or potential accident and have corrected the situation.

Indicators for Area 4.5a

- Number of quality improvement projects completed during the last few years that deal with issues such as health and safety

- Results of safety audits by internal or external organizations

- Absence of any lawsuits or complaints relating to health and safety issues made by regulatory agencies

- How employees feel about the work environment in terms of its health and safety

- What the company does that extends beyond simply complying with existing regulations regarding safety

- Extent to which approach to safety is preventive vs. a focus on detection of problems and follow-up correction of problem-causing situations

- Efforts the organization has employed to make employee work areas pleasant and free of distractions

- Existence of specific improvement goals and strategies for health, safety, and ergonomics

- Efforts the organization has employed to assure that employees are comfortable at work

- Extent to which the company evaluates and improves ergonomics

- Scope and breadth of improvements made in ergonomics

- Programs the company implements to promote the health of employees (e.g., health club, weight loss programs, etc.)

- Existence of a systematic process for analyzing the causes of accidents when they occur

- Thoroughness of cause-analysis process

- Evidence that cause-analysis process is actually followed

- What employees have to say about the degree to which the organization analyzes causes of accidents and acts to correct situations causing problems

- Follow-up evaluations are done on corrective actions relating to safety

- The organization uses a preventive approach to safety, via audits or similar process

- Existence of a process to ensure that audit findings are acted upon and that follow-up occurs, proving that corrective actions have been successful

---

AREA TO ADDRESS   **[APPROACH, DEPLOYMENT]**

4.5b What special services, facilities, activities, and opportunities the company makes available to employees to enhance their work experience and/or to support their overall well-being.

Note:

  (1)   **Special services, facilities, activities and opportunities might include: counseling; recreational or cultural activities; non-work-related education; day care; special leave; safety off the job; flexible work hours; and outplacement.**

What They're Looking For Here

Almost all companies do something in this area. What the examiners are looking for is the breadth and depth of the special services you provide to employees, and the degree to which these services have been tailored to the special needs of the organization's employees. For example, in an organization populated largely by women, child care might be an appropriate and appreciated special service. In a situation in which an organization's surrounding community education system is poor, remedial reading or other similar programs may be needed. If you have done a thorough analysis of your employees and have identified their special needs, and have tailored your employee assistance programs to those needs, you will do well in this area.

Most organizations approach this area either by offering what other companies offer in the way of employee services, or waiting until a problem occurs and then developing a program to deal with the problem (e.g., drugs or alcohol). If, however, you take a proactive/preventive approach to employee assistance, this will be noticed more by the examiners. If you can demonstrate that you offer more than your competitors do in the area of employee services, this too will be of interest to examiners. Your response might consist of a table that lists all employee assistance programs on the left side of the page, and the name of your organization and a few of its competitors along the top. A matrix like the one that follows could then be created to illustrate which employee assistance programs you offer, as compared to your competition.

EMPLOYEE ASSISTANCE PROGRAMS			
	Your Organization	Competitor A	Competitor B
Child Care	X	X	
Home Financing Assistance	X		X
Health Club Membership	X		
Weight Control Program	X		
Stop Smoking Program	X		
Drug/Alcohol Program	X		
Discount Symphony Tickets	X		
Annual Family Picnic	X	X	X
Counseling	X	X	
Outplacement Assistance	X	X	

Indicators For Area 4.5b

- Whether or not a needs analysis has been completed to determine the employee assistance programs that may be needed in the organization

- Number of different employee assistance programs offered

- Breadth/variety of employee assistance and special services offered

- How the organization's employee assistance programs compare to major competitors'

- Employee opinion on the assistance programs offered

AREA TO ADDRESS   **[APPROACH, DEPLOYMENT]**

4.5c How the company determines employee satisfaction. Include a brief description of methods, frequency, and the specific factors for which satisfaction is determined. Describe how these factors relate to employee motivation and productivity. Segment by employee category or type, as appropriate.

Note:

(2)   **Examples of specific factors for which satisfaction might be determined are: safety; employee views of leadership and management; employee development and career opportunities; employee preparation for changes in technology or work organization; work environment; teamwork; recognition; benefits; communications; job security; and compensation.**

What They're Looking For Here

What they are looking for in this Area to Address is that you use a thorough and objective approach to measuring employee satisfaction, and that you do so with reasonable frequency. An annual 10-item morale survey that has been completed by only a portion of employees will not earn you many points in this area. An annual morale survey is a good start, but the Baldrige Examiners will be looking at how thorough and how frequent your survey is, and at the percentage of employees who actually complete it.

Surveys are only one means of measuring employee satisfaction. Other types of data are much better indicators of the level of employee satisfaction in an organization. You should include statistics on:

- Turnover
- Reasons why employees leave the company (obtained via exit interviews or follow-up surveys)
- Absenteeism
- Incidence of stress-related illnesses or disorders
- Requests for lateral transfers

The extent to which your data on employee satisfaction are based upon multiple measures will have a large impact on the score you receive in this area. What your organization does with the data on employee satisfaction is also examined in this area. Many organizations conduct morale surveys that end up being reviewed and thrown away, with the issues never being dealt with. The Baldrige people are looking for evidence that you have a process for reviewing these data and for developing action plans to improve the issues uncovered in the survey. Examples of situations where you uncovered problems relating to employee satisfaction and have corrected them will help make your response more credible.

Indicators For Area 4.5c

- Use of thorough employee morale/satisfaction surveys on a regular basis

- Objectivity of survey methodology and instruments

- Frequency with which employee satisfaction is measured

- Percentage of employees at all levels and in all functions who complete surveys (return rate and sample)

- Use of multiple measures/indices over and above surveys to measure employee satisfaction

- Objectivity of other employee satisfaction data

- Evidence that a systematic process is used to review employee satisfaction data and develop corrective action plans for dealing with problems or situations with which employees are dissatisfied

- Evidence that approach to measuring employee satisfaction is evaluated and continuously improved

- Extent to which safety issues are addressed as part of employee satisfaction measures

---

AREA TO ADDRESS   **[RESULTS]**

4.5d Trends in key measures and/or indicators of well-being and satisfaction. Explain important adverse results, if any. For such adverse results, describe how root causes were determined and corrected, and/or give current status. Compare results on the most significant measures or indicators with appropriately selected companies and/or benchmarks.

Notes:

(3)   **Measures or indicators of well-being and satisfaction (4.5d) include safety, absenteeism, turnover, turnover rate for customer-contact employees, grievances, strikes, worker compensation, and results of satisfaction determinators.**

(4)   **Comparisons (4.5d) might include industry averages, industry leaders, local/regional leaders, and key benchmarks.**

What They're Looking For Here

Note the use of the word "trends" again. This Area to Address, as with the others that call for "trends," should contain multiple graphs depicting your results on the indices noted for the period of the past several years. The typical response for this section is to include a single graph depicting employee morale survey scores for the last three years or so. While this is a good start, the examiners are looking for more than one index. Include graphs depicting at least three or four different indices of employee satisfaction over the last several years. Each of these graphs should show a steady improvement in performance. Further, you should show how your results compare with both your competitors' and with industry leaders'. Without competitor data, the examiners have no way of knowing how impressive your results are. For example, let's say your turnover among customer-contact personnel has gone from 120% per year to 70% per year over the last four years. This piece of data is not very impressive unless you were to show that the industry average is 110% and that your two biggest competitors average around 100% turnover among their customer-contact employees. Now your results in the area of turnover become more significant.

Where there have been adverse trends, you need to explain how the root causes of these problems have been identified and corrected. This would apply even for one-time events such as strikes, negative legal judgments, or charges/penalties assigned by customers or regulatory bodies.

Indicators For Area 4.5d

- Number of different indices of employee satisfaction for which data are collected and presented

- Validity of indices as measures of employee satisfaction

- Amount of historical data presented for each index to depict trends

- Extent to which employees in all locations and functions are represented in the data

- Evidence that employee-satisfaction problems are analyzed to determine their root causes

- Extent to which causes of employee-satisfaction problems are corrected so as not to recur

- Trends that show continuous improvement on all dimensions of employee well-being and satisfaction

- Any adverse trends or anomalies in the data are satisfactorily explained

- How data for employee satisfaction indices compare with major competitors' data and results

- How data on employee satisfaction compares with industry and world leaders outside of industry

- Number of different sources of comparative data presented for each index of employee satisfaction for which the applicant presents data

Chapter 9

Interpreting the Criteria
for Management of
Process Quality

OVERVIEW OF THE MANAGEMENT OF PROCESS QUALITY CATEGORY

Category 5.0 covers Management of Process Quality. This category is worth fourteen percent of the award evaluation, or a possible 140 points. The category addresses how you assure and improve the quality of the products and services you offer to customers through process management strategies. Emphasis should be placed on the word *how*. This category deals with *processes*, not results. Results are assessed in category 6.0, Quality and Operational Results. The Award Criteria define category 5.0 as follows:

> The **Management of Process Quality** category examines the key elements of process management, including design, management of day-to-day production and delivery, improvement of quality and operational performance, and quality assessment. The Category also examines how all work units, including research and development units and suppliers, contribute to overall quality and operational performance requirements. (p. 23).

In this chapter we'll discuss the five Examination Items and the fourteen different Areas to Address that fall within this category. As in previous chapters, each section begins with a double-ruled box containing the Examination Item, the point value, and any applicable Notes*. Areas to Address falling under that Item follow in a single-ruled box. In the upper right corner of each Area to Address box is an indication [brackets] of whether the Area pertains to approach, deployment, or results. All definitions and information appearing within these boxes is taken directly from the Baldrige criteria. Following each Area to Address is an explanation defining what the examiners are looking for in assessing your application. Next, I have supplied a list of indicators or evaluation factors that will assist you in interpreting the criteria in preparing your application.

---

* Item notes that apply to a specific Area to Address are appropriately listed in the box containing that Area.

5.1 DESIGN AND INTRODUCTION OF QUALITY PRODUCTS AND SERVICES

Describe how new and/or modified products and services are designed and introduced and how key production/delivery processes are designed to meet both key product and service quality requirements and company operational performance requirements. **(40 points)**

Notes:

(1) Design and introduction might address modifications and variants of existing products and services and/or new products and services emerging from research and development or other product/service concept development. Design also might address key new/modified facilities to meet operational performance and/or product and service quality requirements.

(2) Applicants' responses should reflect the key requirements for their products and services. Factors that might need to be considered in design include: health; safety; long-term performance; environment; measurement capability; process capability; manufacturability; maintainability; supplier capability; and documentation.

(3) Service and manufacturing businesses should interpret product and service design requirements to include all product- and service-related requirements at all stages of production, delivery, and use.

AREA TO ADDRESS   **[APPROACH, DEPLOYMENT]**

5.1a How products, services, and production/delivery processes are designed.
Describe: (1) how customer requirements are translated into product and
service design requirements; (2) how product and service design requirements,
together with the company's operational performance requirements, are
translated into production/delivery processes, including an appropriate
measurement plan; (3) how all product and service quality requirements are
addressed early in the overall design process by appropriate company units;
and (4) how designs are coordinated and integrated to include all phases of
production and delivery.

Notes:

    (4)   **In 5.1a(2), company operational performance requirements relate to**
        operational efficiency and effectiveness—waste reduction and cycle
        time improvement, for example. A measurement plan should spell out
        what is to be measured, how measurements are to be made, and
        performance levels or standards to ensure that the results of
        measurements will show whether or not production/delivery processes
        are in control.

    (5)   **Results of improvements in design should be reported in 6.1a. Results**
        of improvements in design process quality should be reported in 6.2a.

What They're Looking For Here

The examiners want to see that you employ a systematic approach to gathering
information about customers' requirements and desires, and have a process for translating
this information into product or service characteristics and standards. A well-accepted
technique for doing this is Quality Function Deployment (QFD). The approach is best
explained by Hauser and Clausing (of Harvard and MIT) in the May/June, 1989, issue of
the *Harvard Business Review* (see "The House of Quality," pages 63-73). The process
begins by gathering information on the specific requirements customers have regarding
the components of the products you produce. The example given in the article is about
car doors. Customers make a list of 15 to 20 different characteristics they consider
important in car doors. These characteristics are then prioritized by the customers. The
prioritized list of customer requirements is given to design engineers, who design the new
product or portion of a product (e.g., car door) based upon the list of requirements.

A similar process for defining customer requirements in the design of services is described by me in the May, 1990, issue of the *Journal For Quality and Participation.* The process is similar, except that the customer requirements lead to service characteristics and standards instead of engineering characteristics and product design specifications. It is not necessary that you use either of these approaches, but you should use something similar. Your approach should demonstrate that you collect a great deal of data on customer requirements for various aspects of the products and/or services you offer and that you use that information extensively to guide the design of new or enhanced products/services.

Some applicants respond to this section by explaining that they have a systematic process for defining customers' requirements and using this information to design new products and services, but they don't explain the process. One applicant who received a very high score on this area provided a graphic representation of the phases and steps in its process and described each step in detail. Examples were provided to illustrate the process. Make sure, however, not to use an example as your actual response. Examples should be used only to clarify and illustrate processes.

A frequent problem in large organizations is that individuals and functions that should provide input to product/service designs don't have a chance to do so until it is too late. Each individual or function that will be involved in producing, delivering, or servicing the product/service needs to be able to provide input early in the design process. Don't respond simply by saying that this involvement occurs. Explain how you ensure that everyone's input is gathered and considered. Systems, procedures, and the meeting(s) you have in place to encourage this should be described.

Once you have obtained everyone's input, you also need to ensure that they are involved at key points in the design and introduction cycle. Requiring consensus meetings or sign-offs may be a way of ensuring this. It may be appropriate to present a diagram that shows the major phases in the product/service design cycle, and which functions have responsibility for which phases. For example, engineering may have heavy involvement in the first few phases and lesser degrees of involvement as you're getting ready to introduce the product/service.

If you list the critical process characteristics or measures to be controlled and the methods for controlling each process for your major products and/or services, you will demonstrate to the examiners that you have good control plans.

Indicators For Area 5.1a

- Thoroughness with which data on customer requirements is gathered

- Designs are coordinated and integrated to include all phases of production and delivery

- Use of multiple methodologies and sources of data on customer requirements

- Evidence that company is close to the customer

- Extent to which customer requirements are identified for parts of products/services as well as the products/services as a whole

- Use of sound statistical methods to collect and analyze market research data

- Prioritization of customer requirements is done using large samples of customers

- Evidence that customer requirements have been translated into engineering specifications and characteristics during the design phase of the new product development cycle

- Evidence that customer requirements have been translated into service characteristics and standards during the design phase of the new service development cycle

- Evidence that all appropriate personnel and functions are involved in early stages of the design process—when their input has the most value

- Objectivity and validity of process for using customer requirements as inputs for the product/service design process

- Use of systematic methodology such as Quality Function Deployment to translate customer requirements into product/service characteristics

- Quantity of evidence to suggest that existing products and/or services have been designed based upon customer requirements

---

AREA TO ADDRESS   **[APPROACH, DEPLOYMENT]**

5.1b How product, service, and production/delivery process designs are reviewed and validated, taking into account key factors: (1) overall product and service performance; (2) process capability and future requirements; and (3) supplier capability and future requirements.

What They're Looking For Here

This section of your application should describe the overall process you use to design and test new products and services. You should include a graphic that shows the phases and steps in your product/service development cycle. Most applicants that are manufacturing companies do a pretty good job on this section of their applications. Most organizations have a process defined for developing new products and services. Simply having a systematic product/service development process won't earn you many points by itself. What the examiners are looking for in this Area to Address is the extent to which quality is built into the development process. Moreover, they are looking for evidence of a preventive approach to quality, rather than a production spot-check and correction cycle.

One important criterion for the design phase of a new product or service is that all the important functions that will be involved with the product/service participate in the design process. A major problem in many large companies is the number of changes made to designs, drawings, and specifications due to input from manufacturing, field service, marketing, legal, etc. Every department responsible for some detail of the product or service will offer its input. The problem is that the input is usually too late, causing numerous revisions to the product/service designs. A preventive approach involves getting representatives from each of these functions involved early in the design phase of the product/service and obtaining their input at key points, before all the drawings are done and the specifications finalized.

Another aspect of your development process examined in this area is the number and thoroughness of tests you perform on the product/service. Explain the types of tests you conduct, when they are conducted, and what the test is used to determine. Remember that the Baldrige Examiners may not understand your business or technology well, so make sure you avoid industry jargon and technical terms, if at all possible.

In reviewing your process for designing new products or services, the Baldrige Examiners will be looking for evidence that key factors such as product and service performance, and process and supplier capabilities, are taken into consideration. Capabilities need to be considered in reviewing the feasibility of product and service designs. Involving suppliers in the design review process is critical when outside parts, materials, and/or services are required in order to meet key product/service requirements.

Indicators For Area 5.1b

- Novel ways of improving product design and introduction

- Systematic process for designing new products and/or services

- Suppliers are involved in reviewing product/service designs

- Evidence of a participative approach to the design phase of a new product/service, involving all of the functions/departments that will work with the product/service

- Reviews take into account product/service performance data

- Use of a preventive approach to assuring quality in the design of new products/services

- Reviews involve an assessment of process capabilities when appropriate

- Thorough testing of new products and/or services before they are introduced

- Use of techniques such as Alpha Tests, Beta Tests, and controlled market introductions, if appropriate

- Objectivity and reliability of methods used for testing new products/services

- Number and frequency of changes that occur in product/service designs (changes should be minimized)

- Thoroughness of design reviews

- Continued deployment of the voice of the customer through QFD or similar process

---

AREA TO ADDRESS   **[APPROACH, DEPLOYMENT]**
5.1c How designs and design processes are evaluated and improved so that new product and service introductions and product and service modifications progressively improve in quality and cycle time.

What They're Looking For Here

This Area to Address is more relevant to products than to services. Design of new products often gets bogged down and products end up taking much longer to be released than originally planned. In this area, the examiners are looking for a description of the process or approach you use to evaluate the design process and reduce the amount of time it takes to design, test, and introduce new products and/or services. This is not what is sought in Areas 5.1a and 5.1b. In those areas the examiners want to make sure that your new product/service design process is systematic and thorough. Systematic and thorough is sometimes equated with time-consuming and inefficient, however. Your response to this area should stress the timeliness and efficiency of your process. In addition, you should explain some of the steps you have taken in recent years to minimize product/service design time. Results included here would be helpful in supporting your claims. Cite statistics on the average time required from design to the introduction of new products/services this year in comparison with past years, and you will have a stronger case.

You should also provide evidence that you systematically evaluate your design process. Describe the evaluation procedures, methodologies, and instruments. If you can explain how the process has been improved over the last few years this will be considered a positive sign.

Indicators For Area 5.1c

- Evidence of a systematic plan for evaluating the product/service design process that includes customer feedback on product/service quality

- Evidence of a systematic plan for reducing product/service design time

- Specific actions that have been taken to reduce product/service design time

- Validity and thoroughness of evaluation process

- Data to demonstrate that plans/steps that have been implemented actually have reduced the time it takes to design new products/services

- Number and significance of improvements that have been made in the product/service design process over the last few years

5.2 PROCESS MANAGEMENT: PRODUCT AND SERVICE PRODUCTION AND DELIVERY PROCESSES

Describe how the company's key product and service production/delivery processes are managed to ensure that design requirements are met and that both quality and operational performance are continuously improved.
(35 points)

Note:

(1)   Manufacturing and service companies with specialized measurement requirements should describe how they assure measurement quality. For physical, chemical, and engineering measurements, describe briefly how measurements are made traceable to national standards.

AREA TO ADDRESS   [APPROACH, DEPLOYMENT]
5.2a How the company maintains the quality and operational performance of the production/delivery processes described in Item 5.1. Describe: (1) the key processes, their requirements, and how quality and operational performance are tracked and maintained. Include types and frequencies of in-process and end-of-process measurements used; (2) for significant (out-of-control) variations in processes or outputs, how root causes are determined; and (3) how corrections of variation [from 5.2a (2)] are made, verified, and integrated into process management.

Note:

(2)   Variations [5.2a(2)] might be observed by those working in the process or by customers of the process output. The latter situation might result in formal or informal feedback or complaints. Also, a company might use observers or "mystery shoppers" to provide information on process performance.

What They're Looking For Here

The key to producing quality products and services is to control the processes used to produce and deliver those products and services. To do this, first identify all of the processes involved in the production and delivery of goods and services. For clarity, present this information in a matrix listing the products or services you offer along the left side of the chart, and the processes horizontally along the top of the chart. Indicate the processes involved with each product/service by checking the intersection of the two elements.

Along with listing your key processes on a matrix with your various products/services, you need to define what the requirements are for each process, and what the measures are for each one. All of this information can appear in the matrix chart that was described earlier. The headings on such a matrix might be as follows:

Products/Services	Key Processes	Measures	Requirements

Another word for "requirements" as it is used here is standards. Consider an example. In the hotel business, one service they offer is room service breakfast. A key process is the delivery of guest breakfasts. One important measure is the cycle time between the point at which the order leaves the kitchen and the guest signs the check. The requirement or standard for this process might be 7 minutes or less. Make sure when you define the measures and requirements that you use terminology that will be understandable to the Baldrige Examiners, who may have no background in your industry. As in the rest of the application, avoid jargon and acronyms.

Once you have indicated the processes involved with each product/service, and those responsible for each process, describe how you control the various processes. Obviously there isn't room to discuss each process separately, so provide a general description of how all processes are controlled. A good way of doing this is to use a flowchart or similar graphic accompanied by an explanation. The examiners will be judging your response according to how thorough your control procedures are. The degree to which process control is automated will also be a factor in the evaluation. Automation of process control is obviously easier in some industries than others, so this will be taken into account in the assessment. Most manufacturing businesses have more process automation equipment available to them than do service businesses. However, technology is improving the ability of service companies to control their processes. For example, bar coding has enabled retailers to better track their buying so that they can practically eliminate out-of-stock items.

Your response to this item should explain the various methods you employ to ensure that your product and/or services meet the standards outlined in the design specifications. These approaches might include in-process inspection of components, products, or services as they are delivered, as well as an inspection of the final products or accomplishments. An accomplishment produced by a service might be a repaired car, a served meal, or a completed set of architectural drawings. The examiners will also assess the degree to which your approach is prevention-based. In other words, do you have systems in place for preventing the occurrence of defects, or are your systems focused on the detection and correction of defects?

Some processes, particularly those related to service delivery, are better handled by humans than controlled through automation. In this case, you need to describe your methods for controlling the behaviors of the employees delivering the service. Training them does not qualify as a control process. A control process involves specifying desired performance, tracking performance against standards, providing feedback to employees involved in the process, and setting up positive and negative consequences to encourage meeting or exceeding standards.

Many applicants believe that they must use a specific cause-analysis process such as Ishikawa/fishbone diagramming in order to receive a high score for this Area to Address. This is not true. Remember, the Baldrige criteria are designed to be non-prescriptive. The examiners want to see that you employ a systematic method for analyzing the causes of process upsets. I once worked on a project for Toyota's plant in Georgetown, Kentucky, where we were teaching the American employees to solve problems Japanese-style. When I asked the Japanese managers how their style was different from ours, they said that most of the time Americans do not do any analysis. They go from problem to solution. If one solution doesn't work, they try a different one.

If you use this type of problem-solving technique, you will earn a low score in this section. The Baldrige Examiners want to see that you *thoroughly* and *completely* analyze the root causes of process upsets and other types of quality problems before implementing a solution or countermeasure. The approach you use should be based upon a major model, but it can be customized to fit your own needs. For example, some organizations use the comparative approach to cause analysis as taught by the consulting firm of Kepner-Tregoe. Others use the Ishikawa diagram as the base for their approach. These and other proven models are all appropriate.

A good way of explaining your cause-analysis process is to depict it in graphic format or as a list of steps. Next, explain how, where, when, and by whom the process is used. For example, is this process used in quality improvement team meetings as well as departmental staff meetings? The examiners will be looking for evidence of widespread use of the cause-analysis process. Many organizations have good cause-analysis processes, but fail to use them in all of the situations/functions in which they could be used. You might want to give an example of a situation in which a process upset or deviation has been analyzed using this cause-analysis approach. Explain how you arrived at the root cause, and what actions were implemented to solve the problem.

Within this Area to Address you also need to explain how process deviations are corrected and the corrections verified. Once single or multiple causes have been identified, there are usually several different alternatives for countermeasures. Your response to this area should explain how you decide on the most appropriate countermeasure, how you implement it, and how you verify that the change produced the desired result. As in most other areas, the examiners are looking for evidence of a systematic process.

This area should address your follow-up after the implementation of countermeasures designed to improve quality. Many organizations do not do follow-up. For example, a large bank conducted an experiment that showed that if clerks in the operations area were put on incentive pay, their productivity and quality would improve. Upon implementation of the pay system, they found that the incentive pay worked well only for about three months. After that time, productivity stayed up but quality began to deteriorate. If the bank had not conducted a thorough follow-up evaluation, it might have left the incentive system intact for quite some time before realizing that it was no longer producing the desired results.

One important criterion regarding your follow-up approach is the scope of your follow-up activities. Do you conduct follow-up of *all* changes implemented to improve quality, or only the major ones that impact the whole organization? Do you conduct follow-up assessments in the support organizations as well as in the line organization? Another important criterion is the objectivity of the approach and instruments you use to conduct follow-up evaluations. Conducting a survey of employees' bosses six months after the employees have been through quality training is a poor way of evaluating the impact of training, for example. It's analogous to "the emperor's new clothes." People expect to see a change after the training, so that's how they respond to the survey. Surveys should never be used when it is possible to obtain "hard" data on quality measures.

The duration of your follow-up is also considered important. Some side-effects don't appear immediately. If your evaluation occurs only a couple of months following implementation of a countermeasure, you won't know what happens after six months or a year. The effectiveness of countermeasures may deteriorate significantly after the first few months.

Indicators For Area 5.2a

- Clear identification of all important processes relating to the production and delivery of products and/or services

- Use of statistical process control where appropriate

- Relationships identified between individual products/services and processes

- Approach to process control is preventive in nature

- Process owners and/or accountabilities identified, if appropriate

- Degree to which process control is automated where appropriate and possible

- Frequency of measurement of key process variables

- Thoroughness of control mechanisms used to ensure that processes stay within specified tolerances or guidelines

- Control mechanisms for ensuring that processes based upon employee behavior are systematic and thorough

- Adequate sample sizes used to collect data on end-of-process measures

- Adequacy of in-process quality inspection

- Use of valid statistical procedures for analyzing process data

- Number of different process measures for which data are collected

- Use of established and acceptable model for cause analysis

- Use of different processes for analyzing common-cause and special-cause problems

- Thoroughness and rigor of cause-analysis process

- Examples or evidence to suggest that analysis process is successful for discerning the root causes of process upsets and other quality-related problems

- Appropriateness of cause-analysis process for type of industry and organization

- Percentage of employees who have been effectively trained to use cause-analysis process

- Evidence to suggest that cause-analysis process is used in all appropriate situations in the organizations

- Existence of a systematic process for evaluating corrective measures that may be used to improve performance

- Procedures exist and are used to verify that corrective measures/actions produce desired results

- Follow-up evaluation done in all departments/functions

- Length of time follow-up data are collected

- Follow-up evaluation done with all countermeasures/changes that are designed to improve quality

- Objectivity of methods and instruments to gather follow-up evaluation data

---

AREA TO ADDRESS   **[APPROACH, DEPLOYMENT]**

5.2b How processes are improved to achieve better quality, cycle time, and operational performance. Describe how each of the following is used or considered: (1) process analysis/simplification; (2) benchmarking information; (3) process research and testing; (4) use of alternative technology; (5) information from customers of the processes—within and outside the company; and (6) stretch targets.

Note:

(3)   Results of improvements in product and service production and delivery processes should be reported in 6.2a.

What They're Looking For Here

This section should include an explanation of how you analyze and improve the key processes in your organization. The foundation of any process improvement effort is to begin by documenting current processes. This is often more difficult than it would seem. Getting a group of employees to all agree on how a process is performed is sometimes a time-consuming activity. The most common approach to this effort is to create process models or systems diagrams that depict inputs, outputs, and key process steps. An example of a macro process model is shown in Figure 9.1.

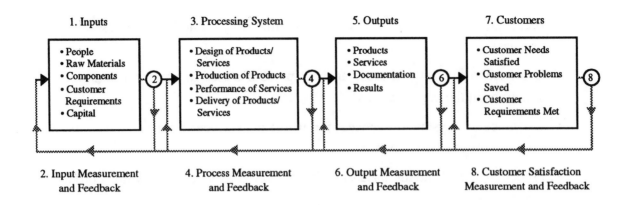

Figure 9.1: Macro Process Model of an Organization

Modeling all processes in an organization is a great way to identify opportunities for improvement. Many processes have never been documented. The act of documenting a process forces employees to question whether all of the steps are really necessary and to see ways in which the processes may be streamlined. Many large and small companies are currently working on modeling all of their processes, which number in the thousands, and are finding that it is a great deal of work. The activity, however, has already produced numerous improvements.

Evaluation of new or updated technology is another way to identify opportunities for improvement. Acquiring new technology may give you the ability to significantly reduce customer processing time in a service business, for example. The clerks at Hertz Rental Car now use hand-held terminals to record your mileage and gas and print out a receipt on the spot. This technology allowed Hertz to greatly reduce the amount of time the customer spends returning a rental car.

Opportunities for continuous improvement are also identified by reviewing competitive and benchmark data. A competitor or company you have benchmarked yourself against may exhibit performance superior to yours on a particular measure. Their level of performance should then become the goal for your company to achieve or surpass.

Your approach to continuous improvement should be well rounded. In other words, do not base all your opportunities for continuous improvement around what the competition is doing. You will never rise to the top using such an approach because you will be too busy playing catch-up. Include data from a variety of sources in your approach, and make your approach proactive as well as reactive. Employees from all levels and functions within the organization should be involved in the continuous improvement process.

Your response for this Area to Address should also explain how you evaluate various process improvement alternatives to decide on the best approach. The Baldrige Examiners are looking for evidence of a systematic approach to deciding on the best way to improve processes. A typical response to this area is to explain that, "We use a participative group process to brainstorm possible process improvements and decide upon the most appropriate approach." This may sound good, but the examiners want more information.

As with many of the Areas to Address relating to quality assurance processes, a good way to respond here is to include a flowchart or similar graphic that depicts the steps in your decision-making process. Describe who uses the process and how and when it is used. If every employee has been trained in the process, state this in your response. Your approach should have certain characteristics. First, it should be participative; the process should allow for input from several employees who have knowledge of any problems. Second, it should involve brainstorming or a similar approach for generating alternative actions. Finally, it should include a process for evaluating alternative actions or countermeasures against specific criteria and constraints found in the work environment. For example, a particular action may be very effective, but if there is not enough time to implement it, or if it costs too much money, it is not a good choice.

This area to address asks for information on a variety of stimuli, which may be used to initiate process improvement. The first segment (1) asks about how simply analyzing a process can serve as a stimulus for improving it. Sometimes all it takes is to draw a flowchart of a process to realize how inefficient it is, and to spot key steps that can be eliminated. Benchmarking, which is asked about in 5.2c (2), often stimulates process improvement since one sees how another company performs the same or a similar process. It may be that you never considered it possible to perform a process the way the benchmarked company does. Process improvements are also sometimes generated based upon research.

Research findings (3) may reveal a new way of performing particular tasks, or of manufacturing a component that was not technically possible before. Similarly, alternative technology (4) may allow you to make improvements in a process. The hand-held computers that I described earlier in the Hertz example are a great illustration of how a new technology was used to greatly improve and simplify the process of returning a car and obtaining a receipt.

Sometimes internal and external customers (5) provide inputs that lead to process improvements. Customers can sometimes see a lack of logic in processes, or opportunities for improvement that those performing the processes can't discern. I recently was a passenger on a foreign airline and was amazed at the approach it used to count the number of passengers on the plane. There were no assigned seats, so everyone rushed into the plane at once, fighting for the best seats. Even when everyone had found a seat, we realized that there was still almost an hour before take-off time. It was a big plane, holding at least a couple of hundred people. In looking around, the plane appeared almost completely full—there were only about 6–8 empty seats in the entire plane. While we waited, a flight attendant walked slowly down the aisle with a hand counter, counting the passengers on the left side of the airplane. Once she got to the back, she walked back toward the front, clicking off the number of passengers on the right side of the plane. The entire process took about ten minutes because she was being very careful. The man next to me was extremely annoyed at the apparent lack of sense to this procedure. He said, "They know how many seats are in this plane. Why don't they just count the number of empty seats—wouldn't that be a lot easier?" While we were all laughing about this silly procedure, another flight attendant started down the aisle, with a hand counter. The man next to me stopped the attendant and said, "What are you doing? Someone already counted the passengers. Why don't you just count the number of empty seats? The plane is almost full." You can just guess the answer: "Our procedure is that we need to do a count of all passengers twice to ensure accuracy. We would not be following the procedure if we did it any other way." With this, he proceeded to walk through the entire plane again, repeating the counting procedure that was performed by the other flight attendant ten minutes before. You may think this is a funny story that would never happen in another airline, or certainly not in your company. But every company I've ever seen has some processes like this one—processes that may have made sense at one time but are laughable under changed circumstances. Listen to your internal and external customers when they ask: "Why do you have to do it this way?"

Using challenge goals (6) is another way of stimulating process improvement. Once a process has been mapped and data are collected on current levels of performance for key process variables, a stretch goal is set to force people to do the process differently. I recently heard the chief financial officer of Motorola talk about how they do this in his function. A process that had always caused them a great deal of grief and overtime was completing the month-end close of the books. Everyone in the department ended up working late at the end of every month, and the antacids flowed freely because of the high stress. After mapping and measuring this process, the CFO set a stretch goal for the process improvement team. They had to figure out how to do the month-end close in half the usual time (labor hours) and without any overtime. They were told that they could change anything they wanted, as long as they didn't violate any regulations or generally accepted accounting practices. Big surprise—they did what they all thought was impossible at first. They did a major overhaul of the process, cutting out many unnecessary steps. Closing the books at the end of the month is no longer a nightmare for those who work in the finance department of Motorola. This is the type of example the examiners want to see in your use of stretch or challenge goals to stimulate process improvements.

Indicators For Area 5.2b

- Use of process modeling as a means for identifying opportunities for improvement in processes and resulting products/services

- Objectivity and methodological rigor of process modeling approach

- Scope of process modeling to include all functions in the organization

- Use of field data, when appropriate, as a way of identifying opportunities for continuous improvement

- Systematic analysis of new and changing technology as a means for identifying quality improvement opportunities

- Number of different stimuli used as impetus for continuous improvement efforts

- Use of competitor or benchmark data as stimuli for identifying opportunities for quality improvement

- Scope of continuous improvement efforts includes all departments/functions and all levels of employees

- Existence of a systematic process for making decisions regarding countermeasures designed to correct quality-related problems or process upsets

- Approach to deciding on process improvement strategy is participative and adaptable for use with groups, as well as with individuals

- Approach to process improvement is based upon one or more established models for systematic decision-making

- Use of brainstorming or similar technique to generate a variety of alternative actions to consider for improving processes

- Evidence that process analysis is used as a stimulus for process improvement

- Breadth and scope of process improvements initiated via process analysis

- Evidence that benchmarking is used as a stimulus for process improvement

- Breadth and scope of process improvements initiated from benchmarking studies

- Evidence that process research and discovery of alternative technologies have led to process improvements

- Breadth and scope of process improvements that have been initiated based upon research, testing, or the use/discovery of alternative technologies

- Evidence that inputs from internal and external customers has led to changes and improvements in processes

- Breadth and scope of changes and improvements to processes that have been initiated based upon internal or external customer inputs

- Evidence that stretch goals or challenge goals have been used to initiate process improvements

- Breadth and scope of process improvements that have been initiated based upon the setting of challenge goals

---

5.3 PROCESS MANAGEMENT: BUSINESS AND SUPPORT SERVICE PROCESSES

Describe how the company's key business and support service processes are designed and managed so that current requirements are met and that quality and operational performance are continuously improved. (30 points)

Notes:

(1) Business and support service processes might include units and operations involving finance and accounting, software services, sales, marketing, public relations, information services, purchasing, personnel, legal services, plant and facilities management, basic research and development, and secretarial and other administrative services.

(2) The purpose of Item 5.3 is to permit applicants to highlight separately the improvement activities for functions that support the product and service design, production, and delivery processes addressed in Items 5.1 and 5.2. The support services and business processes included in Item 5.3 depend on the applicant's type of business and other factors. Thus, this selection should be made by the applicant. Together, Items 5.1, 5.2, 5.3, and 5.4 should cover all operations, processes, and activities of all work units.

AREA TO ADDRESS   **[APPROACH, DEPLOYMENT]**

5.3a How key business and support service processes are designed. Include: (1) how key quality and operational performance requirements for business and support services are determined or set; (2) how the quality and operational performance requirements [from 5.3a (1)] are translated into delivery processes, including an appropriate measurement plan.

What They're Looking For Here

This area to address is similar to Examination Item 5.1, which asks how you design new products and services. This area to address asks how you design products and services that are produced by the support functions in your organization. For example, product literature, accounting reports, and training programs are all products that are produced by support departments in companies. Support functions also frequently introduce new services, or change/improve existing services. The procurement function, for example, might introduce a new simplified process for issuing a purchase order.

What the Baldrige Examiners are looking for in this section is that support functions do a thorough job of identifying the requirements of their internal customers. These customer requirements are then used as the driver to revise existing services/products, or design new ones. Your response for this area to address can be very revealing because usually only the companies that are far along on their quality journey design support services based on internal customer requirements.

The first part of this area to address [5.3a(1)] asks how support functions identify the most important requirements for the products and services they provide. Your response should explain that this process begins by having each support function identify all of their internal and/or customers. Once customers have been identified, explain how requirements are determined for each major product and service area for the support function. It is no expected that your approach will be as formal or systematic as the one you will describe in section 7.1a, but you need at least to define an informal process for determining customer requirements in support areas. Internal customers often want things from support departments that are unreasonable or not possible given resource constraints. For example, an HR function might find out that most managers and supervisors in the company want to get rid of the performance appraisal system—they think it adds no value to the company and takes up valuable time. Does this mean that HR should eliminate the performance appraisal system? Or, to take another example, internal customers might tell the legal department that they want a 48-hour turn around on documents sent to them for review. Should the legal department automatically figure out a way to meet the 48-hour customer requirement? The answer is *not necessarily* in both cases. You need to explain how you take customer requirements and translate these into reasonable and achievable requirements.

The second half of this area to address [5.3a(2)] asks how you take the requirements you defined in 5.3a(1) and turn them into actual services or products. Your response might include a flowchart or similar graphic that outlines the major steps in this design process. To lend credibility to this process description, you might provide a couple of examples of how this was done in several support areas. The example should explain how customer requirements were determined and how these requirements were met by the design of the new product/service. This area to address also asks how you develop measures to evaluate the extent to which customer requirements are being met.

Indicators For Area 5.3a

- A systematic process has been defined that support departments use for identifying their customers, and the requirements of those customers

- Evidence that the process for defining customer requirements is used by *all* support functions in the organization rather than only a few

- Information is presented that explains how conflicting customer requirements are resolved

- A systematic process has been defined for taking customer requirements and using them to design new/enhanced products and services in support functions

- Evidence that the process is actually used by all support functions to design new products and/or services

- Evidence that support functions have an approach for measuring the degree to which customer requirements are being met for the products they produce and the services they provide for internal and/or external customers

- Evidence that measurement plans exit that specify data collection methods, frequencies, and reporting methods

- Standards have been set for each measure based on customer requirements

- Measures of product/service quality in support functions are fed back to appropriate personnel who are empowered to make any necessary changes to improve performance.

AREA TO ADDRESS   **[APPROACH, DEPLOYMENT]**

5.3b How the company maintains the quality and operational performance of business and support service delivery processes. Describe: (1) the key processes, their requirements, and how quality and operational performance are tracked and maintained. Include types and frequencies of in-process and end-of-process measurements used; (2) for significant (out-of-control) variations in processes or outputs, how root causes are determined; and (3) how corrections of variation [from 5.3b(2)] are made, verified, and integrated into process management.

Note:

(3) **Variation [5.3b(2)] might be observed by those working in the process or by customers of the process output. The latter situation might result in formal or informal feedback or complaints.**

What They're Looking For Here

Your response for this Area to Address should be a condensed version of your response to Examination Item 5.2. The examiners want to see that you employ the same process for assuring quality in your support departments as you use in the line function of the organization. This is an area in which many organizations receive a very low score. Applying total quality management in support departments is more difficult and the results obtained are harder to quantify. However, more than half of the personnel and operating costs go to support functions in many of the large companies. This means that a quality improvement effort cannot simply concentrate on the line organization. Similar improvements must also be made in the staff functions.

The first thing that the examiners will look for in your response is your approach. You need to have defined quality indices and standards for each support function based upon internal customer requirements. Not many organizations have done this, so yours will get greater credit if it has. You also need to have process and output measures in place, and a way of feeding these data back to the employees who control the performance measures. While it is probably not necessary that you have actual control plans written, it *is* necessary that you have procedures in place for controlling the key quality variables. In short, your approach to quality assurance of support functions will be judged against the same criteria as those appearing in 5.2a–c.

The second aspect that will be evaluated in your response is your deployment. Make sure that your response explains how and in which support departments/functions you have implemented systems and procedures for assuring quality. In order to receive a high score for this section, you should have fully implemented a quality assurance process in all support/staff functions. Don't state simply that you have "fully implemented Total Quality Management in all of our support departments." Discuss each department and explain which aspects of TQM have been implemented. Again, a table or matrix chart listing the support departments vertically along the left side and the features of your quality system horizontally along the top of the chart offers an excellent way to present this information. An example is shown in Figure 9.2.

QUALITY SYSTEM FEATURES					
Support Departments	Definition of Requirements	Process Measurement	Output Measurement	Control Procedures	Problem Solving
Accounting	X				X
Human Resources	X		X	X	X
Engineering		X	X		
Quality	X		X		X
Maintenance	X	X	X	X	X
Sales	X	X	X		
Marketing			X		X
Information Services		X	X	X	X

Figure 9.2: Example of Matrix Chart Showing Deployment of Quality Systems in Support Departments

Obviously, your approach to root cause analysis in support areas should mirror your response to 5.2a. Cause analysis is often done well in the factory, or in the service delivery functions, but forgotten about in the support functions such as finance, HR, facilities, and procurement. Whatever cause analysis model you use in your primary functions or line organization should also be used in staff or support organizations. Many applicants will be tempted to save valuable space in this section by simply making a brief statement indicating that you use the same approach for cause analysis as you described in 5.2a. While this may be true, you need to convince the examiners that you actually use this model to analyze the causes of problems in support functions.

To make your response credible, you should provide a number of examples that illustrate the widespread use of systematic cause analysis in various support functions in your company. Examples take up space, so be brief, explaining the problem, the process used to analyze the cause, the cause, and the solution or corrective action. You might also want to explain what happened after you implemented the solution or corrective action.

Indicators For Area 5.3b

- Procedures and mechanisms are in place to control key variables associated with quality

- In-process as well as output measures are used to assess quality in support departments

- A systematic cause-analysis process is used to diagnose the causes of quality problems and process deviations that occur in support departments

- Various alternatives are generated and evaluated prior to the implementation of countermeasures or changes designed to solve problems or improve performance

- Quality assurance procedures and systems have been implemented in all support departments

- Support departments and employees within these departments are evaluated according to how well they satisfy internal customer requirements

- Use of established and acceptable model for cause analysis

- Degree to which the cause analysis process is systematic and logical

- Evidence that employees in support functions have been trained to use cause analysis process

- Examples or evidence that suggests that cause analysis process is effective for discerning the root causes of support department problems

- Breadth and scope of evidence to support claims that cause analysis is used to analyze problems in all support functions in the company.

AREA TO ADDRESS   **[APPROACH, DEPLOYMENT]**

5.3c How processes are improved to achieve better quality, cycle time, and overall operational performance. Describe how each of the following are used or considered: (1) process analysis/simplification; (2) benchmarking information: (3) process research and testing; (4) use of alternative technology; (5) information from customers of the business processes and support services—within and outside the company; and (6) stretch targets.

Note:

(4)   Results of improvements in business processes and support services should be reported in Item 6.3a.

What They Are Looking For Here

You should begin your response to this Area to Address by listing the major quality improvement goals that have been developed for each of the major support functions in the organization. You might make a chart like the one shown in Figure 9.3 that depicts support functions, goals, and quality indices.

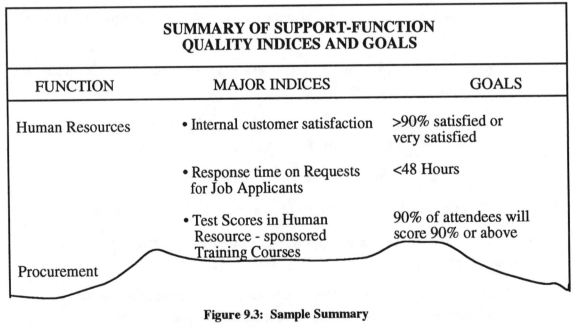

SUMMARY OF SUPPORT-FUNCTION QUALITY INDICES AND GOALS		
FUNCTION	MAJOR INDICES	GOALS
Human Resources	• Internal customer satisfaction	>90% satisfied or very satisfied
	• Response time on Requests for Job Applicants	<48 Hours
	• Test Scores in Human Resource - sponsored Training Courses	90% of attendees will score 90% or above
Procurement		

Figure 9.3: Sample Summary

Chart of Support-Function Quality Indices and Goals

Following your description of measurement indices and goals for each of the major support functions in your organization, you need to explain how processes are examined and improved. Your response should include an examination of performance data, new technologies, and benchmarking as stimuli that lead to process improvement activities. An example or two will help illustrate how this has occurred in your support areas. Your response should also explain how data on internal customer requirements are used to initiate process improvements in support functions. Many organizations' support functions are currently at work to improve their processes, but few are using customer requirements as the stimulus for these improvement actions. Provide some examples to illustrate how internal customer needs and requirements have driven you to make changes or enhancements in support processes, explaining how performance has improved since the changes were made. Finally, explain how and how often progress on quality improvement projects is reviewed in support departments.

Indicators For Area 5.3c

- Identification of quality indices for all support functions

- Validity of indices

- Existence of goals or standards for each of the quality indices in support functions

- Use of a systematic and participative process to define quality indices and set improvement goals

- Approach for ensuring that continuous improvement occurs in all support departments

- Deployment of continuous improvement activities throughout all locations and all support functions

- Defined systematic process for evaluating and improving quality

- Breadth and scope of efforts during last 12 months to improve quality within support departments

- Systematic and planned approach for reviewing progress of quality improvement efforts in support departments

- Frequency of progress reviews

- Use of process modeling/documentation as a means for identifying opportunities for quality improvement in support functions

- Extent to which process models have been created for all support functions

- Use of a proactive and reactive approach to identify opportunities for continuous improvement

- Systematic analysis of new and changing technology as a means of identifying opportunities for improvement in support functions

- Evidence that analysis of business and support processes is used to initiate process improvements

- Breadth and scope of process improvements in support functions initiated via process analysis

- Evidence that benchmarking is used as a stimulus for process improvement in support functions

- Breadth and scope of support process improvements made that were initiated by benchmarking studies

- Evidence that process research, testing, and exploration of alternative technologies have led to improvements in support processes

- Breadth and scope of support process improvements that have been initiated based on input of support function customers—inside and outside of the organization

- Evidence that challenge or "stretch" goals are used to initiate process improvements in support functions

- Breadth and scope of process improvements in support functions that were initiated from the setting of "stretch" or challenge goals

- History and success stories that demonstrate continuous improvement efforts have paid off in various support functions in the organization

- Use of competitor and benchmark data as stimuli for identifying opportunities for quality improvement

- Plans to define internal customer requirements for support functions

- Plans to improve scope or accuracy of quality data collection and feedback systems

- Plans showing increased levels of participation and employee involvement in improving quality in support functions

- Evidence that progress has been made on at least some actions planned to increase the deployment of TQM in support functions

5.4 SUPPLIER QUALITY

Describe how the company assures the quality of materials, components, and services furnished by other businesses. Describe also the company's actions and plans to improve supplier quality. (20 points)

Note:

(1) **The term "supplier" refers to providers of goods and services. The use of these goods and services may occur at any stage in the production, delivery, and use of the company's products and services. Thus, suppliers include businesses such as distributors, dealers, warranty repair services, contractors, and franchises as well as those that provide materials and components.**

(2) **Generally, suppliers are other-company providers of goods and services. However, if the applicant is a subsidiary or division of a company, and other units of that company supply goods/services, this relationship should be described as a supplier relationship.**

AREA TO ADDRESS **[APPROACH, DEPLOYMENT]**

5.4a How the company's quality requirements are defined and communicated to suppliers. Include a brief summary of the principal quality requirements for key suppliers. Also give the measures and/or indicators and expected performance levels for the principal requirements.

What They're Looking For Here

Begin this section with an explanation of your approach to determining quality requirements for goods and services you receive from key suppliers. Many large organizations use hundreds or even thousands of suppliers. If this is true of your company, you may want to identify who your most critical ten to fifty suppliers are, and discuss your efforts with them rather than trying to include all of them. Once you've identified your key or critical suppliers, list the critical quality requirements for perhaps the top ten or so. One way of doing this might be by means of a table or chart. Next, list the critical measures or indicators you use to monitor and evaluate supplier performance.

All of this information could be neatly summarized in a chart like the one shown in Figure 9.4.

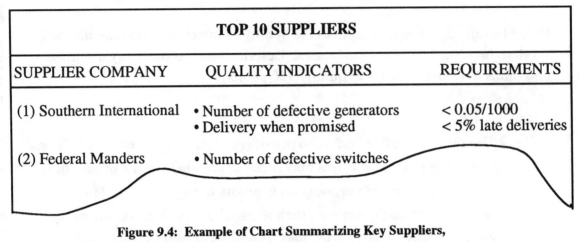

Figure 9.4: Example of Chart Summarizing Key Suppliers, Quality Indicators, and Quality Requirements

Make sure that your response also includes a clear explanation of how you communicate quality indicators and requirements to suppliers. You should also have mechanisms in place to provide regular feedback to key suppliers on how they do in meeting quality requirements. This means that you need to have a thorough approach in place for measuring supplier quality.

Indicators For Area 5.4a

- Identification of critical suppliers, if appropriate

- Extent to which measurable quality indices and requirements/standards have been identified for suppliers

- Percentage of suppliers for which quality indices and requirements/standards have been identified

- Degree to which suppliers are involved in the formulation of indices and standards/requirements

- Existence of an effective system for communicating standards/requirements to suppliers

- Feedback system for keeping key suppliers informed on a regular basis of their performance on key quality indicators

---

AREA TO ADDRESS   **[APPROACH, DEPLOYMENT]**

5.4b How the company determines whether or not its quality requirements are met by suppliers. Describe how performance information is fed back to suppliers.

Note:

  (3)   **Determining how quality requirements are met (5.4b) might include audits, process reviews, receiving inspection, certification, testing and rating systems.**

What They're Looking For Here

It is important that you have a well defined and successful approach for ensuring that your suppliers meet your quality standards. All organizations have suppliers, but in some they play a more important role than in others. For instance, a manufacturing company may buy all of the components for the products it produces from outside suppliers. Hence, supplier performance is critical to the quality of the final products. A service business such as a bank may have relatively few suppliers who perform non-critical services or sell supplies to the bank. The effort your organization puts into ensuring quality from its suppliers should be directly proportional to the degree to which you rely on suppliers for your success.

Begin your response for this area with a general description of the approach you use to assure quality. Explain how you determine your requirements for the goods and services provided by suppliers, and how you communicate these to suppliers. Next, explain how you monitor supplier performance and feed the data back to them so that they may correct existing problems and/or prevent future ones. If you use an audit or periodic assessment, describe how it is conducted, how often it is done, etc.

As in many of the other areas, using a chart or table is a good way to summarize the information. Rather than listing each supply company, you might group them according to the type of products or services you buy from them. Using a matrix, indicate which quality assurance strategies you employ with each group of suppliers. It doesn't matter whether you use certification, testing, audits, or another approach. What matters is that your approach is effective for your organization and suppliers, and is multifaceted. In other words, it should include more than just one strategy/approach.

Indicators For Area 5.4b

- Amount of effort devoted to assurance of supplier quality is appropriately geared to the degree to which organization relies on suppliers

- Use of a multifaceted approach to assure supplier quality

- Organization's requirements have been defined and clearly communicated to suppliers

- Systems exist for measuring supplier performance on a regular basis and for feeding the data back to suppliers to help them improve their performance

- Objectivity and reliability of measures of supplier quality

- Procedures are in place for periodically auditing or assessing supplier processes, products, and services

- Trend of quality-related efforts with suppliers shows continuous improvement over the last several years

---

AREA TO ADDRESS   **[APPROACH, DEPLOYMENT]**
5.4c How the company evaluates and improves its own procurement processes. Include what feedback is sought from suppliers and how it is used in improvement.

What They're Looking For Here

This was a brand-new area to address for 1993, and, in my opinion, a needed one. In the past, this item focused on efforts to improve what outside suppliers do in providing you with high quality goods and services. In this area to address you need to report what you, as the buyer of the goods and services, are doing to improve your own performance in the procurement area. Suppliers always tend to get the blame when things go wrong. Often, it is the buyer who is at fault for failing to communicate requirements to suppliers, or for failing to keep them abreast of changes that will impact their products or services.

In describing how you evaluate your procurement function, the ideal situation would be to get feedback from two sources:

- Internal customers who use procurement to get them the goods and services they need to do their jobs

* External suppliers who must interact with procurement to do business with your company

Procurement functions in many companies seem to forget that their role is to help others in the company obtain the materials and services they need from outside suppliers in a cost-efficient and timely fashion. Procurement people often see themselves as more of a policing function to prevent managers in the company from selecting suppliers that are their friends, or from selecting those suppliers that take them out to lunch and provide them with tickets to sporting events every year. Part of procurement's role is to serve this policing function and to be aware of unethical practices. However, their primary role is to serve the needs of the managers in the organization that need to buy goods and services from outside suppliers. Procurement people also tend to be obsessed with making sure that all the correct forms are filled out and all the appropriate procedures are followed. If you got your parts late because the P.O. didn't go out on time, it was probably your fault because you didn't fill out a few of the lines on the Request for Purchase Order Form.

Not all procurement functions work this way. Northrop Corporation's procurement function is one of the most customer-focused I've dealt with. If the requesting manager doesn't fill out the forms correctly or completely, the buyer or purchasing agent will call him or her and complete it over the phone. The same thing happens if a supplier happens to fill out the forms incorrectly. The manager, who needs the supplies, and the supplier, who sells the supplies, are both coached through the process by the procurement people. This is a perfect example of the type of approach the Baldrige Examiners want to see in your response. Ideally, procurement should seek regular feedback from employees who use their services. In the ideal situation, a number of different methods would be used to seek feedback from internal customers of procurement. Telephone surveys, face-to-face meetings, service pacts or contracts, mail surveys, and other methods might be used to stay in touch with procurement's internal customers' needs. Summarize what you do to obtain feedback from internal customers of procurement in your company. A table or chart like the one shown below might be an efficient way of summarizing this information.

SUMMARY OF CUSTOMER SATISFACTION MEASURES—PROCUREMENT

CUSTOMER GROUP	METHODOLOGY	FREQUENCY	SAMPLE
Senior Executives	Face-to-Face Meetings	Bi-Annually	All
Function Directors	Telephone Survey	Quarterly	50%
2nd & 3rd Level Mgrs.	Mail Survey	Quarterly	20%
2nd & 3rd Level Mgrs.	Focus Group	Bi-Annually	8 Mgrs.

If you choose to use a chart or table like this to summarize how you collect feedback from procurement's internal customers, you need to supplement this with some explanation. Briefly explain why you decided to use the approaches you use, and describe how the satisfaction measures seem to work.

After explaining how you gather internal customer satisfaction data on procurement, you need to explain how you get feedback from suppliers. What is being asked here is not how you rate them, but how they rate you. What kind of a company are you to deal with compared to other companies they sell to? Questions like this can be very revealing. Companies I've worked with often seem to blame the supplier when things go wrong. Being a supplier to big corporations myself, it sometimes seems like the only reason they hire a consultant is to have someone to blame when things go wrong.

Your response for this area to address should explain how you get feedback from your suppliers on how they rate you. Again, you might want to use a chart or table to summarize the various methods you use to obtain feedback. Of course, this will only be appropriate if you use multiple methods. Make sure you explain how many of your total suppliers are contacted, how you decide who gets contacted, and what types of questions get asked. You obviously don't have enough room to include your surveys, but you can describe how many questions are asked and what types of scales are used. In addition to surveys and devices to seek supplier opinions, you may also collect "hard" data on indicators such as the number of suppliers that have refused to deal with your company because of bad experiences, or the average seniority of suppliers. If you've been dealing with the same suppliers for 20 years, both of you must be pretty happy with each other.

Indicators For Area 5.4c

- Number of different sources of data on levels of internal customers' satisfaction with procurement

- Extent to which all users of procurement services are queried as to their satisfaction levels

- Frequency with which internal customer satisfaction is measured

- Reliability and validity of instruments and methods used to gather data on levels of internal customer satisfaction with the procurement function

- Number of different sources of data used to assess suppliers' levels of satisfaction in dealing with your company

- Extent to which all suppliers' feedback is sought

- Use of valid and reliable methods to gather data on supplier satisfaction ratings

- Frequency with which supplier feedback is obtained

- Use of hard data such as loss of key suppliers to supplement opinion data gathered from surveys or interviews

---

AREAS TO ADDRESS   **[APPROACH, DEPLOYMENT]**

5.4d Current actions and plans to improve suppliers' abilities to meet key quality, response time, or other requirements. Include actions and/or plans to minimize inspection, test, audit, or other approaches that might incur unnecessary costs.

Note:

(4)   Actions and plans (5.4d) might include one or more of the following: joint planning, partnerships, training, long-term agreements, incentives, and recognition. They might also include supplier selection. "Other requirements" might include suppliers' price levels. If this is the case, suppliers' abilities might address factors such as productivity and waste reduction.

What They're Looking For Here

The examiners are looking for evidence that you have established solid, cooperative relationships with your suppliers. This can be done in a number of different ways. For example, some organizations develop long-term relationships with suppliers who are able to consistently demonstrate that they meet or exceed quality requirements. Others work together to set goals and develop plans and strategies for reaching the goals.

Your response for this Area to Address should describe all the major efforts you have underway or have planned that will improve your relationship with your suppliers. List those activities and approaches you have employed over the past several years. Discuss joint activities such as training programs and meetings in which employees from your company and from suppliers' organizations have both participated. Describe any incentives or awards you offer to suppliers based upon their quality performance. Some organizations give out awards each year to suppliers who demonstrate exemplary quality.

Another important factor to address in your response to this section are the methods you have employed to improve supplier selection.

Indicators For Area 5.4d

- Evidence that a cooperative relationship exists between applicant's organization and its suppliers

- Joint quality-related activities are performed by applicant's and suppliers' employees (e.g., training, planning meetings, etc.)

- Selection criteria for suppliers indicates that quality is more important than price and other factors

- Evidence to suggest that suppliers are selected based upon quality, and not just price

- Existence of incentives to encourage suppliers to improve their quality

- Awards or recognition programs to reward suppliers for exemplary quality

- Use of long-term partnerships or contracts with suppliers who consistently demonstrate that they can meet or exceed organization's quality standards

- Evidence that inspections of supplier goods have been eliminated or reduced, based on demonstrated good performance

5.5 QUALITY ASSESSMENT

Describe how the company assesses the quality and performance of its systems and processes and the quality of its products and services. (15 points)

Note:

(1) The systems, processes, products, and services addressed in this Item pertain to all company unit activities covered in Items 5.1, 5.2, 5.3, and 5.4. If the assessment approaches differ appreciably for different company processes or units, this should be described in this Item.

AREA TO ADDRESS   **[APPROACH, DEPLOYMENT]**

5.5a How the company assesses: (1) systems and processes; and (2) products and services. For (1) and (2), describe: (a) what is assessed; (b) how often assessments are made and by whom; and (c) how measurement quality and adequacy of documentation of processes are assured.

Note:

(2) Adequacy of documentation should take into account legal, regulatory, and contractual requirements as well as knowledge preservation and knowledge transfer to help support all improvement efforts. Adequacy should take into account completeness, timely update, useability, and other appropriate factors.

What They're Looking For Here

We saw that Examination Item 5.2 addressed the processes you employ to measure and control quality in a more or less "on-line" basis. This Examination Item (5.5) addresses how you periodically *audit or assess* products, services, and the processes used to create them. Theoretically, this item should not be necessary. If you control all of your key processes you shouldn't need to do any periodic audits or inspection. However, the examiners realize that 100% process control is probably not possible—especially when human behavior is a big part of the process. Assuming you need to do periodic audits or inspections, the Examiners want to make sure these are done thoroughly and objectively.

A good way to respond to this Area to Address is to prepare a table or chart summarizing the types of audits or assessments conducted. Suggested headings for such a table are shown in Figure 9.5.

QUALITY AUDITS & ASSESSMENTS				
FUNCTION	TYPE OF AUDIT OR REVIEW	FREQUENCY	METHODOLOGY	AUDITOR

Figure 9.5: Sample Headings for Table Summarizing Quality Audits/Assessments

The first column lists the department or function in which the audit is conducted—for example, purchasing, inventory, production scheduling and control, etc. The second column lists the type of audit or assessment conducted. For example, it might be a safety audit or an inventory of parts. In the third column, indicate how often the audit or assessment is conducted. "Periodically" is not specific enough. Indicate whether the audit is daily, weekly, monthly, annually, or whatever. The fourth column indicates the methodology or approach used to conduct the audit. Use whatever descriptors are most appropriate. For example, you might use one of the following:

- Interviews
- Observations of practices
- Review of data
- Documentation review

Finally, indicate who conducts the audit or assessment. Start by listing those audits or assessments done by customers and outside agencies such as government or regulatory bodies. Then, list the audits done internally, indicating which department or function in your company actually conducts the audit.

A table such as the one described above allows you to summarize information it would take many pages to present in narrative form. In addition to the table, address the objectivity and reliability of the methodologies and instruments used for the audits/assessments. This information is not easily presented in a table. Explain the approaches you use and how you ensure their reliability and validity.

Indicators For Area 5.5a

- Audits/assessments are done on all products and/or services in the organization

- Audits/assessments are done on all major processes involved in the production of services and products

- Audits/assessments are done in support/staff organizations as well as in the line organization

- Reliability and validity of methodologies and instruments used for audits/assessments

- Objectivity of auditors

- Types and frequency of audits/assessments conducted by internal departments/organizations

- Types and frequency of audits/assessments conducted by internal and external customers

- Types and frequency of audits/assessments conducted by government or regulatory agencies/organizations

---

AREAS TO ADDRESS   **[APPROACH, DEPLOYMENT]**
5.5b How assessment findings are used to improve: products and services; systems; processes; supplier requirements; and the assessment processes. Include how the company verifies that assessment findings are acted upon and that the actions are effective.

What They're Looking For Here

Many organizations do a very thorough job of auditing various functions and practices in their organizations. Few do a good job of systematically following up on those audit findings and correcting audit-detected problems. This is an instance where it makes sense to combine your responses to both of these Areas to Address (5.4a and 5.4b). Although they are clearly different, it makes sense to discuss your follow-up procedures along with the success you have had when audits have led to improvements.

Respond to this Area to Address by explaining how information from audits/assessments is disseminated and how plans are created to assign and follow up on audit-driven changes. Once you have described this process, describe how the audits are used as the impetus for changes in policies, procedures, and other areas as part of an effort to continually improve quality. An example or two might substantiate your response.

Your response should also include a discussion of how problems identified in previous audits have been corrected. One applicant presented a graph of the number of problems identified per year in its annual quality audit. The graph showed steady decreases in the problems identified over the last three years. Presenting data such as this will do a great deal to demonstrate to the Baldrige Examiners that you do a thorough job of responding to audit reports and of following up on the problem areas specified in the reports.

Indicators For Area 5.5b

- Thoroughness and readability of reports prepared as a result of audits

- Employee knowledge of findings in audit reports pertaining to their functions/departments

- Evidence that a process exists and is used to assign action items based upon audit/assessment reports

- Results/data to indicate that appropriate corrective actions are taken based upon audit/assessment reports

- Thoroughness of methods for verifying that corrective actions are producing predicted results

- Evidence that further analysis is conducted, or that other corrective actions are implemented when initial ones are not successful

Chapter 10

___

Interpreting the Criteria for Quality
and Operational Results

OVERVIEW OF QUALITY AND OPERATIONAL RESULTS CATEGORY

This sixth category, Quality and Operational Results, is one where organizations are really put to the test. The previous five categories concentrate mainly on processes and activities. A good writer may even make your approach and processes seem like they meet all the criteria in the first five categories, but this section (6.0), and the next one (7.0 Customer Focus and Satisfaction), tell the true tale of the success (or lack thereof) of your quality improvement efforts. In this section, you must provide evidence that all of the processes and programs you employ have really worked to improve quality and overall performance in your organization.

The Baldrige Award Criteria define this category as follows:

> The **Quality and Operational Results** category examines the company's achievement levels and improvement trends in quality, company operational performance, and supplier quality. Also examined are current quality and operational performance levels relative to those of competitors (p. 27).

It is important that you understand the difference between what is being asked for in this section and what is asked for in the section that covers Customer Focus and Satisfaction (7.0). Figure 10.1 depicts a systems diagram of an organization. All organizations have inputs, processes, and outputs. Outputs don't have to be products. In a service business, an output is usually an accomplishment such as a transported passenger, a repaired car, a delivered package, or a meal served. Outputs are received by customers, who then provide information (inputs) on their level of satisfaction with the product or service.

As you can see from Figure 10.1, measurement occurs at four different points:

- Measurement of inputs
- In-process measurement
- Measurement of outputs
- Measurement of customer satisfaction

The quality results asked for in this section of your application pertain to only the *first three* types of measures. Data on customer satisfaction should be discussed in your response to category 7.0.

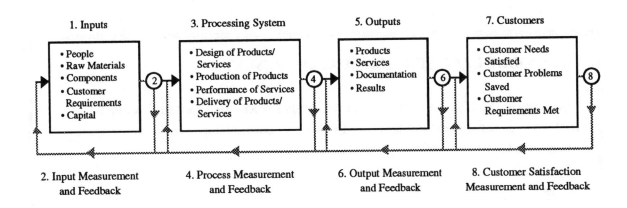

Figure 10.1: Macro Process Model of an Organization

Again we begin with a description of the first Examination Item and Area to Address falling under category 6.0, Quality and Operational Results. Subsequent Examination Items are contained in a double-ruled box together with the point value and any applicable Notes*. Areas to Address falling under that Item follow in a single-ruled box. In the upper right corner of each Area to Address box is an indication [brackets] of whether the Area pertains to approach, deployment, or results. All definitions and information appearing within these boxes is taken directly from the Baldrige criteria. Following each Area to Address is an explanation defining what the examiners are looking for in assessing your application. Next, I have supplied a list of indicators or evaluation factors that will assist you in interpreting the criteria and in preparing your application.

---

* Item notes that apply to a specific Area to Address are appropriately listed in the box containing that Area.

6.1 PRODUCT AND SERVICE QUALITY RESULTS

Summarize trends and current quality levels for key product and service features; compare current levels with those of competitors and/or appropriate benchmarks. (70 points)

Notes:

(1) Key product and service measures are measures relative to the set of all important features of the company's products and services. These measures, taken together, best represent the *most important factors that predict customer satisfaction and quality in customer use*. Examples include measures of accuracy, reliability, timeliness, performance, behavior, delivery, after-sales services, documentation, appearance, and effective complaint management.

(2) Results reported in Item 6.1 should reflect all key product and service features described in the Business Overview and addressed in Items 7.1 and 5.1.

(3) Data reported in Item 6.1 are intended to be objective measures of product and service quality, not the customers' satisfaction or reaction to the products and/or services. Such data may be of several types, including : (a) internal (company) measurements; (b) field performance (when applicable); (c) proactive checks by the company of specific product and service features (7.2d); and (d) data routinely collected by other organizations or on behalf of the company. Data reported in Item 6.1 should provide information on the company's performance relative to the specific product and service features that best *predict* customer satisfaction. These data, collected regularly, are then part of a process for monitoring and improving quality.

AREA TO ADDRESS   **[RESULTS]**

6.1a Trends and current levels for the key measures and/or indicators of product and service quality.

What They're Looking For Here

In this extremely important area, the examiners are looking for a summary of your major quality results over the past several years. In general, the more data you have, the better. If you have ten years' worth of historical quality data, this is good. If you don't have such data, present the data you do have. You should, however, have at least three years' worth of data. An important consideration in evaluating your response to this area is the completeness of your data. In a sample application used to train Baldrige Examiners, a bank claims to collect data for 160 different indices of quality. Yet in this section, it presents data for only three or four indices. This might lead the examiners to think that it selected only those indices that put its performance in a good light, while deliberately ignoring the other 150+ measures that may have indicated declining quality.

While there is not space to include 160 graphs in this section, it is important to provide a summary of data for all major quality indices. A good way of doing this would be to include graphs of data for four to six major measures of quality, and then summarize the remaining statistics in a table such as the one that follows.

SUMMARY OF QUALITY DATA ABC ACCOUNTING, INC., 1989-1993					
Index	1989	1990	1991	1992	1993
% Repeat Business	18%	23%	28%	36%	44%
# of Report Drafts	3.8	3.3	2.5	2.3	1.6
% of Re-Write Time	28%	29%	22%	18%	14%
Number of Points/Audit	127	116	88	72	57
Number of Errors per Page	3.4	3.0	2.5	0.96	0.62

Obviously, you would present more data for more indices than the five included in this example. By using such a table, though, you can include a great deal of information in a limited amount of space. You might even add a "Percent Improvement" column at the far right that lists the improvement percentage over the time period measured (e.g., 26% improvement in repeat business between 1989 and 1993). Using this format, you could present data for 20-30 different indices on a single page of your application.

Graphs and graphics can be used to illustrate information, but be careful how they are drawn. In attempts to save space, some applicants have included four or five different data lines in a single line graph. This makes the graphs confusing and very difficult to read. Never include more than two lines of data on a single graph. Another good rule to follow is to always include a goal or standard line on a graph, like the one shown in Figure 8.2 below. Without a goal or standard on the graph, it is very difficult to evaluate performance.

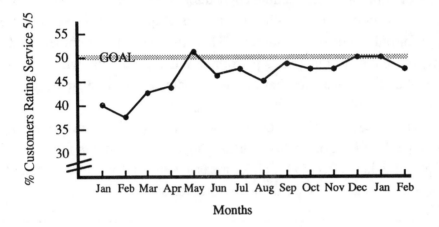

Figure 10.2: Graph with Goal Depicted

Although there are many different types of graphs that can be used to present data, it is best to use either line or bar graphs. Place a time scale on the horizontal axis and some measure of quality performance on the vertical axis. Be sure to adjust the quality performance scale of your graph to depict the maximum amount of improvement. For example, if performance has improved from 82% to 94% over the last four years, the scale should be between 80% and 100% to best show the improvement.

Another common problem to avoid in this section is not adequately explaining your graphs and figures. Explain in the text what the graph depicts and the significance of the results shown. For example: "Figure 6.4 depicts the total number of rejects per thousand in product line A over the last five years. As you can see, rejects have fallen from a high of 73 per thousand to a low of 21 per thousand in 1993." Be careful not to go overboard, as some applicants have done, and describe every piece of data in the graph, point-by-point, year-by-year. This is redundant and wastes valuable space in the application. (Further details on preparing graphics appear in Chapter 2).

If you are presenting data for 25 or more different indices of quality in your organization, there are bound to be some adverse trends or anomalies that may make the organization look bad in certain areas. Indeed, if the data reveal *no* adverse trends, their credibility might be questioned. It is not expected that all trends will be consistently positive. It is expected, however, that *most* of your quality data will show positive trends. When a drop in quality has occurred, you are expected to provide an explanation. It is best if only drops caused by factors outside your control, such as the economy, the environment, regulations, etc., have occurred.

You will be judged in this section on whether you address all adverse trends and anomalies in the data presented for section 6.1a. Furthermore, you will be evaluated on the credibility of your explanations. It is easy to rationalize poor performance as being due to factors lying outside your control. However, the Baldrige Examiners will be looking for strong evidence that your explanations are valid and are not just rationalizations.

Indicators For Area 6.1a

- Number of different quality indices for which data are presented

- Data are presented for all important quality indices, not just a few

- Number of years' worth of historical data presented to show trends

- Degree to which all indices show continuous and steady improvement

- Clarity of graphs included in this section

- Amount of variability in performance.

- Clarity of explanations of quality results

- Measures include inputs, processes, and outputs. (The scope should not be limited to outputs alone)

- Number of adverse trends or anomalies noted in quality data

- Credibility and clarity of explanations for anomalies or adverse trends

- Evidence that when adverse trends are the fault of the organization, the situations causing the problems have been thoroughly investigated and corrected. (This should be indicated by level of performance following the adverse trend.)

AREA TO ADDRESS   **[RESULTS]**

6.1b Comparisons of current quality level with that of principal competitors in the company's key markets, industry averages, industry leaders, and appropriate benchmarks.

Note:

    (4)   **Bases for comparison (6.1b) might include: independent surveys, studies, or laboratory testing; benchmarks; and company evaluations and testing.**

What They're Looking For Here

The number and credibility of data sources you have for comparing your quality results to competitors is important in your response to this Area to Address. The biggest and perhaps most common mistake applicants make in this section is the failure to be specific enough. A typical response for this area is as follows:

> *We use a variety of different sources of data to compare ourselves to our competitors. Market research reports by independent marketing companies, industry reports from professional associations, and our own intelligence gathered by our employees are among the many sources of competitive data.*

A response such as this will earn you very few points in this area because it lacks details and, therefore, credibility. The more specific your response is, the more convincing it is. One applicant who received a very high score for this area began with a statement or two similar to the example above, but followed it with a detailed table in which the various sources of competitive data were listed. An example of such a chart is as follows.

SOURCES AND TYPES OF COMPETITOR DATA Arons Oil Company			
Information Provided	Frequency	Source	Methodology
Quality Data – # Defects 4 major customers	Monthly	Exxon	Laboratory Samples
Market Share Data	Annually	Nat. Petrochemical Association	Survey

A chart such as this shows the examiners the types of data you collect, the objectivity of the data (based upon who collects it), and the number of different sources of information you have on competitors. You might also include a column in your chart that explains how the data are used. For example, the market share data from the National Petroleum Association might be used for goal setting in your planning sessions.

A good way to excel in this Area to Address is to demonstrate that you provide higher quality products and/or services than any of your competitors—locally, nationally, and internationally. In your response, you should provide data on a number of different measurement dimensions to indicate that you are better than all competitors. What many applicants do is provide their own comparisons to results of a few competitors. They pick only those competitors that show a poorer performance than their own companies. Other applicants explain that they are in a very poorly defined market and that it is therefore impossible to gather competitive data for comparison purposes. Being a small company or being in a new field are certainly valid reasons why competitive data are more difficult to gather, but these reasons do not serve as an excuse for having none. Company size and access to competitive data are both taken into consideration in evaluating your application. The complete absence of competitive data, however, makes it virtually impossible to assess your own quality results to determine just how good or impressive they may be.

Remember that this section should address how your quality results compare with those of your competitors. You should *not* provide statistical comparisons on market share, size, number of employees, profits, growth, etc. In order to earn a high score for this area, you will need to provide numerous comparisons of your organization's *quality performance* against a number of your biggest competitors. By comparing yourself to world-class leaders in your field, you give your response additional credibility.

Although your organization does not have to be the best in all areas, you should rank highest in most of the quality measures.

You should present additional data here on how actual results compare with your goals on all important quality indices. Explain whether you are ahead of your goals, behind them, or on target. A table or chart is a good way of summarizing this information, even if some of it was presented in section 6.1. A sample format you could use for your summary table follows.

COMPARISON OF QUALITY RESULTS TO GOALS				
Index	Current Performance	Goal	Difference	Comments
% Comebacks	14%	10%	4% below goal	Showing steady progress
% Correct Diagnoses	92%	90%	2% above goal	
% Jobs Done on Time	94%	98%	4% below goal	10% better than last year

The applicant who prepared the chart in this example has not done especially well in relation to the three quality goals listed, but the format for presentation of the information is good. The examiners will look not only at the extent to which you have met or exceeded each of your quality goals, but also at the level of difficulty of your goals in relation to past performance. For example, if last year you met your deadlines for delivery of customer orders 78% of the time, and this year you met these deadlines 95% of the time, you would get credit for the amount of improvement shown, even if you didn't make your goal of 98% on-time orders.

This section of your application is assessed on the completeness of your data and the degree to which you meet or exceed your goals on each index. If you have 56 quality measures and present data for only 15 of them, you won't receive a very high score. This is not to say that you must present data for all 56 indices. You may choose to present data for only the most critical of the measures. Similarly, if you present data for all 56 indices but have met your goals on only 12 of them, you won't receive a very high score. Finally, make sure that you adequately explain any conditions or situations where you fell significantly short of your goals. Saying that the goal wasn't realistic in the first place is a frequent disclaimer that must be avoided in offering your explanation. Make sure that you explain all adverse trends or failures to meet goals, and that your explanations are both clear and credible.

Indicators For Area 6.1b

- Use of outside sources of data on competitors

- Use of reliable and appropriate sources to gather data on competitors

- Use of ethical and fair methods of gathering data on competitors

- Number of different sources of competitor data

- Number of different aspects of the business that are compared to competitors

- Amount of competitor data relating specifically to quality as against financial or market standing

- How applicant's quality results compare with major competitors

- How much better the applicant's quality results are than those of major competitors

- How applicant's quality results compare to world-class leaders in the field

- Number of different quality indices on which comparisons are made with competitors

- Length of time applicant's quality results have been superior to competitors'

- Percentage of total quality indices (for which data are presented) that relates to leadership goals, objectives, or standards

- Percentage of indices for which performance meets or exceeds goals

- Degree to which performance exceeds goals

- Level of difficulty of goals compared with past performance—how challenging are goals?

- Importance of indices for which performance meets or exceeds goals relative to importance of indices for which performance goals have not been met

6.2 COMPANY OPERATIONAL RESULTS

Summarize trends and levels in overall company operational performance; provide a comparison with competitors and/or appropriate benchmarks. (50 points)

Notes:

(1) Key measures of company operational performance include those that address productivity, efficiency, and effectiveness. Examples should include generic indicators such as use of manpower, materials, energy, capital, and assets. Trends and levels could address productivity indices, waste reduction, energy efficiency, cycle time reduction, environmental improvement, and other measures of improved *overall company performance*. Also include company-specific indicators the company uses to track its progress in improving operational performance. Such company-specific indicators should be defined in tables or charts where trends are presented.

(2) Trends in financial indicators, properly labeled, might be included in Item 6.2. If such financial indicators are used, there should be a clear connection to the quality and operational performance improvement activities of the company.

(3) Include improvements in product and service design and production/delivery processes in this item.

AREA TO ADDRESS   **[RESULTS]**

6.2a Trends and current levels for key measures and/or indicators of company operational performance.

What They're Looking For Here

This is the section where you should present data on all the key operational and financial indices in your organization. As with the other Examination Items, you are expected to provide three to five years' worth of data. The results you present in this section of your application should correspond to the indices that you stated you measure in section 2.1, and the measures on which you set goals as described in section 3.2. What is considered important about your response to this Item is the scope and breadth of the data you present. You should present data for a variety of operational and financial measures. The key here is to select and present data for those measures that reflect *overall company performance*. An error that Baldrige applicants could make in this section (judging from errors made in similar sections in the past) is to present graphs showing only those indices that signal an improving trend. When examiners see this they tend to wonder what performance looks like on the other indices for which there are no graphs. When the criteria refer to "operational results," they are not asking about quality data. Operational measures typically fall into three categories:

- Financial
- Timeliness
- Quantity

Measures of efficiency or productivity, which are a ratio of quantity over cost, are also considered important.

Read over the example indices listed in the criteria for types of indices that should be taken into account. A study that was done by the U.S. General Accounting Office in 1991 on the impact of using the Baldrige criteria to improve organizational performance lists eight operating indices used to evaluate past Baldrige finalists:

- Reliability
- Order processing time
- Product lead time
- Costs of quality

- Timeliness of delivery
- Errors or defects
- Inventory turnover
- Cost savings

The only one of these indices that doesn't fit into a response for Item 6.2 is "Errors or defects." Data on product/service errors or defects are reported in 6.1. The other seven indices are all appropriate, however. I am not suggesting that you need to present data on these indices, only that these should be considered in determining what is appropriate for your company.

Another type of data that should be presented in this section are data on measures that are unique to your industry or your organization. These should be indices by which the company measures itself. Unique measures of customer satisfaction get reported on in section 7.0, not here.

The criteria in this Examination Item also ask for financial data. Financial measures may include some of the following:

- Sales
- Operating expenses
- Return on sales
- Profits
- Return on assets
- Sales per employee

Overall trends in your financial performance over the last five years or so will be examined to determine the degree of improvement and the extent to which improvements have been maintained. Something the examiners will specifically look for is return on investment (ROI) data from your efforts to implement total quality. Many large companies have literally spent millions of dollars on activities relating to implementation of total quality. You should present data in this section that demonstrate the financial benefits that have resulted from your investment in total quality. Part of these data might be all of the financial benefits that can be attributed to the hundreds of individual team projects that have been completed during your implementation of TQ over the last few years. Other financial benefits may have resulted from any macro-level changes implemented. However you present ROI data, the examiners will be interested in the overall level of ROI, as well as the level of confidence in any claim you make about TQ efforts being the key variable responsible for the improvements. It could be that many other variables impacted financial results. For this reason, it is important that you show before-and-after data to help demonstrate that TQ has had a major positive impact on financial measures in your company.

Indicators For Area 6.2a

- Scope and breadth of indices for which operational data are presented

- Correspondence between measures identified in 2.1 and data presented in 6.2

- Extent to which positive trends are demonstrated in productivity, waste, cycle time, and other key operational measures

- Presentation of enough data to establish trends (typically 3-5 years)

- Amount of improvement occurring over the last 3-5 years for key indices

- Extent to which indices are appropriate measures of overall company performance

- Presentation of data on key financial performance measures

- Presentation of financial data shows consistently improving trends over the last 3-5 years

- Levels of financial performance have significantly improved over the last 3-5 years

- Consistency of trends across all different financial indices for which data are presented

- Evidence of ROI from total quality (TQ) investments

- Return on investment results from TQ

AREA TO ADDRESS   **[RESULTS]**

6.2b Comparison of performance with that of competitors, industry averages, industry leaders, and key benchmarks.

What They're Looking For Here

In order to determine how significant or insignificant your results are, you need to present data on competitors and industry averages. What is important about your response to this Area to Address is the extent to which several different comparative statistics are presented for each of the indices presented in 6.2a. A good way of presenting these data is to prepare a chart that lists the various performance indices along the left, and performance of your company and several others in the remainder of the chart. A portion of an example of such a chart is shown below.

Comparison of Operational Results					
Measures	Our Company	Competitor A	Competitor B	Industry Best	Benchmark
Order Processing Time	8 days	14 days	11 days	6 days	3 days
Sales per Employee	$140,000 per employee	$113,000 per employee	$110,000 per employee	$150,000 per employee	N/A
% On-Time Delivery	96%	95%	88%	98%	N/A
Profit (% of total income)	18%	12%	8.4%	20%	N/A

Another way of presenting these data is to present graphs showing trends over the last 3-5 years in your performance as compared with competitors and others. The problem with using a matrix like the one shown above is that only one year's worth of data are presented. The examiners are interested in how your overall levels of results compare with competitors', but they are also interested in how your *trends* compare with others. If other companies have improved at about the same rate as you have, your positive trends will not be nearly as impressive. The sources of your data on competitors and other companies will also be questioned, so make sure that you explain where these data come from.

Obviously, what is important for this Area to Address is that your levels of performance are better than your major competitors', and, in the best-case scenario, than industry leaders' and other benchmarks you use for improvement planning.

Indicators For Area 6.2b

- Percentage of indices for which competitor and industry-leader results-data are presented

- Competitors are the companies against which the applicant most often competes

- Credibility of sources for competitor data and benchmark data

- Extent to which data are presented for major competitors, industry leaders, and benchmarks

- Extent to which current levels of performance by applicant are better than all major competitors', industry leaders', and benchmarks

- Extent to which positive trends exhibited by applicant are significantly better than trends in competitor data

- Length of time (number of years) during which applicant's performance on financial and operational measures is superior to competition

6.3 BUSINESS AND SUPPORT SERVICE RESULTS PROCESS

Summarize trends and current levels in quality and operational performance improvement for business processes and support services; compare results with competitors and/or appropriate benchmarks. (25 points)

Note:

(1)   Business and support services are those as covered in Item 5.3. Key productivity, cycle time, cost and other effectiveness requirements for business and support services. Responses should reflect relevance to the company's principal quality and operational performance objectives addressed in company plans, contributing to the results reported in Items 6.1 and 6.2. Responses should demonstrate broad coverage of company business and support services and work units. Results should reflect the most important objectives of each service or work unit.

AREA TO ADDRESS   **[RESULTS]**

6.3a Trends and current levels for key measures and/or indicators of quality and operational performance of business processes and support services.

What They're Looking For Here

In Examination Item 6.1, you presented data on the quality of your products and services. In 6.2 you presented operational data. In your response for this Examination Item, you need to discuss quality data reflecting business processes and support services. Data should be presented for measures such as accuracy, completeness, timeliness, etc. As mentioned in the item Note, this section should include data for the indices identified in Examination Item 5.3.

Many applicants lose points in this Area to Address because they have no quality data on the work performed by the staff or support departments in the company. Common support departments found in most companies are:

- Accounting/Finance
- Purchasing/Procurement
- Personnel/Human Resources
- Materials/Inventory Control
- Management Information Systems
- Quality Assurance/Control
- Marketing
- Sales
- Legal/Contracts

The Baldrige Examiners expect to see process data and data on the quality of the services performed by these and any other staff functions/departments in your organization. This is the section where you should report data on internal customer satisfaction. Surveys and data collected using other methods to assess customer satisfaction with services performed by individual support departments should be presented. You should also present output data. Examples of this might be errors in reports or defects in other types of outputs produced by support departments. The extent to which maintenance personnel fix problems right the first time would be another example of output data.

The key to quality is to control all of your processes. In many organizations, less than 50% of their financial and human resources are devoted to the line organization. The rest of the resources go toward the staff organizations that "support" the line organization. Given that staff functions make up such a large part of the organization, it stands to reason that the processes performed by these organizations need to be under the same degree of control as those in the line organization.

The examiners are not expecting perfect process data. There will naturally be instances in which adverse conditions were encountered or in which quality fell below standards or goals. However, the examiners do not expect that all trends or instances of below-standard performance will be due to outside forces. Your organization may be at fault for some of the poor performance results. The examiners want to determine whether you know why these trends or drops have occurred and whether the actions you have taken to prevent them from occurring again are appropriate. Your response will be evaluated based upon the thoroughness and credibility of your explanation of such trends and upon the type of corrective actions used to prevent these problems from recurring. The success of your corrective actions will be judged in terms of the quality process data gathered after the corrective actions have been implemented. Refer to any graphs you include in this section and indicate when corrective actions were implemented.

Indicators For Area 6.3a

- Percentage of important processes in support departments for which process data are presented

- Support department process data show little variability and consistently meet or exceed standards

- Presentation of data on the quality of outputs and accomplishments that are produced by support departments

- Scope and breadth of data on outputs/accomplishments of support functions

- Positive trends and overall level of results on graphs of outputs from support departments

- Objectivity of data collection instruments and methods

- Percentage of staff or support organizations/departments on which quality-related process data are presented

- Percentage of important processes in each staff department on which quality-related process data are presented

- Staff organization process data show little variability and consistently meet or exceed standards

- Presentation of process data from the staff departments includes both equipment and behavioral measures

- Presentation of internal customer satisfaction data from all support departments

- Existence of positive trends and overall positive levels of performance in internal customer satisfaction

- Percentage of adverse trends or drops in quality data that are addressed in this section of application

- Credibility of explanations of adverse trends

- Percentage of adverse trends or drops in quality for which corrective actions have been implemented

- Extent to which corrective actions solve the root cause of problems and prevent recurrence (as against being only "band-aid" quick fixes)

AREA TO ADDRESS   **[RESULTS]**
6.3b Comparison of performance with appropriately selected companies and benchmarks.

Note:

   (2)   **Comparisons and benchmarks for business and support services (6.3b) should emphasize best practice performance, regardless of industry.**

What They're Looking For Here

This Area to Address asks to see comparative data on how well your support departments do compared to your competitors. A suggested way of presenting these data is to create a matrix that lists all of your support departments, major quality indices, current performance, and performance of major competitors on the same major indices. What the Baldrige Examiners want to see is that, first of all, you have data on how competitors' support departments do in comparison to your own support departments. Assuming that you do have this data, the next question the examiners will ask is how did you select the competitors with which you compare yourself? Obviously, they want to see that the competitors you select to compare yourself with are the best companies, not simply those to whose data you have the most access.

Another way of presenting comparative data is to select one key performance measure for each support department and present a graph depicting your performance and that of a few competitors over the last few years. On the following page, an example is shown from a hypothetical accounts payable function.

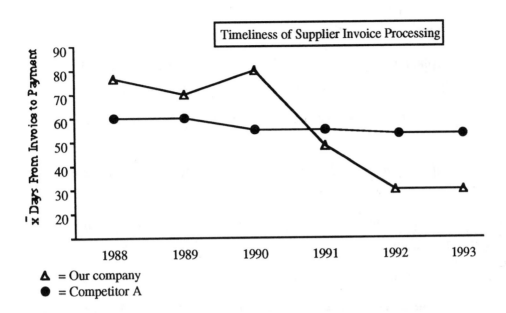

What will be considered important about your results in this section is the trends in your data and the overall level of performance compared with your competitors. If everyone's performance has improved to the same degree over the last few years, your results won't end up being too impressive. To receive a good score, the results from your support department need to be superior to your competitors in the majority of your support departments.

It is also expected that your data comparisons go beyond simply looking at competitors. You are asked how you benchmark the results obtained by your support departments. Benchmarking means comparing yourself to the best, not simply to your competition.

Indicators For Area 6.3b

- Percentage of support departments for which competitive comparison data are presented

- How applicant's level of performance on indices presented compares with competition's

- Extent to which positive trends exhibited by applicant are significantly better than trends in competitor data

- Length of time applicant's support function's performance has been superior to performance of competitors' support departments

- Validity of measurement indices for data presented as overall performance indicators of support functions

- Credibility of sources of competitor data

- Credibility of explanations given to describe reasons why performance of applicant's support organization(s) is not superior to competition

- Competitors for which comparative data are presented are actually the major companies that applicant competes with

- Percentage of support functions/departments for which benchmark data are presented

- Degree to which performance of applicant's support functions is superior to benchmark organization's

- Credibility of sources of benchmark data

6.4 SUPPLIER QUALITY RESULTS

Summarize trends in quality and current quality levels of suppliers; compare the company's supplier quality with that of competitors and/or with appropriate benchmarks. (35 points)

Note:

(1)   The results reported in Item 6.4 derive from quality improvement activities described in Item 5.4. Results should be broken down by major groupings of suppliers and reported using the principal quality measures described in Item 5.4.

AREA TO ADDRESS   [RESULTS]
6.4a Trends and current levels for key measures and/or indicators of supplier quality performance.

What They're Looking For Here

Once again the word "trends" appears in the criteria statement. This should tell you that they want graphs and statistics, not just words. Often, applicants formulate a written response to this area by simply explaining how suppliers' quality has improved due to the applicant's efforts. Without supportive data, however, they end up with a very low score in this area—regardless of how well written the description may be.

The examiners want to see evidence that key measures of supplier quality have improved over the last few years. If you have over 500 suppliers, obviously you don't have room to present data on every one of them. What you might do is select the two or three that you conduct the most business with, and present graphs on their quality performance trends. You could then summarize quality results for other suppliers in a table or chart similar to the one which follows.

SUPPLIER QUALITY DATA					
Company	Measure	1988	1989	1990	1991
Cannon	Photocopiers Uptime	82%	78%	88%	94%
Cleansweeps Janitorial	Cleanliness Ratings	3.4/5	3.7/5	4.3/5	4.6/5
ABC Office Supplies	% On-time Deliveries	82%	88%	90%	90%

Your response for this area will be evaluated both on the amount of supplier data you present, and the degree to which supplier quality shows a trend of continuous improvement. Where there have been drops in supplier quality, you will be expected to provide explanations.

Indicators For Area 6.4a

- Percentage of suppliers for which quality data are presented

- Trend showing continual improvement in supplier quality over the last several years

- Overall levels of supplier quality are high

- Percentage of suppliers showing trend towards improved quality

- Evidence to suggest that actions by applicant to help suppliers improve their quality have resulted in improved performance

- Objectivity and reliability of data presented on suppliers

AREA TO ADDRESS [RESULTS]

6.4b Comparison of the company's supplier quality levels with those of appropriately selected companies and/or benchmarks.

Note:

(2)   **Comparisons (6.4b) might be with industry averages, industry leaders, principal competitors in the company's key markets, and appropriate benchmarks.**

What They're Looking For Here

This Area to Address is designed to give you an opportunity to explain how your suppliers' quality compares to that of your competitors' suppliers, and/or to benchmark organizations. Begin your response for this section by explaining the bases for your comparisons. You should address such questions as:

- How are competitors selected for comparison?
- How are suppliers for which comparative data are presented selected?
- How are benchmark organizations selected for examining supplier performance?

After explaining how you select supplier data from competitors and benchmark organizations, you should present the comparative data. As in the other sections, it is a good idea to present supplier data using graphs. Your response will be judged according to the amount of data you present, and the level of quality your suppliers achieve in relation to competitors' suppliers.

Indicators For Area 6.4b

- Percentage of suppliers for which comparative data are presented

- Importance of suppliers for which comparative data are presented

- Presentation of benchmark data on suppliers

- Degree of difference between quality performance of applicant's suppliers and that of competitors' suppliers

- Number or percentage of suppliers for which applicant's supplier performance is superior to competitors' suppliers

- Trend of quality improvement in applicant's suppliers as compared to competitor's suppliers

Chapter 11

Interpreting the Criteria
for Customer Focus
and Satisfaction

OVERVIEW OF THE CUSTOMER FOCUS AND SATISFACTION CATEGORY

The seventh and final category in the Baldrige Award Criteria is Customer Focus and Satisfaction. This category is worth 300 points, much more than any of the other six categories of criteria. The reason this is the most important category is because customers are the final judge of quality. You might do all the things that quality gurus such as Deming and Juran tell you to achieve impressive quality improvements, but if your customers still think that your products are average or inferior compared to the competition, it is extremely unlikely that you'll become a Baldrige Award winner. Although advertising and other factors can influence customers to buy your product or service the first time, quality is what keeps them coming back. You might buy a certain brand of car because it has great styling and a good price, for example. But you will never buy another one of these cars if the quality is poor and the car is in the shop all of the time. Quality is what keeps people buying your products and services.

According to the 1994 Award Criteria, category 7.0, Customer Focus and Satisfaction, is defined as follows:

> The **Customer Focus and Satisfaction** category examines the company's relationships with customers and its knowledge of customer requirements and of the key quality factors that drive marketplace competitiveness. Also examined are the company's methods to determine customer satisfaction, current trends and levels of customer satisfaction and retention, and these results relative to competitors (p. 29).

Figure 11.1 is repeated from the previous chapter on Quality and Operational Results. Customer satisfaction is measured after the external customers have purchased the products or services produced by the organization. As you can see in the figure, this occurs at point 8, and this information is then fed back to the organization to aid them in producing better quality products and services.

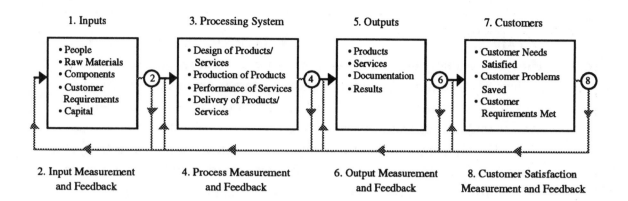

Figure 11.1: Macro Process Model of an Organization

The satisfaction level of internal customers is not addressed in category 7.0. This category relates only to external customer satisfaction. Quality results with internal customers are evaluated in section 6.2 and 6.3.

This chapter describes each of the eight Examination Items in this category of the Award Criteria. As in previous chapters, each section begins with a double-ruled box containing the Examination Item, the point value, and any applicable Notes.* Areas to Address falling under that Item follow in a single-ruled box. In the upper right corner of each Area to Address box is an indication [brackets] of whether the Area pertains to approach, deployment, or results. All definitions and information appearing within these boxes is taken directly from the Baldrige criteria. Following each Area to Address is an explanation defining what the examiners are looking for in assessing your application. Next, I have supplied a list of indicators or evaluation factors that will assist you in interpreting the criteria and in preparing your application.

7.1 CUSTOMER EXPECTATIONS: CURRENT AND FUTURE

Describe how the company determines near-term and longer-term requirements and expectations of customers. (35 points)

---

* Item notes that apply to a specific Area to Address are appropriately listed in the box containing that Area.

AREA TO ADDRESS   **[APPROACH, DEPLOYMENT]**

7.1a How the company determines *current and near-term requirements* **and expectations of customers. Include: (1) how customer groups and/or market segments are determined or selected, including how customers of competitors and other potential customers are considered; (2) how information is collected, including what information is sought, frequency and methods of collection, and how objectivity and validity are assured; (3) how specific product and service features and the relative importance of these features to customer groups or segments are determined; and (4) how other key information and data such as complaints, gains and losses of customers, and product/service performance are used to support the determination.**

Notes:

(1) The distribution between near-term and future depends upon many marketplace factors. The applicant's response should reflect these factors for its market.

(2) The company's products and services might be sold to end users via other businesses such as retail stores or dealers. Thus, "customer groups" should take into account the requirements and expectations of both the end users and these other businesses.

(3) Product and service features refer to all important characteristics and to the performance of products and services that customers experience or perceive throughout their overall purchase and ownership. These include any factors that bear upon customer preference, repurchase loyalty, or view of quality—for example, those features that enhance or differentiate products and services from competing offerings.

(4) Some companies might use similar methods to determine customer requirements/expectations and customer satisfaction (Item 7.4). In such cases, cross-references should be included.

(5) Customer groups and market segments (7.1a, b) should take into account opportunities to select or *create* groups and segments based upon customer- and market-related information.

What They're Looking For Here

What the Baldrige Examiners are looking for in this section is how well you know your current and potential customers. To maintain positive relationships with all of your customers, you need to be in constant touch with their ever-changing wants, desires, and expectations. The first thing you should explain is that you have divided customers into different market segments, which you examine separately, rather than considering all customer needs as identical. While it is true that all of your customers have some common requirements and expectations about the products and services you sell, those in different markets have their own unique requirements as well. You are also expected to explain how and why you segment your customers the way you do. For example, if more than half of your business comes from the automotive industry, and the rest from many other different types of industries, it might make sense to segment your customers into two groups:

- Automotive
- Non-automotive

A manufacturer of printing equipment uses the following segments to categorize its customers:

- Manufacturing companies
- Service companies
- Government
- Educational institutions
- Printers

The Baldrige Examiners are not searching for a specific segmentation strategy. They want to see that you have accurately identified your market segments and that you have sound reasoning for the categories chosen.

Your response for this area should also include an explanation of what the common requirements for all your customers are and what the requirements for customers in the different market segments you serve are. A common way to respond to this area is to make the following statement: "We have identified all of the requirements and expectations unique to each of the different market segments we serve." But as you may have learned by now, using broad statements such as this will not earn many points. Listing the requirements and expectations of your different groups of customers will earn points in this area. A matrix with customer requirements and expectations listed along the left side, and market segments listed horizontally along the top is a great way to show common and unique customer requirements. A sample of a portion of such a chart follows.

CUSTOMER REQUIREMENTS BY MARKET SEGMENT			
CUSTOMER REQUIREMENTS	LARGE COMPUTER MANUFACTURERS	SMALL COMPUTER MANUFACTURERS	OTHERS
Timely Delivery	X	X	X
Assembly of Components	X		X
Special Packaging	X		
Quality Inspection of 25%		X	

You also need to explain how you gather data on customer requirements. Your response will be evaluated according to the objectivity and reliability of your research methodologies and instruments. The examiners will also be looking at factors such as sample size, frequency of data collection, and use of a variety of different methods to gather data on customer requirements. Your own market research should be supplemented with data collected by outside firms to increase the objectivity of your data.

A great many customers may not be a part of your efforts to gather data on customer requirements, and you may not hear from them when they have a service or product complaint. In fact, for every eight customers who are unhappy with a product or service, only one complains. Rather than complain, most unhappy customers simply take their business elsewhere. Two valuable sources of data on customers requirements are complaint data and an analysis of lost customers to determine why they leave. The examiners are looking for evidence that you gather data from customers who decide to buy their product/service elsewhere and that you use both this and customer complaint data to identify customer requirements that may not be apparent from the other market research you do.

Another good source of data is new customers. Surveying new customers to find out why they selected your product or service can provide valuable information. In your response, explain how data on lost and new customers is gathered and directed back through the appropriate channels to serve as input to the product/service design process.

This area to address not only asks how you determine customer requirements, it also asks what you do with them. Question 7.1a (3) asks about the process you use to define product/service features, based upon the customer requirements. In 5.1a I mentioned the approach called Quality Function Deployement for translating customer requirements into product/service design features. This is one very good approach that would earn you points in this section, but it is certainly not a requirement. What the Examiners want to see is that you employ some systematic approach to using the customer requirements as inputs to the product/service design process. Your response should include a flowchart or process description that outlines how you use the customer requirements to determine product/service features. To give your response credibility, you should follow your process description with several examples that illustrate how customer requirements have been used to design product or service features. Explain what the research revealed about high-priority customer needs, and how you met those needs with a new feature or new product/service. Two or three examples should be enough.

Your response for this Area to Address should also explain how you use complaints and performance data as a way of identifying possible customer requirements. For example, a car company may look at the number of warranty repairs that customers have done on their cars during the first year as a set of performance data relevant to customer requirements for reliability.

Indicators For Area 7.1a

- Thoroughness of process for identifying market segments and potential customers

- Data on requirements collected from your own and competitors' customers

- Degree to which customer requirements have been identified for each market segment your company serves

- Identification of the common and unique requirements and expectations for each market segment

- Objectivity of data collection methods used to identify customer requirements and expectations

- Frequency of data collection on each market segment

- Sample sizes are large enough to be adequate representation of customer populations

- How the company provides information to customers to help ensure that their expectations are realistic

- Use of multiple methodologies (e.g., telephone interviews, mail surveys, focus groups, etc.) to gather data on customer requirements

- Use of comparative data for such areas as product/service performance, complaints, and gains/losses of customers to help determine customer requirements

- Use of outside sources of data to supplement applicant's own data on customer requirements

- How the role of and logistical support for customer-contact personnel are determined

- Use of a systematic process for gathering customer requirement data

- Evidence that customer complaint data are summarized and used as input for design or enhancement of products/services

- Use of a systematic process to design product/service features based upon customer requirements

- Evidence that the process for defining products/services based on customer requirements is actually used

- Lost customers are tracked and follow-ups are done to determine their reasons for buying products/services elsewhere and why they were dissatisfied with your products/services

- Thoroughness of system for following up with lost customers

- Data gathered from new customers to determine why they selected the product/services offered by your company

- Use of performance data on products/services to identify customer requirements

- Evidence that data from new or lost customers is used to design, enhance, or change products and/or services

- Extent to which requirements have been identified for all dealers or distributors if appropriate

---

AREA TO ADDRESS   **[APPROACH, DEPLOYMENT]**

7.1b How the company addresses *future requirements* and expectations of customers. Include: (1) the time horizon for the determination; (2) how important technological, competitive, societal, environmental, economic, and demographic factors that may bear upon customer requirements, expectations, preferences, or alternatives are considered; (3) how customers of competitors and other potential customers are considered; (4) how key product and service features and the relative importance of these features are projected; and (5) how changing or emerging market segments and their implications on current or new product/service lines are considered.

What They're Looking For Here

The purpose of this item is to suggest that companies need to focus on determining what customers are likely to want and expect in the future. This may seem a difficult task, but being able to predict future customer demands is what separates the leading companies from the followers. Many large manufacturing companies are designing products now that won't be on the market for several years. These companies need to be aware of how tastes and expectations of customers are likely to change in the future so that their new products will meet or exceed those expectations.

The first portion of your response for this Area to Address should explain the time horizon for determination of future customer requirements. The time horizon should be based upon the trends and frequency of changes in your industry, and a reasonable time frame within which you can predict trends. The amount of time you need to develop and test new products should also be considered in determining the time frame for your predictions. Some pharmaceutical companies are working on drugs that may not be on the market for more than five years. Clothing designers, on the other hand, come up with their product designs about a year or so before they hit the stores. In a fashion-oriented business, it is much more difficult to predict trends and customer tastes more than a couple of years in advance. Your response should explain the logic behind your selection of a particular time frame for predicting future customer expectations.

Your response should explain how needs of current and potential new customers are likely to change. You should also explain how you are in touch with the current and future expectations of competitors' customers. Explain how you predict your existing and potential customers' buying behavior. If you do market research, explain how you ensure that predictions made by this research have turned out to be valid.

The final segment of your response for this Area to Address should list various trends that are relevant to your business, and how each of these trends will impact upon requirements and expectations of your current and potential customers. I suggest preparing a matrix that lists the factors in the first column, the trends for each of the factors in the second column, the impact on your customers' requirements in the third column, and your strategy for capitalizing on each trend in the final column. An example that depicts the relationship between trends and current customer requirements for a real estate firm follows.

Factors	Trends	Customer Requirements	Strategies
Demographics	Move Away From Large Cities	• Better Home Value • Less Traffic • Better Schools • Less Materialistic Values	• Open More Offices in Medium-Sized Cities • Train Agents in Benefits of Small City Living

You also need to explain how you use the information you gather on future customer requirements to design new products and services, or to enhance existing products/services. A very clear way of presenting this information might be to build upon the matrix you presented in 7.1a. List the trends again, and matrix the trends against your products and services, as well as market segments. Your matrix might also show how new features of your products/services will be designed to meet or exceed future customer requirements. The following example chart depicts a portion of a matrix for a fast-food chain that is concerned with the increasing societal trend of eating more healthy foods.

FACTOR	TRENDS	MARKETS/PRODUCTS
Societal	• Less Fat in Diets • Less Cholesterol in Diets	Children—D Adults—A, B, C
Products	A=Salads C=Carrots/Celery Sticks	B=Chicken Sandwich D=Healthy Meal

Explain how data on future trends and customer expectations are used by engineers and/or product/service design teams. Your response should also explain how you evaluate the importance of various future customer requirements so that you concentrate your efforts on designing product/service features that address the most important requirements. Describe the process for incorporating future trends into the design process. You might describe this process using a process model or flowchart. It will also be helpful for you to provide a couple of examples of how you have capitalized on past trends in the way you design new products/services. Your response should also explain how you will capitalize on future trends in order to gain market share and attract a larger customer base.

Indicators For Area 7.1b

- Explanation of time horizon for determination of future customer requirements matches applicant's business, products/services, and technology

- Time frame for determination of future requirements is far enough in the future to allow the organization to capitalize on trends by designing and introducing products and services to meet future customer expectations

- Extent to which projections are made about requirements of existing customers in the future and requirements of potential customers who currently do not buy the organization's products or services

- Identification of important trends in technology, competition, society, economy, demographics, and other factors that may impact the business

- Extent to which the company has identified how each of these trends will impact its business

- Identification of specific strategies the company will use to capitalize on future trends in all areas listed above

- Evidence that future customer requirements are used in the product/service design process

- Use of a systematic process to evaluate the importance of various future customer requirements

- Demonstratation that only the most important future customer requirements are translated into new product/service features

- Clarity and completeness of explanation of how future trends are translated into customer requirements leading to design of new or enhanced products/services

- Extent to which response addresses existing customers and potential future customers

---

AREA TO ADDRESS   **[APPROACH, DEPLOYMENT]**

7.1c How the company evaluates and improves its processes for determining customer requirements and expectations.

Note:

(6)   Examples of evaluations appropriate for 7.1c are:
- **the adequacy of the customer-related information;**
- **the best approaches for getting reliable information—surveys, focus groups, customer-contact personnel, etc., and**
- **increasing and decreasing importance of product/service features among customer groups or segments.**

This evaluation might also be supported by company-level analysis addressed in 2.3a.

<u>What They're Looking For Here</u>

If you've come this far in this book, this Area to Address should look very familiar to you. The last in a sequence of Areas to Address typically calls for evidence that you systematically evaluate and improve a process. This is exactly what is being asked for here. The Baldrige Examiners are looking for evidence that you employ a systematic process to evaluate your market research and other investigations to determine future customer expectations. Begin your response with a list of the various types of research you do to determine customer requirements in the future. Along with a list of the various types of research, you might also mention who does the research, indicating whether you use outside firms or do it all using your own internal resources. For each type of research that is done, list the type of evaluation factors or measures used for assessment. Next, describe the methodology used to gather the evaluation data. Explain how the evaluation data are compiled and how conclusions are drawn.

Following your description of the methods used to evaluate your research approaches, you should explain how you use these evaluation data to improve your research methodology or expand the time horizon for your research. One area you should work on improving is the accuracy of your predictions and the length of your time horizons. The best companies in the future will be those that accurately predict long-range trends. You might end your response with an example or two of how you have used evaluation data to improve your research methodology, leading to improvements in the accuracy of your predictions or in the time horizons of your research.

Indicators For Area 7.1c

- Evidence that a systematic process is used to evaluate the approaches used to determine future customer requirements

- Extent to which evaluations are done on all methodologies employed to conduct research on future customer requirements

- Degree to which evaluation methods are appropriate for the research methods used

- Validity of measurement indices used for evaluation

- Validity of evaluation approaches used

- Clear description of a system to compile evaluation results and follow up on them

- Evidence that evaluation results are acted upon and result in improvements in research approaches

- Evidence to indicate that improvements have been made in the last few years in the accuracy and/or time frames of predictions about future customer requirements

---

7.2 CUSTOMER RELATIONSHIP MANAGEMENT

Describe how the company provides effective management of its interactions and relationships with its customers and uses information gained from customers to improve customer relationship management processes. (65 points)

> **AREA TO ADDRESS**   **[APPROACH, DEPLOYMENT]**
>
> **7.2a For the company's most important contacts between its employees and customers, summarize the key requirements for maintaining and building relationships. Describe how these requirements are translated into key quality measures.**
>
> **Note:**
>
> **(1)   Requirements (7.2a) might include responsiveness, product knowledge, follow-up, ease of access, etc. They do not include product and service requirements addressed in Item 7.1.**

What They're Looking For Here

Begin your response for this Area to Address by outlining the most important inteactions customers have with your employees or representatives. Jan Carlzon, president of SAS, calls these "moments of truth," because these are the make-it-or-break-it opportunities an organization has with the customer. A customer's opinion of your company will depend on how you perform during all of these moments of truth. For an airline, the more important transactions where customers interact with airline employees might be as follows:

- Making a reservation
- Checking baggage
- Buying a ticket and checking in for a flight
- Taking the flight
- Retrieving baggage
- Resolving a problem

These are the points at which most customers interact with airline personnel. For a car company, the two major points of interaction are when the customer buys the car and when the car needs service.

After defining the important customer interaction points/transactions, define what the key customer requirements are. These are the factors that customer care about at this point in their interaction with you. For example, when retrieving our baggage from a flight, most of us care about three things:

1. Did our luggage arrive on the flight we were on?
2. Was our luggage undamaged?
3. How long did we have to wait for the luggage?

In your response, define the major customer requirements or needs for each major point of interaction with customer-contact employees. Finally, explain how you track or measure whether or not you meet the requirements. The question says: "Describe how these requirements are translated into key quality measures." This means, "What do you measure to determine your performance levels in meeting the customer requirements?" Once again, this is a situation where a chart might be a good way of presenting all of the information called for. An example is shown below for an accounting firm that presents all three types of information asked for in this Area to Address.

Major Interaction Points	Key Cust. Requirements	Indicators
Audit planning meeting	• All key players in attendance	Attendance log
	• Major milestones defined	Project plan
	• Labor budget established	Project plan
	• Efficiency of meeting	Customer Satisfaction Survey

Indicators for Area 7.2a

- Extent to which response includes a definition of all important processes and/or transactions where customers come into contact with the organization's employees or representatives

- Identification of key customer requirements for *all* key points of interaction

- Thoroughness and clarity of customer requirements

- Identification of measurement indicators to assess whether or not requirements are being met

- Objectivity and validity of measurement indices

- Degree to which measurement indices have been identified for all key customer requirements for all key interactions

---

AREA TO ADDRESS   **[APPROACH, DEPLOYMENT]**

7.2b How service standards based upon the key quality measures (7.2a) are set and used. Include: 1) how service standards including measures and performance levels, are deployed to customer contact employees and to other company units that provide support for customer-contact employees; and (2) how the performance of the overall service standards system is tracked.

Notes:

(2)   "Service standards" refers to performance levels or expectations the company sets using the quality measures.

(3)   The term "customer-contact employees" refers to employees whose main responsibilities bring them into regular contact with customers— in person, via telephone, or other means.

What They're Looking For Here

This section should build on the indicators or indices you defined in section 7.2a. This is one area in which even service companies receive a low rating because they either fail to list their customer service standards or they list standards that are not well defined or objectively measurable. Many applicants explain that they do set standards, and that those standards are based upon customers requirements, but they never list the standards or the requirements so that the relationship between the two can be seen.

Begin your response for this Area to Address by listing the major customer service standards for your organization. If you have more than ten to fifteen standards, explain how many you have and list the major ones. An effective way to present the standards for your organization may be to categorize them according to the following factors:

- Timeliness
- Courtesy
- Efficiency
- Thoroughness/Completeness

A customer service standard should always have two parts. The first part is the behavior or action the employee should perform, and the second is the standard or criterion that specifies how well the action must be done. Some examples are as follows:

"Approach customers *within three minutes* of the time they enter the department."

"End the transaction by *thanking the customer for using AT&T*."

"Greet members *using their names* when they walk into the club."

The italicized parts of the statements are the criteria or standards that specify how a task should be done or how well it should be done.

Standards should always be stated in a manner that allows conformance to be reliably and objectively measured. Many applicants list standards that include words and phrases such as, "in a friendly manner," "showing empathy for the customer's situation," "promptly," or, "in an efficient manner." While these may all be good adjectives to describe service, they are neither precise nor objectively measurable. My definition of "promptness" may be quite different from yours. Standards need to be very specific and quantified whenever possible.

After listing your customer service standards, the second half of your response to this area should concentrate on how the standards are based upon customer requirements. Many organizations base their standards upon either past performance or industry standards. For example, a medical insurance company uses a standard of 30 days for the time that it should take to process a customer's claim. The 30 days is based upon industry standards. If, on the other hand, the company asked *customers* how long it should take (which it hasn't), customers would probably say one week or so. Your score in this area will be partially based upon how well you demonstrate that your major customer service standards are derived from customer requirements and expectations.

In almost all companies, it is impossible for customer-contact employees to meet customer service standards by themselves. In a restaurant, the waiter must rely upon the host/hostess, food buyer, restaurant manager, cooks, chef and others to help meet customer service standards. In a manufacturing plant, the sales representatives must rely upon production, quality assurance, procurement, accounting, production control, and other departments to help meet customer service standards. In any organization, the people who have the face-to-face contact with the customers must count on the cooperation of many others to help them deliver services and products that meet all of the customers' expectations and needs.

For this to happen, it is essential that all the employees who help the customer-contact people to achieve their goals are knowledgeable of the customer service standards and are held accountable for completing the tasks necessary to enable the customer-contact people to meet those standards. One applicant who received a high score in this area presented a list of customer service standards along the left side of a chart, and a list of the various functions in the organization horizontally along the top of the chart. Codes were used to indicate the degree of influence each support department had in helping to achieve the customer service standard. A portion of such a chart is shown as follows.

ACCOUNTABILITIES – CUSTOMER SERVICE STANDARDS					
STANDARDS	ACCOUNTING	PROCUREMENT	ENGINEERING	PRODUCTION	HRD
Deliver all orders by customer deadline	4	3	4	1	3
Provide appropriate prints and documentation with orders	4	4	1	3	3
Answer technical questions within 24 hours	4	4	1	2	3
Key: 1 = Primary Responsibility 3 = Support Responsibility 2 = Secondary Responsibility 4 = No Responsibility					

This chart is only one way of depicting the level of responsibility each function has in assisting customer-contact employees in meeting customer service standards. Your response needs to explain how support departments and others are made aware of the customer service standards and how they are held accountable for helping to achieve them.

Simply setting customer service standards and communicating them to all employees will not ensure that the standards are met. The expression "you get what you measure" is very true. If you do not track and measure the degree to which standards are met, you can almost guarantee that they will not be met on a consistent basis. Quality improvement is a matter of selecting measurement indices, setting standards, measuring performance against those standards, and sending performance feedback to employees who have influence or control over the indices.

Performance of customer-contact employees compared to established standards needs to be measured and the data fed back to employees in a timely and consistent manner. A great many service and manufacturing companies receive low scores for this area because they do not measure performance against the customer service standards, other than by surveying customers. Surveying customers is a very imprecise way to measure performance against standards. It is important to gather customer opinion about how well you meet satisfaction standards, but you should also have your own internal measurement that gets done.

As customers, the expectations and standards we have for the products and services we buy are constantly changing. Because of the poor on-time performance of airlines in recent years, many of us have lowered our expectations. Other standards have been raised. We expect our cars to be more trouble-free, to need less maintenance, and to run more efficiently than in the past.

Your response for this Area to Address should also briefly explain a process for periodically evaluating the validity of your customer service standards. This should be done through ongoing research into customer requirements and expectations. The requirements and expectations should then be translated into new or revised customer service standards. After describing your approach to evaluating customer service standards, present information on how the standards have evolved or changed over the last several years. A trend indicating that the changes have resulted in more stringent standards will earn you points in this section of your application.

Previous Areas to Address suggest that customer requirements should be the guideline used to set standards. However, what customers expect is sometimes not reasonable or possible given the organization's constraints on resources and the profit margin required. For example, customers may expect never to have to wait in line when they come into a bank branch. Establishing this as a standard may be unrealistic, however, given the constraints on the bank's human resources.

This Area to Address suggests that customer-contact employees should be involved in helping to interpret the customer requirements and setting standards. Standards should not be arbitrarily set by management without a great deal of input from the employees who must perform to the standards. Your response for this area should be specific, outlining exactly how and when employees get involved in setting, evaluating or modifying standards. Many applicants make the mistake of generalizing statements to the effect that, "employees are involved in every step of the process we utilize to set standards for customer service." General statements such as this won't earn many points, because they lack substance and possibly even credibility. Employees should be involved in periodic reviews and adjustments of standards based upon performance, changing business conditions, and changing customer requirements.

Indicators For Area 7.2b

- Response includes a listing of the major customer service standards that the organization has set

- Standards are listed for all important aspects of service, such as timeliness, courtesy, efficiency, etc.

- Standards are specific and conformance can be objectively and reliably measured

- All standards include actions/behaviors and standards/criteria for how or how well the behavior should be performed (action verbs and adjectives)

- Standards are clearly derived from customer expectations and requirements

- Definition of accountabilities for each customer service standard

- Method of deployment of customer service standards information to all company units and functions is systematic and effective for size and type of applicant's organization

- Performance evaluation of all functions in the organization is partially based upon the degree to which these functions assist customer-contact employees in meeting customer service standards

- What customer-contact employees have to say about the amount of support they receive from other departments and functions in helping them to achieve or exceed customer service standards

- Data on behavior of customer-contact employees in relation to standards is collected using internal and external (customer) measurements

- Data on accomplishments of customer-contact employees in relation to standards is collected using internal and external (customer) measurements

- Objectivity of sample sizes and of data collection instruments and methodologies

- Data on performance against customer service standards is fed back to customer-contact employees in a timely manner

- Reports on performance against customer service standards present data on individual and group performance

- Reports on performance against customer service standards are clear and easy to read

- Evidence that a systematic process is used to evaluate customer service standards

- Objectivity and reliability of data collection methodology for evaluating customer service standards

- Frequency of evaluation

- Degree to which evaluation is based upon customer requirements and expectations

- Trend showing that standards have evolved and become more stringent over the past several years

- Percentage of customer service standards on which input from customer-contact employees was sought

- Employees opinion about the amount of input they have in defining customer service standards

- Existence of a formal process for involving customer-contact employees at key decision points in selecting and defining customer service standards

---

AREA TO ADDRESS   **[APPROACH, DEPLOYMENT]**
7.2c How the company provides information and easy access to enable customers to seek assistance, to comment and to complain. Describe the main types of contact and how easy access is maintained for each type.

What They're Looking For Here

This is one area in which many quality-oriented companies have difficulty. Probably the best way of ensuring easy access for customers to comment on an organization's products or services is to have a company representative visit each customer frequently. In some organizations this may not be feasible, so other methods must be used. The key here is to make it easy for the customer. Most organizations place the burden upon the customer to exert the effort and take the initiative to comment on service or product quality. If, however, you take the initiative to determine customer comments rather than waiting for them to complain, you will excel in this section.

Another aspect of your response for this area is that of how easy it is for the customer to take the initiative to comment or complain about your products or services. Many organizations have customer service 800-numbers or hotlines. While this is a great idea, many of that the companies I've dealt with don't adequately staff their customer service phone lines, so that the lines are either busy for hours or you're put on hold forever while waiting for the "next available customer service representative." If you have an 800-number or hotline for customer comments and questions, your response here should include data that indicate the prompt and efficient handling of incoming calls by your staff.

Comment cards are another common technique for allowing customers to voice their opinions. These are frequently used by hotels, restaurants, car dealers, and others. If you make use of these cards or a similar instrument, explain how customers receive or obtain the cards, how much time it takes to fill them out, and what the customers need to do to turn them in. If you simply leave the cards lying out in your place of business for the customer to choose to fill out—in their hotel room, on the seat of a new car, on the restaurant table—only people who are very upset about poor service will take the time to fill them out. If the customer needs to put a stamp on the card and mail it, even fewer of them will bother to fill out and send in the comment card. The same is true of product comment cards that are included with the owners manual of many consumer products. Only people who fill out the cards are part of the sample, so the sample is not representative of all customers.

To receive a high score for your response to this area, you must first have a well-designed and simple system for customers to comment on your products or services, and second, a set of data from customer surveys and interviews that suggest how truly easy it is to comment, complain, or get a question answered. If 98% of your customers say that your customer service department answers the phones in three rings or less and is able to answer questions or resolve problems adequately almost every time, the Baldrige Examiners will take notice. Thus, your approach, deployment, and results are important in this Area to Address.

Indicators For Area 7.2c

- Customers know how and/or whom to contact with questions, comments, or complaints about the products/services offered by the organization

- Applicant uses a variety of approaches to make it easy for customers to comment on the products/services (e.g., 800-number, customer service department, comment cards, etc.)

- Evidence that phone lines and/or customer service departments are adequately staffed for number of calls received

- Amount of effort and time customers have to spend in order to comment, complain, or get questions answered about the applicant's products/services

- Data from customer interviews and/or surveys to suggest that customers are happy with the applicant's ability to handle their comments, questions, or complaints

---

AREA TO ADDRESS   **[APPROACH, DEPLOYMENT]**
7.2d How the company follows up with customers on products, services, and recent transactions to seek feedback and to help build relationships.

What They're Looking For Here

The frequency, thoroughness, and objectivity of the data you gather on how satisfied current customers are with your products and services is important in this Area to Address. A typical response for this area is to explain, "We survey our customers once a year to determine their level of satisfaction with our products/services." Conducting a survey once a year represents a very weak follow-up approach. The examiners look for frequent contact with customers (e.g., quarterly or monthly) to determine how satisfied they are with your products and services. They also want to see that you use a variety of different follow-up methods, such as phone calls, mail surveys, etc. Although the approach should be comprehensive, it is also very important that it minimizes the amount of time the customer must spend giving you feedback. Too much follow-up can be an aggravation to the customer and end up doing more to turn him/her off than anything else. Explain how your approach to follow-up is sensitive to these issues and back it up with any data that indicate customers' opinion of your follow-up system. It is also important that you do informal follow-up with customers—not to collect customer satisfaction data, but simply to build a more positive relationship.

Indicators for Area 7.2d

- Percentage of customers surveyed during follow-up to determine their levels of satisfaction with your products and/or services

- Frequent informal contact is done to build strong relationships with customers

- Use of a variety of different data collection methods as follow-up on customer transactions

- Follow-up approach demonstrates concern for minimizing customer time and hassle

- Proactive follow-up is done for all types of customers and all of the organization's products and services

---

AREA TO ADDRESS   **[APPROACH, DEPLOYMENT]**

7.2e How the company ensures that formal and informal complaints and feedback received by all company units are resolved promptly and effectively. Briefly describe the complaint management process.

Notes:

(6)   Information on trends and levels in measures and indicators of complaint response time, effective resolution, and percent of complaints resolved on first contact should be reported in Item 6.1.

(7)   How feedback and complaint data are aggregated for overall evaluation and how these data are translated into actionable information, should be addressed in 2.3a.

<u>What They're Looking For Here</u>

Most companies have systems for filing and summarizing complaint letters and phone complaints made to customer service departments. However, the majority of customers who have comments on the services and products they buy don't bother writing a letter or calling a customer service department. Many organizations we buy from don't even have customer service departments. The Baldrige Examiners are looking for methods and procedures you have in place to capture the formal and informal customer comments or complaints. Most of the informal data get lost in many organizations, creating an unrealistic picture of actual levels of customer satisfaction. For example, the comments you make to the copier machine repair person or the field support representative from the computer company may never be recorded anywhere. Comments made to salespeople, or even customer-contact employees, are often heard and then forgotten.

In order to receive a high score for this area, you need to demonstrate that you have a comprehensive, yet simple, system for documenting all written and/or verbal comments made by customers about the quality of your products and services. You also need to have a system for summarizing and reporting all formal and informal complaints/ comments received from customers.

Your response should include a combination of process description and results. A flowchart, algorithm, or a list of steps should be included that depict the process for responding to and correcting customer complaints. You should also explain the escalation process that occurs when a customer feels that his/her complaint has not been resolved satisfactorily. Your process will be assessed for its logic, thoroughness, and the degree to which it fits your type of business and the size of your company.

The second part of your response for this area should include data covering a variety of different indices that show you are timely in resolving customer complaints, and that complaints are resolved completely and with a minimum of inconvenience to the customer. Data on the number of complaints received is not really relevant to this Area to Address. The number of complaints received is a measure of the quality of services and/or products offered by the organization. This section should focus on how well you handle and resolve the complaints that do come in. Preventing complaints in the first place is addressed elsewhere.

One of the most common mistakes that applicants make in responding to these "process" items is to write a brief and very general description of how they deal with a particular issue or input. A typical response is as follows.

> *Each complaint received is analyzed by customer service representatives to determine its root cause. The cause of the complaint must be recorded on the Complaint Log form. Once a month, a summary report is prepared that lists the causes of complaints and provides statistics on the number of complaints tied to specific causes. Reports are sent to the department managers who have responsibility for correcting the causes of the complaints.*

The problem with a response such as this is that it is too vague and the process described does not explain:

- The steps a customer service representative follows to analyze the cause(s) of a problem

- The knowledge customer service representatives have to analyze the cause(s) of customer complaints

- How the organization follows up on corrective actions that need to be taken to correct problem situations

Sending a report to managers once a month is not an effective system for resolving problems.

Your response for this Area to Address should also explain how you use your analyses of the causes of customer complaints to improve processes, products, and services in the organization. Describe the process, and perhaps give an example or two of how you have used customer-complaint analyses to modify processes or a product/service.

Indicators For Area 7.2e

- Comprehensiveness of system for tracking customer comments and complaints

- Objectivity of the approach for gathering and documenting data on customer comments and/or complaints

- All employees who have telephone or personal contact with customers have a simple but thorough way of documenting any incidental comments or complaints heard about the company's products or services

- Data on customer comments/complaints from a variety of sources is aggregated for overall evaluation and comparison

- Data on customer comments/complaints is fed back to appropriate personnel in a timely fashion

- Customers believe that the comments/complaints they make to any of the organization's employees will get documented and reported

- Existence of a formal and logical process for resolving customer complaints

- Clearly defined escalation procedures for situations in which customers do not feel their complaint has been resolved by lower level personnel

- Trend showing reductions in the amount of time needed to resolve customer complaints over the past few years

- Current performance on the amount of time needed to resolve complaints is exemplary

- Data showing customer satisfaction with the handling of complaints

- Objectivity and reliability of data on levels of customer satisfaction with the handling of complaints

- Data on the thoroughness with which complaints are handled

- Organized and systematic process for analyzing the causes of customer complaints

- Description of process clearly depicts inputs, process steps, and outputs

- Level of clarity and amount of detail in description of process is appropriate

- Those analyzing the causes of customer complaints have the knowledge and skills to do so

- Information on the causes of customer complaints is fed back to employees who can correct the problems

- Evidence that complaint data are used to initiate improvement projects that prevent the future complaints and potential loss of customers

- Evidence that analyses of causes of customer complaints are used to make changes in processes, products, and/or services

---

AREA TO ADDRESS   **[APPROACH, DEPLOYMENT]**

7.2f   How the following are addressed for customer-contact employees: (1) selection factors; (2) career path; (3) deployment of special training to include: knowledge of products and services; listening to customers; soliciting comments from customers; how to anticipate and handle problems or failures ("recovery"); skills in customer retention; and how to manage expectations; (4) empowerment and decision making; (5) satisfaction; and (6) recognition and reward.

Notes:

(4)   **In addressing "empowerment and decision making" in 7.2f, indicate how the company ensures that there is a common vision or basis to guide the actions of customer-contact employees. That is, the response should make clear how the company ensures that empowered customer-contact employees have a consistent understanding of what actions or types of actions they may or should take.**

(5)   **In addressing satisfaction (7.2f), consider indicators such as turnover and absenteeism, as well as results of employee feedback through surveys, exit interviews, etc.**

What They're Looking For Here

This Area to Address tends to be confusing, and many applicants have difficulty responding to it. A common response is to say, "We put all of our customer contact employees through our extensive orientation program which gives them a clear view of our approach to customer service and quality." Almost all organizations have orientation programs, so orienting your customer-contact employees won't earn you many points. You will, however, earn points if you have a unique or thorough approach to selecting customer-contact employees.

Along with the use of innovative approaches to selecting customer-contact employees, your approach to defining the hiring requirements for these employees will also be examined. One applicant who received a very high score for this area based hiring requirements on a study of its most successful customer-contact employees. By studying these individuals, they were able to determine exactly what skills and abilities they possessed that made them so successful. This list of skills and abilities then became the hiring criteria by which the company evaluated all candidates for customer-contact positions.

Any special training or recognition programs you have in place for customer-contact employees should also be described in this area. Make sure you explain the purpose of the program, how it works (briefly), and the results you have achieved from the program. If it is a special training program on interpersonal skills, for example, describe the course, explain what specific skills it is designed to teach, and list any data you have that demonstrate how effective the course is in providing employees with the needed skills.

Most organizations talk a great deal about empowerment, but few do more than give frontline employees slightly more authority to make decisions. When it comes to empowering customer-contact employees, most organizations don't trust their employees enough to give them any real problem-solving or decision-making authority. Your response to this Area to Address should begin with an overview of your strategies and plans for increasing the degree of empowerment given to frontline employees. You should list specific actions, not just general comments. One applicant that had an outstanding application in many areas received a very poor evaluation for this Area to Address because their response was three sentences long, and provided only very general information suggesting that they empower employees to make decisions and solve problems.

After describing your strategies and plans for increasing empowerment, you should present evidence that you actually do empower customer-contact employees. Evidence can consist of things such as:

- Policies that clearly define limits of authority

- Escalation procedures and different levels of decision-making authority

- Surveys of employees regarding the degree to which they believe the organization empowers them to make decisions and to solve customer problems

- Data on the number of problems that get escalated to management rather than being solved at lower levels.

It is important in your response to show increased degrees of empowerment over the past several years. If you can compare past authority levels and policies to those of the present, this will provide a convincing argument to the examiners about how you've made steady progress in increasing the levels of empowerment. An example or two of extraordinary measures that employees have taken to satisfy customers will also help to convince examiners that you support your employees in their efforts to do whatever it takes to keep customers satisfied.

Indicators For Area 7.2f

- Identification of unique skills or abilities required of customer-contact employees

- Objectivity of process used to assess special hiring requirements of customer-contact employees

- Existence of specific plans and strategies for dealing with attrition of customer-contact personnel

- Thoroughness and effectiveness of selection procedures and instruments used for customer-contact employee positions

- Validation of selection instruments in the organization to make sure they are good predictors of success in customer-contact jobs

- Amount and effectiveness of special training given to customer-contact employees

- Existence of special recognition or reinforcement programs for customer-contact employees

- Extent to which recognition/reward programs promote quality, versus sales, cost control, or other indices

- Strategies and plans to increase levels of empowerment of customer-contact employees

- Degree to which plans and strategies have been effectively deployed throughout the organization

- Amount of authority customer-contact employees have now as compared to in the past

- Policies and procedures to support claims made about degree of empowerment

- Organizational hierarchy, reporting relationships, and levels of authority are indicative of high degrees of empowerment

- Evidence to suggest that customer-contact employees are really empowered to make decisions and solve problems

- What customer-contact employees have to say about their levels of authority and the degree to which the organization empowers them

- Evidence that the organization's management supports frontline employees in their decisions to satisfy customers

- Examples of extraordinary measures or actions that have been taken in efforts to satisfy customers

- Evidence of data gathering to determine levels of satisfaction among customer contact employees

---

AREA TO ADDRESS   **[APPROACH, DEPLOYMENT]**
7.2g How the company evaluates and improves its customer relationship management processes. Include: (1) how the company seeks opportunities to enhance relationships with all customers or with key customers; and (2) how evaluations lead to improvements such as in service standards, access, customer-contact employee training, and technology support; and (3) how customer information is used in the improvement process.

What They're Looking For Here

As with all other Areas to Address that relate to internal evaluation, your response to this item should demonstrate the following pattern:

- Definition of evaluation factors/indices
- Collection of data on indices/factors
- Analysis of data
- Implementation of changes or corrective actions to improve services to customers

A flowchart or graphic would be helpful when presenting this information. Follow the process description with a brief explanation of the types of changes you have implemented as a result of your evaluation data and the success or failure of those changes in improving customer satisfaction.

In order to receive high marks for this Area to Address, you should use multiple indices for evaluating customer relationship management. You should also collect data at multiple points in the relationship with customers. For example, some car companies survey customers 90 days, 3 years, and 5 years after they buy a car to determine how satisfaction may change as the car gets older.

Once you have described how you evaluate your performance in managing your relationships with your customers, you need to explain how these evaluation data are used. Examples of how you have improved training, technology or customer-related practices are all appropriate. You may also use these data as a stimulus for improving the way you evaluate your customer relationship management.

Indicators For Area 7.2g

- Use of a planned and systematic approach to evaluate and improve service to customers, and customer relationship management

- Objectivity of data collection methods used to evaluate customer relationship

- Strategies employed to improve customer relationships are specific and based upon analysis of data

- Number and credibility of examples given to support process description

- Evidence that approach to servicing customers has improved as a result of evaluation data

- Breadth and scope of changes and improvements that have been initiated based on evaluations of customer relationship management

---

7.3 COMMITMENT TO CUSTOMERS

Describe the company's commitments to customers regarding its products/services and how these commitments are evaluated and improved. (15 points)

Note:

> **Examples of commitments are product and service guarantees, warranties, and other understandings, expressed or implied.**

AREA TO ADDRESS　　　　　　　　　　**[APPROACH, DEPLOYMENT]**
7.3a Types of commitments the company makes to promote trust and confidence in its products/services and to satisfy customers when product/service failures occur. Describe these commitments and how they: (1) address the principal concerns of customers; (2) are free from conditions that might weaken customer's trust and confidence; and (3) are communicated to customers clearly and simply.

What They're Looking For Here

This is a very straightforward Area to Address if you are an automobile company or a manufacturer of other consumer products. Most consumer-product firms have clear and written guarantees for their products. The examiners will be assessing the terms of the guarantee/warranty. For example, if you cover only a few components of the product, or if the warranty period is very short (e.g., 90 days or 1 year), you will lose points. Chrysler's 7-year/70,000 mile warranty is the best of all domestic auto manufacturers, and this would earn it a high score for the conditions of its warranty. Chrysler clearly believes in the quality of its products, and its warranty testifies to this fact.

Along with the conditions and comprehensiveness of the guarantees or warranties you offer on your products/services, the understandability of the written guarantee is assessed. In order for this to be reviewed, you have to include the text of your guarantee or warranty in your response. This might seem like common sense, but the majority of applicants do not include the actual warranty or guarantee in their applications. If you have many different guarantees for various products/services, you might select one that is representative of the lot and present this in your response. Clarity and understandability are assessed according to the degree of "legalese" and fine print that are included in the statements.

Another aspect of the examiners' assessment is the credibility of your guarantees/ warranties. Credibility is judged on the basis of the believability of your claims and the degree to which you have followed up on the promises your guarantees/warranties make. Data from customer surveys on how satisfied customers are with your adherence to the conditions of your guaranties/warranties is needed to establish credibility.

If you are a service company, or a supplier of products/components to larger manufacturing companies, you may have more difficulty responding to this Area to Address. You may not have formal and written guarantees or warranties. However, service companies are increasingly offering service guarantees. Domino's Pizza guarantees that your pizza will be delivered in 30 minutes. Hampton Inns guarantee that you will be satisfied, or you do not have to pay for your room. If you have no written guarantee, simply explain your policies and how you stand behind your products/services. Any supporting data you can present will lend credibility to your explanations.

Along with formal guarantees and warranties, you should explain other commitments you make to your customers. How you respond to this area is dependent upon the type of business you are in and the types of actions you can take to encourage customers to believe in the quality of your products/services. For example, Jaguar Cars has a program called "Service On Site." When you purchase a new Jaguar, you receive a card with an 800-number you can call if your car ever breaks down or if you are stranded because it won't operate. Jaguar will dispatch a repair technician to your location and either repair your car on-the-spot or tow it to a dealership for repairs. Cadillac and Mercedes Benz offer a similar service. In fact, Cadillac's commitment to follow-up service was one of the factors that led to its becoming a winner of the Baldrige Award in 1990. Commitments such as these help build the customer's trust in the quality and reliability of a product or service.

Your response for this item should also list any out-of-the-ordinary policies, guarantees, or features you offer on your products/services that demonstrate your commitment to customers. You should mention how your commitment to customers compares with that of major competitors and world-class leaders in your field. Your response will be given a higher score if you go beyond what any of your competitors do to demonstrate commitment to customers.

Indicators For Area 7.3a

- Comprehensiveness of warranty/guarantee coverage

- Comparison of applicant's guarantees/warranties to competition's

- Terms and conditions of guarantees/warranties (exclusions, etc.)

- Amount and objectivity of data indicating customer satisfaction with applicant's performance on terms of warranty/guarantee

- Response includes actual written warranties or guarantees

- Clarity and understandability of written guarantees and warranties (minimum of legalese and fine print)

- Credibility of guarantees/warranties—evidence that organization will follow through on claims

- Number of different programs or features that organization offers to demonstrate its commitment to customers

- How customers value the extra commitments the organization makes to see to the customer's satisfaction

- How innovative the organization's efforts/programs are for demonstrating its commitment to customers

- How applicant's commitment to customers compares to competitors and world-class leaders in the field

---

AREA TO ADDRESS   **[APPROACH, DEPLOYMENT]**

7.3b How the company evaluates and improves its commitments, and the customers' understanding of them, to avoid gaps between expectations and company performance. Include: (1) how information/feedback from customers is used; (2) how product/service performance improvement data are used; and (3) how competitors' commitments are considered.

What They're Looking For Here

The Baldridge Examiners are looking for evidence in this section that you systematically evaluate and improve your guarantees, warranties, or other commitments to customers. Your response should explain the specific measurement indices you use to evaluate your commitments. If you have only one product with only one guarantee, you will be able to evaluate the guarantee very easily. If you have many products and services, your approach to evaluation will be considerably more complex. As in many of the previous sections, I suggest that you prepare a matrix that summarizes how you evaluate various aspects of your commitments to customers.

Product/Service	Guarantee	Measurement Index	Measurement Method

The first column would list your major products and/or services, followed by the specific guarantees, warranties, or other commitments you offer. The third column should list the measurement indices you use. For example, one index may be the number of complaints received that relate to warranty or guarantee performance. Another index may be what customers have to say about the fairness or clarity of the warranties you offer. The final column should be used to list the methodologies you employ to collect the evaluation data. For example, you may ask specific questions about guarantees on customer surveys that you do periodically.

In this Area to Address, the examiners are also looking for a trend of increasing confidence in the quality of your products/services as a result of your offering stronger guarantees and/or warranties. If you used to guarantee your products for 90 days, and now they are guaranteed for two years, this will be of interest to the examiners. Data you present should show a trend of continuous improvements in your warranties, guarantees, and other commitments to customers. If you have not changed or improved any of your commitments or guarantees, you should explain how your current offering is superior to what any competitor offers.

Indicators For Area 7.3b

- Extent to which commitments on all major products/services are evaluated

- Appropriateness of measurement indices selected for evaluation of guarantees, warranties, or other commitments

- Validity, scope, and objectivity of measurement indices

- Use of multiple types of data to evaluate guarantees, warranties, or othercommitments

- Evidence that improvements in clarity and strength of guarantees, warranties, or other commitments have been made over the last few years

- Number and degree of improvements applicant has made in warranties and guarantees over the last three years

- Significance of improvements that have been made in warranties and guarantees

- Trend showing improvement in written or implied warranties and guarantees in their strength and clarity

- Comparison of applicant's customer commitments to major competitors' commitments

- Existence of data that demonstrate that customers completely understand commitments your organization makes regarding its products/services

---

7.4 CUSTOMER SATISFACTION DETERMINATION

Describe how the company determines customer satisfaction, customer repurchase intentions, and customer satisfaction relative to competitors; describe how these determination processes are evaluated and improved. (30 points)

AREA TO ADDRESS   **[APPROACH, DEPLOYMENT]**

7.4a How the company determines customer satisfaction. Include: (1) a brief description of the methods, processes, and measurement scales used; frequency of determination; and how objectivity and validity are assured. Indicate significant differences, if any, in these satisfaction methods, processes, and measurement scales for different customer groups or segments; and (2) how customer satisfaction measurements capture key information that reflects customers' likely market behavior, such as repurchase intentions.

Notes:

   (1)   **Customer satisfaction measurement may include both a numerical rating scale and descriptors assigned to each unit in the scale. An effective (actionable) customer satisfaction measurement system is one that provides the company with reliable information about customer ratings of specific product and service features and the relationship between these ratings and the customer's likely market behavior.**

   (2)   **The company's products and services might be sold to end users via other businesses such as retail stores or dealers. Thus "customer groups" or segments should take into account these other businesses as well as the end users.**

   (3)   **Customer dissatisfaction indicators include complaints, claims, refunds, recalls, returns, repeat services, litigation, replacements, downgrades, repairs, warranty work, warranty costs, misshipments, and incomplete orders.**

What They're Looking For Here

There are many ways to measure customer satisfaction. Most companies rely upon only two methods:

- Comment/Feedback Cards
- Annual mail survey sent to all or a sample of customers

While these two approaches are certainly valid, if this is all you do it is not likely that you are obtaining a clear view of the degree to which customers are satisfied with your products/services. The problem with comment cards and surveys is that most customers can't be bothered to take the time to fill them out. Or if they do fill them out, they do so quickly and carelessly, rating everything average or above average. As consumers of numerous goods and services, we are inundated with requests for our opinions and feedback. Most of us respond to a few of these requests and ignore the rest, unless we are extremely unhappy with the level of service or product quality. And when we are very unhappy, we usually don't bother with filling out a comment card or waiting for the annual survey—we write a letter or make a phone call right away.

The most objective way to measure customer satisfaction is by examining customers' behavior, not their opinions. The fact that Mr. Green traded in his 1988 Ford Taurus for a 1992 model from the same dealership says more about Mr. Green's level of satisfaction than any survey could. In fact, if you surveyed Mr. Green, you might find that there are a number of things he didn't like about his Taurus. The bottom line, though, is that he bought another one. The amount of repeat business an organization receives is one of the best indicators of customer satisfaction. (—Unless you're the only game in town. If you live in Butte, Montana, for example, there may be only one Mercedes dealer who sells or services those cars.)

Market share can be an indicator of customer satisfaction, but it is not a good one. Market share is influenced by too many extraneous factors such as competition, advertising, and pricing. In this Area to Address, the examiners are looking for an approach to measuring customer satisfaction that takes into account a variety of different sources of data. Opinion data should be gathered using several approaches and large representative samples of all the organization's customers. Other measures, such as repeat business, need to be used to supplement opinion data. The specific measures you utilize will depend upon the nature of your products/services. A single measure can be misleading, so the use of multiple indices and data gathering methodologies adds a great deal of objectivity and reliability to your approach.

If you are a large corporation with many products and/or services, chances are that you serve a variety of customers with differing needs and levels of satisfaction with your products/services. For example, a large service company might have hotels, restaurants and amusement parks, each catering to different types of customers. A company that makes only personal computers may have many different types of customers for their single product. Customers may be segmented based upon how they will use their personal computers.

In this Area to Address, the Baldrige Examiners are also looking for evidence that you segment your customers in a logical manner and that your customer satisfaction efforts address the various segments. In some cases, it won't make sense to segment them at all.

However, even if you are a small business you should probably be categorizing your customers somehow. If 60% of your business is conducted with AT&T, for example, and the rest is with miscellaneous small companies, you might segment your customers into two groups: (1) AT&T and (2) all others.

Indicators For Area 7.4a

- Number of different sources of data on customer satisfaction

- Use of objective measures such as repeat business along with opinion data

- Frequency with which customer satisfaction is measured

- Adequate sample sizes used when measuring customer satisfaction

- Extent to which customers in all segments/markets are included in customer satisfaction data

- Validation done with customer satisfaction instruments prior to their use

- Reliability of instruments used to measure customer satisfaction

- Use of multiple approaches to gather customer opinion data, such as surveys, focus groups, etc.

- Logical approach for segmenting customers and customer satisfaction data

- Use of measurement indices and instruments that are unique to each customer group's expectations and needs regarding your products/services

- Separate sets of data collected on levels of customer satisfaction for each major market group or segment

- Use of data collection instruments and methods that minimize the time customers must spend providing you with feedback.

AREA TO ADDRESS   **[APPROACH, DEPLOYMENT]**

7.4b How customer satisfaction relative to that for competitors is determined. Describe: (1) company-based comparative studies; and (2) comparative studies or evaluations made by independent organizations and/or customers. For (1) and (2), describe how objectivity and validity are assured.

Note:

    (4)   **Company-based or independent organization comparative studies (7.4b) might take into account one or more indicators of customer dissatisfaction as well as satisfaction. The extent and types of such studies may depend upon factors such as industry and company size.**

What They're Looking For Here

This Area to Address refers to how you determine how your levels of customer satisfaction compare with those of your competitors. We are not looking for data here; the criteria ask *how* you determine comparative levels of customer satisfaction. Including a question or two on your customer surveys to ask your customers what they think of your competition is a common way of doing this. This is certainly not the most objective way, however. You are surveying your own customers and they may never have bought the competition's products/services, even though they may have an opinion about them. A more complete approach is to use an outside research firm to measure customer satisfaction among your own and your competitors' customers. J. D. Power, the market research firm used by the automotive industry, uses the same instruments to measure customer satisfaction among customers of all car companies. This way, the data are objective and can be easily compared. Your approach need not be as comprehensive as that used by the automotive industry, but you need to demonstrate that you gather reliable data on the levels of customer satisfaction your competitors achieve relative to your own levels.

Indicators For Area 7.4b

- Use of a variety of sources of data on competitors' levels of customer satisfaction

- Objectivity of data gathered on how your customer satisfaction levels compare with competitors

- Amount of data collected on comparison of customer satisfaction levels to those of competitors

- Reliability of data gathering methods used to assess competitors' levels of customer satisfaction

---

AREA TO ADDRESS   **[APPROACH, DEPLOYMENT]**

7.4c How the company evaluates and improves its overall processes and measurement scales for determining customer satisfaction and customer satisfaction relative to that for competitors. Include how other indicators (such as gains and losses of customers) and customer dissatisfaction indicators (such as complaints) are used in this improvement process.

What They're Looking For Here

Since customer satisfaction is the most important index of quality in any organization, it is important that effort be put toward constantly evaluating and improving the methods and instruments used to assess customer satisfaction levels. A common response for this area is written as follows: "We evaluate the usefulness of each item on our customer satisfaction questionnaires annually, and revise the instruments based upon both customer feedback and the usefulness of the data each item generates." A response like this is too vague.

You should begin your response here by listing the indices you use to measure and evaluate the organization's approach to determining customer satisfaction. Explain why these indices have been selected as the best measures of the effectiveness of your customer satisfaction measurement system. Next, list the steps or phases involved in your evaluation process, along with the outputs of each phase. Describe how evaluation data are summarized and reported, and explain who receives the reports. Finally, explain the process you use to review the evaluation results and develop an action plan for improving your approach to measuring customer satisfaction. A description of some of the changes you've made over the years to the customer satisfaction measurement system will help demonstrate that you do, in fact, take action based upon the evaluation data. The Baldrige Examiners are looking for a trend of continuous improvements.

Indicators For Area 7.4c

- Explanation of a well-defined and systematic approach to evaluate customer satisfaction measurement system

- Objectivity and reliability of methodology and instruments used to evaluate customer satisfaction measurement system

- Evaluation data are summarized and sent to appropriate managers and other employees

- Action plans based upon evaluation data are created to identify improvements needed in customer satisfaction measurement system

- Evidence that actions plans are actually implemented and that changes have been made in measurement instruments and/or methodologies based upon evaluation data

- Trend showing continual improvements/enhancements in approach to measuring customer satisfaction over the last several years

- Evidence that improvements have been made in measurement of customer dissatisfaction indicators.

7.5 CUSTOMER SATISFACTION RESULTS

Summarize trends in the company's customer satisfaction and trends in key indicators of customer dissatisfaction. (85 points)

Note:

(1)   Results reported in this Item derive from methods described in Items 7.4 and 7.2.

AREA TO ADDRESS   **[RESULTS]**

7.5a Trends and current levels in key measures and/or indicators of customer satisfaction, including customer retention. Segment by customer group, as appropriate. Trends may be supported by objective information and/or data from customers demonstrating current or recent (past 3 years) satisfaction with the company's products/services.

Note:

  (2)   **Information supporting trends (7.5a) might include customer's assessments of products/services, customer awards, and customer retention.**

What They're Looking For Here

This is the area for which data should be reported that demonstrate how levels of customer satisfaction have improved over the last several years due to quality improvement efforts. This section should include graphs of customer satisfaction data for the different groups of customers you serve. Refer back to the guidelines included in Chapter 2 of this book for a discussion of how to prepare graphs and tables. Don't make the mistake some applicants have made and respond with a single graph of customer satisfaction data. Present several different graphs of customer satisfaction data from at least the past three years. Three data points do not establish much of a trend, so the more historical data you can present, the better.

In evaluating this section, the Baldrige Examiners will be looking for several things. The first is the amount of data you present on customer satisfaction. While you are constrained by the maximum of 75 pages for your entire application, some applicants devote only half a page to this important Area to Address. Include as much data as you can, and don't be afraid to use several pages for this area. It is possible to fit as many as eight separate graphs on one page. Tables or charts also allow you to fit a great deal of data in a small space. (Make sure that your graphs and charts are readable, however.)

Two other related factors examined are the level of customer satisfaction you have achieved and the current level of performance in relation to past levels. If 80% of your customers are satisfied or very satisfied with your quality, a large number (20%) still remain unsatisfied. If only 50% were satisfied three years ago, you will receive some credit for a big improvement, but your overall levels of satisfaction are still low.

Improvement is much more difficult when you are already doing well. It may take more effort and thus be more significant if you have raised customer satisfaction levels from 94% to 98% in three years. A trend showing steady improvement over the last three to five years is considered very positive.

The final factor examined in this Area to Address is the number of different indices and types of data you present on customer satisfaction. Different measures of customer satisfaction (or the same indices among different segments or groups of customers) should be presented. For example, you might present data on overall levels of satisfaction among new customers, existing customers, large company customers, small company customers, government customers, private sector customers, etc. Choose the breakdowns that make the most sense for your products/services and markets.

Indicators for Area 7.5a

- Number of different indices of customer satisfaction for which data are presented

- Presentation of customer satisfaction data by customer or market group

- Trend showing continual improvements over the last several years in all measures of customer satisfaction

- Amount of historical data presented on levels of customer satisfaction

- Overall levels of customer satisfaction (percent of customers satisfied with service, etc.)

- Clarity of graphs and explanations of customer satisfaction data

- Number and types of different breakdowns of customer satisfaction data

---

AREA TO ADDRESS   **[RESULTS]**

7.5b Trends in measures and/or indicators of customer dissatisfaction. Address the most relevant and important indicators for the company's products/ services.

Note:
(3)   Indicators of customer satisfaction are given in Item 7.4, Note 3.

What They're Looking For Here

Obviously, not all of the indices mentioned regarding dissatisfaction will be relevant to your organization. You should respond to this section by presenting data you have for any indicators that are a good gauge of customers' dissatisfaction with your products and/or services. Present the data graphically and include at least three years of statistics. The number of different indices for which data are presented and the degree to which the data show a steadily decreasing trend are the factors that will be evaluated in your response to this section.

It is likely that not all of the results and trends will be entirely positive. Performance on one or more indicators of customer dissatisfaction may not show a consistent downward trend. It is important that you thoroughly explain each of these anomalies or adverse trends. A thorough explanation does not mean that blame should be placed elsewhere for the occurrence of the anomaly. It simply means that you can describe exactly why these phenomena occurred and explain the steps taken to prevent future lapses in performance.

Indicators For Area 7.5b

- Number of different indices for which data are presented

- Data are presented for all important adverse indices or measures of dissatisfaction in industry

- All adverse indicators show steady downward trend over the past three or more years

- Minimum number of anomalies or positive trends in dissatisfaction indicators

- Clear and complete explanations provided for all anomalies in data or positive trends in dissatisfaction indicators

- Overall levels of performance on indicators of dissatisfaction

7.6 CUSTOMER SATISFACTION COMPARISON

Compare the company's customer satisfaction results with those of competitors. (70 points)

Notes:

(1)   Results reported in this Item derive from methods described in Item 7.4.

(2)   Competitors include domestic and international ones in the company's markets, both domestic and international.

AREA TO ADDRESS   **[RESULTS]**

7.6a Trends and current levels in key measures and/or indicators of customer satisfaction relative to competitors. Segment by customer group, as appropriate. Trends may be supported by objective information and/or data from independent organizations, including customers.

Note:

(3)   Objective information and/or data from independent organizations, including customers (7.6a), might include survey results, competitive awards, recognition, and ratings. Such surveys, competitive awards, recognition, and ratings by independent organizations and customers should reflect comparative satisfaction (and dissatisfaction), not comparative performance of products and services. Information on comparative performance of products and services should be included in 6.1b.

What They're Looking For Here

In this section of your application, you should present data demonstrating that your customers are more satisfied with your products and/or services than any of your competitors' customers are with their products/services. Your performance relative to that of your competitors is the most important factor evaluated in your response to this area. This is an Area to Address on which many applicants lose points because they have little comparison data, or their results are not significant when compared to competitors' levels of customer satisfaction. You can earn a high score on Item 7.4 for your customer satisfaction results and still earn a very low score for this Item if your levels of customer satisfaction are not better than most of your competitors'.

It is important in your response for this area that you compare your performance on several dimensions of customer satisfaction to several key competitors. The organizations you compare yourself to are also important. Comparing yourself to a world-class leader instead of local competitors will obviously earn you more points.

Indicators For Area 7.6a

- Number of different competitors to which comparisons are made

- Number of different indices of customer satisfaction on which comparisons are made to the competition

- Status/level of competitors (e.g., world-class leader in field) to which comparisons are made

- Percentage of customer satisfaction indices on which applicant is superior to the competition

- Applicant's superiority to competition in measures of customer satisfaction

- Objectivity of data on how applicant compares to competition

- Extent to which competitors in all major markets and with all major products/services are used for comparison

---

AREA TO ADDRESS   **[RESULTS]**

7.6b Trends in gaining and losing customers, or customer accounts, to competitors.

What They're Looking For Here

In your response for this area, you must first show that you systematically measure gains and losses in customers. It is surprising how many organizations don't track this. In addition, you should have data on why customers decide to buy your products/services or why they decide to buy elsewhere. Present the data on gains and losses of customers in "numbers of customers," not just in "dollars." Obtaining additional sales from an existing customer is not the same as gaining a new customer.

The examiners want to see that your results in the area of quality and customer satisfaction are responsible for gains in new customers and reductions in the number of lost customers. Trends over the past several years should show increases in the number of new customers and decreases in lost customers. Point out correlations in the data between the implementation of quality improvement methods and any increase in new customers. If, however, you began your quality improvement efforts in 1988 but you have been steadily gaining customers since 1985, you can't justifiably say that the quality improvement efforts were solely responsible for the results. Your score for this area will be enhanced if you can demonstrate a cause-and-effect relationship between your quality improvement efforts and data on gains and losses of customers.

Indicators For Area 7.5b

- A systematic and objective method is used to collect data on gains/losses of customers

- Data trends show continual increase in number of new customers over the past three or more years

- Data trends show continual decreases in number of lost customers over the past three or more years

- Extent to which cause/effect relationships are shown between gains/losses of customers and quality improvement efforts of the organization

- Gains in customers are not due to competitors going out of business or no longer being in the same markets

---

AREA TO ADDRESS   **[RESULTS]**
7.6c Trends in gaining or losing market share to competitors.

What They're Looking For Here

This Area to Address is similar to 7.6b. The difference is that we are looking at market share rather than the number of new or lost customers. As in the previous area, the examiners want to see that your market share has increased as a result of your quality improvement results. Data should be presented for all of your major products and/or services in all the major markets you serve. If you present information on only a couple of your products/services or a couple of markets, the examiners will probably suspect that the missing data are negative.

Your results should demonstrate continual increases in your market share and show a cause-effect relationship between improvements in your quality and increases in market share. Market share is determined by many factors that have nothing to do with quality. For example, your market share could have increased because you cut your prices. Or, it could have increased because the size of the market increased and the number of competitors decreased. Advertising, marketing, pricing, product availability, and many other factors influence market share. It is not enough to show that your market share has increased steadily over the last few years. You need to demonstrate that your market share has increased primarily because you offer higher-quality goods/services than your competitors.

Indicators For Area 7.6c

- Trends show gains in shares in key markets over the last several years

- Cause-effect relationships demonstrated between increases in market share and improvements in quality

- Data are presented for all key products/services and for all major markets

- Number of markets in which gains in shares have been demonstrated

- Significance/size of increases in market share

- Competitors show losses in market shares as applicant's shares have increased

- Evidence that increases in market share are not due to loss of competition or other strategies unrelated to quality improvement

Chapter 12

How to Audit Your Organization Against the Baldrige Award Criteria

The purpose of this chapter is to outline a process for designing a quality audit based specifically upon the Baldrige Award Criteria. Chapter 13 explains various ways of using the Baldrige criteria as a strategic planning tool. This chapter provides a detailed explanation of one of the most thorough of such approaches, the quality audit. The audit can be conducted internally by trained quality auditors. They need to assess current performance against the criteria and make recommendations for improvements.

THE AUDIT CYCLE

Regardless of whether you are doing a quality audit, an accounting audit, a safety audit, or some other kind of audit, you generally follow a four-phase process as outlined in Figure 12.1.

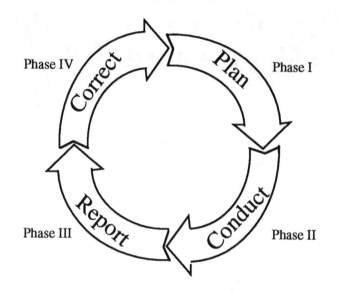

Figure 12.1: Quality Audit Planning Cycle

As you can see, the four phases in the quality audit cycle are Plan, Conduct, Report, and Correct. The majority of the work the audit team has to perform is in the Planning and Conducting phases. Each of these four phases is described in further detail. The first three phases in an audit against the Baldrige criteria could take three to four months to complete. The remainder of the year (eight or nine months) or longer could be spent making corrections based upon the audit findings.

PHASE I: PLANNING THE QUALITY AUDIT

Purpose

The purpose of this phase is to create a detailed plan for completing the audit. This requires a great deal of work for most organizations because you will be starting from scratch. You may already have audited the quality of your products and services periodically or conducted specific audits for safety or regulatory compliance, but you may not have conducted an audit as comprehensive as one based upon the Baldrige criteria. Essentially, you will be looking at all functions and levels of the organization, and examining a great deal of data in order to draw conclusions about the approach, deployment, and results the company is achieving in the area of quality.

Process

The process below outlines the major tasks in planning the quality audit. The specific process you follow may vary slightly.

```
1. Form Audit Teams
2. Write Audit Project Plan
3. Create Audit Instruments
4. Create Data Collection Plan
5. Schedule Interviews and Data Collection Activities
```

Step 1: Form Audit Teams

The size of your audit team will depend upon the size of your organization. If your company has a few hundred employees and sales of under $10 million, an audit team of three or four individuals will probably suffice. If your organization employs thousands of people and has sales of several billion dollars, you might have an audit team of fifty or more. If you are a medium- to large-size company, your audit team should be led by an audit manager. The audit manager is directly responsible for the audit. Beneath the audit manager are several senior auditors. The job of the senior auditors is to supervise and coach the auditors in their collection of data. It makes sense to assign one senior auditor to each of the seven categories in the Baldrige criteria. Each senior auditor then has a team of auditors responsible for auditing the organization's practices and results relating to a single category. Figure 12.2 presents a suggested organizational structure for an audit team in a medium or large company.

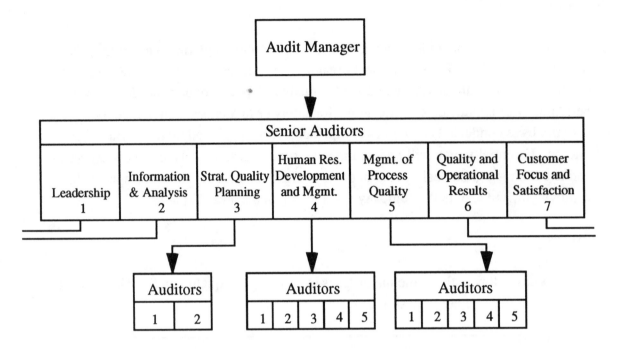

Figure 12.2: Suggested Audit Team Organization Structure for Medium or Large Company

As you can see, there are a total of seven senior auditors, each having responsibility for one of the seven Award Criteria categories. Each senior auditor has a team of auditors reporting to him/her. The number of auditors on the senior auditor's team is shown as being equivalent to the number of Items in the Baldrige criteria for that category. For example, category 3.0, Strategic Quality Planning, is divided into two Items, so there are two auditors on this team. Management of Process Quality, category 5.0, is divided into five Items, so there are five auditors on this team.

If you are auditing a small organization, the audit team might look like the one depicted in Figure 12.3.

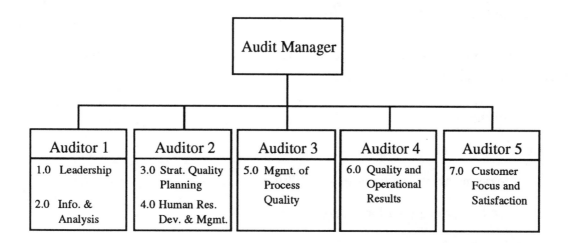

**Figure 12.3: Suggested Audit Team Organization Structure
for Small Organization**

Once you have designed your audit team structure and reporting relationships, you need to select individuals to fill the positions. The audit manager should be someone who has successfully managed large projects in the company, has good rapport and credibility with top management, and has a grasp of the concepts and principles relating to the Baldrige criteria. Senior auditors should be selected based upon their supervisory skills, their attention to detail, and their knowledge of the particular Baldrige category to which they will be assigned. You will not, however, want to assign senior auditors to be in charge of auditing an area in which they currently work. For example, don't take the human resource manager and assign him/her the senior auditor position for category 4.0, Human Resource Development and Management. Even though this person obviously knows a great deal about human resources, he/she is probably too close to it to objectively audit human resource practices and results. Select someone who knows a good deal about human resources or who once worked as a manager in this function, but now works in another function. You want a balance of objectivity and knowledge of the function being audited.

The auditors should be chosen based upon their attention to detail, knowledge of quality concepts, and knowledge of the particular Baldrige category to which they will be assigned. It is not important that those chosen to be auditors or senior auditors be participants from past audits. An audit against the Baldrige criteria will be significantly different from an accounting, safety, or other type of audit conducted in the company.

Step 2: Write Audit Project Plan

Once your audit team has been assembled, the next task is to create a detailed project plan for the audit. The project plan defines the:

- Scope of the audit

- Areas to be examined

- Audit team members and their responsibilities

- Schedule for completion of audit tasks

- Outputs to be produced

- Specific steps or tasks to be completed during each phase of the audit

- Time estimates for each task

- Labor and materials budget for the audit

The project plan should be outlined in a group meeting of the audit manager and the senior auditors. The audit manager facilitates the group in defining both the outputs of each phase of the audit process and the steps involved in producing each of the outputs. Figure 12.4 shows some of the typical outputs that might be listed for the audit phases.

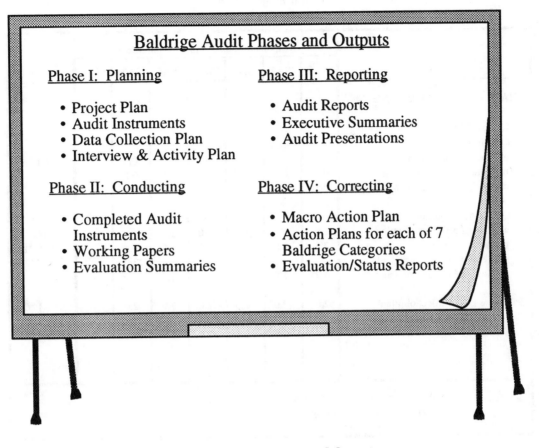

Figure 12.4: Audit Phases and Outputs

Once the outputs for all four phases have been listed, the group must specify the tasks involved in completing the first phase. After the tasks are listed, estimate time requirements for each individual who will be responsible for assisting or completing each task. Figure 12.5 shows a portion of a project plan chart for the first phase of an audit project. Notice that the time estimates are indicated in days or portions of days for each member of the audit team. (The steering committee is a group of top executives who will want to be involved in overseeing the audit.) The final column is used to schedule the various tasks listed. The scheduling is done after listing the tasks and estimating time.

Audit Project Plan

Steps/Tasks	Responsibilities & Time Requirements							Schedule
	SA1	SA2	SA3	SA4	SA5	SAM	SC	
PHASE I: AUDIT PLANNING								
1. Review Project Plan with Steering Committee								
a. Prepare for meeting	0.5	-	-	-	-	0.5	-	11/1
b. Conduct/attend meeting	0.5	0.5	0.5	0.5	0.5	0.5	0.5	11/3
c. Revise Plan Based on SC input	0.5	-	-	-	-	0.25	-	11/4
2. Create Audit Instruments								
a. Planning/Design Meeting	1.0	1.0	1.0	1.0	1.0	1.0	-	11/8
b. Write Audit Instruments	2.5	3.0	3.0	3.0	3.0	1.5	-	11/9-11/12
c. Review Audit Instruments	-	-	-	-	-	3.0	-	11/15-11/18
d. Revise Audit Instruments	0.75	1.0	1.0	1.0	1.0	-	-	11/19
3. Create Data Collection Plan	2.0	2.0	2.0	2.0	2.0	2.0	-	11/21-11/22
4. Schedule Interviews and Activities	2.5	2.5	2.5	2.5	2.5	3.0	-	11/23-11/26

KEY   SA1-SA5 = Senior Auditors 1-5
                     SAM = Senior Audit Manager
                     SC = Steering Committee

Figure 12.5: Audit Project Plan

Once the meeting participants have created work plan charts like the one in Figure 12.5 for all the phases of the project, the project plan itself should be outlined. The format of the written plan is flexible and should be based upon the format used for other types of project plans in your organization. It should address the process to be followed in completing the audit and describe outputs that will be produced. An outline of a typical audit project plan appears below.

```
┌─────────────────────────────────────────────────────────┐
│                                                         │
│                      OUTLINE:                           │
│                                                         │
│                                                         │
│                Typical Audit Project Plan               │
│                                                         │
│                                                         │
│        I.    Introduction and purpose                   │
│        II.   Background                                 │
│        III.  Project scope, goals,  and objectives      │
│        IV.   Audit team                                 │
│        V.    Phase I process and outputs                │
│        VI.   Phase II process and outputs               │
│        VII.  Phase III process and outputs              │
│        VIII. Phase IV process and outputs               │
│                                                         │
└─────────────────────────────────────────────────────────┘
```

Step 3: Create Audit Instruments

The Baldrige Award Criteria consist of a hierarchy of 7 Categories, 28 Examination Items, and 91 Areas to Address. Your first task in creating audit instruments is to take each of the 91 Areas to Address and break them down into 3 to 8 indicators. Chapters 5 through 11 of this book contain breakdowns of each of the 91 Areas to Address together with suggested indicators. Some examples follow for 2.1a.

2.0 INFORMATION AND ANALYSIS (Category)

2.1 Scope and Management of Quality and Performance Data and Information (Item)

2.1a Criteria for selecting data and information for use in quality and operational performance improvement. List key types of data and information used and briefly outline the principal roles of each type in improving quality and operational performance. Include: (1) customer-related; (2) product and service performance; (3) internal operations and performance including business and support services, and employee-related; (4) supplier performance; and (5) cost and financial.

INDICATORS

I.   Existence of specific criteria for selecting measurement indices for products and services produced for external customers.

II. Existence of specific criteria for selecting measurement indices for products and services produced for internal customers.

III. Degree to which measurement indices are selected based upon their impact on customer satisfaction.

IV. Elimination from quality reports of any indices (and corresponding data) that don't meet selection criteria.

V.   Degree to which internal and external customers are involved in identifying criteria for selection of quality measurement indices.

Once indicators have been identified for each of the Areas to Address in the Baldrige criteria, the next task is to create the first-level audit instruments, which include interview questionnaires and checklists. The complete hierarchy of audit instruments and reports is depicted in Figure 12.6.

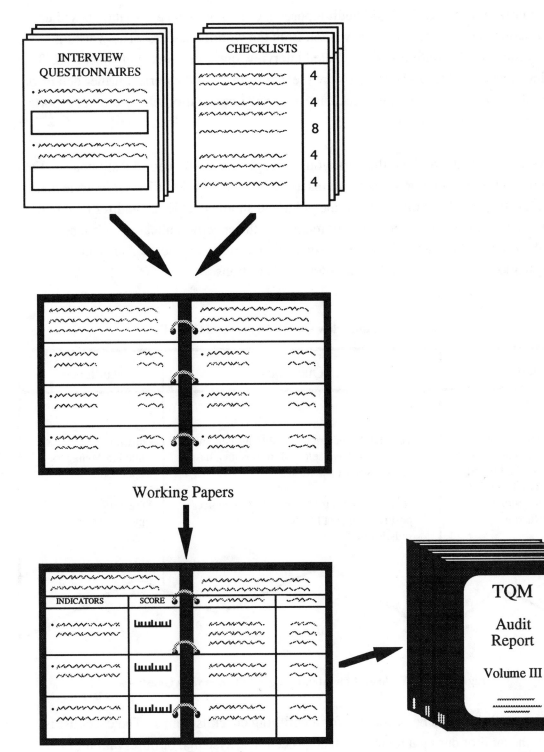

Working Papers

Evaluation Summaries

Figure 12.6: Hierarchy of Audit Instruments

To summarize the figure, the TQM audit reports, the final outputs, are written based upon the evaluation summaries, which are written from the working papers. The working papers summarize the findings of completed interview questionnaires and checklists. The interview questionnaires and checklists are created from the indicators. Further details on the use of the questionnaires and checklists, and on the preparation of these other reports, are covered later in this chapter.

Once you have identified the indicators, you can begin designing your questionnaire. For each indicator, create one or more questions an auditor could ask during an interview. Your questions should be direct and to the point and should enable the auditor to solicit helpful feedback from the interviewee in relation to the specific indicator. Also, be sure to list the titles of those who should be asked each question. Figure 12.7 presents a sample worksheet for identifying audit interview questions.

Creating Audit Interview Questionnaires and Checklists

Indicator	Questions	Audience
2.1.a III Degree to which measurement indices are selected based upon their impact upon customer satisfaction	• To what degree are the quality measurement indices you have selected for this area based upon customer satisfaction? • How would improvements in these indices positively impact levels of customer satisfaction?	Directors Function Managers Supervisors Directors Function Managers

Figure 12.7: Worksheet for Identifying Audit Interview Questions

A similar worksheet can be developed for identifying checklist items. The checklist is used by the auditor during a review of data, procedures, systems, or observation of practices rather than during an interview. Checklists are detailed lists of criteria reflecting what you should find in a well-designed and integrated total quality management system.

Once you have written interview questions or checklist items for each indicator and identified who you will direct each question to, you can formulate specific questionnaires for interviews. You don't want to go back to the same individual six or seven times with various questions about the Baldrige criteria. You should interview each person once, asking all of your questions in that interview. For this reason, it is important to coordinate your interview plans with other members of the audit team. We will discuss this more later.

Step 4: Create Data Collection Plan

At this point, you have written all of your interview questionnaires and checklists. Now you need to figure out who is going to be responsible for completing each questionnaire checklist. Figure 12.8 shows an example of a data collection plan for the 1.0 (Leadership) category. The specific audit instruments are listed vertically along the left side of the sheet, and the auditor's initials are listed horizontally along the top of the sheet.

DATA COLLECTION PLAN

Category: 1.0 Leadership

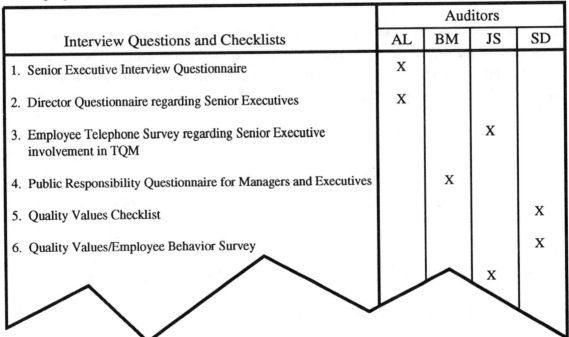

Interview Questions and Checklists	Auditors			
	AL	BM	JS	SD
1. Senior Executive Interview Questionnaire	X			
2. Director Questionnaire regarding Senior Executives	X			
3. Employee Telephone Survey regarding Senior Executive involvement in TQM			X	
4. Public Responsibility Questionnaire for Managers and Executives		X		
5. Quality Values Checklist				X
6. Quality Values/Employee Behavior Survey				X
			X	

Figure 12.8: Example Data Collection Plan

Step 5: Schedule Interviews and Data Collection Activities

The final step in the planning phase of the TQM audit process is to schedule all of the interviews and data collection activities. Allocate interview time according to the number of questionnaires that need to be answered by the interviewee. For example, you might need to ask the top executives over a hundred questions, so you should schedule several hours for these interviews. The schedule for other data collection activities is somewhat more problematic, because it is difficult to estimate the amount of time it will take for a tour, a review of a system, etc.

In a large organization with senior auditors and many auditors, each senior auditor should have a master schedule showing the daily interviews and data collection activities of each auditor. Every auditor should prepare his/her own data collection and interview schedule and submit this to the senior auditor. Schedules should be based upon the major deadlines that have been outlined in the audit project plan.

PHASE II: CONDUCTING THE AUDIT

Purpose

The purpose of this phase is to gather and summarize the data needed to assess the organization against the Baldrige criteria. Even in a small organization, this phase will require a great deal of time. There will be many people to interview, a large amount of data to review, and many systems and procedures to observe.

Process

The specific steps that you follow may be more involved than those listed below, but in a general sense, the following three activities should be completed during this phase:

1. Gather and Document Audit Data
2. Prepare Audit Working Papers
3. Write Evaluation Summaries

Each of these steps is described below.

Step 1: Gather and Document Data

Gathering data involves conducting individual and group interviews, observing systems and procedures, and reviewing data. Various data collection methods used in quality audits are listed as follows.

AUDITING DATA COLLECTION TECHNIQUES

- Individual and Group Interviews
  - Executives
  - Supervisors
  - Customers
  - Managers
  - Employees
  - Suppliers

- Review of Data
  - Product Quality Data
  - Safety Data
  - Benchmark Data
  - Customer Satisfaction
  - Service Quality Data
  - Employee Data
  - Competitive Data
  - Internal Customer Satisfaction

- Review of Resources
  - Programs
  - Documentation/Drawings
  - Surveys
  - Procedure Manuals
  - Audit Reports
  - Plans

- Demonstrations/Work Throughs
  - Tours
  - Observation of Employees as They Perform Operations
  - Examiner/Auditor Works Through Processes

Your goal when conducting the interviews and observations is to find examples of actions and practices that do not meet the Baldrige criteria. The people you will be interviewing and observing will be trying to tell and show you how well they meet or exceed all of the criteria. It's very easy to be persuaded to see only the positive aspects and overlook the negatives. You will be doing your organization a great disservice if you overlook problems or concerns. Problems that are not identified will not get corrected prior to applying for the award, and your organization will lose points with the Baldrige Examiners.

The two major data collection methods used are interviews and observations. When conducting interviews, make sure that you ask the same questions to several different levels of employees. For example, don't just ask executives if they are committed to quality, ask some of the employees how committed to quality the executives are.

Even though your interview questionnaires may contain specific questions, it is better not to run through the questions one at a time. Make the interview a little less structured and ask some open-ended questions to encourage interviewees to talk. Some examples are listed below:

- "Give me some examples of decisions your boss has made that show his commitment to quality."

- "Tell me about the process you use to create the strategic quality plan."

- "How do you determine what training people require on quality topics?"

- "How well do we do in handling customer complaints as compared to our biggest competitors?"

Along with interviews, auditors spend a great deal of time reviewing data and observing practices and procedures. Again, keep in mind that as an auditor you are looking for problems. The people who prepare the data will try to make them look as positive as possible. If there are missing data, this probably means that the auditors are trying to hide something. For example, if data on some dimension are presented from the past five years, but data from only the past two years are presented for other dimensions, the missing data are most likely negative.

When you are conducting tours or observations, people will tend to be on their best behavior. Everyone will know why you are there and will behave accordingly. It will be difficult for you to find anything negative if all of your observations are announced. It is good idea to do some unannounced inspections and observations so you will have a better chance of seeing things the way they really are.

Step 2: Prepare Audit Working Papers

At this point in the audit, you will have generated reams of interview notes, references, graphs, and completed checklists. Your next task is to begin summarizing this information so that it can be reviewed and evaluated. This is done by creating audit working papers. Figure 12.9 presents a sample of what your audit working papers might look like.

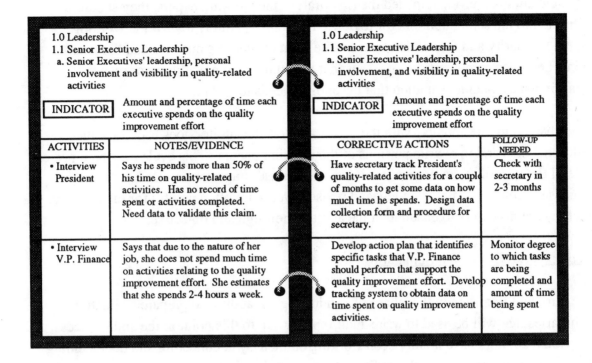

Figure 12.9: Sample Audit Working Papers

As you can see, the page spread covers a single indicator. Data gathering activities such as interviews and observations are listed in the far left column. Notes and evidence relating to the degree to which the indicator is met are written in the next column. Notice that in this example, what the president says about the amount of time he spends on quality-related activities is recorded, but the notes specify that there are no data to back up his claims. On the left side of the facing page you list any corrective actions you think would help improve the organization's or individual's performance on this indicator. In the case of this president, it says that he needs to start tracking the activities and time he spends on the quality improvement effort. For the vice president of finance, it suggests that an action plan be developed that outlines specific activities she should be performing to support the quality improvement effort. The final column on the right side of the facing page is used to list any follow-up needed to collect further data or obtain the answers to questions.

This format for the working papers is simply a suggestion. You should design your own working papers in a way that works best for your organization. The only real guidelines to follow are that the working papers should address each indicator individually and that they should be a summary, and therefore less detailed, than your interview/observation notes.

Once the auditors have completed the first draft of the working papers, they should be submitted to the senior auditors for review. The senior auditors review the working papers for clarity and thoroughness and write what accounting auditors call "points." Points are notes or suggestions of issues that the auditor did not address or notes regarding additional information that the auditor needs to gather.

After discussing the "points" with the senior auditor, the auditor goes back to gather additional data and to rewrite portions of the working papers. This cycle may be repeated several times until the senior auditor is satisfied that all important issues have been addressed properly. These "review and revise" cycles are often painful for the auditors, but they are necessary to ensure that the audit is thorough and objective.

Step 3: Write Evaluation Summaries

The third and final step in this phase of conducting the audit is to prepare evaluation summaries that will be used to write audit reports. Up to this point in the audit process, individual auditors have mainly been working on their own, collecting and documenting data. Now is the time when the audit teams get together to discuss and summarize their findings. In a large organization, you should hold separate meetings—one for each audit team assigned to the seven categories of Baldrige criteria. In a small organization with a single audit team of six to eight people, a series of meetings with the team will be necessary. The purpose of these meetings is to obtain input from all auditors and to reach a consensus regarding the ratings to give the organization against the various Examination Items, Areas to Address, and indicators in the Baldrige Award Criteria. Even though the Baldrige Examiners assign a score only to each of the 28 Examination Items, and then to each of the seven categories, it is recommended that you score all aspects as depicted in Figure 12.10.

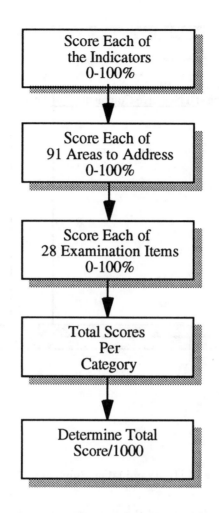

Figure 12.10: Audit Scoring Process

For the sake of the example, let's assume that you work for a large organization that has seven individual audit teams, each consisting of a senior auditor and three to eight auditors. Each of the seven groups will attend a two- to three-day meeting where final scores will be decided and examination summaries written.

Prior to the meeting you should prepare a series of flipcharts, like the one in Figure 12.11, to use in writing the examination summaries.

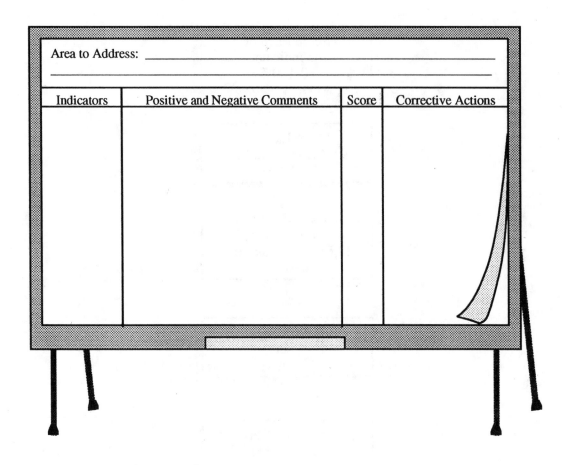

Figure 12.11: Examination Summary Flipchart

It is best to use double-wide easels and flipchart paper for these meetings. If this is not available, two standard flipchart easels can be placed side-by-side so that all four columns of information can fit on one sheet. At the top of the sheet, list one of the Areas to Address that falls under the audit team's participation category. Begin the meeting by explaining that you are going to lead the group in discussing and scoring each indicator, one at a time. Write the first indicator for the first Area to Address at the top of the first column of the flipchart. Ask the team members to refer to their working papers and to volunteer some of the significant positive and negative comments they have regarding the organization's performance on this indicator. Ask for input from all of the auditors that examined this indicator and try to get a balance of positive and negative comments. If performance on an indicator is particularly bad, try to find at least one positive comment to write. Figure 12.12 depicts a portion of a flipchart with information on the indicator and comments filled in.

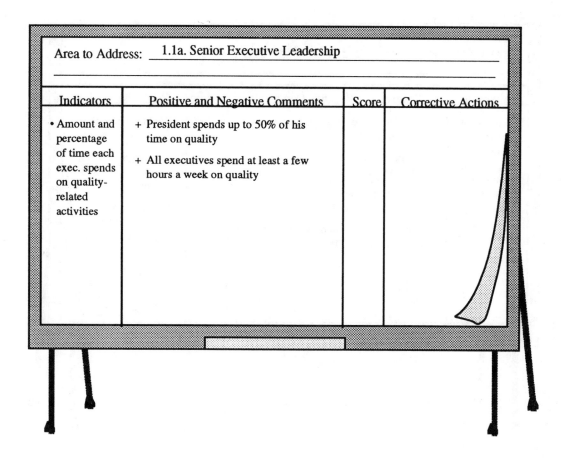

Area to Address:	1.1a. Senior Executive Leadership		
Indicators	Positive and Negative Comments	Score	Corrective Actions
• Amount and percentage of time each exec. spends on quality-related activities	+ President spends up to 50% of his time on quality + All executives spend at least a few hours a week on quality		

Figure 12.12: Examination Summary Flipchart with Indicator

and Comments Filled In

As you are gathering comments from the auditors in the meeting, remember that the goal is to prepare a summary. Therefore, fifteen or twenty comments on a single indicator is probably too many. A better number might be three or four positive and three or four negative comments. Select the ones that are most important and for which you have the most supporting evidence.

Once the comments have been documented, the group must decide on a score for this indicator. A percentage scoring system should be used, similar to the Baldrige evaluation, with 100% indicating perfect performance. The group should reach a consensus on the score, based upon the positive and negative comments that have been listed and discussed. Therefore, even auditors who did not examine a particular indicator can offer their input to the scoring decisions. After deciding on a percentage score for the indicator, the group needs to identify corrective actions that should be taken to improve the organization's score on this indicator. Figure 12.13 shows a portion of an evaluation summary flipchart with this information filled in.

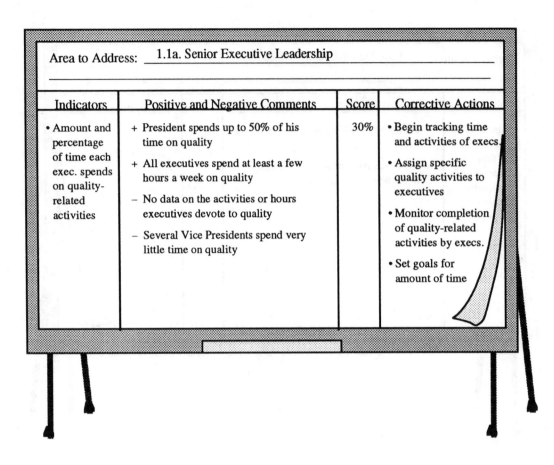

Figure 12.13: Examination Summary Flipchart with all Four Columns Filled In

The corrective actions should come from the auditors' working papers and should be a summary of all of the corrective actions they may have listed. Corrective actions should specify what can be done to improve performance on an indicator, but they should not specify how a particular improvement will be done or by whom it should be done. That will be determined later when action plans are created.

When the group finishes this exercise for the first indicator, post the flipcharts on the meeting room wall, and proceed with the next indicator. You can see why this meeting will require several days. The group could spend a few hours creating the charts on each indicator, and there may be over fifty different indicators to discuss in some of the larger categories, such as Customer Focus and Satisfaction. If you want to shorten the length of the meeting, divide the audit team into subgroups that focus upon specific Examination Items. For example, the 3.0 (Strategic Quality Planning) category is divided into two Examination Items. If the audit team that looked at category 3.0 comprises four members, split the team into two subgroups each responsible for creating the examination summaries for one of the two Examination Items. This will shorten the overall meeting time, but the quality of the documentation will not be as good because fewer auditors can offer their input in creating the summaries. This second phase of the audit process is complete when all meetings have been conducted and all of the evaluation summaries have been written.

PHASE III: REPORTING AUDIT FINDINGS

Purpose

The purpose of this phase is to prepare audit reports for various audiences, present the contents of the reports, and to revise the reports as necessary.

Process

The audit report is written by a team of senior auditors using the examination summaries created in the previous phase. Although the format of the report is flexible, a suggested outline is as follows.

AUDIT REPORT OUTLINE

    I.   Background on the Baldrige Award and Total Quality Management

   II.   Audit Methodology

  III.   Overview of Baldrige Criteria

       A. Categories, Items, and Areas to Address

       B. Scoring System

  IV.   Category 1.0 Leadership

       A. Findings

       B. Recommendations

   V.   Category 2.0 Information and Analysis

       A. Findings

       B. Recommendations

  VI.   Category 3.0 Strategic Quality Planning

       A. Findings

       B. Recommendations

 VII.   Category 4.0 Human Resource Development and Management

       A. Findings

       B. Recommendations

VIII.   Category 5.0 Management of Process Quality

       A. Findings

       B. Recommendations

  IX.   Category 6.0 Quality and Operational Results

       A. Findings

       B. Recommendations

   X.   Category 7.0 Customer Focus and Satisfaction

       A. Findings

       B. Recommendations

The first section of the report should provide some background information on both the Baldrige Award and total quality management. You should explain how and why the award was developed, talk about organizations that have won in the past, and explain how the criteria for the award serve as a national set of standards by which all organizations can evaluate their efforts to improve quality. This section should also contain the reasons your organization became involved in total quality management and some of the major actions that have occurred relating to TQM. Finally, you should explain the organization's intentions in regard to the Baldrige Award. If you intend to apply for the award in 1995, say, state this. For many organizations the results of the audit will determine when they apply for the Baldrige Award.

Section II of the audit report is designed to provide information on how the audit was conducted. Some of the specific questions and issues that should be addressed in this section are:

- How was the audit team organized and who was on it?

- Who was interviewed and what types of questions were asked?

- What types of data and printed materials were reviewed?

- What instruments were developed to gather audit data?

- How were observations and reviews of systems accomplished?

- How were data summarized?

- How were scores and corrective actions determined?

This section of the report should be thorough, but not more than 20 pages in length. To maximize space, details such as the specific instruments used can go into appendices.

Section III of the audit report should provide an overview of the Baldrige criteria.

It should include explanations of the seven different categories, along with the Examination Items and Areas to Address that comprise each category. Explain that each Area to Address is broken down into indicators, which are what auditors look for in their evaluation of the organization. This section of the report should be no more than 15 pages in length. Do not go into great detail explaining each Area to Address and indicator. Detailed information is more useful in the individual sections of the report covering the seven categories of criteria.

The seven remaining sections of the audit report each address the findings and recommendations relevant to a particular category of the award criteria. These sections should use similar formats and include the same headings of information. Begin each section with a description of the category and a definition of the Examination Items covered, followed by a one or two page summary of the findings in this category. The reader ought to be able to get a general feeling of the organization's performance in this category by reviewing this summary. Follow the summary with a discussion of the detailed findings and your recommendations for actions that need to be taken to improve performance (see Figure 12.14).

For example, begin with the first Area to Address under the first Examination Item. Define the Examination Item and Area to Address, using the text from the Baldrige Award Criteria. Next, list and explain the first indicator and provide your evaluation of the organization's performance on this indicator. This information should be presented in narrative style based upon the comments written in the evaluation summaries.

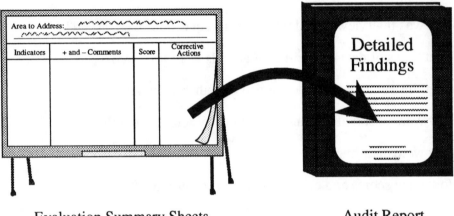

Evaluation Summary Sheets   Audit Report

**Figure 12.14: How to Write Detailed Findings Sections
in the Audit Report**

Follow your discussion of the organization's performance against the first indicator with your recommendations for actions that need to be taken to improve performance. This section can best be presented as a list of recommendations followed by an explanation of each recommendation.

Each of the seven sections presenting the detailed findings and recommendations will be between 30 and 60 pages in length, depending on the number of indicators you address and the amount of information there is to present. This is the body of the report, however, and should include a great deal of detail.

Once a draft of the entire audit report has been written, the audit manager, and perhaps an upper-level manager who has not been involved in the audit, should review it. The report is to be reviewed for completeness and clarity. Have the report edited to make it read as if it were written by one person and to make sure the headings and style of each section are consistent. After the necessary revisions are made, make an executive summary of the report. This document should be 6–10 pages in length, cover the same information covered in the larger report, and address the content from the perspective of top management in the organization. I suggest that the audit manager be the one to write the executive summary. This document should also be edited by an editor and reviewed by several people who have been involved in the audit.

After the abbreviated and full-length versions of the audit report have been completed, the next task is to prepare a list of presentations that need to be made. You will probably need three types of presentations:

- Presentation to the audit team
- Presentation to upper management
- Presentation to middle management and key technical professionals.

It is important to remember that the audit team needs a review of the entire audit findings and recommendations. Up to this point, they have been exposed only to the particular area they were assigned to audit. This presentation to the audit team will last several hours, as each senior auditor presents his or her audit category to the team. The presentation to the audit team should be done first because it serves as a dry run for the remaining presentations.

The next presentation is to upper management. This can be the same presentation you gave to the audit team, or an abbreviated version of it. The length of the presentation and the amount of detail covered depends upon the willingness of management to devote a half day or more of their time to this. Under no circumstances should the presentation to upper management be more than one day in length. Do not attempt to present all of the information contained in the audit report—simply present the highlights.

The final series of presentations to be done are those to function directors, managers, and key technical professionals. Tailor these presentations to the issues that can be dealt with by the individuals in these functions. All groups should get a brief overview of the findings and recommendations that pertain to the entire organization, followed by presentations on the findings and recommendations that are unique to that function.

PHASE IV: CORRECTING AUDIT FINDINGS

Purpose

The purpose of this final phase in the audit cycle is to correct any and all problems and deficits identified during the audit. This is the most critical phase in the audit process; unfortunately, it is also the phase most often done poorly. Accepting the audit findings is difficult enough—none of us likes to hear about our shortcomings. Dealing with the concerns that were identified is time consuming and often quite difficult. Some of the changes required will take several years to properly implement, and are usually resisted.

Process

The major steps in this fourth phase of the audit cycle are outlined and described below.

> 1. Form Steering Committee
> 2. Create Macro Action Plan
> 3. Create Individual Action Plans for Baldrige Categories
> 4. Implement and Evaluate Recommendations

Step 1: Form Steering Committee

After all presentations on the audit findings and recommendations have been completed, the next step is to form a steering committee that will oversee the plans and projects put into action to correct the concerns and problems identified in the audit. The steering committee will provide the resources, impetus, and direction to individuals working on the audit-driven changes, without working on the changes themselves. The steering committee should be made up of six to ten individuals who are members of top management in the organization. Ideally, the steering committee should consist of the president or CEO, along with his/her direct reports. The higher up in the organization the members of the steering committee are, the more likely the audit-driven changes will actually be completed. (If a steering committee was already in place during Phases I through III, you can work with this same committee provided that the members have the necessary authority to bring about change.)

The steering committee members will not need to spend a great deal of time managing the Correction Phase of the audit cycle, but their involvement is critical. Many of the changes needed to correct the concerns identified in the audit will require top management authority to implement. Major changes are often needed in procedures, policies, and practices.

The responsibilities of the steering committee are outlined as follows.

STEERING COMMITTEE RESPONSIBILITIES

- Develop Macro Action Plan for Implementing Audit-Driven Changes
- Assign Responsibilities to Key Managers
- Attend Periodic Status Meetings
- Review Status Reports
- Commit Necessary Resources and Remove Obstacles
- Make Major Policy and Procedure Decisions as Needed

One of the biggest mistakes made when forming a steering committee is to assign individuals to the committee who are at too low a level in the organization. A steering committee made up of function and department managers will not have the clout and decision-making authority to do what it takes to implement the audit-driven changes. Often the top executives don't see why they need to be involved. Implementing total quality management, however, must be done *from the top down.* Every company that has won the Baldrige Award will testify to this. Top management support means more than allocating the necessary resources. Executives must be visibly involved in the quality effort and devote a good portion of their own time to it.

Step 2: Create Macro Action Plan

The steering committee must first meet to create the macro or long-term action plan. The overall goals relating to quality are to be included in this plan. Two types of goals that should be set are:

- Quality results goals
- Quality process goals

Samples of macro results and process goals are shown below.

QUALITY RESULTS GOALS

- Achieve customer satisfaction scores of 94% satisfaction by the end of 1995.
- Achieve goal of no more than 20 defects per million products by the end of 1994.
- Achieve internal customer satisfaction scores averaging 95% by the end of the second quarter of 1994.

QUALITY PROCESS GOALS

- Apply for the Baldrige Award in 1995 and achieve a score of at least 700/1000.
- Implement a comprehensive system for measuring the cost of quality by the end of 1994.
- Achieve an internal TQM Audit score of 700/1000 by the end of 1994.
- All managers and supervisors will devote at least 25% of their time to quality-related efforts by the end of 1994.

After macro goals have been established for the quality improvement effort, the steering committee must review and prioritize the recommendations contained in the audit report. Begin with the Leadership category and list the major recommendations or changes on a flipchart. Number each one as shown in Figure 12.15. Once the recommendations are listed, ask the members of the steering committee to individually prioritize the recommendations from most to least important. Write the steering committee members' initials on the chart as shown, and leave two final columns for the sum of the priorities and the numerical order of the group's priorities.

CATEGORY: 1.0 – LEADERSHIP							
RECOMMENDATIONS	Individual Priorities					Total	Final Priorites
	MG	JS	AT	RM	SV		
1. Executive training in TQM	1	6	2	5	1	15	1
2. Time Tracking System	7	8	7	2	8	32	6
3. Establishing accountabilities for quality results for all executives	6	1	3	1	4	15	1
4. Develop a clear set of quality values	3	3	5	4	2	17	2
5. Create Action Plan for improving executives' involvement in Quality	2	5	1	6	5	19	3
6. Establish goals for improving executives' involvement in public responsibilities relating to quality	8	7	8	3	7	33	7
7. Develop system for evaluating extent to which quality values are demonstrated in employee behavior	4	4	6	7	3	24	4
8. Develop participative process for managing quality	5	2	4	8	6	25	5

Figure 12.15: Prioritizing Recommendations with the Steering Committee

As you can see in Figure 12.15, the individual's ratings are added across the columns, with the sum appearing in the "total" column for each row. The recommendation with the lowest overall score is assigned the highest priority. In the example above, two of the recommendations are tied for top priority: Executive Training in TQM, and Establishing Accountabilities for Quality Results for all Executives. This method of prioritizing works well because it is quick, and everyone has an equal say in establishing the overall priorities. The same process is continued for each of the six remaining Baldrige categories. Once all of the recommendations are prioritized, the steering committee should assign one individual to each of the seven categories to be responsible for carrying out the recommendations. These individuals should be high enough in the organization to make the necessary changes and implement the projects initiated by the recommendations. Each of these managers will form his/her own committee to work on creating more detailed plans for developing and implementing the high-priority recommendations.

Before concluding the steering committee meeting, establish a schedule for development of the seven quality improvement teams and the creation of detailed plans by each team. Also establish dates for periodic review meetings, where team leaders will present their progress to the steering committee. It is a good idea to schedule these meetings once each quarter. Monthly meetings are a possibility if the organization is in a hurry to get the changes implemented.

Step 3: Create Individual Action Plans For Baldrige Categories

Each of the seven quality improvement teams has the responsibility to design and implement the recommendations under one of the Baldrige criteria categories. Those recommendations that cut across categories will be assigned to one of the seven teams. The first task of the teams is to hold a meeting to develop detailed project plans for the recommendations for which they are responsible. Each recommendation may require a separate plan, or several recommendations may be combined into a single project. For example, it might make sense to combine recommendations 3 and 5 from Figure 12.15 into one project . The project plans created at this stage are similar to the project plan that was created for the audit itself. You begin by listing the tasks involved in completing the project, then estimating the time required for project personnel, and finally, assigning deadlines to each of the project tasks.

Figure 12.16 depicts a project plan for creating a set of quality values for the organization.

| Steps/Tasks | Responsibilities & Time Requirements | | | | | Schedule |
	PM	AM	ST	PC	WP	
TEAM: LEADERSHIP						
1. Form Project Committee	0.25	0.5	-	-	-	
2. Review Resources	0.5	0.5	0.5	-	-	
3. Conduct/Attend Meeting to Draft Quality Values						
a. Prepare for meeting	0.25	0.5	0.5	-	-	
b. Conduct/attend meeting	1.0	1.0	1.0	1.0	-	
c. Document meeting outputs	-	1.0	-	-	1.0	
4. Quality Values Feedback Survey						
a. Prepare survey	0.25	0.5	0.5	-	1.0	
b. Administer survey	0.25	1.0	0.25	-	2.0	
c. Document survey results	0.5	1.0	0.5	0	2.0	
5. Project Committee Review Meeting						
a. Prepare for meeting	0.25	0.25	-	-	0.5	
b. Conduct/attend meeting to review feedback and decide on quality values	0.5	0.5	0.5	0.5	-	
c. Document meeting outputs	-	0.5	-	-	0.5	

KEY   PM = Project Manager   PC = Project Committee
               AM = Al Masters   WP = Word Processing
               ST = Sam Turner

Figure 12.16: Project Plan for Creating Quality Values

This is a simple project compared to some of the other recommendations. Notice that there is a project manager and two other team members working on this project. There is also a project committee made up of executives responsible for determining the quality values of the organization. Once the executives have drafted a set of quality values, the values are tested with a cross section of employees to determine people's reactions. Based upon the employees' reactions, the values will be revised as necessary and communicated to all employees.

Step 4: Implement and Evaluate Recommendations

There are no specific steps to follow in implementing the recommendations because the approach depends upon the complexity and nature of the recommendation. For example, the quality values simply need to be communicated to employees to be implemented.

Other recommendations, such as a system for evaluating the degree to which employee behavior is consistent with the values, will require much more work.

Because there will be seven different teams working on developing recommendations to improve quality, it is important that all seven teams work together to come up with an implementation plan. The seven team leaders need to meet to review the status of their projects and discuss implementation plans. It is important that the quality improvement effort be an integrated one rather than be seven different groups working independently of one another. In this meeting the leaders must lay out all of the high-priority recommendations to be implemented for the year, and identify an implementation sequence that makes the most sense. Make sure to note whether the implementation of one recommendation is a prerequisite for another. Many of the recommendations in the Leadership category are prerequisites to those in other categories. Basic quality values need to be established before other activities can be initiated.

It is extremely important to evaluate the impact of each recommendation to determine whether the change or new approach actually improves quality processes or results. Go back to the indicators in the audit report that pertain to a given recommendation. You should be measuring performance on these indicators both before and after introducing the recommendations that pertain to these indicators. Measuring the performance of the indicators before and after implementation of the recommendations will allow you to determine whether they have had the desired effect on the indicators. Plot these before-and-after data on graphs to determine the relative impact the change has had on performance. This type of data is useful not only for demonstrating a return on investment in your quality improvement efforts, but also for diagnostic purposes when a recommendation fails to produce the desired results. Figure 12.17 presents an example of a measure of number of hours per month executives spend on quality-related activities before and after they set goals and started having to report this figure to the president.

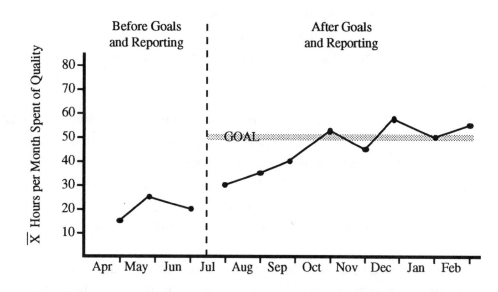

**Figure 12.17: Evaluation of Goals and Reporting on Average Number
of Hours per Month Executives Spend on Quality Related Activities**

The results in Figure 12.17 show that executives averaged about 20 hours a month on quality-related activities before the goals and reporting started, and that they reached the target of 50 hours a month within four months after the goal and reporting began. This graph clearly shows that the strategy employed was successful. It would be difficult to calculate the return on investment for this particular project, but the cause-effect relationship between the changes introduced and the average number of hours devoted to quality is clear.

CONCLUSIONS

In this chapter, I have presented an approach to auditing your organization against the Baldrige criteria. Previous chapters have provided you with lists of indicators that can be used to assess your performance on each of the 91 Areas to Address in the Baldrige criteria. In this chapter, I have explained how to use these indicators to develop audit instruments to audit your own organization against the Baldrige criteria. But, you might ask, why bother? Why not pay the $4,000 and apply for the Baldrige Award so you can have an audit done by actual Baldrige Examiners?

First of all, you will spend a great deal of time and money preparing the application for the award. Xerox, one of the 1989 Baldrige Award winners, claims to have spent 800,000 labor hours preparing their application. Unless you are fairly certain of at least being a finalist, this is a great deal of money to spend. If you do actually apply for the award and receive low scores from the examiners reviewing your application, you will not receive a site visit. A score in the high 600s or better is necessary to warrant a site visit, where a team of Baldrige Examiners spends several days in your company auditing your practices and results.

An internal audit such as the one described in this chapter is more for diagnostic than evaluative purposes. Its goal is to identify areas of weakness and recommend specific actions that can be taken to remedy the areas of weakness. As such, it is much more thorough than a site visit conducted by Baldrige Examiners. The report you receive from the Baldrige Examiners will not include recommendations but only findings regarding the strengths and weaknesses of your quality practices and results.

Once you have conducted several of the internal audits of the sort described in this chapter and have received scores of 600 or more from your internal auditors, you are ready to actually apply for the Malcolm Baldrige Award. I work with a number of companies who think they are a year or two away from applying and possibly winning the Baldrige Award. Going through an audit such as the one described here can be an eye-opening experience for management. Most often they realize they are five or more years away from being ready to apply for the award, and have a great deal of work to do to change their organization to better meet the award criteria.

An audit is valuable only if the organization is willing to make the changes identified and implement the recommendations made by the auditors. I've worked with many organizations that will spend the time and money for a thorough quality audit, but will not commit the resources needed to implement the recommendations that come out of the audit. It is critical to get top management to commit to doing something about the audit findings before embarking upon such a comprehensive evaluation of the organization in the first place. Once management commits to following through on the findings, you may well be on your way to achieving Baldrige award winning quality.

Chapter 13

Using a Baldrige Assessment as a Strategic Planning Tool

ASSESSMENT ALTERNATIVES

The previous chapter presented details on how to audit your organization against the Baldrige criteria. This approach is very thorough, but many organizations don't have the resources to use it to the best effect. Most of the companies I've worked with in conducting Baldrige assessments over the past few years don't use the full-scale audit approach. Rather, a number of other basic methods are used. These are listed below in order of least to most objective and thorough, and of least to most expensive.

1. Survey based on the Baldrige criteria

2. Armchair assessment

3. Mock Baldrige application

4. Formal Baldrige application

5. Audit against the Baldrige criteria

1. Baldrige Survey—The simplest and least expensive method of establishing some baseline data on where you stand in your implementation of TQM is to send out a survey to all or a sample of employees, having them rate the organization on how well it has implemented each of the items making up the Baldrige criteria. A large variety of surveys exist that may be used for this purpose. One that has been written by the author was published in the June 1993 issue of the *Journal for Quality and Participation.*

Using such a survey, or similar ones available through TQM consulting firms, is the least expensive way of evaluating your own status. However, it is also the least reliable, regardless of which survey instrument you are using. The problem with any survey is that it is subjective. People responding to the survey don't usually have the "big picture" of what is happening in the company, and they often mark their responses to the survey items based upon limited and most recent experiences. I've administered Baldrige surveys to 100 or so people in a single organization and gotten scores that ranged from 250 to 800 out of a possible 1000 points. Does this mean that the survey instrument is poor? Perhaps, but I believe that all TQM surveys are at best a very rough and rudimentary indicator. Considering the low cost of the survey, however, this tool does provide you with a basic idea of where you stand, without spending much money or time.

2. Armchair Assessment—The second approach is a good deal more thorough and more useful than a survey, without much added expense. I have used this approach with a number of large organizations and have talked to a number of others that use a variation on it. Here's how it works. A team of senior executives from the business unit or organization being assessed attend a two-day workshop to learn the Baldrige criteria and gain an understanding of how an assessment is done. Next, the executive team attends a one day meeting where they begin to assess their own organization. During the meeting, a facilitator begins by reviewing the first Baldrige Examination Item, explaining what it means. Next, the participants brainstorm a list of the organization's strengths and areas for improvement relating to that Item. The pluses and minuses are listed by the facilitator on a flipchart. After listing a page or so of strengths and areas for improvements, the facilitator asks the group to suggest a percentage score in multiples of 10. The group discusses and reaches consensus on a percentage score, the facilitator writes it on the flipchart, and together they move on to the next Item. This process continues until all 28 Items have been completed. A time limit of 15 minutes is observed for discussing each Item, so the meeting is very fast-moving. After listing comments and scoring each of the 28 Baldrige Items, percentage scores are multiplied by the official point value of each Item to compute the final score. The 28 flipchart pages are typed and become the complete assessment report. Total time commitment for the approach is three days.

While this approach is quick and relatively inexpensive, it does have some problems. First, the objectivity of the senior executives is not always what it should be. The executives sometimes find it easier to list the good things than to spend time thinking of areas for improvement. They also tend to give more credit for partial deployment of systems or approaches than a Baldrige Examiner would. Executives also tend to score a little higher than a Baldrige Examiner might. The personality of the CEO or the most senior executive in the meeting can also make this approach problematic. I've observed a few assessment meetings where the participants simply deferred to what the senior executives said and what he/she said the score was.

Even with its problems, this approach is much better than using any kind of survey. The assessment is more thorough; you end up with a page of strengths, areas for improvement, and a score on each of the 28 items; and executives buy-in to the results of the assessment more readily because they did it. This approach will only work, however, if the senior executives are willing to devote three days for training and assessment. Executives in many organizations don't feel they need to be involved in such training or assessment and prefer to delegate this task to others. The Armchair Assessment will only work if you can get the senior executives to commit to it.

3. Mock Baldrige Application—This is by far the most commonly used approach for assessment against the Baldrige criteria. This approach is currently being used by, among others, AT&T, IBM, Baxter Healthcare, Northrop, McDonnell Douglas, Roadway Express, Whirlpool, Cargill, Westinghouse, Johnson & Johnson, Appleton Papers, and Boise Cascade. The approach involves having business units, facilities, or even departments in a company prepare their own application using the same format as the Baldrige application. Generally, all 28 Items are required to be addressed and the applications are often about the same size (70–85 pages) as an official application. Applications are reviewed and individually scored by a team of examiners from other departments or units, who then get together to reach consensus on the final scores. Examiners are usually company employees who have been trained in a 2–4 day workshop. Some companies use outsiders to supplement their team of internal examiners, adding Baldrige consultants, customers, and suppliers, for example.

In some companies, such as Baxter and IBM, the examiners score the written applications and do site visits on the best (usually the top 15%–20%). Most organizations also have their own quality awards that they give out to the best performers. The major difference between the Armchair Assessment and the Mock Baldrige Application is that one always uses examiners from one business unit or department to evaluate another business unit or department. Some organizations have gotten senior executives involved as part of their team of examiners. Cargill, a major agricultural firm with 70,000 employees, has a team of about 50 examiners that includes about 15 senior executives. Most senior executives in Northrop Corporation also have spent at least one year serving as an examiner for their award. A side benefit of getting executives to be examiners is that they almost always come away from the experience as staunch believers in the value of the Baldrige criteria as a tool for running a better organization.

The advantage of this approach over the previous two, then, is the objectivity and thoroughness of the assessment and feedback. The approach can give you the same level of analysis and feedback that a company would get by applying for the Baldrige Award. The approach also does a great deal to help move the organization toward being a Total Quality company. Examiners become internal experts on the Baldrige criteria, and can help others to work toward satisfying the criteria. Another advantage is that you can get near immediate feedback on your application and probe the examiners for details if the feedback is unclear. Examiners can provide recommendations about what the organization should do to improve the areas for improvement that were uncovered in the assessment.

The only real disadvantage of this approach is that it is much more expensive than the other two. You will recall from Chapter 2 that it takes a great deal of time to write an application. In this case, time will also need to be spent in training examiners, having them review and score the applications, and possibly go on site visits. Examiners in many companies that use this approach can be expected to spend the following amount of time on the activities listed:

- Attend examiner training
- Score written applications
- Reach consensus on scores
- Prepare and conduct site visit
- Prepare and present feedback report

3 days
2 days × 3 applications = 6 days
.5 days × 3 applications = 1.5 days
5 days
2 days
17.5 days

When you consider that some large companies such as AT&T have over 100 examiners, this can add up to a major investment. If you supplement your team of internal examiners with consultants or other outsiders, the cost can become even greater.

4. Formal Baldrige Application—A fourth and less commonly used approach for assessment is to formally apply for the Baldrige Award to see where you stand. This strategy was used by a number of organizations that later went on to win the award. (They applied and failed to win at least once before finally winning the award.) Miliken, Federal Express, Cadillac, and others all used the initial feedback they received to then go on to win. The $4,000 it costs to apply for the award for a large organization is minimal compared to the value of the feedback received. For $4,000 ($1,200 for small companies) you get a team of 6–8 official examiners who will individually score your application, reach consensus on your scores, and present you with a feedback report that gives you a page of strengths, areas for improvement and scores for each of the 28 Baldrige Items. If you are lucky enough to receive a site visit, a team of examiners will spend up to a week in your organization doing a further assessment. If you were to pay an outside consulting firm to conduct such an assessment, you would probably pay $30,000–$50,000 or more. Applying for the Baldrige Award to receive feedback is perhaps one of the government's biggest bargains.

If formally applying for the award offers such advantages, why don't more companies do it? Besides the initial cost (relatively small though it may be), the disadvantages are as follows. First, there is the long delay between the time you send in the application (April 1) and the time you receive feedback (November or December). This means that you can't use the feedback for planning purposes until the following year. A second disadvantage is that the approach forces you to apply as an entire company, or at least its major business units; Units or facilities that have fewer than 500 employees are not allowed to apply for the Baldrige Award. A third disadvantage is that you do not receive your final score—only ranges are provided. This makes it difficult to gauge the level of improvement each year. Another problem is that you are not allowed to talk to anyone about your feedback. I know of one Baldrige applicant that received a feedback report which was extremely vague. One page had three positive comments, an area for improvement, and a score of 20%. When the organization called the Baldrige office and asked to speak to the examiners or someone who could explain their feedback and scores, they were informed that no one was allowed to talk to them about these matters. One final reason why applying for the award as an assessment method may not be a good idea is that a low score might have a negative impact on employee morale. Imagine how the results would play if you received a score of 175 out of 1000 (when you may have been expecting around 600). Such results will be used as ammunition by those employees who believe Total Quality Management is just another passing fad.

5. Audit Against the Baldrige Criteria—The most thorough and most expensive way of evaluating your implementation of total quality management is to prepare and conduct an audit of the organization's practices and results based upon the Baldrige criteria (see Chapter 12). This involves developing a detailed audit plan, creating audit instruments, and spending many hours interviewing various levels of employees, reviewing quality data, and observing processes and practices. The advantage of this approach over the other four is its objectivity and the level of detailed feedback provided. The scope of the audit can vary considerably, and can be tailored to the organization's resource constraints. Some large organizations devote thousands of hours to such audits, and assign 10 to 20 employees to work full time for several months on the audit. Another organization I know of assigned a task force of seven people, and each spent a total of about 10 person-days on the audit.

The audit is very similar to the approach taken by the Baldrige Examiners when they do a site visit. However, you don't need to prepare a mock or real Baldrige application to conduct a TQM audit. The audit instruments are developed using the Baldrige criteria and the assessments are done based upon interviews, observations, and reviews of data rather than by reading a 75-page summary of the organization's approach to quality. (Again, see Chapter 12 of this book for details on how to conduct an audit against the Baldrige criteria.)

USING THE BALDRIGE ASSESSMENT TO DRIVE IMPROVEMENT

Getting assessed against the Baldrige criteria is the organizational equivalent of getting a three-day physical. The problem, however, is that many organizations have not figured out how to take the information from a Baldrige-style assessment and use it for improvement planning. An organization I'm familiar with has been doing Baldrige assessments of each of its business units for the last three years; each year teams of examiners spend a great deal of time on site visits to evaluate the organization's approaches, deployment, and results. Findings of the assessment are presented to senior management, and the examiners are thanked for doing such an honest and thorough evaluation. In 1991, when this was first done, each of the business units received a score of around 300 points out of a possible 1000. In 1992, the same type of assessment was done on the same business units, and, once again, the organizations all received scores of around 300 points. Some areas were slightly better, some had gotten worse. In 1993, a team of examiners did the third Baldrige assessment, and the scores once again ended up being around 300.

The problem is that this company, like many others, has not figured out how to put *teeth* into the assessment and assure that areas for improvement end up getting addressed in the overall business plan of the organization. This is what I will attempt to provide guidance on here.

Trying to Fix Everything at the Same Time

One commonly used approach in trying to make improvements is to take each area identified in the Baldrige assessment as lacking and developing an action plan for addressing the problem. Committees and task forces are formed and hundreds of people are involved in trying to improve the organization's performance in, often, more than 100 different areas. A year is spent and thousands of dollars in labor are expended working on the various improvement projects. The assessment is done again the following year, and, to everyone's surprise, the overall score does not improve much. The reason for the failure is that such an approach is too diluted, too uncoordinated, too lacking tie-in to the company's strategic business plan. Teams end up stepping on each others' toes, perhaps improving performance in one area only to make it worse in another.

A Smarter Approach—Selecting a Few Major Areas to Work on Improving

A better improvement planning approach is to prioritize the areas for improvement before proceeding to develop action plans. With this approach, you take the 120 or so areas for improvement from the Baldrige assessment and select the most important 10–20 to work on over the next year. Senior executives may assign a score to each area for improvement, using the following variables and scale:

- IMPACT—to what extent will fixing this weakness impact our performance on key measures of quality, customer satisfaction, or financial performance? (1 = no impact; 10 = great impact on a number of performance measures.)

- URGENCY—to what extent do we have to address this weakness immediately? (1 = can be postponed for several years; 10 = this needs to be fixed *now*.)

- TREND—is performance in this area currently getting worse, stable, or better? (1 = performance is improving rapidly; 10 = performance is getting worse all the time.)

By adding the scores for each area for improvement as given by each member of the senior executive team, you should be able to list the 100 or so areas in order of their priority. You then take the top ten and develop action plans for improving performance in these areas. A project manager is assigned to each action plan, and specific tasks and deadlines are developed for each improvement project.

Breaking Into The Next Level

Organizations performing Baldrige assessments often reach a plateau at between 300 and 400 points on the Baldrige scale. It is fairly easy for an organization that does some training, implements some process improvement teams, and starts measuring customer satisfaction to earn a score in this range. Getting a score of 500–600, on the other hand, generally requires some major changes in an organization's leadership, culture, and overall systems. Changing these features in an organization requires risk—and taking risks is something most organizations don't do well, especially if they are not in trouble. Companies that are unwilling or unable to make the changes needed to break out of the 300–400 point range are unlikely to stick with a Total Quality effort and the results of training and process improvement teams will tend to be short-lived. In companies that score above 500, Total Quality is not a program or initiative; it is, or is becoming, the way the organization is run.

Linking a Baldrige Assessment With Your Strategic Business Plan

A strategic business plan should focus on *results* before defining strategies and activities. Because two thirds of the Baldrige criteria deal with an organization's approaches or activities rather than with results, it is sometimes difficult to use a Baldrige assessment as a strategic planning tool. However, the assessment can provide important input to your business plan—as long as you avoid using it simply to outline projects or activities rather than concrete goals. For example, I've seen a number of organizations that set goals such as the following:

• Implement a comprehensive system for tracking customer satisfaction levels using a telephone survey by the end of the third quarter, 19_ _.

• All employees will have an individualized training plan by the end of the year.

• Implement QFD in all design functions in the company by the end of 19 _ _.

In this case, all of these goals were written in direct response to areas for improvement identified in a Baldrige assessment. None of them, however, are really *goals*—they are projects or activities. A goal should include a meaningful *measure* of performance such as ROI, profit, customer satisfaction, market share, or employee satisfaction, and should specify the desired level of performance on the measure. A strategy defines how the goal will be achieved. The results sections of a Baldrige assessment (6.0, 7.5 and 7.6) provide information on current performance and past trends for all key measures in an organization. Data from these sections of an assessment can be used to set annual goals for the following year, and longer-term goals for three to five years. Benchmarking studies, noted in section 2.2 of the Baldrige assessment, can also supply input for setting stretch goals. Once such goals have been set for all key results measures, the remaining sections of the Baldrige assessment can be used to help articulate strategies for accomplishing the goals. For example, you might set a goal to improve employee satisfaction by 40% over current levels during the following two years. To achieve this goal, look at the areas for improvement that were identified in section 4.5 of the assessment report. This should tell you where some holes exist in your approach to making your organization a good place to work. It won't tell you how to fix the problems, but it will tell you where to begin. Similarly, let's say that you develop a long term goal of reducing the number of customers you lose because of poor service by 75% over the next three years. Look at areas for improvement that were identified in section 7.1, 7.2, and 7.3 of the Baldrige assessment.

In short, a Baldrige assessment can usefully be linked to the business planning process of an organization as long as the data are used to develop concrete business goals and the weaknesses in the company's approach are identified and used as input for the development of improvement strategies.

Developing a Plan to Improve Your Baldrige Assessment Score

An approach used by a number of organizations to improve their score is to develop a separate plan focused on this. Organizations such as Northrop and McDonnell Douglas even set goals for business unit executives to improve their Baldrige assessment score by a certain percentage from one year to the next. The latter kind of goal setting is, in my view, a good idea. The score on a Baldrige assessment is an excellent indication of the overall health of a business unit or organization. It includes an evaluation of all important business results as well as the approaches used to achieve the results. What I would not recommend, however, is developing a separate plan for improving the score. Meeting the Baldrige criteria does not require a separate set of activities distinct from those involved in running the organization. The Baldrige criteria outline a comprehensive approach for running an organization. Goals to improve performance in the areas of customer satisfaction, quality, and other "results" areas need to go into the company's overall business plan—not produced as a separate document.

The Key to Success

Doing assessments against the Baldrige criteria can be an expensive and time consuming activity. Most organization's today have had their staffs cut back, so that there is no longer time for "busy" work such as conducting an audit that doesn't seem to result in any immediate benefits to the organization. Unless your organization is serious about making the changes necessary to satisfy the Baldrige criteria, I wouldn't waste time on doing an assessment. Even if you are serious about using the assessment to improve, you still need a system for making this happen. This system is in using the Baldrige assessment along with other data to develop your strategic business plan. The key to making it all happen is to get senior executives involved in the assessment and the review of findings. A common thread running through all of the organizations that have won the Baldrige Award is a strong commitment among and the active involvement of senior executives. Only then can the organization travel on its journey toward reaching the ideals set by the Baldrige criteria.

FURTHER READING

Brown, Mark Graham. *Baldrige Quick Reference Guide.* White Plains, NY: Quality Resources, 1994.

Brown, Mark Graham. "Commitment: It's Not The Whether, It's The How To." *Journal For Quality and Participation*, December, 1989, p. 38–42.

―――― "Measuring Your Company Against the Baldrige Criteria." *Journal for Quality and Participation*, June, 1992, p. 82–88.

―――― "The Baldrige Award: How Do You Win?" *Automation*, October, 1991, p. 34–37.

Brown, Mark Graham, Darcy Hitchcock, and Marsha Willard. *Why TQM Fails and What to Do About It.* Burr Ridge, IL: Irwin Professional Publishing, 1994.

Brown, Mark Graham, and Ray Svenson. "What Doing TQM Really Means." *Journal For Quality and Participation*, September, 1990, p. 32–38.

DeCarlo, Nell J., and Kent J. Sterett. "History of the Malcolm Baldrige National Quality Award." *Quality Progress*, March, 1990 p. 41–50.

Fisher, Donald. *The Simplified Baldrige Award Organization Assessment.* New York: Lincoln-Bradley, 1993.

Garvin, David A. "How the Baldrige Award Really Works." *Harvard Business Review*, November/December, 1991, p. 80–95.

Hart, Christopher W.L., and Christopher E. Bogan. *The Baldrige: What It Is, How It's Won, How to Use It to Improve Quality in Your Company.* New York: McGraw-Hill Inc., 1992.

Hauser, John R., and Don Clausing. "The House of Quality." *Harvard Business Review*, May/June, 1989, p. 63–73.

Helton, B. Ray. "Investing in Quality Pays Off " *QPMA's Discover*, Sept/Oct., 1993, p. 4–11.

Henry, Craig A. "Does the United States Need Quality Awards?" *Quality Progress*, December, 1990, p. 26–27.

Kendrick, John J. "Customers Win in Baldrige Award Selections." *Quality*, January, 1991, p. 23–31.

Main, Jeremy. "How to Win the Baldrige Award." *Fortune*, April 23, 1990, p. 101–116.

———— "Is the Baldrige Overblown?" *Fortune*, July 1, 1991, p. 62–65.

Rohan, Thomas M. "Do You Really Want a Baldrige?" *Industry Week*, April, 1991.
Schaffer, Robert H., and Thomson, Harvey A. "Successful Change Programs Begin with Results." *Harvard Business Review*, January/February, 1992, p. 80–89.

Stratton, Brad. "Four to Receive 1990 Baldrige Awards." *Quality Progress*, December, 1990, p. 19–21.

U. S. General Accounting Office. "Management Practices—U. S. Companies Improve Performance Through Quality Efforts." U. S. General Accounting Office Publication GAO/NSIAD–91–190, May, 1991.

Wolff, Michael. "Pushing to Improve Quality." *Research and Technology Management*, May/June, 1990, p. 19–22.

Malcolm Baldrige
National
Quality
Award

1994 Award Criteria

"To meet the challenges of the global economy…our most successful companies have been eliminating unnecessary layers of management, empowering front-line workers, becoming more responsive to their customers and seeking constantly to improve the products they make, the services they provide, and the people they employ."

William J. Clinton

> *"Sharing by past Baldrige Award winners — large and small, manufacturing and service — has inspired and challenged others to join the national effort to improve quality."*
>
> **Ronald H. Brown**
> **Secretary of Commerce**

The Award, composed of two solid crystal prismatic forms, stands 14 inches tall. The crystal is held in a base of black, anodized aluminum with the Award winner's name engraved on the base. A solid bronze, 22-karat, gold-plated, die-struck medallion is captured in the front section of the crystal. The medal bears the inscriptions: "Malcolm Baldrige National Quality Award" and "The Quest for Excellence" on one side and the Presidential Seal on the other.

Awards traditionally are presented by the President of the United States at a special ceremony in Washington, D.C.

Awards are made annually to recognize U.S. companies that excel in quality management and quality achievement. Awards may be given in each of three eligibility categories:

- Manufacturing companies
- Service companies
- Small businesses

Award recipients may publicize and advertise receipt of the Award. The recipients are expected to share information about their successful quality strategies with other U.S. organizations.

Crystal by Steuben
Medal by The Protocol Group

CONTENTS

ii THE MALCOLM BALDRIGE NATIONAL QUALITY AWARD:
A PUBLIC-PRIVATE PARTNERSHIP

1 INTRODUCTION

2 DESCRIPTION OF THE 1994 AWARD CRITERIA

2 AWARD CRITERIA PURPOSES

2 CORE VALUES AND CONCEPTS

5 AWARD CRITERIA FRAMEWORK

6 THE STRATEGIC QUALITY PLANNING CATEGORY —
INTEGRATING QUALITY AND OPERATIONAL PERFORMANCE
REQUIREMENTS WITH BUSINESS STRATEGY

7 THE INFORMATION AND ANALYSIS CATEGORY —
THE BASIS FOR ANALYSIS OF RESULTS, PROCESS
IMPROVEMENT, AND MAINTAINING ALIGNMENT OF
PROCESSES WITH BUSINESS STRATEGY

8 THE PIVOTAL ROLE OF THE QUALITY AND
OPERATIONAL RESULTS CATEGORY

9 KEY CHARACTERISTICS OF THE AWARD CRITERIA

10 LINKAGE OF THE AWARD CRITERIA TO QUALITY-
AND PERFORMANCE-RELATED CORPORATE ISSUES

12 CHANGES FROM THE 1993 CRITERIA

12 KEY THEMES STRENGTHENED IN THE 1994 CRITERIA

13 1994 AWARD EXAMINATION CRITERIA — ITEM LISTING

14 1994 AWARD EXAMINATION CRITERIA
14 1.0 LEADERSHIP
16 2.0 INFORMATION AND ANALYSIS
18 3.0 STRATEGIC QUALITY PLANNING
20 4.0 HUMAN RESOURCE DEVELOPMENT AND MANAGEMENT
23 5.0 MANAGEMENT OF PROCESS QUALITY
27 6.0 QUALITY AND OPERATIONAL RESULTS
29 7.0 CUSTOMER FOCUS AND SATISFACTION

33 SCORING SYSTEM: APPROACH, DEPLOYMENT, RESULTS

34 SCORING GUIDELINES

35 1994 EXAMINATION RESPONSE GUIDELINES

39 ELIGIBILITY CATEGORIES AND RESTRICTIONS

41 HOW TO ORDER COPIES OF 1994 AWARD MATERIALS

41 FEES FOR THE 1994 AWARD CYCLE

42 HOW TO ORDER AWARD EDUCATIONAL MATERIALS

42 QUEST FOR EXCELLENCE VI CONFERENCE

THE MALCOLM BALDRIGE NATIONAL QUALITY AWARD: A PUBLIC-PRIVATE PARTNERSHIP

Building active partnerships in the private sector, and between the private sector and government, is fundamental to the success of the Award in improving quality in the United States.

Support by the private sector for the Award Program in the form of funds, volunteer efforts, and participation in information transfer is strong and rapidly growing.

To ensure the continued growth and success of these partnerships, each of the following organizations plays an important role:

The Foundation for the Malcolm Baldrige National Quality Award

The Foundation for the Malcolm Baldrige National Quality Award was created to foster the success of the Program. The Foundation's main objective is to raise funds to permanently endow the Award Program.

Prominent leaders from U.S. companies serve as Foundation Trustees to ensure that the Foundation's objectives are accomplished. Donor organizations vary in size and type, and are representative of many kinds of businesses and business groups. To date, the Foundation has raised approximately $11 million.

National Institute of Standards and Technology (NIST)

Responsibility for the Award is assigned to the Department of Commerce. NIST, an agency of the Department's Technology Administration, manages the Award Program.

NIST's goals are to aid U.S. industry through research and services; to contribute to public health, safety, and the environment; and to support the U.S. scientific and engineering research communities. NIST conducts basic and applied research in the physical sciences and engineering and develops measurement techniques, test methods, and standards. Much of NIST's work relates directly to quality and to quality-related requirements in technology development and technology utilization.

American Society for Quality Control (ASQC)

ASQC assists in administering the Award Program under contract to NIST.

ASQC is dedicated to facilitating continuous improvement and increased customer satisfaction by identifying, communicating and promoting the use of quality principles, concepts, and technologies. ASQC strives to be recognized throughout the world as the leading authority on, and champion for, quality. ASQC recognizes that continuous quality improvement will help the favorable repositioning of American goods and services in the international marketplace.

Board of Overseers

The Board of Overseers is the advisory organization on the Award to the Department of Commerce. The Board is appointed by the Secretary of Commerce and consists of distinguished leaders from all sectors of the U.S. economy.

The Board of Overseers evaluates all aspects of the Award Program, including the adequacy of the Criteria and processes for making Awards. An important part of the Board's responsibility is to assess how well the Award is serving the national interest. Accordingly, the Board makes recommendations to the Secretary of Commerce and to the Director of NIST regarding changes and improvements in the Award Program.

Board of Examiners

The Board of Examiners evaluates Award applications, prepares feedback reports, and makes Award recommendations to the Director of NIST. The Board consists of quality experts primarily from the private sector. Members are selected by NIST through a competitive application process. For 1994, the Board consists of more than 270 members. Of these, 9 serve as Judges, and approximately 50 serve as Senior Examiners. The remainder serve as Examiners. All members of the Board take part in an examiner preparation course.

In addition to their application review responsibilities, Board members contribute significantly to building awareness of the importance of quality and to information transfer activities. Many of these activities involve the hundreds of professional, trade, community, and state organizations to which Board members belong.

Award Recipients' Responsibilities and Contributions

Award recipients are required to share information on their successful quality strategies with other U.S. organizations. However, recipients are not required to share proprietary information, even if such information was part of their Award application. The principal mechanism for sharing information is the annual Quest for Excellence Conference, highlighted on page 42.

Award recipients in the first six years of the Award have been very generous in their commitment to improving U.S. competitiveness, and manufacturing and service quality. They have shared information on their successful quality strategies with hundreds of thousands of companies, educational institutions, government agencies, health care organizations, and others. This sharing far exceeds expectations and Program requirements. Award winners' efforts have encouraged many other organizations in all sectors of the U.S. economy to undertake their own quality improvement efforts.

INTRODUCTION

The Malcolm Baldrige National Quality Award is an annual Award to recognize U.S. companies that excel in quality management and quality achievement.

The Award promotes:

- awareness of quality as an increasingly important element in competitiveness,
- understanding of the requirements for quality excellence, and
- sharing of information on successful quality strategies and the benefits derived from implementation of these strategies.

Award Participation

The Award has three eligibility categories:

- Manufacturing companies
- Service companies
- Small businesses

Awards may be given in each category each year. Award recipients may publicize and advertise their Awards. In addition to publicizing the receipt of the Award, recipients are expected to share information about their successful quality strategies with other U.S. organizations.

Companies participating in the Award process are required to submit application packages that include completion of the Award Examination.

The Award Examination

The Award Examination is based upon quality excellence criteria created through a public-private partnership. In responding to these criteria, each applicant is expected to provide information and data on the company's improvement processes and results. Information and data submitted must be adequate to demonstrate that the applicant's approaches could be replicated or adapted by other companies.

The Award Examination is designed not only to serve as a reliable basis for making Awards but also to permit a diagnosis of each applicant's overall management system.

The Application Package

A complete Application Package consists of several components. Detailed information and the necessary forms are contained in the Application Forms and Instructions document. Ordering instructions for this document are given on page 41.

The objective of the Application Package is to provide sufficient information on management of products and services and results of improvement processes to permit a rigorous evaluation by the Board of Examiners. The Application Package consists of: an approved Eligibility Determination Form, with a listing of applicant company sites; a completed Application Form; a Business Overview, addressing the applicant's key business factors; the Application Report, responding to all Award Examination Criteria; and, Supplemental Sections, submitted by applicants whose application includes units that are in different businesses.

Application Review

Applications are reviewed and evaluated by members of the Board of Examiners in a four-stage process:

Stage 1 – independent review and evaluation by at least five members of the Board

Stage 2 – consensus review and evaluation for applications that score well in Stage 1

Stage 3 – site visits to applicants that score well in Stage 2

Stage 4 – Judges' review and recommendations

Board members are assigned to applications taking into account the nature of the applicants' businesses and the expertise of the Examiners. Assignments are made in accord with strict rules regarding conflict of interest.

Applications are reviewed without funding from the United States government. Review expenses are paid primarily through application fees; partial support for the reviews is provided by the Foundation for the Malcolm Baldrige National Quality Award.

Feedback to Applicants

Each applicant receives a feedback report at the conclusion of the review process. The feedback is based upon the applicant's responses to the Award Examination Criteria.

Purpose of This Booklet

This booklet contains the Award Criteria, a description of the Criteria, scoring guidelines, and other information. In addition to serving as the basis for submitting an Award application, organizations of all kinds use the Criteria for self-assessment, planning, training, and other purposes.

If you plan to apply for the Award in 1994, you will also need the document entitled *1994 Application Forms and Instructions.* Ordering instructions are given on page 41.

Eligibility Determination Forms due — March 4, 1994

Award applications due — April 4, 1994

DESCRIPTION OF THE 1994 AWARD CRITERIA

Award Criteria Purposes

The Malcolm Baldrige National Quality Award Criteria are the basis for making Awards and for giving feedback to applicants. In addition, the Criteria have three important roles in strengthening U.S. competitiveness:

- to help raise quality performance practices and expectations;

- to facilitate communication and sharing among and within organizations of all types based upon a common understanding of key quality and operational performance requirements; and

- to serve as a working tool for planning, training, assessment, and other uses.

Award Criteria Goals

The Criteria are designed to help companies enhance their competitiveness through focus on dual, results-oriented goals:

- delivery of ever-improving value to customers, resulting in improved marketplace performance; and

- improvement of overall company operational performance.

Core Values and Concepts

The Award Criteria are built upon a set of core values and concepts. These values and concepts are the foundation for integrating the overall customer and company operational performance requirements.

These core values and concepts are:

Customer-Driven Quality

Quality is judged by customers. All product and service characteristics that contribute value to the customer and lead to customer satisfaction and preference must be the focus of a company's management system. Value, satisfaction, and preference may be influenced by many factors throughout the customer's overall purchase, ownership, and service experiences. These factors include the company's relationship with customers that helps build trust, confidence, and loyalty. This concept of quality includes not only the product and service characteristics that meet basic customer requirements, but it also includes those characteristics that enhance them and differentiate them from competing offerings. Such enhancement and differentiation may be based upon new offerings, combinations of product and service offerings, rapid response, or special relationships.

Customer-driven quality is thus a strategic concept. It is directed toward customer retention and market share gain. It demands constant sensitivity to emerging customer and market requirements, and measurement of the factors that drive customer satisfaction and retention. It also demands awareness of developments in technology and of competitors' offerings, and rapid and flexible response to customer and market requirements.

Success requires more than defect and error reduction, merely meeting specifications, and reducing complaints. Nevertheless, defect and error reduction and elimination of causes of dissatisfaction contribute significantly to the customers' view of quality and are thus also important parts of customer-driven quality. In addition, the company's success in recovering from defects and errors ("making things right for the customer") is crucial to building customer relationships and to customer retention.

A company's customer-driven focus needs to address all stakeholders — customers, employees, suppliers, stockholders, the public, and the community.

Leadership

A company's senior leaders must create a customer orientation, clear and visible quality values, and high expectations. Reinforcement of the values and expectations requires substantial personal commitment and involvement. The leaders' basic values and commitment need to include areas of public responsibility and corporate citizenship. The leaders must take part in the creation of strategies, systems, and methods for achieving excellence. The systems and methods need to guide all activities and decisions of the company. The senior leaders must commit to the growth and development of the entire work force and should encourage participation and creativity by all employees. Through their regular personal involvement in visible activities, such as planning, communications, review of company performance, and recognizing employees for quality achievement, the senior leaders serve as role models, reinforcing the values and encouraging leadership in all levels of management.

Continuous Improvement

Achieving the highest levels of quality and competitiveness requires a well-defined and well-executed approach to continuous improvement. The term "continuous improvement" refers to both incremental and "breakthrough" improvement. The approach to improvement needs to be "embedded" in the way the company functions. Embedded means that: (1) improvement is part of the daily work of all work units; (2) improvement processes seek to eliminate problems at their source; and (3) improvement is driven by opportunities to do better, as well as by problems that must be corrected. Opportunities for improvement have four major sources: employee ideas; R&D; customer input; and benchmarking or other comparative information on processes and performance.

Improvements may be of several types: (1) enhancing value to customers through new and improved products and services; (2) reducing errors, defects, and waste; (3) improving responsiveness and cycle time performance; (4) improving productivity and effectiveness in the use of all resources; and (5) improving the company's performance and leadership position in fulfilling its public responsibilities and serving as a role model in corporate citizenship. Thus improvement is driven not only by the objective to provide better product and service quality, but also by the need to be responsive and efficient — both conferring additional marketplace advantages. To meet all of these objectives, the process of continuous improvement must contain regular cycles of planning, execution, and evaluation. This requires a basis — preferably a quantitative basis — for assessing progress, and for deriving information for future cycles of improvement. Such information should provide direct links between desired performance and internal operations.

Employee Participation and Development
A company's success in improving performance depends increasingly on the skills and motivation of its work force. Employee success depends increasingly on having meaningful opportunities to learn and to practice new skills. Companies need to invest in the development of the work force through education, training, and creating opportunities for continuing growth. Such opportunities might include classroom and on-the-job training, job rotation, and pay for demonstrated skills. Structured on-the-job training offers a cost effective way to train and to better link training to work processes. Increasingly, training, development, and work organizations need to be tailored to a more diverse work force and to more flexible, high performance work environments.

Major challenges in the area of work force development include: (1) integration of human resource management — selection, performance, recognition, training, and career advancement; and (2) aligning human resource management with business plans and strategic change processes. Addressing these challenges requires acquisition and use of employee-related data on skills, satisfaction, motivation, safety, and well-being. Such data need to be tied to indicators of company or unit performance, such as customer satisfaction, customer retention, and productivity. Through this approach, human resource management may be better integrated and aligned with business directions, using continuous improvement processes to refine integration and alignment.

Fast Response
Success in competitive markets increasingly demands ever-shorter cycles for new or improved product and service introduction. Also, faster and more flexible response to customers is now a more critical requirement. Major improvement in response time often requires simplification of work organizations and work processes. To accomplish such improvement, the time performance of work processes should be measured. There are other important benefits derived from this focus: response time improvements often drive simultaneous improvements in organization, quality, and productivity. Hence it is beneficial to consider response time, quality, and productivity objectives together.

Design Quality and Prevention
Business management should place strong emphasis on design quality — problem and waste prevention achieved through building quality into products and services and into production processes. In general, costs of preventing problems at the design stage are much lower than costs of correcting problems which occur "downstream". Design quality includes the creation of fault-tolerant (robust) or error resistant processes and products.

A major issue in the competitive environment is the design-to-introduction ("product generation") cycle time. Meeting the demands of ever-more rapidly changing markets requires that companies carry out stage-to-stage coordination and integration ("concurrent engineering") of functions and activities from basic research to commercialization.

From the point of view of public responsibility, the design stage involves decisions regarding resource use and manufacturing processes. Such decisions affect process waste streams and the composition of municipal and industrial wastes. The growing demand by consumers and others for a cleaner environment means that companies will need to develop design strategies that place greater weight on environmental factors.

Consistent with the theme of design quality and prevention, continuous improvement and corrective action need to emphasize interventions "upstream" — at early stages in processes. This approach yields the maximum overall benefits of improvements and corrections. Such upstream intervention also needs to take into account the company's suppliers.

Long-Range Outlook
Achieving quality and market leadership requires a company to have a strong future orientation and a willingness to make long-term commitments to all stakeholders — customers, employees, suppliers, stockholders, the public, and the community. Planning needs to determine or anticipate many types of changes including those that may affect customers' expectations of products and services, technological developments, changing customer segments, evolving regulatory requirements and community/societal expectations, or thrusts by competitors. Plans, strategies, and resource allocations need to reflect these commitments and changes. A major part of the long-term commitment is development of employees and suppliers, fulfilling public responsibilities, and serving as a corporate citizenship role model.

Management by Fact

A modern business management system needs to be built upon a framework of measurement, data and analysis. Measurements must derive from the company's strategy and encompass all key processes and the outputs of those processes. Facts and data needed for quality improvement and quality assessment are of many types, including: customer, product and service performance, operations, market, competitive comparisons, supplier, employee-related, and cost and financial. Analysis refers to the process of extracting larger meaning from data to support evaluation and decision making at various levels within the company. Such analysis may entail using data to reveal information — such as trends, projections, and cause and effect — that might not be evident without analysis. Facts, data, and analysis support a variety of company purposes, such as planning, reviewing company performance, improving operations, and comparing company quality performance with competitors' or with "best practices" benchmarks.

A major consideration relating to use of data and analysis to improve performance involves the creation and use of performance measures or indicators. Performance measures or indicators are measurable characteristics of products, services, processes, and operations the company uses to track and improve performance. The measures or indicators should be selected to best represent the factors that lead to improved customer satisfaction and operational performance. A system of measures or indicators tied to customer and/or company performance requirements represents a clear and objective basis for aligning all activities with the company's strategy and goals. Through the analysis of data from the tracking processes, the measures or indicators themselves may be evaluated and changed. For example, measures or indicators selected to track product and service quality may be judged by how well improvement relative to the quality measures or indicators correlates with improvement in customer satisfaction.

Partnership Development

Companies should seek to build internal and external partnerships to better accomplish their overall goals.

Internal partnerships might include those that promote labor-management cooperation, such as agreements with unions. Agreements might entail employee development, cross-training, or new work organizations, such as high performance work teams. Internal partnerships might also involve creating network relationships among company units to improve flexibility and responsiveness.

Examples of external partnerships include those with customers, suppliers, and education organizations. An increasingly important kind of external partnership is the strategic partnership or alliance. Such partnerships might offer a company entry into new markets or a basis for new products or services. A partnership might also permit the blending of a company's core competencies or leadership capabilities with complementary strengths and capabilities of partners, thereby enhancing overall capability, including speed and flexibility.

Partnerships should seek to develop longer-term objectives, thereby creating a basis for mutual investments. Partners should address the key requirements for success of the partnership, means of regular communication, approaches to evaluating progress, and means for adapting to changing conditions.

Corporate Responsibility and Citizenship

A company's management objectives should stress corporate responsibility and citizenship. Corporate responsibility refers to basic expectations of the company — business ethics and protection of public health, public safety, and the environment. Health, safety and environmental considerations need to take into account the company's operations as well as the life cycles of products and services. Companies need to address factors such as resource conservation and waste reduction at their source. Planning related to public health, safety, and environment should anticipate adverse impacts that may arise in facilities management, production, distribution, transportation, use and disposal of products. Plans should seek to prevent problems, to provide a forthright company response if problems occur, and to make available information needed to maintain public awareness, safety, trust, and confidence. Inclusion of public responsibility areas within a quality system means meeting all local, state, and federal laws and regulatory requirements. It also means treating these and related requirements as areas for continuous improvement "beyond mere compliance."

Corporate citizenship refers to leadership and support — within reasonable limits of a company's resources — of publicly important purposes, including the above-mentioned areas of corporate responsibility. Such purposes might include education, environmental excellence, resource conservation, community services, improving industry and business practices, and sharing of nonproprietary quality-related information. Leadership as a corporate citizen entails influencing other organizations, private and public, to partner for these purposes.

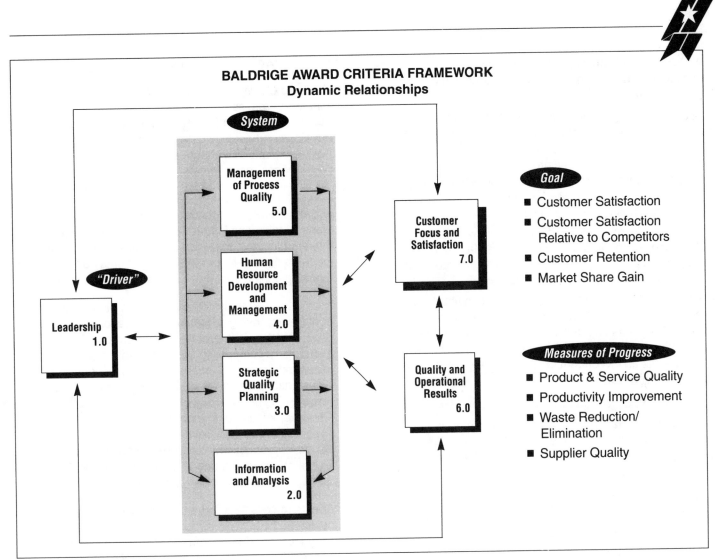

BALDRIGE AWARD CRITERIA FRAMEWORK
Dynamic Relationships

System

| Management of Process Quality 5.0 |
| Human Resource Development and Management 4.0 |
| Strategic Quality Planning 3.0 |
| Information and Analysis 2.0 |

"Driver"

Leadership 1.0

Customer Focus and Satisfaction 7.0

Quality and Operational Results 6.0

Goal
- Customer Satisfaction
- Customer Satisfaction Relative to Competitors
- Customer Retention
- Market Share Gain

Measures of Progress
- Product & Service Quality
- Productivity Improvement
- Waste Reduction/ Elimination
- Supplier Quality

Award Criteria Framework

The core values and concepts are embodied in seven categories, as follows:

1.0 Leadership
2.0 Information and Analysis
3.0 Strategic Quality Planning
4.0 Human Resource Development and Management
5.0 Management of Process Quality
6.0 Quality and Operational Results
7.0 Customer Focus and Satisfaction

The framework connecting and integrating the categories is given in the figure above.

The framework has four basic elements:

Driver

Senior executive leadership creates the values, goals, and systems, and guides the sustained pursuit of customer value and company performance improvement.

Goal

The basic aim of the quality process is the delivery of ever-improving value to customers.

System

The System comprises the set of well-defined and well-designed processes for meeting the company's customer, quality, and performance requirements.

Measures of Progress

Measures of progress provide a results-oriented basis for channeling actions to delivering ever-improving customer value and company performance.

The seven Criteria Categories shown in the figure are subdivided into Examination Items and Areas to Address:

Examination Items

There are 28 Examination Items, each focusing on a major management requirement. Item titles and point values are given on page 13. The Examination Item format is shown on page 35.

Areas to Address

Examination Items consist of sets of Areas to Address (Areas). Information is submitted by applicants in response to specific requirements of these Areas.

The Strategic Quality Planning Category — Integrating Quality and Operational Performance Requirements with Business Strategy

Strategic Quality Planning (Category 3.0) addresses business planning and deployment of plans, with special focus on customer and operational performance requirements. The Category stresses that customer-driven quality and operational performance excellence are key strategic business issues which need to be an integral part of overall business planning. Specifically:

- customer-driven quality is a strategic view of quality. The focus is on the drivers of customer satisfaction, customer retention and market share — key factors in competitiveness and business success;

- operational performance improvement contributes to short-term productivity growth and cost/price competitiveness. The focus on building operational capability — including speed, responsiveness, and flexibility — also represents an investment in strengthening longer-term competitiveness.

Overall, the Criteria emphasize that continuous improvement be an integral part of the daily activity of all work units. The special role of Category 3.0 is to provide a better planning focus for most daily work, aligning it with the company's strategic directions.

In particular, planning is needed to:

- understand the key customer and operational requirements as input to setting strategic directions. This will help ensure that ongoing process improvements will be aligned with the company's strategic directions.

- optimize the use of resources and ensure bridging between short-term and longer-term requirements which may entail capital expenditures, training, etc.

- ensure that deployment will be effective — that there are mechanisms to transmit understanding and alignment on three basic levels: (1) company/executive level; (2) the key process level; and (3) the work-unit/individual-job level.

- ensure that work organizations and structures will effectively serve the accomplishment of strategic plans and set the stage for integrating breakthrough and incremental improvement.

The Category requirements do not imply highly formalized planning systems, departments, or specific planning cycles. Nor do the planning requirements imply that all improvements could or should be planned. Finally, the planning requirements in Category 3.0 address basic company strategy and directions, not specific product/service designs. Such designs are addressed in Item 5.1.

Category 3.0 consists of two Items:

3.1 *Strategic Quality and Company Performance Planning Process*
This Item calls for information on how the company develops and deploys customer-focused strategy and business plans that integrate customer and operational performance requirements.

Area 3.1a calls for information on the key influences and requirements that affect business strategy and plans — taking as long a view as possible. Although the main focus of this Area is customer satisfaction leadership, such leadership requirements need an overall planning context — addressed in this Area.

Area 3.1b calls for information on how plans explicitly address improving and enabling operational performance. One key factor in this Area is structural — ensuring that company plans address the customer focus and "leanness" of company and work unit organizations. Accomplishing the plans may require restructuring or "re-engineering" of business processes. The other key factor in this Area highlights three important and closely-related business improvement issues — productivity, waste reduction, and cycle time. The term "waste" as used here refers to waste in all forms — materials, energy, labor, and capital.

Area 3.1c calls for information on how plans are deployed. Strategy and plans developed at the company level need to be translated simply and effectively into requirements for all work units. Of central importance is how alignment and consistency are achieved — for example, via key processes and key measurements which define requirements and indicators of effectiveness for work units. Such definition of requirements at the process and work unit level provides a basis for priorities for ongoing improvement actions. The Area also calls for information on how resources are committed to support process improvements, which may entail new resource commitments or changed resource allocations.

Area 3.1d calls for information on how the company evaluates and improves the overall planning process and the deployment of plans. This involves input from work units. This input could affect the content of plans, such as training and development needs. It could also provide key information on the effectiveness of deployment — how well plans have been translated into specific requirements and measures throughout the company.

3.2 Quality and Performance Plans

This Item calls for information on actual plans which integrate key customer and operational requirements. The main focus of the Item is on effective translation of plans, including resources, to specific requirements for work units and suppliers. The time horizon for this plan implementation is divided into two parts: a 1-3 year period for specific plans, and 3 years or more for an outline of plans. This approach is used to ensure that short-term actions are guided by factors that reflect the company's longer-term directions.

The Item calls for a projection (3.2d) of the company's key performance levels using the most important measures of quality and operational performance. It also calls for comparing projected performance versus competitors and key benchmarks. This projection/comparison is intended to help companies improve their understanding of dynamic, competitive quality and operational factors and to encourage them to use their *rates of improvement* as a management tool.

The Information and Analysis Category — The Basis for Analysis of Results, Process Improvement, and Maintaining Alignment of Processes with Business Strategy

Information and Analysis (Category 2.0) is the focal point within the Criteria for all key information to drive improvement of quality and operational performance. In simplest terms, Category 2.0 is the "brain center" for the alignment of a company's information system with its strategic directions. The Category addresses the requirements for organizational improvement based upon the improvement of key processes.

Category 2.0 consists of three Items:

2.1 Scope and Management of Quality and Performance Data and Information

This Item calls for a description of how the company selects data and information and the roles of such data and information in improving quality and operational performance. Major emphasis is placed upon the adequacy of data — from customers and processes — to drive process improvement. Though cost and financial data provide useful support, process improvement is driven primarily through nonfinancial indicators — indicators linked to requirements derived from customers and from company operational performance. The Item addresses other key issues in information management, including: data reliability; broad and rapid access; data review and update; and improvement of all aspects of the scope and management of data and information.

2.2 Competitive Comparisons and Benchmarking

This Item addresses external drivers of improvement — data and information related to competitive factors and to best practices. The major premises underlying this Item are: (1) companies need to "know where they stand" relative to competitors and to best practices performance for similar activities; (2) comparative and benchmarking information provides impetus for significant (sometimes "breakthrough") improvement, and alerts companies to competitive threats, and new practices; and (3) companies need to understand their own processes, the processes of others, and the performance levels associated with these processes. The Item addresses the key issues in management of competitive comparisons and benchmarking. These are: criteria for selection; scope, sources and principal uses of comparative and benchmarking information; how benchmarking and comparative information are used to understand processes, stimulate innovation, and elevate expectations; and how the process for obtaining and using competitive comparison and benchmarking information is improved.

2.3 Analysis and Uses of Company-Level Data

Management by fact is a core concept in the Criteria. The Criteria call for a wide variety of data — nonfinancial and financial — to guide a company's courses of action toward beneficial results. Despite their importance, however, individual facts do not usually provide a sound basis for action or priorities. Action depends upon understanding cause/effect connections among processes and between processes and results. Process actions may have many resource implications; results may have many cost and revenue implications as well. Given that resources for improvement are limited, and cause/effect connections are often unclear, there is a critical need to provide a sound, analytical basis for decisions. In the Criteria, this role is fulfilled by analyses of many types. Item 2.3 plays a key linkage role in an integrated data strategy.

Item 2.3 has three analysis components:

Area 2.3a calls for the aggregation and analysis of customer-related data (from Category 7.0) and other key data to focus on improving customer-related decision making and priorities. This is the only Area within the Criteria that addresses the interrelationships among all customer-related sources of information. Together with product and service quality data (Item 6.1), the data in Category 7.0 provide a basis for identifying key drivers of customer satisfaction, customer retention, and market share gain. Inasmuch as Item 6.1 is linked to key processes (Category 5.0), the analysis carried out in 2.3a translates the "voice of the customer" into internal process improvement requirements. These requirements ensure that priority is given to process improvements that lead to marketplace success, captured in Items 7.5 and 7.6.

Area 2.3b calls for the aggregation and analysis of operations-related data (from Category 6.0) and other key data to focus on improving operations-related decision making and priorities. This is the only Area within the Criteria that addresses the interrelationships among operations-related sources of information. It is thus the principal basis for optimizing overall operational improvement consistent with improving customer-related indicators. Inasmuch as the Items of Category 6.0 are tied directly to key processes (Category 5.0) and to human resource processes and data (Category 4.0), the analyses carried out in 2.3b help to align all internal process improvement.

Area 2.3c calls for linking overall quality and operational performance improvement data to changes in overall company financial performance. This is the only Area within the Criteria that addresses this key linkage. Thus, it is an important source of information for allocating limited resources among potential improvement projects based upon improvement potential and financial impact.

The Pivotal Role of the Quality and Operational Results Category

Quality and Operational Results (Category 6.0) provides a results focus for all improvement activities. Through this focus, the Criteria's dual purpose — superior value of offerings as viewed by the customer and the marketplace, and superior company performance reflected in productivity and effectiveness indicators — is maintained. Category 6.0 thus provides "real-time" information (measures of progress) for evaluation and improvement of processes, aligned with overall business strategy.

Category 6.0 consists of four Items:

6.1 Product and Service Quality Results

This Item calls for reporting quality levels and improvements for key product and service features — **features that matter to the customer and to the marketplace**. These features are derived from customer-related Items ("listening posts") which make up Category 7.0. If the features have been properly selected, improvements in them should show a strong positive correlation with customer and marketplace improvement indicators — captured in Items 7.5 and 7.6. The correlation between quality and customer indicators is a critical management tool. It is a device for focusing on key features. In addition, the correlation

may reveal emerging or changing market segments, changing importance of features, or even potential obsolescence of products and/or services.

6.2 Company Operational Results

This Item calls for reporting performance and improvements in internal operations and productivity of the company. Paralleling Item 6.1, which focuses on features that matter to the customer, Item 6.2 focuses on **factors that best reflect overall company operational performance**. Such factors are of two types: (1) generic — common to all companies; and (2) business-specific. Generic factors include cycle time and productivity, as reflected in use of labor, materials, energy, capital, and assets. Indicators of productivity, cycle time, or internal quality should reflect overall company performance. Business- or company-specific effectiveness indicators vary greatly. Examples include rates of invention, environmental quality, export levels, new markets, percent of sales from recently introduced products or services, and shifts toward new segments.

6.3 Business and Support Service Results

This Item calls for reporting performance and improvements in quality, productivity, and effectiveness of business and support services. This permits a demonstration of how support units contribute to overall improvement in quality (reported in Item 6.1) and overall improvement in company operational performance (reported in Item 6.2). This Item is thus a useful device in aligning support activities with the company's overall principal quality, productivity, and business objectives. Through this Item, progress in meeting special requirements, which may differ among work units and which define work-unit effectiveness, can be measured.

6.4 Supplier Quality Results

This Item calls for reporting quality levels and improvements in key measures of supplier quality. The term "supplier" refers to external providers of products and services, "upstream" and/or "downstream" from the company. The focus should be on the most critical quality attributes from the point of view of the company — the buyer of the products and services. Trends and levels of quality should reflect results by whatever means they occur — via improvements by suppliers within the supply base, through selection of better suppliers, or both.

Key Characteristics of the Award Criteria

1. The Criteria are directed toward results.

The Criteria focus principally on seven key areas of business performance, given below.

> Results are a composite of:
> (1) customer satisfaction/retention
> (2) market share, new market development
> (3) product and service quality
> (4) productivity, operational effectiveness, and responsiveness
> (5) human resource performance/development
> (6) supplier performance/development
> (7) public responsibility/corporate citizenship

Improvements in these seven results areas contribute significantly to company performance, including financial performance. The results indicators also recognize the importance of contributions to improving suppliers and to the national well-being.

The use of a composite of indicators helps to ensure that strategies are appropriately balanced — that they do not trade off among important stakeholders, objectives, or responsibilities. The composite of indicators also helps to ensure that company strategies bridge short-term and long-term considerations.

2. The Criteria are nonprescriptive.

The Criteria are a set of 28 basic, interrelated, results-oriented requirements. However, the Criteria imply wide latitude in how requirements are met. Accordingly, the Criteria do not prescribe:

- specific quality tools, techniques, technologies, systems, or starting points;
- that there should or should not be within a company a separate quality department or organization; or
- how the company itself should be organized.

The Criteria do emphasize that these and other factors be regularly evaluated as part of the company's improvement processes. The factors listed are important and are very likely to change as needs and strategies evolve.

The Criteria are nonprescriptive because:

(1) The Criteria's focus is on requirements that produce results, not on procedures, tools or organizations. Through this approach, companies are encouraged to develop and *demonstrate* creative, adaptive and flexible approaches to meeting basic requirements. The nonprescriptive nature of the requirements thus fosters incremental and major ("breakthrough") improvement.

(2) Selection of tools, techniques, systems and organizations usually depends upon many factors such as business size, business type, the company's stage of development, and employee capabilities.

(3) Focus on common requirements within a company rather than on specific procedures fosters better understanding, communication, and sharing, while encouraging diversity and creativity in approaches.

3. The Criteria are comprehensive.

The Criteria address all internal and external requirements of the company, including those related to fulfilling its public responsibilities. Accordingly, all processes of all company work units are tied to these requirements. New or changing strategies or directions of the company may be readily adapted within the same set of Criteria requirements.

4. The Criteria include interrelated (process→results) learning cycles.

The arrows in the figure on page 5 indicate dynamic linkage among the Criteria requirements. Learning (and action based upon that learning) takes place via feedback among the process and results elements as outlined above (The Pivotal Role of the Quality and Operational Results Category, 6.0).

The learning cycles have four, clearly-defined stages:

(1) planning, including design of processes, selection of indicators, and deployment of requirements;

(2) execution of plans;

(3) assessment of progress, taking into account internal and external (results) indicators; and

(4) revision of plans based upon assessment findings.

5. The Criteria emphasize quality system alignment.

The Criteria call for improvement (learning) cycles at all levels and in all parts of the company. To ensure that improvement cycles carried out in different parts of the company support one another, overall aims need to be consistent or *aligned*. Alignment in the Criteria is achieved via interconnecting and mutually reinforcing measures and indicators, derived from overall company requirements. These measures and indicators tie directly to customer value and to operational performance. The use of measures and indicators thus channels different activities in agreed-upon directions. Use of measures and indicators avoids the need for detailed procedures or unnecessary centralization of decision making or process management. Measures and indicators thus provide a communications tool and a basis for deploying consistent customer and operational performance requirements to all work units. Such alignment ensures consistency of purpose while at the same time supporting speed, innovation, and empowerment.

6. The Criteria are part of a diagnostic system.

The Criteria and the scoring guidelines make up a two-part diagnostic (assessment) system. The Criteria are a set of 28 basic, interrelated, results-oriented requirements (Examination Items). The scoring guidelines spell out the assessment dimensions — Approach, Deployment, and Results — and the key factors used in assessment relative to each dimension. An assessment thus provides a profile of strengths and areas for improvement relative to the 28 requirements. In this way, the assessment directs attention to processes and actions that contribute to the results composite described above.

Linkage of the Award Criteria to Quality- and Performance-Related Corporate Issues

Incremental and Breakthrough Improvement

Nonprescriptive, results-oriented Criteria and key measures and indicators focus on *what* needs to be improved. This approach helps to ensure that improvements throughout the organization contribute to the organization's overall objectives. In addition to fostering creativity in approach and organization, results-oriented Criteria and key measures and indicators encourage "breakthrough thinking" — openness to the possibility for major improvements as well as to incremental ones. However, if key measures and indicators are tied too directly to existing work organizations and processes, breakthrough changes may be discouraged. For this reason, analysis of processes and progress should focus on the selection of and the value of the measures and indicators themselves. This will help to ensure that measure and indicator selection does not stifle creativity and prevent beneficial changes ("re-engineering") in organization or work processes.

Benchmarks may also serve a useful purpose in stimulating breakthrough thinking. Benchmarks offer the opportunity to achieve significant improvements based on adoption or adaptation of current best practice. In addition, benchmarks help encourage creativity through exposure to alternative approaches. Also, benchmarks represent a clear challenge to "beat the best," thus stimulating the search for major improvements rather than only incremental refinements of existing approaches. As with key measures and indicators, benchmark selection is critical, and benchmarks should be reviewed periodically for appropriateness.

Business Strategy and Decisions

The focus on superior offerings and lower costs of operation means that the Criteria's principal route to improved financial performance is through requirements that seek to channel company activities toward producing superior overall value. Delivering superior value — an important part of business strategy — also supports other business strategies such as pricing. For example, superior value offers the possibility of price premiums or competing via lower prices. Pricing decisions may enhance market share and asset utilization, and thus may also contribute to improved financial performance.

Business strategy usually addresses factors in addition to quality and value. For example, strategy may address market niche, alliances, facilities location, diversification, acquisition, export development, research, technology leadership, and rapid product turnover. The Criteria support the development, deployment, and evaluation of business decisions and strategies, even though these involve many factors other than product and service quality. Examples of applications of the Criteria to business decisions and strategies include:

- quality management of the information used in business decisions and strategy — scope, validity, and analysis;
- quality requirements of niches, new businesses, and export target markets;
- use of benchmarking information in decisions relating to outsourcing, alliances and acquisitions;
- analysis of factors — societal, regulatory, economic, competitive, and risk — that may bear upon the success or failure of strategy;
- development of scenarios built around possible outcomes of strategy or decisions, including risks and consequences of failures; and
- lessons learned from previous strategy developments — within the company or available through research.

Financial Performance

The Criteria address financial performance via three major avenues: (1) emphasis on quality requirements that lead to superior offerings and thus to better market performance, market share gain, and customer retention; (2) emphasis on improved productivity, asset utilization, and lower overall operating costs; and (3) support for business strategy development, business decisions, and innovation.

The Criteria and evaluation system take into account market share, customer retention, customer satisfaction, productivity, asset utilization, and other factors that contribute to financial performance. However, the Criteria do not require direct reporting of aggregate financial information such as quarterly or annual profits. The Criteria *do encourage* the use of financial information, including profit trends, in analyses and reporting of results derived from performance improvement strategies. That is, companies are encouraged to demonstrate the connection between quality, operational performance improvement, and financial performance.

The exclusion of profit information that does not have a clear connection to quality and operational performance improvement is made for the following reasons — technical, fairness, and procedural:

- Short-term profits may be affected by factors such as accounting practices, business decisions, write-offs, dividends, and investments.

- Some industries historically have higher profit levels than others.

- The time interval between quality improvement and overall financial improvement depends upon many factors. This interval is not likely to be the same from industry to industry or even for companies in the same industry.

- The Criteria measure performance relative to rigorous, customer-oriented, company-performance criteria. Though improved quality and productivity are likely to improve a company's overall financial performance, its financial performance depends also on the performance of competitors — which the Award process cannot measure directly. The inclusion of aggregate financial indicators in evaluations would thus place at a disadvantage applicants in the most competitive businesses. Such applicants may have the most to offer from the point of view of sharing management strategies.

- Financial performance depends upon many external factors, such as local, national, and international economic conditions and business cycles. Such conditions and cycles do not have the same impact on all types of businesses or on individual companies.

- Some companies would not participate in the Award process if required to provide financial information.

Innovation and Creativity

Innovation and creativity — new products, novel changes to existing products, and imaginative approaches — are important aspects of delivering ever-improving value to customers and of maximizing productivity. State of technology may play a key role in corporate involvement in research. Innovation and creativity are crucial features in company competitiveness and can be applied to products, processes, services, human resource development, and work organization at all stages of the technological maturity of products and services.

The Criteria encourage innovation and creativity in all aspects of company decisions and in all work areas. Examples of mechanisms used in the Criteria to encourage such activities include:

- Nonprescriptive criteria, supported by benchmarks and indicators, encourage creativity and breakthrough thinking as they channel activities toward purpose, not toward following procedures.

- Customer-driven quality places major emphasis on the "positive side of quality," which stresses enhancement, new services, and customer relationship management. Success with the positive side of quality depends heavily on creativity — usually more so than steps to reduce errors and defects which tend to rely more on well-defined techniques.

- Human resource utilization stresses employee involvement, development, and recognition, and encourages creative approaches to improving employee effectiveness, empowerment, and motivation.

- Continuous improvement and cycles of learning are stressed as integral parts of the activities of all work units. This requires analysis and problem solving everywhere within the company.

- Strong emphasis on cycle time reduction in all company operations encourages companies to analyze work paths, work organizations, and the value-added contributions of all process steps. This fosters change, innovation, and creative thinking in how work is organized and conducted.

- Focus on future requirements of customers, customer segments, and customers of competitors encourages companies to seek innovative and creative ways to serve needs.

Examples of specific process management mechanisms to improve new product and process innovation include:

- strong emphasis on cycle time in the design phase to encourage rapid introduction of new products and services derived from company research. Success requires stage-to-stage coordination of functions and activities ranging from basic research to commercialization.

- quality system requirements for research and development units that address: climate for innovation, including research opportunities and career advancement; unit awareness of fundamental knowledge that bears upon success; unit awareness of national and world leadership centers in universities, government laboratories, and other companies; shortening the patenting cycle; effectiveness of services to research and development by other units including procurement, facilities management, and technical support; key determinants in project success and project cancellation; company communication links, including internal technology transfer; key technical and reporting requirements and communications; and key measures of success — such as problem-solving effectiveness and responsiveness — for research and development units.

Changes from the 1993 Award Criteria

The 1994 Award Criteria are built upon the seven-category framework used in previous years. However, a number of changes have been made in the Criteria booklet to strengthen key themes and to clarify requirements. Changes are:

- The number of Areas to Address has been reduced from 92 to 91. (The number of Examination Items remains at 28.)

- More Item Notes have been added to improve clarity.

- The Examination Response Guidelines have been re-written and integrated with the Business Overview to help applicants and other users of the Criteria focus better on key business requirements. These Guidelines stress the importance of including information of the type that permits assessment and feedback.

- The Description of the Award Criteria has been revised and expanded. The major addition is: The Strategic Quality Planning Category — Integrating Quality and Operational Performance Requirements with Business Strategy.

- The description of the Scoring System has been expanded and clarified. Sections added are: Item Classification and Scoring Dimensions; and "Relevance and Importance" as a Scoring Factor. The latter section is intended to help applicants and other users of the Criteria to focus better on key business factors given in the Business Overview.

Key Themes Strengthened in the 1994 Criteria

The principal theme strengthened in 1994 is integration/linkage, with particular focus on the integration of quality and operational performance issues with overall business planning. This integration is reinforced throughout the Criteria booklet, including the booklet's four major sections: Description of the 1994 Award Criteria; 1994 Award Examination Criteria; Scoring System and Guidelines; and the 1994 Examination Response Guidelines.

A summary of the relationships between 1994 and 1993 requirements, by Category, follows:

Leadership

- The basic requirements in this Category are unchanged. Notes have been added and/or clarified.

Information and Analysis

- The basic requirements in this Category are unchanged. Notes have been added and/or clarified. Descriptions of the Items in this Category are given on pages 7-8.

Strategic Quality Planning

- The basic requirements in this Category are unchanged. Notes have been added and/or clarified. The importance of the Category is stressed in the expanded Description of the 1994 Award Criteria. The intent is to emphasize the need to fully integrate quality and operational requirements with business planning. Descriptions of the Items in this Category are given on pages 6-7.

Human Resource Development and Management

- The basic requirements in this Category are unchanged. Notes have been added and/or clarified. All changes respond to two concerns: (1) the need for greater alignment between business plans and human resource plans and practices; and (2) the need to improve integration of the individual elements of human resource practices — selection, performance, recognition, and training, for example.

Management of Process Quality

- The basic requirements in this Category are unchanged. Notes have been added and/or clarified.

- One Area has been eliminated from Item 5.2, leaving two Areas — one addressing process maintenance, and the other, process improvement. The design of the processes addressed in Item 5.2 is part of Item 5.1. Item 5.3 retains three Areas — those addressing process design, process maintenance, and process improvement.

- The title of Item 5.3 has been changed to Process Management: Business and Support Service Processes.

- The intent of Item 5.4 has been clarified to include other units of the applicant's company in its supplier relationships, if appropriate.

Quality and Operational Results

- The basic requirements in this Category are unchanged. Notes have been added and/or clarified. Descriptions of the Items in this Category are given on page 8.

- The title of Item 6.3 has been changed to Business and Support Service Results. This is parallel to the title change of the closely-related Item, 5.3.

Customer Focus and Satisfaction

- The basic requirements in this Category are unchanged. Notes have been added and/or clarified.

- Item 7.2 (Customer Relationship Management) has been focused better on the requirements of the customer relationship. The overlap with Item 2.3 (Analysis and Uses of Company-Level Data) has been clarified through the requirement that *complaint aggregation and analysis* be part of Item 2.3. The complaint management process, including complaint resolution, remains part of Item 7.2. Also in Item 7.2, 7.2f addresses customer-contact employee requirements for all the customer relationship issues addressed in 7.2a, b, c, d, and e.

- Items 7.5 and 7.6 now include the requirement for trends *and current levels* of satisfaction.

Applicants and other users of the Award Criteria are cautioned to note that some changes in wording have been made in most Items.

1994 Examination Categories/Items	Point Values
1.0 Leadership	**95**
1.1 Senior Executive Leadership	45
1.2 Management for Quality	25
1.3 Public Responsibility and Corporate Citizenship	25
2.0 Information and Analysis	**75**
2.1 Scope and Management of Quality and Performance Data and Information	15
2.2 Competitive Comparisons and Benchmarking	20
2.3 Analysis and Uses of Company-Level Data	40
3.0 Strategic Quality Planning	**60**
3.1 Strategic Quality and Company Performance Planning Process	35
3.2 Quality and Performance Plans	25
4.0 Human Resource Development and Management	**150**
4.1 Human Resource Planning and Management	20
4.2 Employee Involvement	40
4.3 Employee Education and Training	40
4.4 Employee Performance and Recognition	25
4.5 Employee Well-Being and Satisfaction	25
5.0 Management of Process Quality	**140**
5.1 Design and Introduction of Quality Products and Services	40
5.2 Process Management: Product and Service Production and Delivery Processes	35
5.3 Process Management: Business and Support Service Processes	30
5.4 Supplier Quality	20
5.5 Quality Assessment	15
6.0 Quality and Operational Results	**180**
6.1 Product and Service Quality Results	70
6.2 Company Operational Results	50
6.3 Business and Support Service Results	25
6.4 Supplier Quality Results	35
7.0 Customer Focus and Satisfaction	**300**
7.1 Customer Expectations: Current and Future	35
7.2 Customer Relationship Management	65
7.3 Commitment to Customers	15
7.4 Customer Satisfaction Determination	30
7.5 Customer Satisfaction Results	85
7.6 Customer Satisfaction Comparison	70
TOTAL POINTS	**1000**

1.0 Leadership (95 pts.)

The *Leadership* Category examines senior executives' *personal* leadership and involvement in creating and sustaining a customer focus and clear and visible quality values. Also examined is how the quality values are integrated into the company's management system, including how the company addresses its public responsibilities and corporate citizenship.

1.1 Senior Executive Leadership (45 pts.)

Describe the senior executives' leadership, personal involvement, and visibility in developing and maintaining an environment for quality excellence.

A   D   R

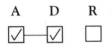

(See page 33 for a description of these symbols.)

AREAS TO ADDRESS

a. senior executives' leadership, personal involvement, and visibility in quality-related activities of the company. Include: (1) creating and reinforcing a customer focus and quality values; (2) setting expectations and planning; (3) reviewing quality and operational performance; (4) recognizing employee contributions; and (5) communicating quality values outside the company.

b. brief summary of the company's customer focus and quality values that serve as a basis for consistent understanding and communication within and outside the company

c. how senior executives regularly communicate and reinforce the company's customer focus and quality values with managers and supervisors

d. how senior executives evaluate and improve the effectiveness of their personal leadership and involvement

Notes:

(1) "Senior executives" means the applicant's highest-ranking official and those reporting directly to that official.

(2) Activities of senior executives (1.1a) might also include leading and/or receiving training, communicating with employees, benchmarking, customer and supplier interactions, and mentoring other executives, managers, and supervisors.

(3) Communication by senior executives outside the company [1.1a(5)] might involve: national, state, and community groups; trade, business, and professional organizations; and education, health care, government, standards, and public service/charitable groups. It might also involve the company's stockholders and board of directors.

1.2 Management for Quality (25 pts.)

Describe how the company's customer focus and quality values are integrated into day-to-day leadership, management, and supervision of all company units.

A   D   R

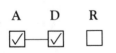

AREAS TO ADDRESS

a. how the company's customer focus and quality values are translated into requirements for all managers and supervisors. Describe: (1) their principal roles and responsibilities within their units; and (2) their roles and responsibilities in fostering cooperation with other units.

b. how the company's customer focus and quality values (1.1b) are communicated and reinforced throughout the entire work force

c. how overall company and work unit quality and operational performance are reviewed. Describe: (1) types, frequency, content, and use of reviews and who conducts them; and (2) how the company assists units that are not performing according to plans.

d. how the company evaluates and improves managers' and supervisors' effectiveness in reinforcing the company's customer focus and quality values

Notes:

(1) Communication throughout the entire work force (1.2b) should emphasize the overall company approach and deployment. Some of this communication may be done by senior executives, as addressed in Item 1.1.

(2) The evaluation (1.2d) might utilize employee input or feedback on managers' and supervisors' leadership skills in reinforcing a customer focus and quality values.

1.3 Public Responsibility and Corporate Citizenship *(25 pts.)*

Describe how the company includes its responsibilities to the public in its quality policies and improvement practices. Describe also how the company leads as a corporate citizen in its key communities.

A   D   R

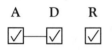

AREAS TO ADDRESS

a. how the company integrates its public responsibilities into its quality values and practices. Include: (1) how the company considers risks, regulatory and other legal requirements in setting operational requirements and targets; (2) a summary of the company's principal public responsibilities, key operational requirements and associated targets, and how these requirements and/or targets are communicated and deployed throughout the company; and (3) how and how often progress in meeting operational requirements and/or targets is reviewed.

b. how the company looks ahead to anticipate public concerns and to assess possible impacts on society of its products, services, and operations. Describe briefly how this assessment is used in planning.

c. how the company leads as a corporate citizen in its key communities. Include: (1) a brief summary of the types and extent of leadership and involvement in key communities; (2) how the company promotes quality awareness and sharing of quality-related information; (3) how the company seeks opportunities to enhance its leadership; and (4) how the company promotes legal and ethical conduct in all that it does.

d. trends in key measures and/or indicators of improvement in addressing public responsibilities and corporate citizenship. Include responses to any sanctions received under law, regulation, or contract.

Notes:

(1) The public responsibility issues addressed in 1.3a and 1.3b relate to the company's impacts and possible impacts on society associated with its products, services, and company operations. They include business ethics, environment, and safety as they relate to any aspect of risk or adverse effect, whether or not these are covered under law or regulation.

(2) The term "targets" as used in Item 1.3 and elsewhere in the Criteria refer to specific performance levels, based upon appropriate measures or indicators.

(3) Major public responsibility or impact areas should be addressed in planning (Item 3.1) and in the appropriate process management Items of Category 5.0.

(4) Health and safety of employees are not included in Item 1.3. They are covered in Item 4.5.

(5) The corporate citizenship issues appropriate for inclusion in 1.3c relate to actions by the company to strengthen community services, education, health care, environment, and practices of trade or business associations. Such involvement would be expected to be limited by the company's available human and financial resources.

(6) If the company has received sanctions under law, regulation, or contract during the past three years, include the current status in responding to 1.3d. If no sanctions have been received, so indicate. If settlements have been negotiated in lieu of potential sanctions, give explanations.

2.0 Information and Analysis (75 pts.)

The *Information and Analysis* Category examines the scope, management, and use of data and information to maintain a customer focus, to drive quality excellence, and to improve operational and competitive performance.

2.1 Scope and Management of Quality and Performance Data and Information (15 pts.)

Describe the company's selection and management of data and information used for planning, day-to-day management, and evaluation of quality and operational performance.

A   D   R

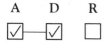

AREAS TO ADDRESS

a. criteria for selecting data and information for use in quality and operational performance improvement. List key types of data and information used and briefly outline the principal roles of each type in improving quality and operational performance. Include: (1) customer-related; (2) product and service performance; (3) internal operations and performance, including business and support services, and employee-related; (4) supplier performance; and (5) cost and financial.

b. how reliability, consistency, and rapid access to data are assured throughout the company. If applicable, describe how software accuracy and reliability are assured.

c. how the company evaluates and improves the scope and management of data and information. Include: (1) review and update; (2) shortening the cycle from data gathering to access; (3) broadening access to all those requiring data for day-to-day management and improvement; and (4) aligning data and information with process improvement plans and needs.

Notes:

(1) Item 2.1 permits the applicant to demonstrate the <u>breadth and depth</u> of its data. Applicants should give brief descriptions of the data under major headings such as "internal operations and performance" and subheadings such as "support services". Note that information on the scope and management of competitive and benchmark data is requested in Item 2.2.

(2) Actual data should not be reported in Item 2.1. These data are requested in other Items. Accordingly, all data reported in other Items should be part of the base of data and information to be described in Item 2.1.

(3) Improving the management of data and information (2.1c) might also include company mechanisms and/or incentives for units to contribute and to share data and information.

2.2 Competitive Comparisons and Benchmarking (20 pts.)

Describe the company's processes, current sources and scope, and uses of competitive comparisons and benchmarking information and data to support improvement of quality and operational performance.

A   D   R

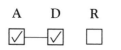

AREAS TO ADDRESS

a. how competitive comparisons and benchmarking information and data are used to help drive improvement of quality and operational performance. Describe: (1) how needs are determined; and (2) criteria for seeking appropriate competitive comparisons and benchmarking information — from within and outside the company's industry.

b. brief summary of current scope, sources, and principal uses of each type of competitive comparisons and benchmarking information and data. Include: (1) customer-related; (2) product and service quality; (3) internal operations and performance, including business and support services and employee-related; and (4) supplier performance.

c. how competitive comparisons and benchmarking information and data are used to improve understanding of processes, to encourage breakthrough approaches, and to set "stretch" targets

d. how the company evaluates and improves its overall processes for selecting and using competitive comparisons and benchmarking information and data to improve planning and operational performance

---

Notes:

(1) Benchmarking information and data refer to processes and results that represent superior practices and performance and set "stretch" targets for comparison.

(2) Sources of competitive comparisons and benchmarking information might include: (1) information obtained from other organizations through sharing; (2) information obtained from the open literature; (3) testing and evaluation by the company itself; and (4) testing and evaluation by independent organizations.

2.3 Analysis and Uses of Company-Level Data (40 pts.)

Describe how data related to quality, customers and operational performance, together with relevant financial data, are analyzed to support company-level review, action and planning.

A   D   R

☑——☑ ☐

AREAS TO ADDRESS

a. how customer-related data and results (from Category 7.0) are aggregated with other key data and analyses and translated via analysis into actionable information to support: (1) developing priorities for prompt solutions to customer-related problems; and (2) determining key customer-related trends and correlations to support reviews, decision making, and longer-term planning

b. how quality and operational performance data and results (from Category 6.0) are aggregated with other key data and analyses and translated via analysis into actionable information to support: (1) developing priorities for improvements in products/services and company operations, including cycle time, productivity and waste reduction; and (2) determining key operations-related trends and correlations to support reviews, decision making, and longer-term planning

c. how the company relates overall improvements in product/service quality and operational performance to changes in overall financial performance to support reviews, decision making, and longer-term planning

d. how the company evaluates and improves its analysis for use as a key management tool. Include: (1) how analysis supports improved data selection and use; (2) how analysis strengthens the integration of overall data use for improved decision making and planning; and (3) how the analysis-access cycle is shortened.

Notes:

(1) Item 2.3 focuses primarily on analysis for company-level purposes, such as reviews (1.2c) and strategic planning (Item 3.1). Data for such analysis come from all parts of the company. Other Items call for analyses of specific sets of data for special purposes. For example, the Items of Category 4.0 require analyses to demonstrate effectiveness of training and other human resource practices. Such special-purpose analyses are assumed to be part of the overall information base of Category 2.0, available for use in Item 2.3. These specific sets of data and special-purpose analyses are referred to in 2.3a and 2.3b as "other key data and analyses."

(2)"Actionable" means that the analysis provides information that can be used for priorities and decisions leading to allocation of resources.

(3) Solutions to customer-related problems [2.3a(1)] at the company level involve a process for: (1) aggregation of formal and informal complaints from different parts of the company; (2) analysis leading to priorities for action; and (3) use of the resulting information throughout the company. Note the connections to 7.2e, which focuses on day-to-day complaint management, including prompt resolution.

(4) The focus in 2.3a is on analysis to improve customer-related decision making and planning. This analysis is intended to provide additional information to support such decision making and planning that result from day-to-day customer information, feedback, and complaints.

Examples of analysis appropriate for inclusion in 2.3a are:
- *how the company's product and service quality improvement correlates with key customer indicators such as customer satisfaction, customer retention, and market share;*
- *cross-comparisons of data from complaints, post-transaction follow-up, and won/lost analyses to identify improvement priorities;*
- *relationship between employee satisfaction and customer satisfaction;*
- *cost/revenue implications of customer-related problems and problem resolution effectiveness;*
- *rates of improvements of customer indicators;*
- *customer loyalty (or positive referral) versus level of satisfaction; and*
- *customer loyalty versus level of satisfaction with the effectiveness of problem resolution.*

(5) The focus in 2.3b is on analysis to improve operations-related decision making and planning. This analysis is intended to support such decision making and planning that result from day-to-day observations of process performance.

Examples of analysis appropriate for inclusion in 2.3b are:
- *how product/service improvement priorities are determined;*
- *evaluation of the productivity and cost impacts of improvement initiatives;*
- *rates of improvement in key operational indicators;*
- *evaluation of trends in key operational efficiency measures such as productivity;*
- *comparison with competitive and benchmark data to identify improvement opportunities and to set improvement priorities and targets.*

(6) The focus in 2.3c is on the linkages between improvements in product/service quality and operational performance and overall financial performance for company goal and priority setting. Analyses in 2.3c might incorporate the results of analyses described in 2.3a and 2.3b, and draw upon other key data and analyses.

Examples of analysis appropriate for inclusion in 2.3c are:
- *relationships between product/service quality and operational performance indicators and overall company financial performance trends as reflected in indicators such as operating costs, revenues, asset utilization, and value added per employee;*
- *comparisons of company financial performance versus competitors based on quality and operational performance indicators;*
- *allocation of resources among alternative improvement projects based on cost/revenue implications and improvement potential;*
- *net earnings derived from quality/operational performance improvements;*
- *comparisons among business units showing how quality and operational performance improvement have improved financial performance; and*
- *contributions of improvement activities to cash flow and/or shareholder value.*

3.0 Strategic Quality Planning (60 pts.)

The *Strategic Quality Planning* Category examines the company's planning process and how all key quality and operational performance requirements are integrated into overall business planning. Also examined are the company's short- and longer-term plans and how plan requirements are deployed to all work units.

3.1 Strategic Quality and Company Performance Planning Process
(35 pts.)

Describe the company's business planning process for the short term (1-3 years) and longer term (3 years or more) for customer satisfaction leadership and overall operational performance improvement. Include how this process integrates quality and operational performance requirements and how plans are deployed.

A   D   R

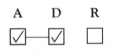

AREAS TO ADDRESS

a. how the company develops strategies and business plans to address quality and customer satisfaction leadership for the short term and longer term. Describe how plans consider: (1) customer requirements and the expected evolution of these requirements; (2) projections of the competitive environment; (3) risks: financial, market, technological, and societal; (4) company capabilities, such as human resource and research and development to address key new requirements or market leadership opportunities; and (5) supplier capabilities.

b. how strategies and plans address operational performance improvement. Describe how the following are considered: (1) realigning work processes ("re-engineering") to improve customer focus and operational performance; and (2) productivity and cycle time improvement and reduction in waste.

c. how plans are deployed. Describe: (1) how the company deploys plan requirements to work units and to suppliers, and how it ensures alignment of work unit plans and activities; and (2) how resources are committed to meet plan requirements.

d. how the company evaluates and improves: (1) its planning process; (2) deploying plan requirements to work units; and (3) receiving planning input from work units

Notes:

(1) Item 3.1 addresses overall company strategies and business plans, not specific product and service designs. Strategies and business plans that might be addressed as part of Item 3.1 include operational aspects such as manufacturing and/or service delivery strategies, as well as new product/service lines, new markets, outsourcing, and strategic alliances.

(2) Societal risks and impacts are addressed in Item 1.3.

(3) Productivity and cycle time improvement and waste reduction (3.1b) might address factors such as inventories, work in process, inspection, downtime, changeover time, set-up time, and other examples of utilization of resources such as materials, equipment, energy, capital, and labor.

(4) How the company reviews quality and operational performance relative to plans is addressed in 1.2c.

3.2 Quality and Performance Plans

(25 pts.)

Summarize the company's specific quality and operational performance plans for the short term (1-3 years) and the longer term (3 years or more).

A   D   R

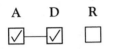

AREAS TO ADDRESS

a. for planned products, services, and customer markets, summarize: (1) key quality requirements to achieve or retain leadership; and (2) key company operational performance requirements

b. outline of the company's deployment of principal short-term quality and operational performance plans. Include: (1) a summary of key requirements and associated operational performance measures or indicators deployed to work units and suppliers; and (2) a brief description of resources committed for key needs such as capital equipment, facilities, education and training, and new hires.

c. outline of how principal longer-term (3 years or more) quality and operational performance requirements (from 3.2a) will be addressed

d. two-to-five-year projection of key measures and/or indicators of the company's quality and operational performance. Describe how quality and operational performance might be expected to compare with key competitors and key benchmarks over this time period. Briefly explain the comparisons, including any estimates or assumptions made regarding the projected quality and operational performance of competitors or changes in benchmarks.

Notes:

(1) The focus in Item 3.2 is on the translation of the company's business plans, resulting from the planning process described in Item 3.1, to requirements for work units and suppliers. The main intent of Item 3.2 is alignment of short- and long-term operations with business directions. Although the deployment of these plans will affect products and services, design of products and services is not the focus of Item 3.2. Such design is addressed in Item 5.1.

(2) Area 3.2d addresses projected progress in improving performance and in gaining advantage relative to competitors. This projection may draw upon analysis (Item 2.3) and data reported in results Items (Category 6.0 and Items 7.5 and 7.6). Such projections are intended to support reviews (1.2c), evaluation of plans (3.1d), and other Items.

4.0 Human Resource Development and Management (150 pts.)

The *Human Resource Development and Management* Category examines the key elements of how the work force is enabled to develop its full potential to pursue the company's quality and operational performance objectives. Also examined are the company's efforts to build and maintain an environment for quality excellence conducive to full participation and personal and organizational growth.

4.1 Human Resource Planning and Management (20 pts.)

Describe how the company's overall human resource management, plans and processes are integrated with its overall quality and operational performance plans and how human resource planning and management address fully the needs and development of the entire work force.

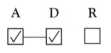

A   D   R

☑—☑   ☐

AREAS TO ADDRESS

a. brief description of the most important human resource plans (derived from Category 3.0). Include: (1) development, including education, training and empowerment; (2) mobility, flexibility, and changes in work organization, work processes or work schedules; (3) reward, recognition, benefits, and compensation; and (4) recruitment, including possible changes in diversity of the work force. Distinguish between the short term (1-3 years) and the longer term (3 years or more), as appropriate.

b. how the company improves key personnel processes. Describe key improvement methods for processes such as recruitment, hiring, personnel actions, and services to employees, including support services to managers and supervisors. Include a description of key performance measures or indicators, including cycle time, and how they are used in improvement.

c. how the company evaluates and improves its human resource planning and management using all employee-related data. Include: (1) how selection, performance, recognition, job analysis, and training are integrated to support improved performance and development of all categories and types of employees; and (2) how human resource planning and management are aligned with company strategy and plans.

Notes:

(1) Human resource plans (4.1a) might include one or more of the following:
- *mechanisms for promoting cooperation such as internal customer/supplier techniques or other internal partnerships;*
- *initiatives to promote labor-management cooperation, such as partnerships with unions;*
- *creation and/or modification of recognition systems;*
- *creation or modification of compensation systems based on building shareholder value;*
- *mechanisms for increasing or broadening employee responsibilities;*
- *creating opportunities for employees to learn and use skills that go beyond current job assignments through redesign of processes;*
- *creation of high performance work teams;*
- *education and training initiatives; and*
- *forming partnerships with educational institutions to develop employees or to help ensure the future supply of well-prepared employees.*

(2) The personnel processes referred to in 4.1b are those commonly carried out by personnel departments or by personnel specialists. Improvement processes might include needs assessments and satisfaction surveys. Improvement results associated with the measures or indicators used in 4.1b should be reported in Item 6.3.

(3) "Categories of employees" (4.1c) refers to the company's classification system used in its personnel practices and/or work assignments. It also includes factors such as union or bargaining unit membership. "Types of employees" takes into account other factors, such as work force diversity or demographic makeup. This includes gender, age, minorities, and the disabled.

(4) "All employee-related data" (4.1c) refers to data contained in personnel records as well as data described in Items 4.2, 4.3, 4.4, and 4.5. This might include employee satisfaction data and data on turnover, absenteeism, safety, grievances, involvement, recognition, training, and information from exit interviews.

(5) The evaluation in 4.1c might be supported by employee-related data such as satisfaction factors (Item 4.5), absenteeism, turnover, and accidents. It might also be supported by employee feedback.

4.2 Employee Involvement
(40 pts.)

Describe how all employees are enabled to contribute effectively to meeting the company's quality and operational performance plans; summarize trends in effectiveness and extent of involvement.

A   D   R

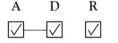

AREAS TO ADDRESS

a. how the company promotes ongoing employee contributions, individually and in groups, to improvement in quality and operational performance. Include how and how quickly the company gives feedback to contributors.

b. how the company increases employee empowerment, responsibility, and innovation. Include a brief summary of principal plans for all categories of employees, based upon the most important requirements for each category.

c. how the company evaluates and improves the effectiveness, extent, and type of involvement of all categories and all types of employees. Include how effectiveness, extent and types of involvement are linked to key quality and operational performance improvement results.

d. trends in key measures and/or indicators of the <u>effectiveness</u> and <u>extent</u> of employee involvement

Notes:

(1) The company might use different involvement methods and measures or indicators for different categories of employees or for different parts of the company, depending on needs and responsibilities of each employee category or part of the company. Examples include problem-solving teams (within work units or cross-functional); fully-integrated, self-managed work groups; and process improvement teams.

(2) Trend results (4.2d) should be segmented by category of employee, as appropriate. Major types of involvement should be noted.

4.3 Employee Education and Training *(40 pts.)*

Describe how the company determines quality and related education and training needs for all employees. Show how this determination addresses company plans and supports employee growth. Outline how such education and training are evaluated, and summarize key trends in the effectiveness and extent of education and training.

A   D   R

AREAS TO ADDRESS

a. how the company determines needs for the types and amounts of quality and related education and training for all employees, taking into account their differing needs. Include: (1) linkage to short- and long-term plans, including company-wide access to skills in problem solving, waste reduction, and process simplification; (2) growth and career opportunities for ernployees; and (3) how employees' input is sought and used in the needs determination.

b. how quality and related education and training are delivered and reinforced. Include: (1) description of education and training delivery for all categories of employees; (2) on-the-job application of knowledge and skills; and (3) quality-related orientation for new employees.

c. how the company evaluates and improves its quality and related education and training. Include how the evaluation supports improved needs determination, taking into account: (1) relating on-the-job performance improvement to key quality and operational performance improvement targets and results; and (2) growth and progression of all categories and types of employees.

d. trends in key measures and/or indicators of the <u>effectiveness</u> and <u>extent</u> of quality and related education and training

Notes:

(1) Quality and related education and training address the knowledge and skills employees need to meet their objectives as part of the company's quality and operational performance improvement. This might include quality awareness, leadership, project management, communications, teamwork, problem solving, interpreting and using data, meeting customer requirements, process analysis, process simplification, waste reduction, cycle time reduction, error-proofing, and other training that affects employee effectiveness, efficiency, and safety. In many cases, this might include job enrichment skills and job rotation that enhance employees' career opportunities. It might also include basic skills such as reading, writing, language, arithmetic, and basic mathematics that are needed for quality and operational performance improvement.

(2) Education and training delivery might occur inside or outside the company and involve on-the-job or classroom delivery.

(3) The overall evaluation (4.3c) might compare the relative effectiveness of structured on-the-job training with classroom methods. It might also address how to best balance on-the-job training and classroom methods.

(4) Trend results (4.3d) should be segmented by category of employee (including new employees), as appropriate. Major types of training and education should be noted.

4.4 Employee Performance and Recognition

(25 pts.)

Describe how the company's employee performance, recognition, promotion, compensation, reward, and feedback approaches support the improvement of quality and operational performance.

A   D   R

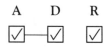

Notes:

(1) The company might use a variety of reward and recognition approaches — monetary and non-monetary, formal and informal, and individual and group.

(2) Employee satisfaction (4.4b) might take into account employee dissatisfaction indicators such as turnover and absenteeism.

(3) Trend results (4.4c) should be segmented by employee category, as appropriate. Major types of recognition, compensation, etc., should be noted.

4.5 Employee Well-Being and Satisfaction *(25 pts.)*

Describe how the company maintains a work environment conducive to the well-being and growth of all employees; summarize trends in key indicators of well-being and satisfaction.

A   D   R

Notes:

(1) Special services, facilities, activities, and opportunities (4.5b) might include: counseling; recreational or cultural activities; non-work-related education; day care; special leave; safety off the job; flexible work hours; and outplacement.

(2) Examples of specific factors for which satisfaction might be determined (4.5c) are: safety; employee views of leadership and management; employee development and career opportunities; employee preparation for changes in technology or work organization; work environment;

teamwork; recognition; benefits; communications; job security; and compensation.

(3) Measures or indicators of well-being and satisfaction (4.5d) include safety, absenteeism, turnover, turnover rate for customer-contact employees, grievances, strikes, worker compensation, and results of satisfaction determinations.

(4) Comparisons (4.5d) might include industry averages, industry leaders, local/regional leaders, and key benchmarks.

5.0 Management of Process Quality (140 pts.)

The *Management of Process Quality* Category examines the key elements of process management, including design, management of day-to-day production and delivery, improvement of quality and operational performance, and quality assessment. The Category also examines how all work units, including research and development units and suppliers, contribute to overall quality and operational performance requirements.

5.1 Design and Introduction of Quality Products and Services (40 pts.)

Describe how new and/or modified products and services are designed and introduced and how key production/delivery processes are designed to meet both key product and service quality requirements and company operational performance requirements.

A D R
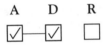

AREAS TO ADDRESS

a. how products, services, and production/delivery processes are designed. Describe: (1) how customer requirements are translated into product and service design requirements; (2) how product and service design requirements, together with the company's operational performance requirements, are translated into production/delivery processes, including an appropriate measurement plan; (3) how all product and service quality requirements are addressed early in the overall design process by appropriate company units; and (4) how designs are coordinated and integrated to include all phases of production and delivery.

b. how product, service, and production/delivery process designs are reviewed and validated, taking into account key factors: (1) overall product and service performance; (2) process capability and future requirements; and (3) supplier capability and future requirements

c. how designs and design processes are evaluated and improved so that new product and service introductions and product and service modifications progressively improve in quality and cycle time

Notes:

(1) Design and introduction might address modifications and variants of existing products and services and/or new products and services emerging from research and development or other product/service concept development. Design also might address key new/modified facilities to meet operational performance and/or product and service quality requirements.

(2) Applicants' responses should reflect the key requirements for their products and services. Factors that might need to be considered in design include: health; safety; long-term performance; environment; measurement capability; process capability; manufacturability; maintainability; supplier capability; and documentation.

(3) Service and manufacturing businesses should interpret product and service design requirements to include all product- and service-related requirements at all stages of production, delivery, and use.

(4) In 5.1a(2), company operational performance requirements relate to operational efficiency and effectiveness — waste reduction and cycle time improvement, for example. A measurement plan should spell out what is to be measured, how measurements are to be made, and performance levels or standards to ensure that the results of measurements will show whether or not production/delivery processes are in control.

(5) Results of improvements in design should be reported in 6.1a. Results of improvements in design process quality should be reported in 6.2a.

5.2 Process Management: Product and Service Production and Delivery Processes

(35 pts.)

Describe how the company's key product and service production/delivery processes are managed to ensure that design requirements are met and that both quality and operational performance are continuously improved.

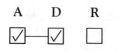

A   D   R

AREAS TO ADDRESS

a. how the company maintains the quality and operational performance of the production/delivery processes described in Item 5.1. Describe: (1) the key processes, their requirements, and how quality and operational performance are tracked and maintained. Include types and frequencies of in-process and end-of-process measurements used; (2) for significant (out-of-control) variations in processes or outputs, how root causes are determined; and (3) how corrections of variation [from 5.2a(2)] are made, verified, and integrated into process management.

b. how processes are improved to achieve better quality, cycle time, and operational performance. Describe how each of the following is used or considered: (1) process analysis/simplification; (2) benchmarking information; (3) process research and testing; (4) use of alternative technology; (5) information from customers of the processes — within and outside the company; and (6) stretch targets.

Notes:

(1) Manufacturing and service companies with specialized measurement requirements should describe how they assure measurement quality. For physical, chemical, and engineering measurements, describe briefly how measurements are made traceable to national standards.

(2) Variations [5.2a(2)] might be observed by those working in the process or by customers of the process output. The latter situation might result in formal or informal feedback or complaints. Also, a company might use observers or "mystery shoppers" to provide information on process performance.

(3) Results of improvements in product and service production and delivery processes should be reported in 6.2a.

5.3 Process Management: Business and Support Service Processes

(30 pts.)

Describe how the company's key business and support service processes are designed and managed so that current requirements are met and that quality and operational performance are continuously improved.

A	D	R

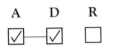

AREAS TO ADDRESS

a. how key business and support service processes are designed. Include: (1) how key quality and operational performance requirements for business and support services are determined or set; (2) how these quality and operational performance requirements [from 5.3a(1)] are translated into delivery processes, including an appropriate measurement plan.

b. how the company maintains the quality and operational performance of business and support service delivery processes. Describe: (1) the key processes, their requirements, and how quality and operational performance are tracked and maintained. Include types and frequencies of in-process and end-of-process measurements used; (2) for significant (out-of-control) variations in processes or outputs, how root causes are determined; and (3) how corrections of variation [from 5.3b(2)] are made, verified, and integrated into process management.

c. how processes are improved to achieve better quality, cycle time, and overall operational performance. Describe how each of the following are used or considered: (1) process analysis/simplification; (2) benchmarking information; (3) process research and testing; (4) use of alternative technology; (5) information from customers of the business processes and support services — within and outside the company; and (6) stretch targets.

Notes:

(1) Business and support service processes might include units and operations involving finance and accounting, software services, sales, marketing, public relations, information services, purchasing, personnel, legal services, plant and facilities management, basic research and development, and secretarial and other administrative services.

(2) The purpose of Item 5.3 is to permit applicants to highlight separately the improvement activities for functions that support the product and service design, production, and delivery processes addressed in Items 5.1 and 5.2. The support services and business processes

included in Item 5.3 depend on the applicant's type of business and other factors. Thus, this selection should be made by the applicant. Together, Items 5.1, 5.2, 5.3, and 5.4 should cover all operations, processes, and activities of all work units.

(3) Variations [5.3b(2)] might be observed by those working in the process or by customers of the process output. The latter situation might result in formal or informal feedback or complaints.

(4) Results of improvements in business processes and support services should be reported in 6.3a.

5.4 Supplier Quality

(20 pts.)

Describe how the company assures the quality of materials, components, and services furnished by other businesses. Describe also the company's actions and plans to improve supplier quality.

A   D   R

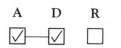

AREAS TO ADDRESS

a. how the company's quality requirements are defined and communicated to suppliers. Include a brief summary of the principal quality requirements for key suppliers. Also give the measures and/or indicators and expected performance levels for the principal requirements.

b. how the company determines whether or not its quality requirements are met by suppliers. Describe how performance information is fed back to suppliers.

c. how the company evaluates and improves its own procurement processes. Include what feedback is sought from suppliers and how it is used in improvement.

d. current actions and plans to improve suppliers' abilities to meet key quality, response time, or other requirements. Include actions and/or plans to minimize inspection, test, audit, or other approaches that might incur unnecessary costs.

Notes:

(1) The term "supplier" refers to providers of goods and services. The use of these goods and services may occur at any stage in the production, delivery, and use of the company's products and services. Thus, suppliers include businesses such as distributors, dealers, warranty repair services, contractors, and franchises as well as those that provide materials and components.

(2) Generally, suppliers are other-company providers of goods and services. However, if the applicant is a subsidiary or division of a company, and other units of that company supply goods/services, this relationship should be described as a supplier relationship.

(3) Determining how quality requirements are met (5.4b) might include audits, process reviews, receiving inspection, certification, testing, and rating systems.

(4) Actions and plans (5.4d) might include one or more of the following: joint planning, partnerships, training, long-term agreements, incentives, and recognition. They might also include supplier selection. "Other requirements" might include suppliers' price levels. If this is the case, suppliers' abilities might address factors such as productivity and waste reduction.

5.5 Quality Assessment

(15 pts.)

Describe how the company assesses the quality and performance of its systems and processes and the quality of its products and services.

A   D   R

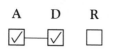

AREAS TO ADDRESS

a. how the company assesses: (1) systems and processes; and (2) products and services. For (1) and (2), describe: (a) what is assessed; (b) how often assessments are made and by whom; and (c) how measurement quality and adequacy of documentation of processes are assured.

b. how assessment findings are used to improve: products and services; systems; processes; supplier requirements; and the assessment processes. Include how the company verifies that assessment findings are acted upon and that the actions are effective.

Notes:

(1) The systems, processes, products, and services addressed in this Item pertain to all company unit activities covered in Items 5.1, 5.2, 5.3, and 5.4. If the assessment approaches differ appreciably for different company processes or units, this should be described in this Item.

(2) Adequacy of documentation should take into account legal, regulatory, and contractual requirements as well as knowledge preservation and knowledge transfer to help support all improvement efforts. Adequacy should take into account completeness, timely update, useability, and other appropriate factors.

6.0 Quality and Operational Results *(180 pts.)*

The ***Quality and Operational Results*** Category examines the company's achievement levels and improvement trends in quality, company operational performance, and supplier quality. Also examined are current quality and operational performance levels relative to those of competitors.

6.1 Product and Service Quality Results *(70 pts.)*

Summarize trends and current quality levels for key product and service features; compare current levels with those of competitors and/or appropriate benchmarks.

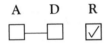

AREAS TO ADDRESS

a. trends and current levels for the key measures and/or indicators of product and service quality

b. comparisons of current quality levels with that of principal competitors in the company's key markets, industry averages, industry leaders, and appropriate benchmarks

Notes:

(1) Key product and service measures are measures relative to the set of all important features of the company's products and services. These measures, taken together, best represent the most important factors that predict customer satisfaction and quality in customer use. Examples include measures of accuracy, reliability, timeliness, performance, behavior, delivery, after-sales services, documentation, appearance, and effective complaint management.

(2) Results reported in Item 6.1 should reflect all key product and service features described in the Business Overview and addressed in Items 7.1 and 5.1.

(3) Data reported in Item 6.1 are intended to be objective measures of product and service quality, not the customers'

satisfaction or reaction to the products and/or services. Such data might be of several types, including: (a) internal (company) measurements; (b) field performance (when applicable); (c) proactive checks by the company of specific product and service features (7.2d); and (d) data routinely collected by other organizations or on behalf of the company. Data reported in Item 6.1 should provide information on the company's performance relative to the specific product and service features that best predict customer satisfaction. These data, collected regularly, are then part of a process for monitoring and improving quality.

(4) Bases for comparison (6.1b) might include: independent surveys, studies, or laboratory testing; benchmarks; and company evaluations and testing.

6.2 Company Operational Results *(50 pts.)*

Summarize trends and levels in overall company operational performance; provide a comparison with competitors and/or appropriate benchmarks.

A   D   R

AREAS TO ADDRESS

a. trends and current levels for key measures and/or indicators of company operational performance

b. comparison of performance with that of competitors, industry averages, industry leaders, and key benchmarks

Notes:

(1) Key measures of company operational performance include those that address productivity, efficiency, and effectiveness. Examples should include generic indicators such as use of manpower, materials, energy, capital, and assets. Trends and levels could address productivity indices, waste reduction, energy efficiency, cycle time reduction, environmental improvement, and other measures of improved overall company performance. Also include company-specific indicators the company uses to track its progress in improving operational performance. Such

company-specific indicators should be defined in tables or charts where trends are presented.

(2) Trends in financial indicators, properly labeled, might be included in Item 6.2. If such financial indicators are used, there should be a clear connection to the quality and operational performance improvement activities of the company.

(3) Include improvements in product and service design and production/delivery processes in this Item.

6.3 Business and Support Service Results (25 pts.)

Summarize trends and current levels in quality and operational performance improvement for business processes and support services; compare results with competitors and/or appropriate benchmarks.

a. trends and current levels for key measures and/or indicators of quality and operational performance of business and support services

b. comparison of performance with appropriately selected companies and benchmarks

A   D   R

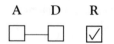

Notes:

(1) Business and support services are those covered in Item 5.3. Key measures of performance should reflect the principal quality, productivity, cycle time, cost, and other effectiveness requirements for business and support services. Responses should reflect relevance to the company's principal quality and operational performance objectives addressed in company plans, contributing to the results reported in Items 6.1 and 6.2. Responses

should demonstrate broad coverage of company business and support services and work units. Results should reflect the most important objectives for each service or work unit.

(2) Comparisons and benchmarks for business and support services (6.3b) should emphasize best practice performance, regardless of industry.

6.4 Supplier Quality Results (35 pts.)

Summarize trends in quality and current quality levels of suppliers; compare the company's supplier quality with that of competitors and/or with appropriate benchmarks.

AREAS TO ADDRESS

a. trends and current levels for key measures and/or indicators of supplier quality performance

b. comparison of the company's supplier quality levels with those of appropriately selected companies and/or benchmarks

A   D   R

Notes:

(1) The results reported in Item 6.4 derive from quality improvement activities described in Item 5.4. Results should be broken down by major groupings of suppliers and reported using the principal quality measures described in Item 5.4.

(2) Comparisons (6.4b) might be with industry averages, industry leaders, principal competitors in the company's key markets, and appropriate benchmarks.

7.0 Customer Focus and Satisfaction (300 pts.)

The *Customer Focus and Satisfaction* Category examines the company's relationships with customers, and its knowledge of customer requirements and of the key quality factors that drive marketplace competitiveness. Also examined are the company's methods to determine customer satisfaction, current trends and levels of customer satisfaction and retention, and these results relative to competitors.

7.1 Customer Expectations: Current and Future

(35 pts.)

Describe how the company determines near-term and longer-term requirements and expectations of customers.

A   D   R

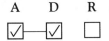

AREAS TO ADDRESS

a. how the company determines *current and near-term requirements* and expectations of customers. Include: (1) how customer groups and/or market segments are determined or selected, including how customers of competitors and other potential customers are considered; (2) how information is collected, including what information is sought, frequency and methods of collection, and how objectivity and validity are assured; (3) how specific product and service features and the relative importance of these features to customer groups or segments are determined; and (4) how other key information and data such as complaints, gains and losses of customers, and product/service performance are used to support the determination.

b. how the company addresses *future requirements* and expectations of customers. Include: (1) the time horizon for the determination; (2) how important technological, competitive, societal, environmental, economic, and demographic factors that may bear upon customer requirements, expectations, preferences, or alternatives are considered; (3) how customers of competitors and other potential customers are considered; (4) how key product and service features and the relative importance of these features are projected; and (5) how changing or emerging market segments and their implications on current or new product/service lines are considered.

c. how the company evaluates and improves its processes for determining customer requirements and expectations

Notes:

(1) The distinction between near-term and future depends upon many marketplace factors. The applicant's response should reflect these factors for its market.

(2) The company's products and services might be sold to end users via other businesses such as retail stores or dealers. Thus, "customer groups" should take into account the requirements and expectations of both the end users and these other businesses.

(3) Product and service features refer to all important characteristics and to the performance of products and services that customers experience or perceive throughout their overall purchase and ownership. These include any factors that bear upon customer preference, repurchase loyalty, or view of quality — for example, those features that enhance or differentiate products and services from competing offerings.

(4) Some companies might use similar methods to determine customer requirements/expectations and customer satisfaction (Item 7.4). In such cases, cross-references should be included.

(5) Customer groups and market segments (7.1a,b) should take into account opportunities to select or <u>create</u> groups and segments based upon customer- and market-related information.

(6) Examples of evaluations appropriate for 7.1c are:
- *the adequacy of the customer-related information;*
- *improvement of survey design;*
- *the best approaches for getting reliable information — surveys, focus groups, customer-contact personnel, etc.; and*
- *increasing and decreasing importance of product/service features among customer groups or segments.*

The evaluation might also be supported by company-level analysis addressed in 2.3a.

7.2 Customer Relationship Management (65 pts.)

Describe how the company provides effective management of its interactions and relationships with its customers and uses information gained from customers to improve customer relationship management processes.

A D R

☑—☑ ☐

AREAS TO ADDRESS

a. for the company's most important contacts between its employees and customers, summarize the key requirements for maintaining and building relationships. Describe how these requirements are translated into key quality measures.

b. how service standards based upon the key quality measures (7.2a) are set and used. Include: (1) how service standards, including measures and performance levels, are deployed to customer-contact employees and to other company units that provide support for customer-contact employees; and (2) how the performance of the overall service standards system is tracked.

c. how the company provides information and easy access to enable customers to seek assistance, to comment, and to complain. Include the main types of contact and how easy access is maintained for each type.

d. how the company follows up with customers on products, services, and recent transactions to seek feedback and to help build relationships

e. how the company ensures that formal and informal complaints and feedback received by all company units are resolved effectively and promptly. Briefly describe the complaint management process.

f. how the following are addressed for customer-contact employees: (1) selection factors; (2) career path; (3) deployment of special training to include: knowledge of products and services; listening to customers; soliciting comments from customers; how to anticipate and handle problems or failures ("recovery"); skills in customer retention; and how to manage expectations; (4) empowerment and decision making; (5) satisfaction; and (6) recognition and reward

g. how the company evaluates and improves its customer relationship management processes. Include: (1) how the company seeks opportunities to enhance relationships with all customers or with key customers; and (2) how evaluations lead to improvements such as in service standards, access, customer-contact employee training, and technology support; and (3) how customer information is used in the improvement process.

Notes:

(1) Requirements (7.2a) might include responsiveness, product knowledge, follow-up, ease of access, etc. They do not include product and service requirements addressed in Item 7.1.

(2) "Service standards" refers to performance levels or expectations the company sets using the quality measures.

(3) The term "customer-contact employees" refers to employees whose main responsibilities bring them into regular contact with customers — in person, via telephone, or other means.

(4) In addressing "empowerment and decision making" in 7.2f, indicate how the company ensures that there is a common vision or basis to guide the actions of customer-contact employees. That is, the response should make clear how the company ensures that empowered customer-contact employees have a consistent understanding of what actions or types of actions they may or should take.

(5) In addressing satisfaction (7.2f), consider indicators such as turnover and absenteeism, as well as results of employee feedback through surveys, exit interviews, etc.

(6) Information on trends and levels in measures and indicators of complaint response time, effective resolution, and percent of complaints resolved on first contact should be reported in Item 6.1.

(7) How feedback and complaint data are aggregated for overall evaluation and how these data are translated into actionable information, should be addressed in 2.3a.

7.3 Commitment to Customers *(15 pts.)*

Describe the company's commitments to customers regarding its products/services and how these commitments are evaluated and improved.

A   D   R

Note: *Examples of commitments are product and service guarantees, warranties, and other understandings, expressed or implied.*

AREAS TO ADDRESS

a. types of commitments the company makes to promote trust and confidence in its products/services and to satisfy customers when product/service failures occur. Describe these commitments and how they: (1) address the principal concerns of customers; (2) are free from conditions that might weaken customers' trust and confidence; and (3) are communicated to customers clearly and simply.

b. how the company evaluates and improves its commitments, and the customers' understanding of them, to avoid gaps between customer expectations and company performance. Include: (1) how information/feedback from customers is used; (2) how product/service performance improvement data are used; and (3) how competitors' commitments are considered.

7.4 Customer Satisfaction Determination *(30 pts.)*

Describe how the company determines customer satisfaction, customer repurchase intentions, and customer satisfaction relative to competitors; describe how these determination processes are evaluated and improved.

A   D   R

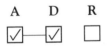

AREAS TO ADDRESS

a. how the company determines customer satisfaction. Include: (1) a brief description of processes and measurement scales used; frequency of determination; and how objectivity and validity are assured. Indicate significant differences, if any, in processes and measurement scales for different customer groups or segments; and (2) how customer satisfaction measurements capture key information that reflects customers' likely future market behavior, such as repurchase intentions or positive referrals.

b. how customer satisfaction relative to that for competitors is determined. Describe: (1) company-based comparative studies; and (2) comparative studies or evaluations made by independent organizations and/or customers. For (1) and (2), describe how objectivity and validity of studies are assured.

c. how the company evaluates and improves its overall processes and measurement scales for determining customer satisfaction and customer satisfaction relative to that for competitors. Include how other indicators (such as gains and losses of customers) and customer dissatisfaction indicators (such as complaints) are used in this improvement process.

Notes:

(1) Customer satisfaction measurement might include both a numerical rating scale and descriptors assigned to each unit in the scale. An effective (actionable) customer satisfaction measurement system is one that provides the company with reliable information about customer ratings of specific product and service features and the relationship between these ratings and the customer's likely future market behavior.

(2) The company's products and services might be sold to end users via other businesses such as retail stores or dealers. Thus, "customer groups" or segments should take into account these other businesses as well as the end users.

(3) Customer dissatisfaction indicators include complaints, claims, refunds, recalls, returns, repeat services, litigation, replacements, downgrades, repairs, warranty work, warranty costs, misshipments, and incomplete orders.

(4) Company-based or independent organization comparative studies (7.4b) might take into account one or more indicators of customer dissatisfaction as well as satisfaction. The extent and types of such studies may depend upon factors such as industry and company size.

7.5 Customer Satisfaction Results *(85 pts.)*

Summarize trends in the company's customer satisfaction and trends in key indicators of customer dissatisfaction.

A   D   R

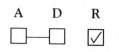

AREAS TO ADDRESS

a. trends and current levels in key measures and/or indicators of customer satisfaction, including customer retention. Segment by customer group, as appropriate. Trends may be supported by objective information and/or data from customers demonstrating current or recent (past 3 years) satisfaction with the company's products/services.

b. trends in measures and/or indicators of customer dissatisfaction. Address the most relevant and important indicators for the company's products/services.

Notes

(1) Results reported in this Item derive from methods described in Items 7.4 and 7.2.

(2) Information supporting trends (7.5a) might include customers' assessments of products/services, customer awards, and customer retention.

(3) Indicators of customer dissatisfaction are given in Item 7.4, Note 3.

7.6 Customer Satisfaction Comparison *(70 pts.)*

Compare the company's customer satisfaction results with those of competitors.

A   D   R

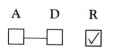

AREAS TO ADDRESS

a. trends and current levels in key measures and/or indicators of customer satisfaction relative to competitors. Segment by customer group, as appropriate. Trends may be supported by objective information and/or data from independent organizations, including customers.

b. trends in gaining and losing customers, or customer accounts, to competitors

c. trends in gaining or losing market share to competitors

Notes:

(1) Results reported in Item 7.6 derive from methods described in Item 7.4.

(2) Competitors include domestic and international ones in the company's markets, both domestic and international.

(3) Objective information and/or data from independent organizations, including customers (7.6a), might include survey results, competitive awards, recognition, and ratings. Such surveys, competitive awards, recognition, and ratings by independent organizations and customers should reflect comparative satisfaction (and dissatisfaction), not comparative performance of products and services. Information on comparative performance of products and services should be included in 6.1b.

SCORING SYSTEM: APPROACH, DEPLOYMENT, RESULTS

The system for scoring applicant responses to Examination Items and for developing feedback is based upon three evaluation dimensions: (1) Approach; (2) Deployment; and (3) Results. All Examination Items require applicants to furnish information relating to one or more of these dimensions. Specific factors associated with the evaluation dimensions are described below. Scoring Guidelines are given on page 34.

Approach

"Approach" refers to how the applicant addresses the requirements given in the Examination Items. The factors used to evaluate approaches include *one or more* of the following:

- appropriateness of the methods, tools, and techniques to the requirements
- effectiveness of use of methods, tools, and techniques
- degree to which the approach is systematic, integrated, and consistently applied
- degree to which the approach embodies effective evaluation/improvement cycles
- degree to which the approach is based upon quantitative information that is objective and reliable
- evidence of unique and innovative approaches. This includes significant and effective adaptations of approaches, tools, and techniques used in other applications or types of businesses

Deployment

"Deployment" refers to the extent to which the applicant's approaches are applied to all relevant work units and activities given in the responses to Examination Items. The factors used to evaluate deployment include *one or more* of the following:

- appropriate and effective use of the approach in key processes
- appropriate and effective use of the approach in the development and delivery of products and services
- appropriate and effective use of the approach in interactions with customers, employees, suppliers of goods and services, and the public

Results

"Results" refers to outcomes in achieving the purposes given in the Examination Items. The factors used to evaluate results include *one or more* of the following:

- current performance levels
- performance levels relative to appropriate comparisons and/or benchmarks
- rate of performance improvement
- demonstration of sustained improvement and/or sustained high-level performance
- breadth and importance of performance improvements

Item Classification and Scoring Dimensions

Award Examination Items are classified according to the kinds of information and/or data applicants are expected to furnish.

The three types of Items and their designations are:

	A	D	R
1. Approach/Deployment	☑	☑	☐

	A	D	R
2. Results	☐	☐	☑

	A	D	R
3. Approach/Deployment/Results	☑	☑	☑

Approach and Deployment are linked to emphasize that Items requesting information on Approach always require information to convey Deployment — consistent with the specific requirements of the Item. Although Approach and Deployment dimensions are linked, feedback to the applicant would reflect strengths and/or areas for improvement in either or both dimensions.

Results Items depend primarily on data. However, the evaluation factor, "breadth and importance of performance improvements", is concerned with how widespread and how significant an applicant's improvement results are. This is directly related to the Deployment dimension. That is, if improvement processes are widely deployed, there should be corresponding results. A score for a Results Item is a composite based upon overall performance, also taking into account the breadth and importance of performance improvements.

Approach/Deployment/Results Items focus mainly on Approach/Deployment. The results requested are those most directly derived from the Approach/Deployment and hence most important for use in the evaluation of the effectiveness of the Approach/Deployment. Such results are used in process improvement.

"Relevance and Importance" as a Scoring Factor

The three evaluation dimensions described above are all critical to the assessment and feedback processes. However, evaluations and feedback must also consider the relevance and importance to the applicant's business of improvements in Approach, Deployment, and Results. The areas of greatest relevance and importance are addressed in the Business Overview, and are a primary focus of Items such as 3.1, 5.1, and 7.1.

SCORING GUIDELINES

SCORE	APPROACH / DEPLOYMENT
0%	■ no systematic approach evident; anecdotal information
10% to 30%	■ beginning of a systematic approach to the primary purposes of the Item ■ early stages of a transition from reacting to problems to a general improvement orientation ■ major gaps exist in deployment that would inhibit progress in achieving the primary purposes of the Item
40% to 60%	■ a sound, systematic approach, responsive to the primary purposes of the Item ■ a fact-based improvement process in place in key areas; more emphasis is placed on improvement than on reaction to problems ■ no major gaps in deployment, though some areas or work units may be in very early stages of deployment
70% to 90%	■ a sound, systematic approach, responsive to the overall purposes of the Item ■ a fact-based improvement process is a key management tool; clear evidence of refinement and improved integration as a result of improvement cycles and analysis ■ approach is well-deployed, with no major gaps; deployment may vary in some areas or work units
100%	■ a sound, systematic approach, fully responsive to all the requirements of the Item ■ a very strong, fact-based improvement process is a key management tool; strong refinement and integration — backed by excellent analysis ■ approach is fully deployed without any significant weaknesses or gaps in any areas or work units

SCORE	RESULTS
0%	■ no results or poor results in areas reported
10% to 30%	■ early stages of developing trends; some improvements *and/or* early good performance levels in a few areas ■ results not reported for many to most areas of importance to the applicant's key business requirements
40% to 60%	■ improvement trends *and/or* good performance levels reported for many to most areas of importance to the applicant's key business requirements ■ no pattern of adverse trends *and/or* poor performance levels in areas of importance to the applicant's key business requirements ■ some trends *and/or* current performance levels — evaluated against relevant comparisons *and/or* benchmarks — show areas of strength *and/or* good to very good relative performance levels
70% to 90%	■ current performance is good to excellent in most areas of importance to the applicant's key business requirements ■ most improvement trends *and/or* performance levels are sustained ■ many to most trends *and/or* current performance levels — evaluated against relevant comparisons *and/or* benchmarks — show areas of leadership and very good relative performance levels
100%	■ current performance is excellent in most areas of importance to the applicant's key business requirements ■ excellent improvement trends *and/or* sustained excellent performance levels in most areas ■ strong evidence of industry and benchmark leadership demonstrated in many areas

Introduction

This section provides guidelines and recommendations for writing the Business Overview and for responding to the requirements of the 28 Examination Items of the Award Criteria. The section consists of four parts: (1) Description of the Business Overview; (2) Description of an Examination Item; (3) Guidelines for Preparing the Business Overview; and (4) Guidelines for Responding to the Examination Items.

Description of the Business Overview

The Business Overview is an outline of the applicant's business, addressing what is most important to the business and the key factors that influence how the business operates.

The Award Examination is designed to permit evaluation of any kind of business. However, individual Items and Areas to Address may not be equally applicable or equally important to all businesses, even to businesses of comparable size in the same industry. The Business Overview is intended to "set the stage" for the Examiners' evaluation. It should help Examiners to understand what is relevant and important to the applicant's business.

The Business Overview is used by the Examiners in all stages of the application review. For this reason, this Overview is a vital part of the overall application.

Description of an Examination Item

Writing an application for the Award requires responding to the requirements given in the 28 Examination Items. Each Item and its key components are presented in the same format as illustrated in the figure below.

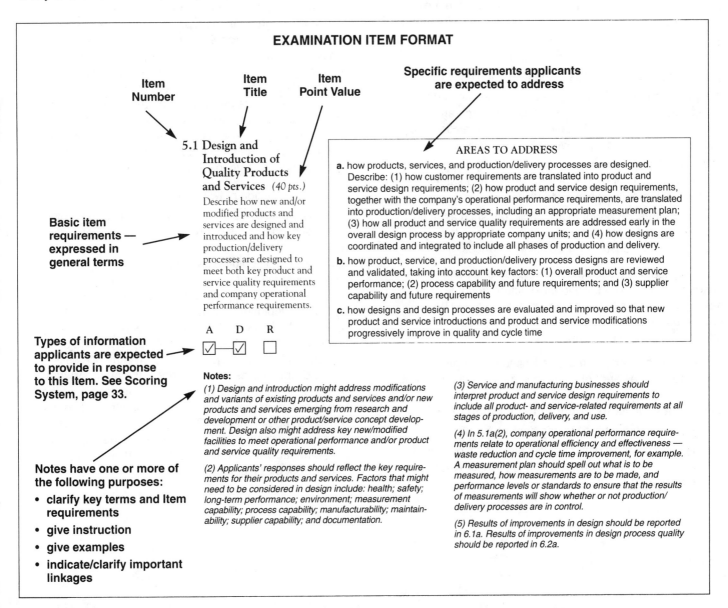

EXAMINATION ITEM FORMAT

Item Number

Item Title

Item Point Value

Specific requirements applicants are expected to address

5.1 Design and Introduction of Quality Products and Services (40 pts.)

Describe how new and/or modified products and services are designed and introduced and how key production/delivery processes are designed to meet both key product and service quality requirements and company operational performance requirements.

A   D   R
☑—☑   ☐

Basic item requirements — expressed in general terms

Types of information applicants are expected to provide in response to this Item. See Scoring System, page 33.

AREAS TO ADDRESS

a. how products, services, and production/delivery processes are designed. Describe: (1) how customer requirements are translated into product and service design requirements; (2) how product and service design requirements, together with the company's operational performance requirements, are translated into production/delivery processes, including an appropriate measurement plan; (3) how all product and service quality requirements are addressed early in the overall design process by appropriate company units; and (4) how designs are coordinated and integrated to include all phases of production and delivery.

b. how product, service, and production/delivery process designs are reviewed and validated, taking into account key factors: (1) overall product and service performance; (2) process capability and future requirements; and (3) supplier capability and future requirements

c. how designs and design processes are evaluated and improved so that new product and service introductions and product and service modifications progressively improve in quality and cycle time

Notes:

(1) Design and introduction might address modifications and variants of existing products and services and/or new products and services emerging from research and development or other product/service concept development. Design also might address key new/modified facilities to meet operational performance and/or product and service quality requirements.

(2) Applicants' responses should reflect the key requirements for their products and services. Factors that might need to be considered in design include: health; safety; long-term performance; environment; measurement capability; process capability; manufacturability; maintainability; supplier capability; and documentation.

(3) Service and manufacturing businesses should interpret product and service design requirements to include all product- and service-related requirements at all stages of production, delivery, and use.

(4) In 5.1a(2), company operational performance requirements relate to operational efficiency and effectiveness — waste reduction and cycle time improvement, for example. A measurement plan should spell out what is to be measured, how measurements are to be made, and performance levels or standards to ensure that the results of measurements will show whether or not production/delivery processes are in control.

(5) Results of improvements in design should be reported in 6.1a. Results of improvements in design process quality should be reported in 6.2a.

Notes have one or more of the following purposes:

- **clarify key terms and Item requirements**
- **give instruction**
- **give examples**
- **indicate/clarify important linkages**

Guidelines for Preparing the Business Overview

A Business Overview fully responsive to the Examiners' requirements should describe:

- the nature of the applicant's business: products and services

- principal customers (consumers, other businesses, government, etc.) and their special requirements. Special relationships with customers or customer groups should be noted.

- a description of the applicant's major markets (local, regional, national, or international)

- key customer quality requirements (for example, on-time delivery or low defect levels) for products and services. Include all important quality requirements. Briefly note significant differences in requirements among customer groups or markets, if any.

- the applicant's position (relative size, growth) in the industry and key factors in the competitive environment

- the applicant's employee base, including: number, type, educational level, bargaining units, etc.

- major equipment, facilities, and technologies used

- types and numbers of suppliers of goods and services. Indicate the importance of suppliers, dealers, and other businesses, and any limitations or special relationships that may exist in dealing with such businesses.

- the regulatory environment within which the applicant operates, including occupational health and safety, environmental, financial regulations, etc.

- other factors important to the applicant, such as major new thrusts for the company, major changes taking place in the industry, new business alliances, etc.

If the applicant is a subsidiary or division of a company, a description of the organizational structure and key management links to the parent company should be presented. Also include percent of employees and relationships of products and services.

The Business Overview must be limited to four pages. These four pages are not counted in the overall page limit.

Guidelines for Responding to the Examination Items

1. Read the entire Award Criteria booklet.

   The main sections of the booklet provide an overall orientation to the Criteria and how applicants' responses are evaluated.

2. Understand the meaning of "how".

   All Items that request information on Approach include Areas to Address that begin with the word "how". Responses to such Areas should provide as complete a picture as possible to enable meaningful evaluation and feedback. Responses should outline key process details such as methods, measures, deployment, and evaluation factors. Information lacking sufficient detail to permit an evaluation and feedback, or merely providing an example, is referred to in the Criteria booklet as anecdotal information.

3. Understand the meaning of measures and/or indicators.

   All Items calling for results require data using "key measures and/or indicators". Measures and indicators both involve measurement related to performance. When the performance can be measured directly, such as cycle time and on-time delivery, the term "measure" is used. When the overall performance may not be evaluated in terms of one type of measurement, and two or more measurements are used to provide ("indicate") a more complete picture, the term "indicator" is used. For example, innovation success is not easily described in terms of a single measurement. Patents and patent citations provide two measurements which are indicators of innovation success, but completing the picture requires other indicators, such as cycle time for bringing new products to market and market share gain from introduction of innovative products or services.

4. Note the distinction between data and results.

   There is a critical distinction between data and results — a distinction that is often misunderstood. Data are numerical information; results are the outcomes of activities. Data could be used as inputs to activities, as well as outcomes of activities. Results Items require data to demonstrate progress and achievement. Approach/Deployment Items, focused on processes, may benefit from data to provide a clearer and more complete picture of key aspects of Approach and/or Deployment. For example, a company may use self-directed work teams in its approach. It may report that 5 such teams involving 75 percent of the people on the shop floor undertook 11 projects during the past year to reduce scrap and rework. These data are input data giving deployment information related to the approach (self-directed work teams). These teams reducing scrap and rework by 17 percent is a result.

5. Understand specific Item requirements.

Review each Item classification and the specific requirements given under Areas to Address and in Item Notes.

6. Gather and organize relevant information for a response.

Most of the Items require summaries of information gathered from different parts of the company.

7. Select relevant/important information.

In preparing Item responses, focus on information that is *both* directly responsive to the Item requirements and to key business requirements spelled out in the Business Overview. Information and data included should be relevant and important to both the Item and to the applicant's business.

8. Anticipate assessment and feedback.

A well-written response is one that lends itself to Examiner or other feedback. A response that facilitates assessment gives clear information on how (approach) and on the relevant use (deployment) of the approach. Anecdotal information or information lacking overall context should not be given as it is usually not possible to prepare meaningful feedback. Examples are, of course, helpful but examples often do not convey a picture of overall approach and deployment. If examples are used, make certain that they illustrate a more complete response already presented.

9. Make responses concise.

The application page limits (85 pages for companies in the Manufacturing and Service Categories and 70 pages for companies in the Small Business Category) do not permit lengthy narrative or inclusion of information not directly responsive to Item requirements. For this reason, applicants are urged to make all responses concise and factual. Statements should be supported with data whenever appropriate.

10. Cross-reference when appropriate.

Although applicants should seek to make individual responses self-contained, there may be instances when responses to different Items are mutually reinforcing. In such cases it is appropriate to reference responses to other Items, rather than to repeat information presented elsewhere. In doing so, applicants should make the reference specific by using Item and Area designators, for example, see 4.2c.

11. Review each response.

Each response should be reviewed to make certain that it addresses the Item requirements and is consistent with the applicant's key business requirements spelled out in the Business Overview. It is also important to ensure that a response is consistent with information reported in Items that are closely linked.

Reporting Results and Trend Data

1. Results Items require data to demonstrate progress (trend data), achievement (performance levels), and breadth of deployment. Evaluation of achievement is usually based upon two factors: (1) that the performance level has been sustained or is the current result of a favorable trend; and (2) that the performance level can be compared with that of other appropriate organizations.

2. Applicants are required to report trend data to show progress and to show that improvements or outstanding performance levels are sustained. No minimum period of time is specified for trend data. Time periods may span five years or more for some results. Trends may be much shorter in areas where improvement efforts are new. In cases where the trend line is short, the Examiners' evaluation will take into account the demonstrated levels of performance.

3. The spacing between data points on a trend line (annual, monthly, etc.) should reflect a natural measurement/use scheme for such results. That is, how the data are used in process management should determine the spacing between data points. For example, measurement frequency should support timely improvement.

4. In reporting trend data, applicants should be aware that breadth of results is a major factor in the Examiners' evaluation. For this reason, it is important to report data reflecting wide deployment of improvement activities. Use of graphs and tables offers a good means to present many results compactly.

5. Graphs and tables should be integrated into the body of the text, wherever possible.

The following graph illustrates data an applicant might present as part of a response to Item 6.1, Product and Service Quality Results. The applicant has indicated, in the Business Overview and in Item 7.1, on-time delivery as a key customer requirement.

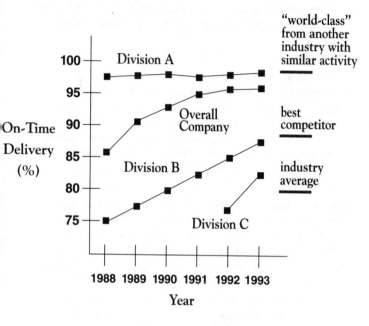

Using the graph, the following characteristics of clear and effective data presentation are illustrated:

- the trend lines report data for a key business requirement

- both axes and units of measure are clearly labeled

- results are presented for several years

- meaningful comparisons are clearly shown

- the company shows, using a single graph, that its three divisions separately track on-time delivery

To help interpret the scoring guidelines (page 34), the following comments on the graphed results would be appropriate:

- the current overall company performance level is excellent. This conclusion is supported by the comparison with competitors and with a "world class" level

- the company exhibits an overall excellent improvement record

- Division A is the current performance leader — showing sustained high performance and a slightly positive trend. Division B shows rapid improvement. Its current performance is near that of the best industry competitor, but trails the "world class" level.

- Division C — a new division — shows rapid progress. Its current performance is not yet at the level of the best industry competitor.

Reviewing the Overall Set of Item Responses

1. It is helpful to review, as a whole, the complete set of 28 Item responses. There are four main considerations in this review:

   a. emphasis on the applicant's most important business requirements. This emphasis should be clear throughout the set of responses, and consistent with the Business Overview.

   b. balance in the use of page limits. Ample page space should be given to results Items which are weighed heavily in the Examiners' evaluation. Items and Areas that address factors particularly important to the applicant's business should receive relatively more emphasis.

   c. overall consistency. Responses should be checked to ensure that responses to related Items are consistent, and that there is appropriate cross-referencing to minimize duplication of information.

   d. final check on deployment information. The overall application should convey widespread and consistent implementation, not merely an outline of approaches. The final review allows an assessment of how well the application as a whole covers all key company requirements, responsibilities, and processes.

ELIGIBILITY CATEGORIES AND RESTRICTIONS

Basic Eligibility

Public Law 100-107 establishes the three eligibility categories of the Award: Manufacturing, Service, and Small Business. Any for-profit business located in the United States or its territories may apply for the Award. Eligibility for the Award is intended to be as open as possible to all U.S. companies. Minor eligibility restrictions and conditions ensure fairness and consistency in definition. For example, publicly or privately owned, domestic or foreign-owned, joint ventures, incorporated firms, sole proprietorships, partnerships, and holding companies may apply. Not eligible are: local, state, and national government agencies; not-for-profit organizations; trade associations; and professional societies.

Award Eligibility Categories

1. Manufacturing
Companies or subsidiaries (defined below) that produce and sell manufactured products or manufacturing processes, and those companies that produce agricultural, mining, or construction products.

2. Service
Companies or subsidiaries that sell services.

- Proper classification of companies that perform both manufacturing and service is determined by the larger percentage of sales.

3. Small Business
Complete businesses with not more than 500 full-time employees. Business activities may include manufacturing and/or service. A small business must be able to document that it functions independently of any other businesses which are equity owners. For example, a small business owned by a holding company would be eligible if it can document its independent operation and that other units of the holding company are in different businesses.

If there are equity owners with some management control, at least 50% of the small business' customer base (dollar volume for products and services) must be from other than the equity owners, or other businesses owned by the equity owners.

Subsidiaries

For purposes of the Malcolm Baldrige National Quality Award application, a subsidiary will be taken to mean an actual subsidiary, business unit, division, or like organization. In the Manufacturing and Service categories, subsidiary units of a company may be eligible for the Award. Small businesses must apply as a whole; subsidiary units of small businesses are not eligible.

The following application conditions apply for subsidiary units:

- The unit must have existed one year or more prior to the Award application date (April 4, 1994).

- The unit must have clear definition of organization as reflected in corporate literature, e.g., organization charts, administrative manuals, and annual reports. That is, the unit must function as a business entity, not as a collection of activities aggregated for purposes of writing an Award application.

- The unit must have more than 500 full-time employees, OR

  The unit must have 25% of all employees in the worldwide operations of the parent company. ("Parent company" refers to the company that owns or controls subsidiary units through the ownership of voting stock.)

- The entire unit must be included in the application; no parts of the unit may be excluded.

Restrictions on Eligibility

The intent of Public Law 100-107 is to create an Award process incorporating rigorous and objective evaluation of the applicant's management of its products, services, and operations. *Award recipients are to serve as appropriate models of quality achievement for other U.S. companies.* Customer satisfaction is to play a major role in the Examination. Site visits are required to verify descriptions given in written applications.

The nature of some companies' activities is such that the central purposes and requirements of Public Law 100-107 cannot be fulfilled through their participation in the Award Program; companies or subsidiaries whose businesses cannot fulfill these purposes are not eligible. Specifically, four restrictions apply:

1. A company or its subsidiary is eligible only if the practices associated with all major business functions of the applicant are inspectable in the United States or its territories. One or both of the following conditions must apply:

   - more than 50% of the applicant unit's employees must be located in the U.S. or its territories, OR

     more than 50% of the applicant unit's physical assets must be located in the U.S. or its territories

   Note: *The functions/activities of foreign sites must be included in the Application Report in the appropriate Examination Items.*

2. At least 50% of a subsidiary unit's customer base (dollar volume for products and services) must be free of direct financial and line organization control by the parent company. For example, a subsidiary unit is not eligible if its parent company or other subsidiary of the parent company is the customer for more than one-half of its total products and services.

3. Individual units or partial aggregations of units of "chain" organizations (such as hotels, retail stores, banks, or restaurants) are not eligible.

For purposes of this application, a chain organization is defined as an organization where each unit (e.g., subsidiary or franchise) performs a similar function or manufactures a similar product. Accordingly, a potential applicant is not eligible if the parent company or another unit of the parent company provides similar products or services for substantially the same customer base. Similarly, an individual unit is not eligible if customers would be unable to distinguish easily which unit of the company provides the products or services to them.

4. Company units performing any of the business support functions of the company are not eligible. Examples of business support functions include: Sales/Marketing/ Distribution, Customer Service, Finance and Accounting, Human Resources, Environmental-Health-Safety of Employees, Purchasing, Legal Services, and Research and Development.

Multiple-Application Restrictions

1. A subsidiary and its parent company may not both apply for Awards in the same year.

2. Only one subsidiary unit of a company may apply for an Award in the same year in the same Award category.

Future Eligibility Restrictions

1. If a company receives an Award, the company and all its subsidiary units are ineligible to apply for an Award for a period of five years.

2. If a subsidiary unit receives an Award, it is ineligible to apply for an Award for a period of five years.

3. If a subsidiary unit consisting of more than one-half of the total sales of a company receives an Award, neither that company nor any of its other subsidiary units is eligible to apply for another Award for a period of five years.

Eligibility Determination

In order to ensure that Award recipients meet all reasonable requirements and expectations in representing the Award throughout the U.S., potential applicants must have their eligibility approved prior to applying for the Award.

Determination takes into account the following factors:

- small business status
- subsidiary unit status and subsidiary functions performed
- customer base
- sales to a parent company or another unit or units of the parent company
- status as a company operating in the U.S. and/or its territories
- relationship of products and services to those of the parent company or other units of the parent company
- number and type of support services provided by the parent company or other units of the parent company

Potential applicants for the 1994 Award are encouraged to submit their Eligibility Determination Form as early as possible and no later than March 4, 1994. This form is contained in the 1994 Application Forms and Instructions booklet. For information on how to obtain a copy of this booklet, see page 41.

HOW TO ORDER COPIES OF 1994 AWARD MATERIALS

> **Note:** The **1994 Award Criteria** and the **1994 Application Forms and Instructions** are two separate documents.

Individual Orders

Individual copies of either document can be obtained free of charge from:

Malcolm Baldrige National Quality Award
National Institute of Standards and Technology
Route 270 and Quince Orchard Road
Administration Building, Room A537
Gaithersburg, MD 20899-0001
Telephone: 301-975-2036
Telefax: 301-948-3716

Bulk Orders

Multiple copies of the **1994 Award Criteria** may be ordered in packets of 10:

American Society for Quality Control
Customer Service Department
P.O. Box 3066
Milwaukee, WI 53201-3066
Toll free: 800-248-1946
Telefax: 414-272-1734

Order Item Number T998

Cost: $29.95 per packet of 10 plus postage and handling

Postage and handling charges are:

	U.S.	Canada
1 packet	$ 3.75	$ 8.75
2-4 packets	6.00	11.00
5 or more	12.00*	17.00

For orders shipped outside of the continental United States, there is a fee of 25 percent of order value to cover postage and handling. This fee does not apply to Canada.

Payment

Payment options include check, money order, purchase order, VISA, MasterCard, or American Express.

Payment must accompany all mail orders.

Payment must be made in U.S. currency. Checks and money orders must be drawn on U.S. institutions.

Make checks payable to ASQC.

Shipment

Orders delivered within the continental United States and Canada will be shipped UPS or first class mail.

If actual shipping charges exceed $12.00, ASQC will invoice the customer for additional expense.

FEES FOR THE 1994 AWARD CYCLE

Eligibility Determination Fees

The eligibility determination fee is $50 for all potential applicants. This fee is nonrefundable.

Application Fees

- Manufacturing Company Category—$4000
- Service Company Category—$4000
- Small Business Category—$1200
- Supplemental Sections—$1500

These fees cover all expenses associated with distribution of applications, review of applications, and development of feedback reports. A brief description of companies required to submit Supplemental Sections is given on page 1. Detailed information is given in the **1994 Application Forms and Instructions** document.

Site Visit Review Fees

Site visit fees will be set when the visits are scheduled. Fees depend upon the number of sites to be visited, the number of Examiners assigned, and the duration of the visit. Site visit fees for applicants in the Small Business category will be charged at one-half of the rate for companies in the Manufacturing and Service categories.

These fees cover all expenses and travel costs associated with site visit participation and development of site visit reports. Site visit fees are paid only by those applicants reaching the site visit stage.

Eligibility Determination Forms due — March 4, 1994
Award Applications due — April 4, 1994

HOW TO ORDER AWARD EDUCATIONAL MATERIALS

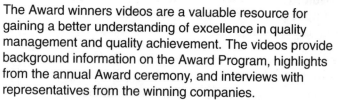

Each year, the Award Program develops materials for use in training members of the Board of Examiners, and for sharing information on the successful quality strategies of the Award winners. The listed materials and information may be obtained from the American Society for Quality Control (toll free: 800-248-1946). Prices and/or availability dates for all materials are given below.

Case Studies

The case studies are used to prepare Examiners for the interpretation of the Award Criteria and the Scoring System. The case studies, when used with the Award Criteria, illustrate the Award application and review process. The case studies are sample applications written for fictitious companies applying for the Baldrige Award. The case studies can provide valuable insights into the Award Criteria and Scoring System for companies interested in making application, as well as for self-assessment, planning, training, and other uses.

Varifilm Case Study Packet

The Varifilm Case Study Packet is based on the 1993 Examiner Preparation Course. Associated with the Varifilm Case Study are the Varifilm Evaluation Notes and the Varifilm Feedback Report. In addition, the Case Study Packet also includes: an Executive Summary; the 1993 Application Scorebook; the 1993 Site Visit Evaluation Book; the 1993 Handbook for the Board of Examiners and the 1993 Award Criteria.

    1993 – Item Number T515: $49.95

Alpha Telco/Herton Technology Case Study Packet

Based on the 1991 Award Criteria, the packet includes the case studies and Senior Examiners' reports for Alpha Telco and Herton.

    1991 – Item Number T508: $25.00

Award Winners Videos

The Award winners videos are a valuable resource for gaining a better understanding of excellence in quality management and quality achievement. The videos provide background information on the Award Program, highlights from the annual Award ceremony, and interviews with representatives from the winning companies.

    1993 – *Available February 22, 1994.*
    1992 – Item Number TA512: $20.00
    1991 – Item Number TA996:   15.00
    1990 – Item Number T992:   15.00
    1989 – Item Number T502:   10.00
    1988 – Item Number T993:   10.00

1992 Expanded Video

An expanded, 55-minute video, entitled "Quality Leadership: A Culture For Continuous Improvement", is available. The video highlights each 1992 Award Winner — AT&T Network Systems Group, Transmission Systems Business Unit; Texas Instruments, Defense Systems and Electronics Group; AT&T Universal Card Services; The Ritz-Carlton Hotel Company; and the Granite Rock Company.

    Item Number TA914: $249.95

1991 Expanded Video

An expanded, 46-minute video, featuring the three 1991 Award winners — Solectron Corporation, Zytec Corporation, and Marlow Industries, shows the viewer the ingredients for successful implementation of a quality system within their organization.

    Item Number TA910: $195.00

QUEST FOR EXCELLENCE VI CONFERENCE

The Annual Quest for Excellence Conference provides a unique opportunity to hear firsthand the Award-winning quality strategies of the past year's winners. Presentations are made by the CEOs and other key individuals who are transforming their organizations. The annual Quest for Excellence Conference is the principal forum for Award winners to present their overall strategies in detail.

The two and one-half day Quest for Excellence VI Conference will provide ample opportunities to explore the Award Criteria in depth, network with executive-level individuals from around the country, and view displays of each of the Award-winning organizations.

The Conference dates are February 7-9, 1994. The Conference will be held at the Washington Hilton and Towers, in Washington, D.C. For further information, contact the Association for Quality and Participation (AQP). (Toll-free: 800-733-3310 or FAX: 513-381-0070)

THE MALCOLM BALDRIGE NATIONAL QUALITY IMPROVEMENT ACT OF 1987 – PUBLIC LAW 100-107

The Malcolm Baldrige National Quality Award was created by Public Law 100-107, signed into law on August 20, 1987. The Award Program, responsive to the purposes of Public Law 100-107, led to the creation of a new public-private partnership. Principal support for the program comes from the Foundation for the Malcolm Baldrige National Quality Award, established in 1988.

The Award is named for Malcolm Baldrige, who served as Secretary of Commerce from 1981 until his tragic death in a rodeo accident in 1987. His managerial excellence contributed to long-term improvement in efficiency and effectiveness of government.

The Findings and Purposes Section of Public Law 100-107 states that:

" 1. the leadership of the United States in product and process quality has been challenged strongly (and sometimes successfully) by foreign competition, and our Nation's productivity growth has improved less than our competitors' over the last two decades.

2. American business and industry are beginning to understand that poor quality costs companies as much as 20 percent of sales revenues nationally and that improved quality of goods and services goes hand in hand with improved productivity, lower costs, and increased profitability.

3. strategic planning for quality and quality improvement programs, through a commitment to excellence in manufacturing and services, are becoming more and more essential to the well-being of our Nation's economy and our ability to compete effectively in the global marketplace.

4. improved management understanding of the factory floor, worker involvement in quality, and greater emphasis on statistical process control can lead to dramatic improvements in the cost and quality of manufactured products.

5. the concept of quality improvement is directly applicable to small companies as well as large, to service industries as well as manufacturing, and to the public sector as well as private enterprise.

6. in order to be successful, quality improvement programs must be management-led and customer-oriented, and this may require fundamental changes in the way companies and agencies do business.

7. several major industrial nations have successfully coupled rigorous private-sector quality audits with national awards giving special recognition to those enterprises the audits identify as the very best; and

8. a national quality award program of this kind in the United States would help improve quality and productivity by:

   A. helping to stimulate American companies to improve quality and productivity for the pride of recognition while obtaining a competitive edge through increased profits;

   B. recognizing the achievements of those companies that improve the quality of their goods and services and providing an example to others;

   C. establishing guidelines and criteria that can be used by business, industrial, governmental, and other organizations in evaluating their own quality improvement efforts; and

   D. providing specific guidance for other American organizations that wish to learn how to manage for high quality by making available detailed information on how winning organizations were able to change their cultures and achieve eminence. "

The Malcolm Baldrige National Quality Award

Managed by:

United States Department of Commerce
Technology Administration
National Institute of Standards and Technology
Route 270 and Quince Orchard Road
Administration Building, Room A537
Gaithersburg, MD 20899-0001

Administered by:

American Society for Quality Control
P.O. Box 3005
Milwaukee, WI 53201-3005

Malcolm Baldrige
National
Quality
Award

1994

*Application
Forms &
Instructions*

The Award, composed of two solid crystal prismatic forms, stands 14 inches tall. The crystal is held in a base of black, anodized aluminum with the Award winner's name engraved on the base. A solid bronze, 22-karat, gold-plated, die-struck medallion is captured in the front section of the crystal. The medal bears the inscriptions: "Malcolm Baldrige National Quality Award" and "The Quest for Excellence" on one side and the Presidential Seal on the other.

Awards traditionally are presented by the President of the United States at a special ceremony in Washington, D.C.

Awards are made annually to recognize U.S. companies that excel in quality management and quality achievement. Awards may be given in each of three eligibility categories:

■ Manufacturing companies
■ Service companies
■ Small businesses

Award recipients may publicize and advertise receipt of the Award. Award recipients are expected to share information about their successful quality strategies with other U.S. organizations.

Crystal by Steuben
Medal by The Protocol Group

CONTENTS

ii   THE MALCOLM BALDRIGE NATIONAL QUALITY AWARD:
A PUBLIC-PRIVATE PARTNERSHIP

1   INTRODUCTION

2   KEY DATES IN THE 1994 AWARD CYCLE
2   OVERVIEW OF THE APPLICATION AND REVIEW PROCESSES

4   1994 ELIGIBILITY CATEGORIES AND RESTRICTIONS
6   1994 ELIGIBILITY DETERMINATION FORM – INSTRUCTIONS
9   1994 ELIGIBILITY DETERMINATION FORM

16   1994 APPLICATION FORM – INSTRUCTIONS
17   1994 APPLICATION FORM
18   1994 APPLICATION REPORT – INSTRUCTIONS

23   1994 APPLICATION PACKAGE SUBMISSION

24   STANDARD INDUSTRIAL CLASSIFICATION (SIC) CODES

25   HOW TO ORDER COPIES OF 1994 AWARD MATERIALS
25   FEES FOR THE 1994 AWARD CYCLE
26   HOW TO ORDER AWARD EDUCATIONAL MATERIALS
26   QUEST FOR EXCELLENCE VI CONFERENCE

If you plan to apply for the Award in 1994, you will also need the document entitled
1994 Award Criteria. Ordering instructions are given on page 25.

1994 Eligibility Determination Forms due — March 4, 1994
1994 Award Applications due — April 4, 1994

To learn about the successful quality strategies of the 1993 Baldrige Award winners, attend
the Quest for Excellence VI Conference, February 7-9, 1994. Further information is on page 26.

THE MALCOLM BALDRIGE NATIONAL QUALITY AWARD: A PUBLIC-PRIVATE PARTNERSHIP

Building active partnerships in the private sector, and between the private sector and government, is fundamental to the success of the Award in improving quality in the United States.

Support by the private sector for the Award Program in the form of funds, volunteer efforts, and participation in information transfer is strong and rapidly growing.

To ensure the continued growth and success of these partnerships, each of the following organizations plays an important role:

The Foundation for the Malcolm Baldrige National Quality Award

The Foundation for the Malcolm Baldrige National Quality Award was created to foster the success of the Program. The Foundation's main objective is to raise funds to permanently endow the Award Program.

Prominent leaders from U.S. companies serve as Foundation Trustees to ensure that the Foundation's objectives are accomplished. Donor organizations vary in size and type, and are representative of many kinds of businesses and business groups. To date, the Foundation has raised approximately $11 million.

National Institute of Standards and Technology (NIST)

Responsibility for the Award is assigned to the Department of Commerce. NIST, an agency of the Department's Technology Administration, manages the Award Program.

NIST's goals are to aid U.S. industry through research and services; to contribute to public health, safety, and the environment; and to support the U.S. scientific and engineering research communities. NIST conducts basic and applied research in the physical sciences and engineering and develops measurement techniques, test methods, and standards. Much of NIST's work relates directly to quality and to quality-related requirements in technology development and technology utilization.

American Society for Quality Control (ASQC)

ASQC assists in administering the Award Program under contract to NIST.

ASQC is dedicated to facilitating continuous improvement and increased customer satisfaction by identifying, communicating and promoting the use of quality principles, concepts, and technologies. ASQC strives to be recognized throughout the world as the leading authority on, and champion for, quality. ASQC recognizes that continuous quality improvement will help the favorable repositioning of American goods and services in the international marketplace.

Board of Overseers

The Board of Overseers is the advisory organization on the Award to the Department of Commerce. The Board is appointed by the Secretary of Commerce and consists of distinguished leaders from all sectors of the U.S. economy.

The Board of Overseers evaluates all aspects of the Award Program, including the adequacy of the Criteria and processes for making Awards. An important part of the Board's responsibility is to assess how well the Award is serving the national interest. Accordingly, the Board makes recommendations to the Secretary of Commerce and to the Director of NIST regarding changes and improvements in the Award Program.

Board of Examiners

The Board of Examiners evaluates Award applications, prepares feedback reports, and makes Award recommendations to the Director of NIST. The Board consists of quality experts primarily from the private sector. Members are selected by NIST through a competitive application process. For 1994, the Board consists of more than 270 members. Of these, 9 serve as Judges, and approximately 50 serve as Senior Examiners. The remainder serve as Examiners. All members of the Board take part in an examiner preparation course.

In addition to their application review responsibilities, Board members contribute significantly to building awareness of the importance of quality and to information transfer activities. Many of these activities involve the hundreds of professional, trade, community, and state organizations to which Board members belong.

Award Recipients' Responsibilities and Contributions

Award recipients are required to share information on their successful quality strategies with other U.S. organizations. However, recipients are not required to share proprietary information, even if such information was part of their Award application. The principal mechanism for sharing information is the annual Quest for Excellence Conference, highlighted on page 26.

Award recipients in the first six years of the Award have been very generous in their commitment to improving U.S. competitiveness, and manufacturing and service quality. They have shared information on their successful quality strategies with hundreds of thousands of companies, educational institutions, government agencies, health care organizations, and others. This sharing far exceeds expectations and Program requirements. Award winners' efforts have encouraged many other organizations in all sectors of the U.S. economy to undertake their own quality improvement efforts.

INTRODUCTION

The Malcolm Baldrige National Quality Award is an annual Award to recognize U.S. companies that excel in quality management and quality achievement.

The Award promotes:

- awareness of quality as an increasingly important element in competitiveness,
- understanding of the requirements for quality excellence, and
- sharing of information on successful quality strategies and the benefits derived from implementation of these strategies.

Award Participation

The Award has three eligibility categories:

- Manufacturing companies
- Service companies
- Small businesses

Awards may be given in each category each year. Award recipients may publicize and advertise their Awards. In addition to publicizing the receipt of the Award, recipients are expected to share information about their successful quality strategies with other U.S. organizations.

Companies participating in the Award process are required to submit application packages that include completion of the Award Examination.

The Award Examination

The Award Examination is based upon quality excellence criteria created through a public-private partnership. In responding to these criteria, each applicant is expected to provide information and data on the company's improvement processes and results. Information and data submitted must be adequate to demonstrate that the applicant's approaches could be replicated or adapted by other companies.

The Award Examination is designed not only to serve as a reliable basis for making Awards but also to permit a diagnosis of each applicant's overall quality management.

Application Review

Applications are reviewed and evaluated by members of the Board of Examiners in a four-stage process:

Stage 1 – independent review and evaluation by at least five members of the Board

Stage 2 – consensus review and evaluation for applications that score well in Stage 1

Stage 3 – site visits to applicants that score well in Stage 2

Stage 4 – Judges' review and recommendations

Board members are assigned to applications taking into account the nature of the applicants' businesses and the expertise of the Examiners. Assignments are made in accord with strict rules regarding conflict of interest.

Applications are reviewed without funding from the United States government. Review expenses are paid primarily through application fees; partial support for the reviews is provided by the Foundation for the Malcolm Baldrige National Quality Award.

Feedback to Applicants

All applicants receive feedback reports at the conclusion of the review process. The feedback is based upon the applicants' responses to the Award Examination Criteria.

Feedback reports are prepared by members of the Board of Examiners. Many applicants use the feedback reports as a guidance document in company planning.

Non-Disclosure

Names of applicants, individual applications, commentary, and scoring information developed during the review of applications are regarded as proprietary and are kept confidential. Such information is available only to those individuals directly involved in the evaluation and application distribution processes. Board of Examiner members are assigned to applications following strict conflict of interest rules and receive no information regarding the content or status of applications to which they are not assigned.

Purpose of This Document

The purpose of this document is to provide the necessary forms and instructions for those companies who wish to apply for the Malcolm Baldrige National Quality Award in 1994. Detailed information is provided on the Eligibility Determination Process, the Award Application Process, and the Application Report. Information on the fees and key dates in the Award cycle is also given.

The 1994 Award Criteria, a companion document, includes a description of the Award processes and requirements, the Award Examination and the Scoring System, and provides a basis for submitting an Award application. Organizations of all kinds use the document for self-assessment, planning, training, and other purposes.

KEY DATES IN THE 1994 AWARD CYCLE

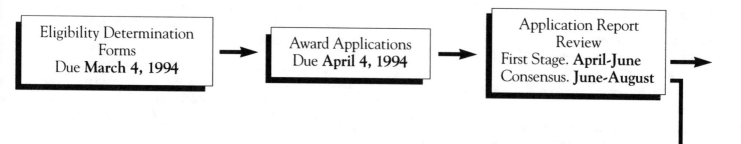

Eligibility Determination Forms
Due **March 4, 1994**

→

Award Applications
Due **April 4, 1994**

→

Application Report Review
First Stage. **April-June**
Consensus. **June-August**

→

OVERVIEW OF THE APPLICATION AND REVIEW PROCESSES

Making Application

Application for the Award is a two-step process:

1. Eligibility Determination Process

First, potential applicants must establish their eligibility in one of the three Award Categories (Manufacturing, Service, or Small Business). Applicants must submit the 1994 Eligibility Determination Form prior to submitting an application. Within 14 days of receipt of the 1994 Eligibility Determination Form, applicants will be notified of their eligibility status. An eligibility determination fee is required of all potential applicants. (See page 25 for information on fees). The eligibility determination fee is nonrefundable.

The 1994 Eligibility Determination Form submission must be postmarked or consigned to an overnight mail delivery service on or before March 4, 1994, to be considered for the 1994 Award. If a question arises about the deadline having been met, you will be asked to supply a dated receipt from the postal or overnight carrier.

Note: *As part of the Eligibility Determination Process, potential applicants must be able to demonstrate that they existed as an organizational unit on or before April 4, 1993.*

2. Award Application Process

Second, applicants must prepare a 1994 Application Form and the 1994 Application Report (see pages 16-22). To be accepted into the Application Review Process, applicants must provide 20 copies of the complete 1994 Application Package (see page 23) along with payment of the application review fees (see page 25).

Applications must be postmarked or consigned to an overnight mail delivery service on or before April 4, 1994, to be eligible for the 1994 Award. If a question arises about the deadline having been met, you will be asked to supply a dated receipt from the postal or overnight carrier.

How Applications are Reviewed

Applications are reviewed by the Board of Examiners in a four-stage process:

1. First-Stage Review

A review of the 1994 Application Report is conducted independently by at least five members of the Board of Examiners. At the conclusion of the first-stage review, the Panel of Judges determines which applications should be referred for consensus review.

2. Consensus Review

A joint review of the 1994 Application Report is conducted by at least five members of the Board of Examiners and led by a Senior Examiner. At the conclusion of the consensus review, the Panel of Judges determines which applicants should receive site visits.

Note: *A wide margin of safety is built into the decisions made at the conclusion of the first-stage review and at the conclusion of the consensus review to ensure that all applicants receive every reasonable consideration to advance to the next stage. The Judges consider applications case by case and review scoring and scoring profiles. Each Award Category — Manufacturing, Service, and Small Business — is considered separately. Strict conflict of interest rules apply and are carefully monitored at all four stages of review.*

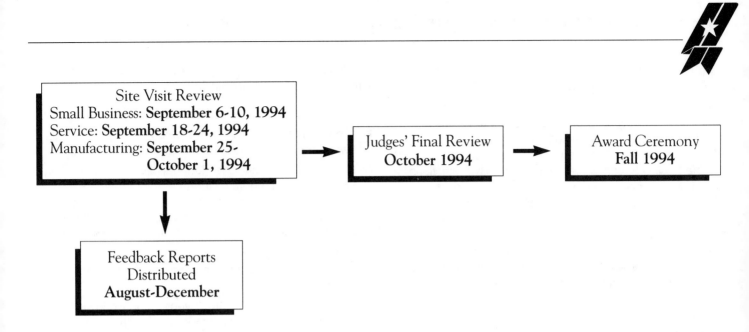

3. Site Visit Review

An on-site verification of the 1994 Application Report is conducted by at least five members of the Board of Examiners and led by a Senior Examiner. The site visit review team develops a report for the Panel of Judges.

Note: *The highest-scoring candidates for the Award undergo site visits by members of the Board of Examiners. The primary objectives of the site visits are to verify the information provided in the 1994 Application Report and to clarify issues and questions raised during review of the Report. In submitting an application, every applicant agrees to host and pay the costs of a site visit, if the applicant is selected. No site visits will be scheduled for sites outside of the United States or its territories. If selected for a site visit, the applicant will be given the names of Examiners scheduled to participate. Site visits consist primarily of interviews by Examiner teams and team reviews of pertinent records and data. Applicants are permitted to make an introductory presentation.*

4. Judges' Final Review

A final review of all evaluation reports on site visited applicants is conducted by the Panel of Judges to recommend Award recipients. The Panel of Judges develops a set of recommendations and presents them to the Director of the National Institute of Standards and Technology (NIST).

Role Model Determination

The Secretary of Commerce and the Director of NIST are responsible for determining that a candidate would be an appropriate role model and therefore should be approved as a Baldrige Award winner. The purpose of this determination is to help ensure that the Award's integrity is preserved.

For the role model determination, NIST conducts records checks on potential Award winners. The check includes: Internal Revenue Service records, field visits to police, district attorney, and court offices in the local jurisdiction of company headquarters — including checks for compliance with environmental, public health and safety regulations; and reviews of Federal Bureau of Investigation, Bureau of Export Administration, and General Services Administration banned list records. No new or independent investigations are conducted.

Award Ceremony

Awards traditionally are presented by the President of the United States at a special ceremony in Washington, D.C.

Feedback Reports

All applicants receive feedback reports commenting on their strengths and areas for improvement.

Basic Eligibility

Public Law 100-107 establishes the three eligibility categories of the Award: Manufacturing, Service, and Small Business. Any for-profit business located in the United States or its territories may apply for the Award. Eligibility for the Award is intended to be as open as possible to all U.S. companies. Minor eligibility restrictions and conditions ensure fairness and consistency in definition. For example, publicly or privately owned, domestic or foreign-owned, joint ventures, incorporated firms, sole proprietorships, partnerships, and holding companies may apply. Not eligible are: local, state, and national government agencies; not-for-profit organizations; trade associations; and professional societies.

Award Eligibility Categories

1. Manufacturing

Companies or subsidiaries (defined below) that produce and sell manufactured products or manufacturing processes, and those companies that produce agricultural, mining, or construction products. (See SIC Codes on page 24.)

2. Service

Companies or subsidiaries that sell services. (See SIC Codes on page 24.)

Note: *Proper classification of companies that perform both manufacturing and service is determined by the larger percentage of sales.*

3. Small Business

Complete businesses with not more than 500 full-time employees. Business activities may include manufacturing and/or service. A small business must be able to document that it functions independently of any other businesses which are equity owners. For example, a small business owned by a holding company would be eligible if it can document its independent operation and that other units of the holding company are in different businesses.

If there are equity owners with some management control, at least 50% of the small business' customer base (dollar volume for products and services) must be from other than the equity owners, or other businesses owned by the equity owners.

Subsidiaries

For purposes of the 1994 Malcolm Baldrige National Quality Award application, a subsidiary will be taken to mean an actual subsidiary, business unit, division, or like organization. In the Manufacturing and Service categories, subsidiaries of a company may be eligible for the Award.

Small businesses must apply as a whole; subsidiaries of small businesses are not eligible.

The following application conditions apply for subsidiary units:

- The subsidiary must have existed one year prior to the Award application date (April 4, 1994).

- The subsidiary must have clear definition of organization as reflected in corporate literature, e.g., organization charts, administrative manuals, and annual reports. That is, the unit must function as a business entity, not as a collection of activities aggregated for purposes of writing an Award application.

- The subsidiary must have more than 500 full-time employees, OR

- It must have 25% of all employees in the worldwide operations of the parent company. ("Parent company" refers to the company that owns or controls subsidiaries through the ownership of voting stock.)

Restrictions on Eligibility

The intent of Public Law 100-107 is to create an Award process incorporating rigorous and objective evaluation of the applicant's total quality system underlying its products and services. *Award recipients are to serve as appropriate models of total quality achievement for other U.S. companies.* Customer satisfaction is to play a major role in the Examination. Site visits are required to verify descriptions given in written applications.

The nature of some companies' activities is such that the central purposes and requirements of Public Law 100-107 cannot be fulfilled through their participation in the Award Program; companies or subsidiaries whose businesses cannot fulfill these purposes are not eligible. Specifically, four restrictions apply:

1. A company or its subsidiary is eligible only if the quality practices associated with all major business functions of the applicant are inspectable in the United States or its territories. One or both of the following conditions must apply:

   - more than 50% of the applicant's employees must be located in the U.S. or its territories, or

   - more than 50% of the applicant's physical assets must be located in the U.S. or its territories

   Note: *The functions/activities of foreign sites must be included in the 1994 Application Report in the appropriate Examination Items.*

2. At least 50% of the subsidiary's customer base (dollar volume for products and services) must be free of direct financial and line organization control by the parent company. For example, a subsidiary is not eligible if its parent company or other subsidiary of the parent company is the customer for more than one-half of its total products and services.

3. Individual units or partial aggregations of units of "chain" organizations (such as hotels, retail stores, banks, or restaurants) are not eligible.

   For purposes of this application, a chain organization is defined as an organization where each unit (e.g., subsidiary or franchise) performs a similar function or manufactures a similar product. Accordingly, a potential applicant is not eligible if the parent company or another unit of the parent company provides similar products or services for substantially the same customer base. Similarly, an individual unit is not eligible if customers would be unable to distinguish easily which unit of the company provides the products or services to them.

4. Subsidiaries performing any of the business support functions of the company are not eligible. Examples of business support functions include: Sales, Marketing, Distribution, Customer Service, Finance and Accounting, Human Resources, Environmental-Health-Safety of Employees, Purchasing, Legal Services, and Research and Development.

Multiple-Application Restrictions

1. A subsidiary and its parent company may not both apply for Awards in the same year.

2. Only one subsidiary of a company may apply for an Award in the same year in the same Award category.

Future Eligibility Restrictions

1. If a company receives an Award, the company and all its subsidiaries are ineligible to apply for another Award for a period of five years.

2. If a subsidiary receives an Award, it is ineligible to apply for another Award for a period of five years.

3. If a subsidiary consisting of more than one-half of the total sales of a company receives an Award, neither that company nor any of its other subsidiaries is eligible to apply for another Award for a period of five years.

Eligibility Determination

In order to ensure that potential Award recipients meet all reasonable requirements and expectations in representing the Award throughout the U.S., applicants must have their eligibility approved prior to applying for the Award.

Determination takes into account the following factors:

- small business status
- subsidiary status and subsidiary functions performed
- customer base
- sales to a parent company or another unit or units of the parent company
- status as a U.S. company
- relationship of products and services to those of the parent company or other units of the parent company
- number and type of support services provided by the parent company or other units of the parent company

Potential applicants for the 1994 Award are encouraged to submit their 1994 Eligibility Determination Form as early as possible and no later than March 4, 1994.

General Instructions

A potential applicant should submit the 1994 Eligibility Determination Form only if they intend to apply in 1994. Type all information requested. The 1994 Eligibility Determination Form may be duplicated. In addition, page 2 of the 1994 Eligibility Determination Form (Item 9, Site Listing and Descriptors) should be duplicated if all sites cannot be listed on a single page. Attach a line and box organization chart of the business. Send a letter of transmittal on company stationery along with the completed form and fee to:

Malcolm Baldrige National Quality Award
c/o American Society for Quality Control
P.O. Box 3005
Milwaukee, WI 53201-3005

Overnight Mailing Address:
Malcolm Baldrige National Quality Award
c/o American Society for Quality Control
611 East Wisconsin Avenue
Milwaukee, WI 53202
(414) 272-8575

Notes:

(1) Applicants must submit a copy of the approved 1994 Eligibility Determination Form with each copy of the 1994 Application Report submitted (see pages 18-22).

(2) If the applicant is a subsidiary or owned by a holding company, include a line and box organization chart for the parent company or the holding company which shows where the applicant fits into the overall organization.

Item Instructions

Item 1. Applicant
Provide the official name and mailing address of the organization applying for the Award. Check whether or not the applicant has existed for at least one year. (See the Note on page 2 for details.) If the answer is no, briefly explain.

Item 2. Highest-Ranking Official
Provide the name, title, mailing address, and telephone number of the applicant's highest-ranking official.

Item 3. For-Profit Designation
Check the appropriate box. Only for-profit organizations are eligible for an Award.

Item 4. Size of Applicant
Give the estimated number of employees of the applying unit as of the date the 1994 Eligibility Determination Form is submitted.

Note: *Where there is a significant proportion of part-time employees, count employees in proportion to the time they work (e.g., 75 employees who work one-third time would count as 25 full-time equivalents).*

State the approximate percent (to the nearest whole number) of employees of the applicant located in the United States or its territories. State the approximate percent (to the nearest whole number) of physical assets of the applicant located in the United States or its territories.

Give the number of different sites of all units involved with the products or services sold by the applicant. Separate sites need not be counted for offices or other work areas located near each other if the company considers them as one location for business and personnel purposes.

Check the appropriate range for sales of the applicant for the preceding fiscal year. (The applicant is reminded that all information is confidential and that only a range is being requested.)

Item 5. Industrial Classification
From page 24 choose up to three two-digit SIC Codes that best describe the applicant's products and/or services.

Note: *Applicants may substitite three- or four-digit SIC Codes, if such information is available.*

Item 6. Award Category
Based on the information given on pages 4 and 24, indicate which one of the three Award categories pertains.

Item 7. Supplier and Dealer Networks
Indicate the number of suppliers of goods and services used by the applicant.

If the applicant relies on external sales organizations, indicate the approximate number of each type.

Item 8. Percent Customer Base
Check the appropriate box. If the answer is no, briefly describe these customers and their relationship to the applicant.

Item 9. Site Listing and Descriptors

(a) Provide the complete address of each site (including foreign sites).

(b) Provide the approximate percent of the applicant's employees at each site. Provide the approximate percent of the applicant's sales accounted for by the output of each site. Use not applicable (N/A) for percent sales of headquarters or similar offices, when appropriate.

(c) Describe the types of products or services that are the output of the site. It may be necessary to state the relationship between the output of the site and the applicant's final products and services. It is not necessary to list every product or service.

Notes:

(1) In cases where the applicant has many sites performing the same function, these sites may be aggregated under one listing. Instead of the addresses for each, a summary statement about the locations may be made. If a site visit is to be conducted, a more detailed listing will be requested when the visit is planned.

(2) If the applicant has foreign sites, these sites must be included. The 1994 Application Report must address activities in foreign sites in the appropriate Examination Items. Applicants should be aware that no visits will be scheduled for sites outside the United States or its territories.

Item 10. Business Factors

Provide a brief description of the following key business factors:

(a) Nature of the applicant's business (products, services, and technology);

(b) Nature of major markets (local, regional, national, and international); and

(c) Importance of suppliers, dealers, distributors, and franchises.

Notes:

(1) Include a list of major competitors as part of the response to Item 10(a).

(2) Include a list of major customers as part of the response to Item 10(b).

(3) Include a list of major suppliers as part of the response to Item 10(c).

Item 11. Subsidiary Designation

If the applicant is a subsidiary, then responses to Item 11(a) through 11(h) are required; otherwise, go to Item 12.

(a) If the applying organization is a component of a company, then the name and address of the parent company and the name and title of the highest official of the parent company must be supplied. Provide the number of worldwide employees of the parent company including all its subsidiaries. Do not include joint ventures.

(b) Check the appropriate box.

(c) Check the appropriate box.

(d) Check the appropriate box. If two or more subsidiaries from a parent company are planning to apply, provide a brief explanation. Only one can be accepted per category.

(e) Submit a short document such as an annual report or the appropriate page(s) from a company publication showing the organization of the parent company and its relationship to the applying unit. This publication must show that the applying unit has existed for at least one year. Indicate the title of this document.

(f) Briefly describe the organizational structure and management links to the parent company.

(g) The potential for marketplace confusion is a key factor in deciding eligibility for one of a set of similar units within companies, especially in the case of chain organizations. If yes is checked, provide a brief description of the market and product or service similarity and the organizational relationships of all units providing the same or similar products and services.

(h) Briefly describe the major business support functions provided to the applicant by the parent company or by other units of the parent company.

Item 12. Ownership by a Holding Company

If the applicant is owned by a holding company, then responses to Item 12(a) through 12(d) are required; otherwise, go to Item 13.

(a) If the applying organization is owned by a holding company, then the name and address of the holding company and the name and title of the highest official of the holding company must be supplied.

(b) Check the appropriate box. If two or more units from the holding company are planning to apply, provide a brief explanation. Only one can be accepted per category.

(c) Briefly describe the organizational structure and management links to the holding company.

(d) If yes is checked, provide a brief description of the market and product or service similarity and the organizational relationships of all units providing the same or similar products and services.

Item 13. Use of Supplemental Sections

If the applicant intends to submit one or more Supplemental Sections (see page 20 for description), then responses to Item 13(a) and 13(b) are required; otherwise, go to Item 14.

(a) Indicate the number of Supplemental Sections the applicant intends to submit.

(b) Briefly describe the material to be included in each Supplemental Section.

Note: *Applicants must first receive approval from the Administrator to ensure that your intended use of Supplemental Sections will be allowed as part of your 1994 Application Package. The Administrator will return your 1994 Eligibility Determination Form with an official determination for each Supplemental Section described in Item 13(b).*

Item 14. Fee

A nonrefundable fee (see page 25 for information on fees) must be included with the 1994 Eligibility Determination Form and letter of transmittal.

Item 15. Official Inquiry Point

While reviewing the 1994 Eligibility Determination Form and associated materials, the Administrator may need to contact the applicant for additional information. Give the name, address, telephone, and telefax numbers of the official inquiry person.

Item 16. Signature, Authorizing Official

The signature of the applicant's highest-ranking official or designee is required.

1994 Eligibility Determination

The Administrator will return your form with an official determination written in this box. Submit the approved 1994 Eligibility Determination Form as part of the 1994 Application Package.

1994 Eligibility Determination Form Checklist

Use the following checklist to ensure that all required parts of the 1994 Eligibility Determination Form are complete.

( ) 1. All items completed.

( ) 2. Signature, Authorizing Official.

( ) 3. Item 9, Site Listing and Descriptors, filled out, including foreign sites, if any.

( ) 4. Line and box Organization Chart of applicant included.

( ) 5. If applicable, submit a short document showing the organization of the parent company and its relationship to the applicant.

( ) 6. Letter of transmittal attached.

( ) 7. Check or money order in the amount of $50 enclosed, payable to The Malcolm Baldrige National Quality Award.

( ) 8. Send Eligibility Determination Form to:

Malcolm Baldrige National Quality Award
c/o American Society for Quality Control
P.O. Box 3005
Milwaukee, WI 53201-3005

Overnight Mailing Address:
Malcolm Baldrige National Quality Award
c/o American Society for Quality Control
611 East Wisconsin Avenue
Milwaukee, WI 53202
(414) 272-8575

( ) 9. Completed 1994 Eligibility Determination Form consigned to carrier not later than March 4, 1994. It is suggested that applicants obtain a receipt from the carrier showing date of consignment.

Malcolm Baldrige National Quality Award

1 **Applicant**

Company Name _____

Address _____

_____

_____

Has the applicant officially or legally existed for at least one year?
(See the Note on page 2 for details.)

(Check one.) ___Yes ___No (Briefly explain.)

_____

_____

2 **Highest-Ranking Official**

Name _____

Title _____

Address _____

_____

_____

Telephone No. _____

3 **For Profit Designation**

Is the applicant a for-profit business?
(Check one.) ___Yes ___No

4 **Size of Applicant**

Total number of employees _____

Percent employees in the U.S. and/or territories _____

Percent physical assets in U.S. and/or territories _____

Total number of sites _____

Sales Preceding Fiscal Year *(Check one.)*

☐ 0-$1M   ☐ $10M-$100M   ☐ $500M-$1B

☐ $1M-$10M   ☐ $100M-$500M   ☐ Over $1B

5 **Industrial Classification**

List up to three most descriptive two-digit SIC Codes.
(See page 24.)

_____   _____   _____

6 **Award Category** (Check one.)

☐ Manufacturing   ☐ Service   ☐ Small Business

7 **Supplier and Dealer Networks**

Number of Suppliers _____

Number of External Sales Organizations:

Dealers _____   Distributors _____

Franchises _____   Other (Type/Number) _____

_____

8 **Percent Customer Base**

Is over 50% of the sales of the applicant to customers outside
of the applicant's organization, its parent company, or other
companies with financial or organizational control of the
applicant or parent company? (Check one.)

___Yes ___No (Briefly explain.)

OMB Clearance #0693-0006
Expiration Date: September 30, 1994

*This form may be copied and attached to,
or bound with, other application materials.*

Malcolm Baldrige National Quality Award

9 | **Site Listing and Descriptors**

a. Address of Site	b. Relative Size — Percent of Applicant's		c. Description of Products or Services
	Employees	Sales	

Provide all the information for each site except where multiple sites produce similar products or services. For such multiple site cases, see page 7.

This page may be copied and attached to, or bound with, other application materials.

10

Malcolm Baldrige National Quality Award

10 **Business Factors**

Provide a brief description of the following key business factors:

a. Nature of the applicant's business (products, services, and technologies); conclude with a list of major competitors

b. Nature of major markets (local, regional, national, and international); conclude with a list of major customers

Malcolm Baldrige National Quality Award

10 **Business Factors** (Continued)

c. Importance of suppliers, dealers, distributors, and franchises; conclude with a list of major suppliers

11 **Subsidiary Designation**

Is applicant a subsidiary, business unit, division, or like organization? ___Yes (Continue) ___No (Go to Item 12.)

a. Parent Company

Company Name _____

Address _____

_____

_____

Highest Official _____

Title _____

Number of worldwide employees of the

parent company _____

b. Does applicant comprise over 25% of the worldwide employees of the parent company? (Check one.)

___Yes ___No

c. Does the applicant consist of more than 50% of the worldwide sales of the parent company? (Check one.)

___Yes ___No

d. Is the applicant's parent company or another subsidiary of the parent company intending to apply? (Check one.)

___Yes (Briefly explain.) ___No ___Don't know

Malcolm Baldrige National Quality Award

11 ## Subsidiary Designation (Continued)

e. Name the document supporting the subsidiary designation.

_____

_____

Include a copy of the document with this application. See instructions on page 7 for limit on materials to be submitted.

f. Briefly describe the organizational structure and management links to the parent company.

g. Do other units within the parent company provide similar products or services? (Check one.)

___Yes (Briefly explain.)   ___No

h. Briefly describe the major business support functions provided to the applicant by the parent company or by other units of the parent company.

Malcolm Baldrige National Quality Award

12 Ownership by a Holding Company

Is the applicant owned by a holding company?
___Yes (Continue)   ___No (Go to Item 13.)

a. Holding Company

Company Name _____

Address _____

_____

_____

Highest Official _____

Title _____

b. Is the holding company or another unit of the holding company intending to apply? (Check one.)

___Yes (Briefly explain.)   ___No   ___Don't know

c. Briefly describe the organizational structure and management links to the holding company.

d. Do other units within the holding company provide similar products or services? (Check one.)

___Yes (Briefly explain.)   ___No

13 Use of Supplemental Sections

Does the applicant intend to submit one or more Supplemental Sections?   ___Yes (Continue)   ___No (Go to Item 14.)

a. Number of Supplemental Sections proposed _____

b. Briefly describe the material to be included in each Supplemental Section.

Malcolm Baldrige National Quality Award

14 Fee (See page 25 for instructions.)

Enclosed is $_____ to cover the eligibility determination.

Make check or money order payable to:

The Malcolm Baldrige National Quality Award

15 **Official Inquiry Point**

Name _____

Title _____

Mailing Address _____

_____

_____

Overnight
Mailing Address _____

_____

Telephone No. _____

Telefax No. _____

16 **Signature, Authorizing Official**

Date _____

X _____

Name _____

Title _____

Address _____

_____

_____

Telephone No. _____

1994 Eligibility Determination Form Mailing Address

Malcolm Baldrige National Quality Award
c/o American Society for Quality Control
P.O. Box 3005
Milwaukee, WI 53201-3005

Overnight Delivery Address:
Malcolm Baldrige National Quality Award
c/o American Society for Quality Control
611 East Wisconsin Avenue
Milwaukee, WI 53202
(414) 272-8575

_____

DO NOT WRITE BELOW THIS LINE

Note: This form will be returned to you with the eligibility determination indicated below. An approved 1994 Eligibility Determination Form must be submitted as part of each copy of the 1994 Application Package.

☐ Manufacturing   ☐ Service
☐ Small Business   ☐ Ineligible

For Official Use Only

General Instructions

Type all information requested. The 1994 Application Form may be duplicated and single-sided pages submitted. Applicants must submit a copy of the 1994 Application Form with each copy of the 1994 Application Report submitted. Send the completed 1994 Application Package (see page 23) and fee to:

Malcolm Baldrige National Quality Award
c/o American Society for Quality Control
P.O. Box 3005
Milwaukee, WI 53201-3005

Overnight mailing address:
Malcolm Baldrige National Quality Award
c/o American Society for Quality Control
611 East Wisconsin Avenue
Milwaukee, WI 53202
(414) 272-8575

Item Instructions

Item 1. Applicant
Provide the official name and mailing address of the organization applying for the Award.

Item 2. Award Category
From the approved 1994 Eligibility Determination Form, indicate the category in which eligibility was approved.

Item 3. Highest-Ranking Official
Provide the name, title, mailing address, and telephone number of the applicant's highest-ranking official.

Item 4. Official Inquiry Point
As the examination proceeds, the Administrator may need to contact the applicant for additional information.

Give the name, address, and telephone number of the corporate official with authority to provide additional information or to arrange a site visit.

If this official contact point changes during the course of the application process, please inform the Administrator.

Item 5. Application Components
Indicate all forms, reports, and Supplemental Sections submitted as part of the total application. Use the 1994 Application Package Checklist (see page 23) to ensure that all required parts of the 1994 Application Report are complete.

Item 6. Fee
See page 25 for information on fees.

Payment must be submitted with the application.

Item 7. Release Statement
Please read this section carefully.

A signed application indicates that the applicant agrees to the terms and conditions stated there.

Item 8. Signature, Authorizing Official
The signature of the applicant's highest-ranking official or designee is required and indicates the applicant will comply with the terms and conditions stated in the document.

1994 APPLICATION FORM

Malcolm Baldrige National Quality Award

1 Applicant

Company Name _____

Address _____

_____

_____

2 Award Category (Check one.)

☐ Manufacturing ☐ Service ☐ Small Business

3 Highest-Ranking Official

Name _____

Title _____

Address _____

_____

_____

Telephone No. _____

4 Official Inquiry Point

Name _____

Title _____

Mailing Address _____

_____

Overnight
Mailing Address _____

_____

Telephone No. _____

Telefax No. _____

5 Application Components

1994 Eligibility Determination Form with confirmation _____
(check)

1994 Application Report only_____
(check)

1994 Application Report and _____ Supplemental Sections
(number)

6 Fee (See page 25 for instructions.)

Enclosed is $_____ to cover one
Application Report and _____ Supplemental Sections.

Make check or money order payable to:

The Malcolm Baldrige National Quality Award

7 Release Statement

We understand that this application will be reviewed by
members of the Board of Examiners. Should our company
be selected for a site visit, we agree to host the site visit
and to facilitate an open and unbiased examination. We
understand that the company must pay reasonable costs
associated with a site visit.

8 Signature, Authorizing Official

Date _____

X _____

Name _____

Title _____

Address _____

_____

_____

Telephone No. _____

OMB Clearance #0693-0006
Expiration Date: September 30, 1994

*This form may be copied and attached to,
or bound with, other application materials.*

1994 APPLICATION REPORT – INSTRUCTIONS

Objective

The objective of the Application Report is to allow applicants to provide information on quality management of products and services and on results of quality improvement processes to permit a rigorous evaluation to be performed by the Board of Examiners.

Purpose

The purpose of this section is to provide applicants with instructions for preparing the 1994 Application Report. These instructions include information on typing, page limits, organization, assembly, and other format considerations. Guidelines for responding to Examination Items are also given.

Requirements

Each applicant must submit a 1994 Application Report consisting of: (1) a brief Overview of the applicant's business; and (2) responses to the 28 Examination Items in the Award Examination.

Notes:

(1) All units/subunits of the applicant must be included in the 1994 Application Report.

(2) Submissions which do not meet the requirements given in the section entitled Format for the 1994 Application Report will be returned along with the fee payment.

Introduction to Key Business Factors and their use in Evaluation of Applications

The Award Examination is designed to permit evaluation of any quality system for manufacturing and service companies of any size, type of business, or scope of market. The 28 Items and 91 Areas to Address have been selected because of their importance to virtually all businesses. Nevertheless, the importance of the Items and Areas to Address may not be equally applicable to all businesses, even to businesses of comparable size in the same industry. The specific business factors that may bear upon the evaluation and that are described below must be presented in the Business Overview and will be considered at every stage of evaluation.

Preparation of the Business Overview

The Business Overview is an outline of the applicant's business, addressing what is most important to the business and the key factors that influence how the business operates.

The Business Overview is intended to "set the stage" for the Examiners' evaluation. It should help Examiners to understand what is relevant and important to the applicant's business.

The Business Overview is used by the Examiners in all stages of the application review. For this reason, this Overview is a vital part of the overall application.

A Business Overview fully responsive to the Examiners' requirements should describe:

- the nature of the applicant's business: products and services

- principal customers (consumers, other businesses, government, etc.) and their special requirements. Special relationships with customers or customer groups should be noted.

- a description of the applicant's major markets (local, regional, national, or international)

- key customer quality requirements (for example, on-time delivery or low defect levels) for products and services. Include all important quality requirements. Briefly note significant differences in requirements among customer groups or markets, if any.

- the applicant's position (relative size, growth) in the industry and key factors in the competitive environment

- the applicant's employee base, including: number, type, educational level, bargaining units, etc.

- major equipment, facilities, and technologies used

- types and numbers of suppliers of goods and services. Indicate the importance of suppliers, dealers, and other businesses, and any limitations or special relationships that may exist in dealing with such businesses.

- the regulatory environment within which the applicant operates, including occupational health and safety, environmental, financial regulations, etc.

- other factors important to the applicant, such as major new thrusts for the company, major changes taking place in the industry, new business alliances, etc.

If the applicant is a subsidiary or division of a company, a description of the organizational structure and key management links to the parent company should be presented. Also include percent of employees and relationships of products and services.

The Business Overview must be limited to four pages. These four pages are not counted in the overall page limit.

Format for the 1994 Application Report

Typing Instructions

The 1994 Application Report should contain the same Category and Item numerical designations as in the 1994 Award Examination. A table of contents with the page number of each Category and Item should be provided. The 1994 Application Report must be typed on standard 8½ by 11-inch paper using a fixed pitch font of 12 or fewer characters per inch or a proportional spacing font of point size 10 or larger. Any type may be used. Helvetica and Times or equivalent type fonts are preferred. There should be the equivalent of two points of lead between lines. The number of lines per page should not exceed 60, including the page headings and page numbers. Pages set up in two-column format are preferred. *Type on pages including picture captions, graphs, figures, data tables, and appendices must also meet the requirements for size and spacing.* Pages may be printed on both sides. For purpose of illustration, the text of this paragraph is printed in 10 point Helvetica with 2 points of lead between lines.

Note: *One point of lead equals 1/72, or 0.0138, inch.*

Page Limits and Exclusions

For the **Manufacturing category** and the **Service category**, the Application Report is limited to a maximum of **85 single-sided pages** including pictures, graphs, figures, data tables, and appendices. **Supplemental Sections** are limited to a maximum of **50 single-sided pages**. For **Small Businesses**, the Application Report is limited to **70 single-sided pages**.

Though not required, the use of labeled section tabs would be appreciated. A glossary of terms and abbreviations should be included. In all cases, the Business Overview, dividers, covers, tab separators, glossaries, title pages, organization charts, and tables of contents are not counted as part of the page limit. All remaining pages should be consecutively numbered from start to finish.

The use of bulky binders or similar heavy covers is discouraged. Their use decreases the ease of handling in all phases of the evaluation process. Copies of video or audio tape or other information aids should not be submitted.

Note: *Lists of terms and abbreviations used in a section of the 1994 Application Report may be included on tab separators or dividers without being counted as part of the page limit. However, any text, graphs, figures, or data tables included on tab separators or dividers must be repeated in that section of the 1994 Application Report in order not to be counted as part of the page limit.*

Organization of Responses to Examination Items

Responses to Examination Items should be organized as follows:

- Respond to each Examination Item as a whole. Address the set of Areas in an order and with an emphasis that reflects the applicant's business and quality system. However, to facilitate review by the Board of Examiners, applicants are encouraged to respond to the Areas in the order given in the Items.

- Applicants should denote responses to Areas with the letters a, b, c, etc., corresponding to each Area. Applicants should denote responses to Areas by underlining the Item/Area (e.g., <u>4.2d</u>). If an Area does not pertain to the applicant's business or quality system, the applicant must provide a statement of one or two sentences explaining why the Area is not applicable. This statement should be given at the end of the overall response to the Item. The Item/Area designator should be used as described above.

Document Assembly

A complete 1994 Application Report contains the following components:

- Title Page
- Table of Contents
- Business Overview
- Organization Chart
- 1994 Eligibility Determination Form
- 1994 Application Form
- Summary of Supplemental Sections, if applicable
- Glossary of Terms and Abbreviations
- Categories/Items/Areas (i.e., 1.1a through 7.6c)

All components of the 1994 Application Report should be securely fastened together to prevent separation during handling.

The applicant must provide a line and box organization chart with sufficient detail for Examiners to understand the relationships between subunits of the applicant which are mentioned in the 1994 Application Report. The organization chart is not counted as part of the page limit. The applicant must provide a brief description of each Supplemental Section submitted. This information should include the site's products and services and SIC Codes; it is not counted as part of the page limit.

Use of Supplemental Sections

All applicants must prepare a 1994 Application Report addressing all of the Examination Items. In order to maintain an equivalent level of detail for all sizes and types of companies and subsidiaries, certain applicants may also need to provide Supplemental Sections. The use of Supplemental Sections is required when the applicant comprises units of a company that are essentially different businesses. They are not necessary when similar products or services are produced or delivered by different divisions using similar quality systems. Below is an outline of the key factors and guidelines for Supplemental Sections.

Note: *There is a fee for each Supplemental Section submitted. See page 25 for information on fees.*

■ **Single or related product and service lines served by a single quality system**
Only the 1994 Application Report is required if the applicant has a single quality system that supports all its product or service lines and if the products or services are essentially similar in terms of customers, technology, types of employees, planning, and quality.

■ **Two or more diverse product or service lines and/or dissimilar quality systems**
In such cases, the 1994 Application Report and one or more Supplemental Sections are required. The 1994 Application Report should encompass the largest aggregation of similar product or service lines, as described above, that are supported by a single quality system. Together, the 1994 Application Report and the Supplemental Sections must cover all products and/or services and all quality systems of the applicant.

A complete Supplemental Section contains the following components:

■ Title Page
■ Table of Contents
■ Business Overview
■ Organization Chart
■ Summary of Supplemental Section(s)
■ Glossary of Terms and Abbreviations
■ Categories/Items/Areas (i.e., 1.1a through 7.6c)

All components of the Supplemental Section should be securely fastened together to prevent separation during handling. The applicant must provide a brief description of each Supplemental Section submitted. This information should include the site's products and services and SIC Codes; it is not counted as part of the page limit.

Note: *Supplemental sections are limited to a maximum of 50 single-sided pages.*

Guidelines for Responding to the Examination Items

1. Read the entire *1994 Award Criteria* booklet.

   The main sections of the booklet provide an overall orientation to the Criteria and how applicants' responses are evaluated.

2. Understand the meaning of "how".

   All Items that request information on Approach include Areas to Address that begin with the word "how". Responses to such Areas should provide as complete a picture as possible to enable meaningful evaluation and feedback. Responses should outline key process details such as methods, measures, deployment, and evaluation factors. Information lacking sufficient detail to permit an evaluation and feedback, or merely providing an example, is referred to in the *1994 Award Criteria* booklet as anecdotal information.

3. Understand the meaning of measures and/or indicators.

   All Items calling for results require data using "key measures and/or indicators". Measures and indicators both involve measurement related to performance. When the performance can be measured directly, such as cycle time and on-time delivery, the term "measure" is used. When the overall performance may not be evaluated in terms of one type of measurement, and two or more measurements are used to provide ("indicate") a more complete picture, the term "indicator" is used. For example, innovation success is not easily described in terms of a single measurement. Patents and patent citations provide two measurements which are indicators of innovation success, but completing the picture requires other indicators, such as cycle time for bringing new products to market and market share gain from introduction of innovative products or services.

4. Note the distinction between data and results.

   There is a critical distinction between data and results — a distinction that is often misunderstood. Data are numerical information; results are the outcomes of activities. Data could be used as inputs to activities, as well as outcomes of activities. Results Items require data to demonstrate progress and achievement. Approach/Deployment Items, focused on processes, may benefit from data to provide a clearer and more complete picture of key aspects of Approach and/or Deployment. For example, a company may use self-directed work teams in its approach. It may report that 5 such teams involving 75 percent of the people on the shop floor undertook 11 projects during the past year to reduce scrap and rework. These data are input data giving deployment information related to the approach (self-directed work teams). These teams reducing scrap and rework by 17 percent is a result.

5. Understand specific Item requirements.

   Review each Item classification and the specific requirements given under Areas to Address and in Item Notes.

6. Gather and organize relevant information for a response.

   Most of the Items require summaries of information gathered from different parts of the company.

7. Select relevant/important information.

   In preparing Item responses, focus on information that is *both* directly responsive to the Item requirements and to key business requirements spelled out in the Business Overview. Information and data included should be relevant and important to both the Item and to the applicant's business.

8. Anticipate assessment and feedback.

   A well-written response is one that lends itself to Examiner or other feedback. A response that facilitates assessment gives clear information on how (approach) and on the relevant use (deployment) of the approach. Anecdotal information or information lacking overall context should not be given as it is usually not possible to prepare meaningful feedback. Examples are, of course, helpful but examples often do not convey a picture of overall approach and deployment. If examples are used, make certain that they illustrate a more complete response already presented.

9. Make responses concise.

   The application page limits (85 pages for companies in the Manufacturing and Service categories and 70 pages for companies in the Small Business category) do not permit lengthy narrative or inclusion of information not directly responsive to Item requirements. For this reason, applicants are urged to make all responses concise and factual. Statements should be supported with data whenever appropriate.

10. Cross-reference when appropriate.

    Although applicants should seek to make individual responses self-contained, there may be instances when responses to different Items are mutually reinforcing. In such cases it is appropriate to reference responses to other Items, rather than to repeat information presented elsewhere. In doing so, applicants should make the reference specific by using Item and Area designators, for example, see 4.2c.

11. Review each response.

    Each response should be reviewed to make certain that it addresses the Item requirements and is consistent with the applicant's key business requirements spelled out in the Business Overview. It is also important to ensure that a response is consistent with information reported in Items that are closely linked.

Reporting Results and Trend Data

1. Results Items require data to demonstrate progress (trend data), achievement (performance levels), and breadth of deployment. Evaluation of achievement is usually based upon two factors: (1) that the performance level has been sustained or is the current result of a favorable trend; and (2) that the performance level can be compared with that of other appropriate organizations.

2. Applicants are required to report trend data to show progress and to show that improvements or outstanding performance levels are sustained. No minimum period of time is specified for trend data. Time periods may span five years or more for some results. Trends may be much shorter in areas where improvement efforts are new. In cases where the trend line is short, the Examiners' evaluation will take into account the demonstrated levels of performance.

3. The spacing between data points on a trend line (annual, monthly, etc.) should reflect a natural measurement/use scheme for such results. That is, how the data are used in process management should determine the spacing between data points. For example, measurement frequency should support timely improvement.

4. In reporting trend data, applicants should be aware that breadth of results is a major factor in the Examiners' evaluation. For this reason, it is important to report data reflecting wide deployment of improvement activities. Use of graphs and tables offers a good means to present many results compactly.

5. Graphs and tables should be integrated into the body of the text, wherever possible.

The following graph illustrates data an applicant might present as part of a response to Item 6.1, Product and Service Quality Results. The applicant has indicated, in the Business Overview and in Item 7.1, on-time delivery as a key customer requirement.

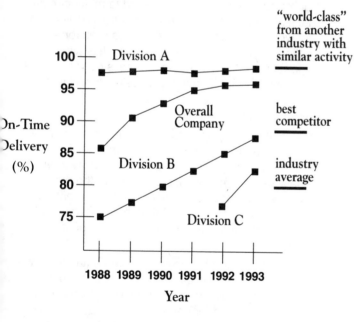

Using the graph, the following characteristics of clear and effective data presentation are illustrated:

- the trend lines report data for a key business requirement
- both axes and units of measure are clearly labeled
- results are presented for several years
- meaningful comparisons are clearly shown
- the company shows, using a single graph, that its three divisions separately track on-time delivery

To help interpret the scoring guidelines (see page 34 of the *1994 Award Criteria*), the following comments on the graphed results would be appropriate:

- the current overall company performance level is excellent. This conclusion is supported by the comparison with competitors and with a "world class" level
- the company exhibits an overall excellent improvement record
- Division A is the current performance leader — showing sustained high performance and a slightly positive trend. Division B shows rapid improvement. Its current performance is near that of the best industry competitor, but trails the "world class" level.
- Division C — a new division — shows rapid progress. Its current performance is not yet at the level of the best industry competitor.

Reviewing the Overall Set of Item Responses

1. It is helpful to review, as a whole, the complete set of 28 Item responses. There are four main considerations in this review:

   a. emphasis on the applicant's most important business requirements. This emphasis should be clear throughout the set of responses, and consistent with the Business Overview.

   b. balance in the use of page limits. Ample page space should be given to results Items which are weighed heavily in the Examiners' evaluation. Items and Areas that address factors particularly important to the applicant's business should receive relatively more emphasis.

   c. overall consistency. Responses should be checked to ensure that responses to related Items are consistent, and that there is appropriate cross-referencing to minimize duplication of information.

   d. final check on deployment information. The overall application should convey widespread and consistent implementation, not merely an outline of approaches. The final review allows an assessment of how well the application as a whole covers all key company requirements, responsibilities, and processes.

1994 APPLICATION PACKAGE SUBMISSION

A complete 1994 Application Package consists of the 1994 Application Report and, if applicable and approved by the Administrator, one or more Supplemental Sections. Send **20 copies** of the complete 1994 Application Package along with the fee payment to:

Malcolm Baldrige National Quality Award
c/o American Society for Quality Control
P.O. Box 3005
Milwaukee, WI 53201-3005

Overnight Mailing Address:
Malcolm Baldrige National Quality Award
c/o American Society for Quality Control
611 East Wisconsin Avenue
Milwaukee, WI 53202
(414) 272-8575

Notes:
(1) Check or money order should be made payable to **The Malcolm Baldrige National Quality Award***.*

(2) Award applications must be postmarked or consigned to an overnight mail delivery service by April 4, 1994, to be eligible for the 1994 Award. If a question arises about the deadline having been met, you will be asked to supply a dated receipt from the postal or overnight carrier.

(3) Submissions which do not meet the requirements given in the section entitled Format for the 1994 Application Report will be returned along with the fee payment.

1994 Application Package Checklist

Use the following checklist to ensure that the required specifications have been met prior to submitting the 1994 Application Package.

( ) 1. 1994 Eligibility Determination Form has been approved.

( ) 2. 1994 Application Form is complete.

( ) 3. Table of Contents is included.

( ) 4. Business Overview addresses all key business factors.

( ) 5. Glossary of Terms and Abbreviations is included.

( ) 6. Organization Chart is included.

( ) 7. Summary of Supplemental Sections, if applicable, is included.

( ) 8. Categories/Items/Areas (i.e., 1.1a through 7.6c) are addressed and properly labeled. (Use of labeled section tabs is encouraged.)

( ) 9. Document size meets requirements. (See section on page limits.)

( ) 10. Pages are consecutively numbered.

( ) 11. Type size meets requirements (including picture captions, graphs, figures, data tables, and appendices).

( ) 12. Signature of Authorizing Official.

( ) 13. Supplemental Sections, if applicable, are included.

( ) 14. Check or money order enclosed, payable to The Malcolm Baldrige National Quality Award.

STANDARD INDUSTRIAL CLASSIFICATION (SIC) CODES

Manufacturing and Products

Code	Sector
01	Agriculture – crops
02	Agriculture – livestock
08	Forestry
09	Fishing, hunting, and trapping
10	Metal mining
12	Coal mining
13	Oil and gas extraction
14	Mineral quarrying
15	General building contractors
16	Heavy construction contractors
17	Special trade contractors
20	Food products
21	Tobacco products
22	Textile mill products
23	Apparel
24	Lumber and wood products
25	Furniture and fixtures
26	Paper and allied products
27	Printing and publishing
28	Chemicals
29	Petroleum refining
30	Rubber and plastics
31	Leather and leather products
32	Stone/clay/glass/concrete products
33	Primary metal industries
34	Fabricated metal products
35	Machinery/computer equipment
36	Electrical/electronic equipment
37	Transportation equipment
38	Instruments/watches and clocks/optical goods
39	Miscellaneous manufacturing

Services

Code	Sector
07	Agricultural services
40	Railroad transportation
41	Local & interurban transport
42	Trucking and warehousing
44	Water transportation
45	Air transportation
46	Pipelines, except natural gas
47	Transportation services
48	Communications
49	Electric/gas/sanitary services
50	Wholesale trade/durable goods
51	Wholesale trade/nondurable goods
52	Retail building materials
53	General merchandise stores
54	Food stores
55	Auto dealers & service stations
56	Apparel and accessory stores
57	Furniture stores
58	Eating and drinking places
59	Miscellaneous retail
60	Banking
61	Credit agencies
62	Security & commodity brokers
63	Insurance carriers
64	Insurance agents
65	Real estate
67	Holding & other investment offices
70	Hotels and lodging places
72	Personal services
73	Business services
75	Auto repair and services
76	Miscellaneous repair services
78	Motion pictures
79	Amusement and recreation
80	Health services
81	Legal services
82	Educational services
83	Social services
84	Museum and art galleries
86	Membership organizations
87	Professional services
89	Miscellaneous services

HOW TO ORDER COPIES OF 1994 AWARD MATERIALS

> **Note:** The *1994 Award Criteria* and the *1994 Application Forms and Instructions* are two separate documents.

Individual Orders

Individual copies of either document can be obtained free of charge from:

Malcolm Baldrige National Quality Award
National Institute of Standards and Technology
Route 270 and Quince Orchard Road
Administration Building, Room A537
Gaithersburg, MD 20899
Telephone: 301-975-2036
Telefax: 301-948-3716

Bulk Orders

Multiple copies of the *1994 Award Criteria* may be ordered in packets of 10 (Order Item Number T998):

American Society for Quality Control
Customer Service Department
P.O. Box 3066
Milwaukee, WI 53201-3066
Toll free: 800-248-1946
Telefax: 414-272-1734

Cost: $29.95 per packet of 10 plus postage and handling

Postage and handling charges are:

	U.S.	Canada
1 packet	$ 3.75	$ 8.75
2-4 packets	6.00	11.00
5 or more	12.00*	17.00

For orders shipped outside of the continental United States, there is a fee of 25 percent of order value to cover postage and handling. This fee does not apply to Canada.

Payment

Payment options include check, money order, purchase order, VISA, MasterCard, or American Express.

Payment must accompany all mail orders.

Payment must be made in U.S. currency. Checks and money orders must be drawn on U.S. institutions.

Make checks payable to ASQC.

Shipment

Orders delivered within the continental United States and Canada will be shipped UPS or first class mail.

If actual shipping charges exceed $12.00, ASQC will invoice the customer for additional expense.

FEES FOR THE 1994 AWARD CYCLE

Eligibility Determination Fees

The eligibility determination fee is $50 for all potential applicants. This fee is nonrefundable.

Application Fees

- Manufacturing Company Category—$4000
- Service Company Category—$4000
- Small Business Category—$1200
- Supplemental Sections—$1500

These fees cover expenses associated with distribution of applications, review of applications, and development of feedback reports. The fees must accompany the 1994 Application Form. Information on Supplemental Sections is given on page 20.

Site Visit Review Fees

Site visit fees will be set when the visits are scheduled. Fees depend upon the number of sites to be visited, the number of Examiners assigned, and the duration of the visit. Site visit fees for applicants in the Small Business category will be charged at one-half of the rate for companies in the Manufacturing and Service categories.

These fees cover all expenses and travel costs associated with site visit participation and development of site visit reports. Site visit fees are paid only by those applicants reaching the site visit stage.

1994 Eligibility Determination Forms due: March 4, 1994

1994 Award Applications due: April 4, 1994

HOW TO ORDER AWARD EDUCATIONAL MATERIALS

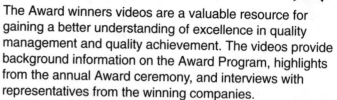

Each year, the Award Program develops materials for use in training members of the Board of Examiners, and for sharing information on the successful quality strategies of the Award winners. The listed materials and information may be obtained from the American Society for Quality Control (toll free: 800-248-1946). Prices and/or availability dates for all materials are given below.

Case Studies

The case studies are used to prepare Examiners for the interpretation of the Award Criteria and the Scoring System. The case studies, when used with the Award Criteria, illustrate the Award application and review process. The case studies are sample applications written for fictitious companies applying for the Baldrige Award. The case studies can provide valuable insights into the Award Criteria and Scoring System for companies interested in making application, as well as for self-assessment, planning, training, and other uses.

Varifilm Case Study Packet

The Varifilm Case Study Packet is based on the 1993 Examiner Preparation Course. Associated with the Varifilm Case Study are the Varifilm Evaluation Notes and the Varifilm Feedback Report. In addition, the Case Study Packet also includes: an Executive Summary; the 1993 Application Scorebook; the 1993 Site Visit Evaluation Book; the 1993 Handbook for the Board of Examiners and the 1993 Award Criteria.

> 1993 – Item Number T515: $49.95

Award Winners Videos

The Award winners videos are a valuable resource for gaining a better understanding of excellence in quality management and quality achievement. The videos provide background information on the Award Program, highlights from the annual Award ceremony, and interviews with representatives from the winning companies.

> 1993 – *Available February 22, 1994.*
> 1992 – Item Number TA512: $20.00
> 1991 – Item Number TA996:   15.00
> 1990 – Item Number T992:   15.00
> 1989 – Item Number T502:   10.00
> 1988 – Item Number T993:   10.00

1992 Expanded Video

An expanded, 55-minute video, entitled "Quality Leadership: A Culture For Continuous Improvement", is available. The video highlights each 1992 Award Winner — AT&T Network Systems Group, Transmission Systems Business Unit; Texas Instruments, Defense Systems and Electronics Group; AT&T Universal Card Services; The Ritz-Carlton Hotel Company; and the Granite Rock Company.

> Item Number TA914: $249.95

1991 Expanded Video

An expanded, 46-minute video, featuring the three 1991 Award winners — Solectron Corporation, Zytec Corporation, and Marlow Industries, shows the viewer the ingredients for successful implementation of a quality system within their organization.

> Item Number TA910: $195.00

QUEST FOR EXCELLENCE VI CONFERENCE

The Annual Quest for Excellence Conference provides a unique opportunity to hear firsthand the Award-winning quality strategies of the past year's winners. Presentations are made by the CEOs and other key individuals who are transforming their organizations. The annual Quest for Excellence Conference is the principal forum for Award winners to present their overall strategies in detail.

The two and one-half day Quest for Excellence VI Conference will provide ample opportunities to explore the Award Criteria in depth, network with executive-level individuals from around the country, and view displays of each of the Award-winning organizations.

The Quest for Excellence VI Conference will feature:
- Eastman Chemical Company
- Ames Rubber Corporation

The Conference dates are February 7-9, 1994. The Conference will be held at the Washington Hilton and Towers, in Washington, D.C. The registration fee is $695.00 until January 10, 1994. Effective January 11, 1994, the fee is $795.00. The registration fee inc[l]udes conference handout materials and participation in all conference activities. For further information, contact the Association for Quality and Participation (AQP). (Toll-free: 800-733-3310 or FAX: 513-381-0070)

THE MALCOLM BALDRIGE NATIONAL QUALITY IMPROVEMENT ACT OF 1987 – PUBLIC LAW 100-107

The Malcolm Baldrige National Quality Award was created by Public Law 100-107, signed into law on August 20, 1987. The Award Program, responsive to the purposes of Public Law 100-107, led to the creation of a new public-private partnership. Principal support for the program comes from the Foundation for the Malcolm Baldrige National Quality Award, established in 1988.

The Award is named for Malcolm Baldrige, who served as Secretary of Commerce from 1981 until his tragic death in a rodeo accident in 1987. His managerial excellence contributed to long-term improvement in efficiency and effectiveness of government.

The Findings and Purposes Section of Public Law 100-107 states that:

" 1. the leadership of the United States in product and process quality has been challenged strongly (and sometimes successfully) by foreign competition, and our Nation's productivity growth has improved less than our competitors' over the last two decades.

2. American business and industry are beginning to understand that poor quality costs companies as much as 20 percent of sales revenues nationally and that improved quality of goods and services goes hand in hand with improved productivity, lower costs, and increased profitability.

3. strategic planning for quality and quality improvement programs, through a commitment to excellence in manufacturing and services, are becoming more and more essential to the well-being of our Nation's economy and our ability to compete effectively in the global marketplace.

4. improved management understanding of the factory floor, worker involvement in quality, and greater emphasis on statistical process control can lead to dramatic improvements in the cost and quality of manufactured products.

5. the concept of quality improvement is directly applicable to small companies as well as large, to service industries as well as manufacturing, and to the public sector as well as private enterprise.

6. in order to be successful, quality improvement programs must be management-led and customer-oriented, and this may require fundamental changes in the way companies and agencies do business.

7. several major industrial nations have successfully coupled rigorous private-sector quality audits with national awards giving special recognition to those enterprises the audits identify as the very best; and

8. a national quality award program of this kind in the United States would help improve quality and productivity by:

   A. helping to stimulate American companies to improve quality and productivity for the pride of recognition while obtaining a competitive edge through increased profits;

   B. recognizing the achievements of those companies that improve the quality of their goods and services and providing an example to others;

   C. establishing guidelines and criteria that can be used by business, industrial, governmental, and other organizations in evaluating their own quality improvement efforts; and

   D. providing specific guidance for other American organizations that wish to learn how to manage for high quality by making available detailed information on how winning organizations were able to change their cultures and achieve eminence. "

The Malcolm Baldrige National Quality Award

Managed by:

United States Department of Commerce
Technology Administration
National Institute of Standards and Technology
Route 270 and Quince Orchard Road
Administration Building, Room A537
Gaithersburg, MD 20899-0001

Administered by:

American Society for Quality Control
P.O. Box 3005
Milwaukee, WI 53201-3005

704015